An Introduction to

DYNAMIC PSYCHIATRY

An Introduction to

DYNAMIC PSYCHIATRY

C. KNIGHT ALDRICH, M.D.

Professor of Psychiatry,
University of Chicago School of Medicine

Foreword by
G. MORRIS CARSTAIRS
Professor of Psychiatry,
University of Edinburgh

The Blakiston Division
McGRAW-HILL BOOK COMPANY
New York   Toronto   Sydney   London

TO

Julie and Carol

FOREWORD

For well over a generation, the development of psychiatry has taken somewhat different directions in Europe and in the United States. In the United States, more than in any other country, the psychodynamic theories concerning normal personality development and the psychopathology of emotional disorders—theories derived from the basic concepts of Sigmund Freud and his successors—have become an accepted part of medical teaching. Most European schools of medicine, on the other hand, offer very little instruction in psychologic factors and devote relatively more time to the study of organic factors in mental illness. They emphasize physical treatment and social rehabilitation much more strongly than psychotherapy. This difference in emphasis has led to some mutual misunderstanding and even at times to recriminations. American psychiatrists, psychologists, and social workers are frequently appalled by the neglect of psychologic factors in European treatment services; and European visitors to the United States have been struck by the preoccupation of so many American psychiatrists with private office practice in which every patient seems to be treated with the same psychotherapeutic approach.

The Atlantic does not create a similar dichotomy in teaching and practice in other fields, such as heart surgery or internal medicine. That it does so in psychiatry is an indication of the immaturity of this discipline, in which schools of thought still play an important part because there is as yet relatively little firm knowledge on which to base testable scientific hypotheses. Since the end of World War II, there has been a great expansion of research activity in this field. Because research knows no frontiers, we can look forward to a rapprochement between the teachers of psychiatry, although social factors may continue to encourage different emphases in treatment. In the meantime, however, there is a clear need for a balanced presentation which emphasizes the common elements rather than the divergences in psychiatric understanding of the causes and treatment of emotional disorders. Dr. Knight Aldrich is uniquely qualified by training and experience to bridge the gulf between the different schools of thought, and his book does precisely this.

His approach to psychiatry is eclectic, firmly based on human biology and on clinical medicine but informed by a clear and confident exposition of the theory of personality development.

Human behavior is complex, and to understand fully its complexities in health and in sickness is far from easy. Nor does Dr. Aldrich try to make it appear easy. He does, however, succeed in showing that it can be understood, however imperfectly; and he demonstrates with many clinical illustrations how this knowledge can be used in treatment. His book is not simply an introduction to short-term psychotherapy, although it can be used as such to advantage by physicians, nurses, clergymen, or social workers—by anyone, indeed, who is engaged professionally in the "helping agencies" of society. It is also an extremely lucid and thoughtful account of the interplay of genetic, biologic, interpersonal, and social factors in the causation of the wide range of mental illness, from the organic psychoses to the behavior disorders. Dr. Aldrich has deliberately given much attention to the minor forms of emotional distress and disability, because they are so widespread that psychiatrists will never be able to deal with more than a fraction of these cases. Already general practitioners, family physicians, and members of the other helping professions find themselves confronted with these problems in ever-increasing numbers. This book will help them to deal competently with the emotional crises of normal family development, from the crises of childhood, adolescence, and marriage to the crises accompanying physical illness, old age, and the prospect of death. More particularly, the book discusses in straightforward language how a physician can undertake simple measures of psychotherapy, showing when and how a patient can be helped by "empathic listening," by clarification of his problems, by judicious use of medication, and even—although rarely— by reassurance and advice.

Dr. Aldrich respects the intelligence of his readers and does not hesitate to point out that certain conditions demand highly specialized treatment, either in hospital or in intensive psychotherapy. Nor does he lose sight of the constant interaction between physical and emotional factors. It is this which makes it so important that a medically trained person always play a responsible part in patient care, even when he delegates the psychotherapeutic task to a lay colleague. Dr. Aldrich reiterates the need to test our hypotheses by experimental verification, and he advances his own hypotheses with such modesty and evident respect for clinical observation that his book will make good sense to readers on both sides of the Atlantic.

G. Morris Carstairs

PREFACE

Until about the beginning of World War II, the status of psychiatry in the American medical profession was generally low. Although over half the hospital beds in the country were in mental hospitals [1], the hospitals were for the most part located in isolated areas, relics of the days when society considered the major problem of mental illness to be the protection of the healthy from the sick. Psychiatry was primarily taught as a branch of neurology, with the major emphasis on description and classification, and hospital psychiatrists were overburdened with enormous case loads of patients for whom sedation and work assignments were virtually the only forms of treatment.

Outpatient psychiatric care was limited and superficial, and the average psychiatrist had little practical help to give general practitioners who were attempting to carry on most of the day-to-day management of psychoneurotic patients. The clinical efforts of the psychologist were for the most part devoted to diagnostic testing; the majority of social workers were occupied with the administration of direct relief and with other tangible services; nurses were offered little instruction about individualized nursing care; and most counseling, whether by physicians, clergymen, or members of other helping professions, consisted primarily of advice and exhortation.

There were exceptions to the typical descriptive, hospital-centered, limited-scope prewar psychiatry. Two schools of thought about the causes of mental illness—the psychobiologic, following Adolph Meyer [2], and the psychoanalytic, following Sigmund Freud [3]—had developed beachheads in medical schools and training programs. Psychoanalysis had established training institutes independent of medical centers and had begun to influence social-work training. Child-guidance clinics, developing out of the mental-hygiene movement, had experimented with multidisciplinary therapeutic teams. None of these influences, however, had a major impact on American medicine and American medical education until World War II.

Many influences contributed to the spectacular development of psychiatry during and after the war [4]. As physicians in the armed services observed the development of psychiatric illness at close quarters, psychodynamic formulations began to make more sense [5]. New treatment techniques removed some of the fatalism from the atmosphere in mental hospitals, and as society overcame some of its fear of mental illness, psychiatry began to move into the community and into general hospitals, on a par with other medical specialties.

The idea that emotional troubles could be overcome by talking them out was not exactly new, but the new idea that insight into a patient's unconscious conflict might be the key to his treatment made psychotherapy a more meaningful and scientific procedure. Psychiatrists became more interested in a psychotherapy based on a diagnosis of causes and structured to counteract specific causative factors than they had been in the earlier hit-or-miss, authoritarian, or suggestive techniques. As psychiatry became more acceptable to the public, more patients sought outpatient treatment, and the demand attracted other students of personality, particularly clinical psychologists, into the practice of psychotherapy. Social workers, influenced by psychiatrists as teachers and consultants, turned more and more to psychoanalytically based social casework [6].

Psychotherapy as traditionally practiced, however, is a time-consuming process, applicable primarily to well-motivated, verbal, and affluent patients. The public's developing demand is for preventive and treatment procedures available to the total community, at the time and place they can be most effectively applied. The most effective application is usually at the point of first recognition, usually long before the psychiatrist enters the picture. Family physicians and clergymen are the traditional first ports of call for help with such feelings as anxiety, grief, guilt, and shame; and they, as well as other community care-givers, look to psychiatrists not only for understanding of everyday emotional illness but for practical methods of care [7].

Psychiatrists have been placed in somewhat of a dilemma by these developments. The uncritical application of an understanding of unconscious elements in the personality can be dangerous to patients, and yet the family physician and clergyman cannot devote the time in training that most psychiatrists believe is needed to provide adequate safeguards. On the other hand, the psychiatrists and their colleagues, the psychologists and social workers, certainly cannot take over the care of more than a small proportion of all the people who suffer from emotional troubles.

Psychiatrists have tried to resolve this dilemma by communicating to all the helping professions a background of basic dynamic psychiatry that emphasizes both its usefulness and the dangers of its uncritical or inappropriate application. Unfortunately, the lines of demarcation between what is safe and what is unsafe are not always clear, and occasionally the psychiatrist may seem to be signaling stop and go simultaneously.

The signals can be clarified by a substantial extension of consultation between psychiatrists and other professional people. Models for interprofessional consultation have been developed by Caplan, Balint, and others [8], and there is still plenty of room for experimentation in the consultation format. Whatever the format, a basic understanding of dynamic psychiatry should help the "firing-line professional" to know when and how best to use psychiatric consultation.

The purpose of this book is to provide an introduction to dynamic psychiatry that will help in the use of consultation as well as in the evaluation and management of people with emotional problems, whether the help is given in the form of medical practice, casework, counseling, or nursing care. The book is an extended, revised edition of a previous book, *Psychiatry for the Family Physician* [9]. Although its new title indicates that it is directed to a wider audience, its primary focus remains the physician and the medical student. Psychiatry is a medical specialty, based on the principle of indivisibility of body and mind, and its psychologic and social aspects cannot be logically separated from its biologic aspects. In most of the examples in the book, therefore, a medical setting is assumed. I have not tried to enumerate all the ways in which the nonmedical professional can undertake ongoing medical liaison to protect his client or parishioner; the procedure may vary in different settings, but the principle is the same: Since the mind cannot be separated from the body, treatment of the mind cannot be carried out unless there is a constant concern with the interaction of physical and psychologic factors.

In order to demonstrate the relevance of an understanding of personality to any helping relationship, the book starts off with an exploration of the emotional significance of illness in general, using examples of acute, chronic, and fatal illness without specific psychiatric overtones. The first chapter will be of particular interest to physicians, nurses, and medical social workers, although many of the aspects of fear, helplessness, denial, and grief discussed in the chapter have general relevance.

The final case illustration in the first chapter introduces the subject of psychiatric illness and serves as a bridge between primarily "medical" cases and the psychiatric material discussed in the rest of the book. A schematic outline of personality structure in cross section follows, to give the reader a frame of reference for applying developmental concepts to the adult patient. The first part closes with a description of the process and tools of diagnosis.

The second part of the book is a step-by-step outline of emotional growth and development. At each step, developmental problems that frequently occur are discussed and the effects on personality of interrupted emotional growth are described. The descriptions introduce the reader to Part Three, which describes the symptoms and psychopathology of neurotic reactions, psychotic reactions, organic conditions, delinquency, and mental retardation. The material on psychopathology, generally limited to aspects of particular practical interest, serves mainly as a preview of the more extensive discussions found in standard textbooks.

The final part consists of a chapter on outpatient treatment that covers primarily the methods which the physician, social worker, pastoral counselor, and nurse can adapt to their uses.

A selected bibliography appears at the end of each chapter for readers interested either in more extensive explorations of the subject matter or in the original source material.

This revision of *Psychiatry for the Family Physician* was made possible by the University of Chicago and the Commonwealth Fund, who underwrote my combined sabbatical and teaching fellowship at the University of Edinburgh in 1963–1964. I am greatly indebted to my colleagues at both universities for their suggestions and criticisms—Prof. G. Morris Carstairs and Dr. and Mrs. Henry Walton at Edinburgh; Dr. William Offenkrantz, Dr. Robert Daniels, Dr. Ralph Heine, Dr. Harry Trosman, and Mr. John Ham at Chicago.

REFERENCES

There are several general textbooks in psychiatry which provide amplification of the material in this book. These include, among others:

Engel, G. L.: *Psychological Development in Health and Disease*, Philadelphia, W. B. Saunders Company, 1962.

English, O. S., and S. M. Finch: *Introduction to Psychiatry*, 3d ed., New York, W. W. Norton & Company, Inc., 1964.

Ewalt, J. R., E. A. Strecker, and F. G. Ebaugh: *Practical Clinical Psychiatry*, 8th ed., New York, McGraw-Hill Book Company, 1957.

Masserman, J. H.: *Principles of Dynamic Psychiatry*, 2d ed., Philadelphia, W. B. Saunders Company, 1961.

Nemiah, J. C.: *Foundations of Psychopathology*, Fairlawn, N.J., Oxford University Press, 1961.

Noyes, A., and L. C. Kolb: *Modern Clinical Psychiatry*, 6th ed., Philadelphia, W. B. Saunders Company, 1963.

As a general reference for a more extensive and detailed treatment of individual topics, see:

Arieti, Silvano (ed.): *American Handbook of Psychiatry*, New York, Basic Books, Inc., Publishers, 1959, vols. I and II.

In child psychiatry:

Caplan, G. (ed.): *Prevention of Mental Disorders in Children*, New York, Basic Books, Inc., Publishers, 1961.

Chess, S.: *An Introduction to Child Psychiatry*, New York, Grune & Stratton, Inc., 1959.

Finch, S. M.: *Fundamentals of Child Psychiatry*, New York, W. W. Norton & Company, Inc., 1960.

Shirley, H.: *Pediatric Psychiatry*, Cambridge, Mass., Harvard University Press, 1963.

In the developing field of prevention:

Caplan, G.: *Principles of Preventive Psychiatry*, New York, Basic Books, Inc., Publishers, 1964.

1. The extent of the problem of mental illness in the United States is documented in *Action for Mental Health: Final Report of the Joint Commission on Mental Illness and Health*, New York, Basic Books, Inc., Publishers, 1961.

2. The contributions of Adolf Meyer and the psychobiologic school are summarized in:

    Meyer, Adolf: *The Commonsense Psychiatry of Dr. Adolf Meyer*, New York, McGraw-Hill Book Company, 1948.

    ————: *Psychobiology: A Science of Man*, Springfield, Ill., Charles C Thomas, Publisher, 1957.

3. A basic survey of psychoanalytic theory is given in:

    Brenner, Charles: *An Elementary Textbook of Psychoanalysis*, Garden City, New York, Doubleday & Company, Inc., 1957.

    Freud's voluminous writings are contained in the twenty-three–volume *Standard Edition of the Complete Psychological Works of Sigmund Freud*, London, The Hogarth Press Ltd., 1953 et seq., hereafter abbreviated as *Standard Edition*.

    Freud summarized much of his theory in:

    Freud, Sigmund: *A General Introduction to Psychoanalysis*, New York, Garden City Books, 1938.

    ————: *Outline of Psychoanalysis*, New York, W. W. Norton & Company, Inc., 1949.

4. The development of dynamic psychiatry in the postwar education of psychiatrists can best be reviewed by reading:

    The Psychiatrist, His Training and Development, Washington, American Psychiatric Association, 1953.

    Training the Psychiatrist to Meet Changing Needs, Washington, American Psychiatric Association, 1963.

5. Grinker, R. R., and J. P. Spiegel: *Men Under Stress*, New York, McGraw-Hill Book Company, 1945.

6. Perlman, H. H.: *Social Casework: A Problem-Solving Process*, Chicago, The University of Chicago Press, 1957.

7. *Proceedings of the Second Colloquium for Postgraduate Teaching of Psychiatry:* Washington, American Psychiatric Association, 1963.
   Draper, E.: *Psychiatry and Pastoral Care,* Englewood Cliffs, N.J., Prentice-Hall, Inc., 1965.
8. Caplan, G.: *Principles of Preventive Psychiatry,* New York, Basic Books, Inc., Publishers, 1964, Chapters 8 and 9.
   Balint, M.: *The Doctor, His Patient and the Illness,* New York, International Universities Press, Inc., 1957.
   Kiesler, F.: "Is This Psychiatry?", in Goldston, S. E. (ed.): *Concepts of Community Psychiatry,* Bethesda, Md., Public Health Service Publication No. 1319, p. 147.
9. Aldrich, C. K.: *Psychiatry for the Family Physician,* New York, McGraw-Hill Book Company, 1955.

CONTENTS

Part One

THE BACKGROUND AND TECHNIQUES
OF PSYCHIATRIC DIAGNOSIS

Chapter 1

EMOTIONS AND ILLNESS

When the average man develops the sniffles, a mild sore throat, a cough, and a low-grade fever, he makes his own diagnosis. He decides that he has a cold in the head, takes some aspirin, drinks fluids, samples a few remedies suggested by his wife or his mother-in-law, and perhaps stays in bed for a day or so. Ordinarily, he recovers and returns to work, and his physician never knows that he has been ill.

The physician sees him only if his symptoms persist or get worse or if new and unfamiliar symptoms develop. If he loses confidence in his own diagnosis or if he suspects a serious illness, he calls for help, primarily because he is worried or afraid. If he puts his specific worry into words, he may say: "Doctor, I am afraid I might be getting a strep throat," "Doctor, I am afraid I might have pneumonia," or "Doctor, there's cancer in my family; don't you think I should have my chest X-rayed?" If he is then asked what it is about strep throat, pneumonia, or cancer that scares him, his answer might include one or more of the following reactions:

1. He fears the *pain* and suffering that he believes these illnesses cause.

2. He worries about being *helpless;* he does not like being a burden to others.

3. He fears *loss* of income, or perhaps of a bodily function or a part of his body.

4. He may fear *death.*

In most cases, his fear determines the timing of his visit to the doctor; he calls for an appointment when his fear of pain, of helplessness, of loss, or of death counterbalances the disadvantages of seeing his doctor. These disadvantages may include the expense, the nuisance, a disinclination to "make a fuss" about something that might be considered trivial, or the possibility that his worst fears might be confirmed.

In patients with more acute conditions, pain or disability may seem to be the primary motive for seeking medical care. Fear, however, is almost always associated with disability and is usually associated with pain; even the patient whose previous bouts of kidney colic have been relieved by

3

medical means will have some fear that this time the medication will not be effective. Pain relief does not automatically relieve fear, particularly if the patient expects his pain to return or believes that his illness is more serious than the physician says it is.

For his fear to be relieved, the patient needs confidence in his doctor—confidence that his doctor understands his problem and that he will know what to do about it. Part of his confidence stems from the doctor's degrees and training, part from his reputation, and part from the success of past treatment. Equally important, however, in determining the patient's confidence is the quality of the relationship the physician has developed with him.

The quality of this relationship is not entirely a function of the physician's experience, reputation, and therapeutic success; medical students may be surprised to discover their importance to the patients they are studying. For example, in the days when the details of a patient's case were discussed in the patient's hearing, a distinguished professor was asked to diagnose and suggest treatment for a middle-aged woman in a charity ward. Her case had puzzled the interns and residents, who clustered around the patient's bed as the attending man first reviewed the findings and then integrated them into the logical and comprehensive steps that lead both to a diagnosis and to an appropriate treatment plan. As he finished, everyone was silent, impressed by the professor's display of erudition and clinical acumen. The silence was broken by the patient, who, catching the eye of the medical student who had painstakingly taken her history and performed a thorough if inexperienced physical examination, asked him: "Do you think that's right, Doctor? Do you think that's what ought to be done?" The student, in some confusion, reminded the patient that he was only a student, whereas the professor was a great medical authority. To which the patient replied: "I know all that, Doctor; he's the one that knows all the books, but you're the one that knows me!"

In this case, the student's interest, thoroughness, and empathy with the patient had given her more confidence in him than in the professor. This relationship technique would perhaps suffice for every patient if fear were always expressed directly and proportionately and if it always responded to appropriate reassurance. But many patients avoid facing their fears, others exaggerate, and still others disguise them; and in most cases, the avoidance, exaggeration, or disguise is not apparent to the patient. For example, suppose the man with the cold in the head notices a fleck of blood in his sputum and associates the blood with possible tuberculosis. The objective course would be to call it to his physician's attention, follow whatever advice is given, and await the results. The patient who avoids facing his fear, however, seems to forget that he ever saw the blood and never tells the doctor. The patient who exaggerates becomes panicky, convinced beyond all possibility of doubt that he has tuberculosis and that he is going to die. The patient who disguises his fears may do so in one of a variety of ways; he may, for example, develop a great deal of unrealistic concern about an apparently unrelated subject—his eyes, perhaps, or his business—while showing appropriate, or perhaps less than appropriate, concern about the question of tuberculosis.

The frequency, extent, and variations of avoidance, exaggeration, and disguise complicate the physician's job. In order to diagnose the illness of almost any patient, the physician needs to recognize the various ways patients have of expressing fear or of avoiding the expression of fear; and in order to treat almost any patient, the physician should know how to manage the fears that accompany illness.

Managing the fears that accompany illness means managing the fears of pain, helplessness, loss, and death and requires an understanding of the underlying psychology. Each fear has a specific symbolic meaning to the particular patient beyond its general connotation, a meaning which can be understood, at least in part, by understanding the patient's past life experiences. Pain, for example, may be associated with punishment if corporal punishment was the usual disciplinary measure in the patient's childhood. Pain may have other, more complex associations, some of which will be mentioned in later chapters. The other three major sources of fear associated with illness will be discussed in the rest of this chapter, with particular emphasis on the ways in which patients cope with them —the helplessness and dependency associated with illness; disability and the need for its acceptance as a prelude to rehabilitation; and the implications of death, both to the patient and to his friends and relatives.

HELPLESSNESS

Severe pain or serious illness produces a *crisis* in a patient's life. A crisis is a situation that overtaxes, or threatens to overtax, the usual problem-solving resources at an individual's command. To cope with the crisis, he must realign old resources or find new resources; in the process, some of his usual activities may be neglected. Thus, in the crisis of severe pain or serious illness, the patient's fears for his health and for his life take priority over external interests. The more he suffers, the more he is concerned with himself and the less emotional energy he has left over for the needs of others. As Charles Lamb put it, "How sickness enlarges the dimensions of a man's self to himself; he is his own exclusive object. Supreme selfishness is inculcated upon him as his only duty ... he keeps his sympathy, like some curious vintage, under trusty lock and key, for his own use only." *

In some degree the patient's condition resembles the helplessness of infancy. The infant, unable himself to relieve his hunger or discomfort, must depend on his mother; in the same way the adult patient, unable to relieve his anxiety or pain, must depend on his physician. Unless his illness is overwhelming, however, his return to a dependent state is not complete. He usually becomes dependent only with respect to his illness, while maintaining his adult capacity to meet his other problems.

His emotional response to his dependent situation is affected to a considerable degree by emotions he experienced in earlier dependent situations. For example, if a person is thrown from a high-spirited horse, he will probably be advised to remount immediately. If he does not soon counteract by a successful ride the anxiety resulting from the fall and if he is predisposed by factors in his earlier emotional development, he may develop a severe fear of riding horseback even though he is an expert rider. The frightening effect of the single experience seems enough to overcome the confidence gained from repeated experiences of mastery. This type of fear, unless counteracted, is likely to increase as time goes on. Eventually, he may be seized with so much anxiety whenever he anticipates riding that he gives it up altogether. If he continues to postpone counteracting his fear, even the sight of a horse or of something that reminds him of a horse may frighten him. In the same way, a frightening incident, situation, or condition in childhood may, if not counteracted, lead to a recurrence of anxiety later on when an incident, situation, or condition reminiscent of the original source of fear is encountered.

Fear is not the only emotion that can be reactivated in this manner. Grief may be reawakened by the sight of a picture or memento of a departed friend, and later in this chapter I will discuss the importance of taking early steps to express and resolve grief to prevent it from persisting indefinitely in exaggerated form. Anger and embarrassment can also be touched off by reminiscent cues and symbols, and the phenomenon is not limited to unpleasant emotions. Anniversaries and trips to childhood scenes bring nostalgic feelings as well as memories, and often the feeling is present without the memory, as the original situation has been forgotten (or repressed—see page 42). For example, the adult patient with an exaggerated fear of doctors or hypodermic needles usually *assumes* that

* Lamb, Charles: *The Convalescent.*

as a child he was frightened by doctors and inoculations, but he seldom *remembers* the incidents. Most if not all children find inoculations frightening, however, even when the physician and parents have reduced their impact by careful preparation, and in the majority of people these fears "wear out," or become extinct. Therefore, the persistence of the fear in the minority cannot be completely explained by simple conditioning. The additional element that determines persistence rather than extinction of the fear as time goes on is the *symbolic significance* of the incident, its meaning to the child in terms of basic emotions and relationships over and above its meaning as a specific incident. Thus, a sudden painful stab in the arm by a man in authority has a different symbolic significance to a child who anticipates unprovoked brutality from his father than it has to a child who regards his father's discipline as reasonable.

Even if he does not recall his childhood *experiences,* therefore, the sick and relatively helpless adult will reexperience some of the *feelings* associated with earlier periods of dependency, so that his reaction to illness is affected by his experience during his infancy and childhood. If he felt secure and loved through infancy, the helplessness of illness will not in itself be threatening and he will trust his physician or his nurse readily and naturally. If, on the other hand, he felt insecure and unloved in infancy, the helplessness of illness will frighten him and he will find it difficult to have confidence in his doctor. Such a patient usually does not recognize the cause of his fears; he tries to accept the doctor's reassurances, but his fear persists and often interferes with the treatment program. A patient who suffers from coronary disease, rheumatic fever, or tuberculosis needs rest, but if he fears the dependency that rest requires, his fear will accelerate his heart, increase his rate of respiration, and produce other physiologic changes which deprive him of the benefits rest should provide. To the patient who fears dependency, surgical procedures are particularly threatening; he is terrified by the total surrender which submission to general anesthesia demands, and his fear may seriously impair his physiologic reserves. The particular terror which poliomyelitis has always inspired is related in part, at least, to the extreme and obvious helplessness it can cause, culminating in the total dependency of the patient in the respirator.

Systematic clinical studies, as well as casual observations, suggest that a child who did not receive the security he needed while he was still dependent resents his parents for their failure to provide it. As he matures, he carries over his resentment to anyone he must depend upon, so that the enforced dependency of illness will again bring out anger. The anger is then directed toward the people who are trying to care for him: the doctor, the nurse, or members of his family. The doctor may be unaware of the anger, since the patient may realize that it is unrealistic or at least unwelcome and may conceal it in some way. Furthermore, many doctors, preferring appreciation to resentment, tend to overlook or rationalize evidence of a patient's irritation when it emerges. In doing so, however, they may also overlook significant evidence that the patient's emotional integration is disturbed.

The following case shows how angry and dependent feelings may interfere with a treatment program.

> A twenty-five-year-old man with severe rheumatic heart disease had been a model patient for five years. He had followed prescribed routines, and although before his illness he had been an active athlete who preferred outdoor work, he adapted himself to a completely sedentary existence without complaint.
>
> His physician was surprised, therefore, when the patient suddenly became depressed, tearful, resentful of restrictions, and determined to abandon all medical routines. His dramatic reversal of attitude followed the doctor's suggestion that he remove salt from his diet, a suggestion which seemed hardly enough of a restriction to justify such an explosion.
>
> When the doctor reevaluated the emotional aspects of the case, however, he saw several reasons for the change. He discovered that the patient had made unusually early and aggressive attempts to emancipate himself from his family, which suggested that he had been going out of his way to avoid dependency. When he first developed joint pains, his parents had called them "growing pains," recommending that he "work them out." Later, however, a doctor told him that his exercise had brought about the damage to his heart. In spite of these circumstances, he had accepted the dependency forced by his illness, concealing the anger he felt toward his parents for misleading him.
>
> At the time of his outburst he was working as a draftsman among healthy and friendly coworkers. His illness excluded him from their recreation after work—dancing, bowling, hunting, and so on—but during the workday he felt himself part of the group, particularly at lunch, which they all ate together at a certain restaurant. When the physician learned this, he remembered that during their discussion of the diet prescription, the patient had been quite anxious to find out where in town he could obtain saltfree meals. It was after he had received a list of such establishments—which did not include the restaurant patronized by the draftsmen—that he became depressed.
>
> When the physician recognized the significance of the diet restriction and the anger behind the patient's outburst, he encouraged him to express his hidden resentment at his illness, his parents, and his restricted life. The doctor carefully explained the rationale of the saltfree diet, making it clear

that he appreciated the importance to the patient of keeping the one social situation in which he did not have to feel different from everyone else. By this time, the patient had become less depressed. He talked to the restaurant chef and found he could obtain a reasonable facsimile of a saltfree diet, which the doctor decided would suffice under the circumstances.

In many cases of this type, a doctor's willingness to work out compromises between the strictly medical indications and the emotional needs of the patient results in better response to treatment. Compromise may be particularly valuable when the medical indication is rest.

A farmwife who had gone to work at fourteen and married at eighteen had for years done all the work of maintaining a home and bringing up six children as well as gardening, raising chickens, and winning prizes at the state fair. She had never been ill and had never taken a vacation.

When she suffered a coronary thrombosis, her physician prescribed bed rest. She adapted reasonably well in the hospital, and when she returned home, her children, relatives, and neighbors competed with each other in taking care of her. They assured her that she had long ago more than earned a rest and that they welcomed the chance to repay, at least in part, some of the help she had given to them.

In spite of their loving care, however, she became tense and unhappy; and although she conscientiously followed orders, her tension increased the load on her heart and retarded her progress. As her doctor talked to her, he realized that all her life she had felt secure only when she was being productive. She had just been close to death, and he knew that it was not the time to try to alter the basis of her emotional security, even if it were possible to do so. Therefore, he decided on a compromise and permitted her to use her electric sewing machine.

With something constructive and useful to do, she felt less like a parasite and found it easier to tolerate seeing others doing her cooking, baking, and scrubbing. Her peace of mind seemed to reduce her cardiac output, more than balancing the slight increase caused by using the sewing machine.

This woman is typical of a large group of patients who are afraid or ashamed of being dependent and who adopt an attitude of apparent independence, or *pseudoindependence*, to avoid and conceal dependency (page 100). When a patient's resistance to dependency is particularly strong, he may become a serious problem in medical management. As long as he is able to struggle, he will fight off anything that suggests that he cannot take care of himself. He always has too much to do to go to bed. When he finally succumbs, he makes his own rules about bathroom privileges and diet. He argues with the nurses and second-guesses the doctors. If his illness becomes too severe for these maneuvers, he may give up the fight, but forced to surrender to dependency, he is likely to become depressed or anxious.

DENIAL

When a symptom of illness frightens a patient, he may avoid facing his fear by *denying* the significance or even the existence of the symptom. Denial is a psychologic protective mechanism in which a disturbing aspect of reality is not acknowledged as real. For denial to be effective, the individual cannot be aware of (or conscious of) either the process of denial or the fact that is denied. Ordinarily, distortion of reality to such an extent is considered evidence of severe emotional disturbance, but when the threat is serious enough, almost anyone will use denial.

Denial can be a major obstacle both to diagnosis and to treatment [1]. For example, a man may know that fever, cough, night sweats, and weight loss often mean tuberculosis. He knows that if anyone develops these signs, he should go at once to a physician. If, however, he uses denial to avoid facing their significance when he develops them, he may seem to ignore their existence, and so he will postpone seeking medical care and will risk infecting others while allowing his lesion to become more extensive. He is most likely to deny the significance of his symptoms if he is accustomed to using denial, if tuberculosis has a particularly frightening connotation to him (as when a relative has died of it), or if the prospect of a long period of dependency is unusually disturbing to him. People who habitually use denial often attempt to avoid the fear of a particular illness or situation by denying not only its relevance to themselves but anything that would remind them of its existence. In this way, an otherwise well-informed person who uses denial and whose relative died of tuberculosis may not have any knowledge of the progress made in its treatment since that time and may still think that treatment requires years of bed rest, with an uncertain outcome.

The physician should always watch for signs of denial as well as for fear, anger, or depression when he must confront a patient with a potentially distressing diagnosis. First of all, he should not overestimate the patient's background in medical information. But even when he carefully explains the nature of the disease and the treatment plan, the patient may be so overwhelmed by the implications of the diagnosis that he will not comprehend any of the explanation. The patient needs a chance to discuss his understanding of his illness and his emotional reactions to it. During these discussions, the physician can help the patient accept his illness, thereby reducing the likelihood of denial, with its consequent dangerous flight from treatment.

When a patient finally accepts the fact that he has a chronic disease, particularly when the disease is permanently incapacitating, he usually becomes depressed. To let him down slowly by telling the bad news little by little may postpone his depression, but it will also delay the ultimate acceptance of his illness and may in the long run prolong and intensify his emotional problems. Observations of blinded soldiers have demonstrated this point [2]. Although most of the men who were informed as soon as practicable that their sight was irrevocably lost became depressed, in time they were able to accept their blindness and take constructive steps toward rehabilitation. On the other hand, those who gradually came to the realization that their blindness was permanent found the condition more difficult to accept and were much more inclined to resist rehabilitative measures.

Where rehabilitation is possible, a kind but realistic statement of the truth, followed by ample opportunity for the patient to ventilate his feelings, is the most satisfactory technique for handling patients with serious diseases and disabilities. A man must know where he stands before he can take constructive action. A patient's attitude toward rehabilitation, however, depends to a considerable extent on his attitudes toward dependency. The passive, dependent person who welcomes illness as a justification for helplessness may resist rehabilitation, since recovery will jeopardize the security of his retreat. On the other hand, the patient who fights off dependency may overdo his rehabilitative efforts or may leave the hospital before he is ready. Personality diagnosis and appropriate psychosocial planning at the onset of a chronic illness can reduce the chances of either an unnecessary prolongation of invalidism or a premature discharge against medical advice [3]. When rehabilitation is *not* possible, however, as in an inoperable cancer, the situation is somewhat changed (this contingency will be discussed in the next section).

Whether to tell a patient that he has cancer or to disguise the diagnosis by using words like "tumor" or "neoplasm" depends on the particular meaning the words have for the patient. Once the diagnosis has been made, it is a bit awkward to try to determine this meaning, so the physician should have included in his initial history taking an inquiry into the patient's own ideas and fears about his illness. For example, a patient who feels guilty about past sins may consider his cancer a deserved punishment. In a case of this kind, reassuring him that his cancer can be treated may have no effect on him, because he believes he ought to die. When a physician sees no response to legitimate reassurance, he should reexamine the specific meaning the disease has for the patient.

Patients of any age should be informed of all contemplated medical or surgical procedures and should be told enough about the nature of the unpleasant experiences and about the amount of postoperative pain they can expect so that they will not be caught unawares [4]. Children particularly need a frank explanation of what to expect. Although a child may be temporarily disturbed when he is told that a painful or frightening experience is in store for him, the long-term ill effects of deception will far outweigh any inconvenience to the physician or nurse that is caused by telling the truth [5]. Children who have been deceived until the last moment about tonsillectomies, for example, frequently develop persistent fears of doctors and other people in authority, as well as signs of anxiety such as night terrors [6]. When possible, surgery should be postponed until the age of six, since younger children cannot completely comprehend even the most careful explanations. Every child should have the security afforded by the presence of his parents before and immediately after surgery, and whenever feasible the physician should choose induction anesthetics which are not terrifying.

A child's emotional needs require particular consideration whenever hospitalization is necessary [7]. Hospitalization forces him into the care of strangers at a time when he is most helpless and most needs his parents. To maintain his security, he requires hospital personnel who understand his fears and the reassurance of frequent visits or even a temporary move into his hospital room by his mother. Children who are not completely immobilized by their insecurity protest vigorously at the end of visiting hours; consequently, a child's parents or doctor may assume that the visits are disturbing to him and should be reduced in frequency, when actually he is frightened by the hospital experience and needs even more emotional support. A child who exploits his illness to gain attention is also showing signs of insecurity which should be investigated, although the doctor can limit the exploitation as he searches for the cause.

Since parents often communicate their own anxiety to their child during visiting hours, the doctor should not begrudge time spent explaining the child's illness to them. Such explanations are important whenever a child is hospitalized, but they are particularly necessary in cases of dramatically dangerous illnesses such as rheumatic fever and tuberculosis. Should the illness be fatal, the doctor's previous concern for the parents' feelings makes it easier for him to help them during their period of grief.

Physicians who know by personal experience the suffering of major illness usually are tolerant and understanding of their patients' reactions to dependency [8]. However, familiarity with the concepts of emotional growth and development (as outlined in the middle chapters of this book), may steer the physician by a different path toward a similar goal of recognition, understanding, and treatment of the emotional reactions to illness.

GRIEF

Grief is the appropriate reaction to the temporary or permanent loss of someone or something dear. Although we usually think of grief in relation to the loss of a relative or friend, the term fits reactions to other losses—of a part of the body, of a home, of a business, or even of a keepsake. If the person or object lost is of major importance to the individual, the loss represents a crisis in his life. As in severe illness, the crisis of important loss overtaxes his problem-solving resources, and in attempting to cope with the loss, some of his usual activities may be neglected.

Much of the drama of a doctor's professional life is concerned with grief [9]. When he tells relatives that a patient is worse or will die or must lose a limb, he precipitates *anticipatory* grief; if later he must inform them that the patient is dead, he reactivates their grief. He arouses grief when he tells a patient that he must have an amputation. If he tells a patient that he has no chance to live, the grief he engenders may be overwhelming. None of these situations is easy for the physician, because he feels a personal sense of loss at his patient's misfortune. He also may have a feeling of failure or even of guilt as he looks back over his management of the case to see if somehow he might have prevented or at least delayed the current calamity.

In many instances, the physician does not see the relatives of a dead patient except during the period of shock that ordinarily lasts for a few days immediately after a loss—before the expression of grief begins. During this period, the relatives superficially appear to have adjusted to the loss, reassuring their friends and their physician by their capacity to attend competently to funeral details and the demands of continuing existence. A few days later, however, when the ceremonies and formalities are over, they begin to feel the full impact of the loss. The physician can often be of most help to the bereaved if he makes a follow-up visit about ten days later.

Cultural factors to some extent determine the external manifestations of grief. Some cultures value an attitude of stoical acceptance, while others expect weeping and tearing of hair and clothes by both men and women. Whether or not the person who has lost a close friend or relative reveals his feelings to others, he is absorbed in his loss as he goes through a period of painful separation, almost as if he were saying farewell, one by one, to each memory and reminder of the loved one. Typically, he accuses himself of having failed to do enough or of having neglected the loved one. He cannot be hurried in his leave-taking, and he often irritably brushes off his friends when they attempt to console him. In his grief, he identifies with the deceased and may develop some of the symptoms of the fatal illness of the loved one. He is apt either to slow down his activity or to be restlessly active without purpose.

Since the grief-stricken relative usually is in close contact with the physician in charge before and at the time of a death, the doctor can help him face his grief, express his feelings, and gradually withdraw much of the investment of love and affection that he has made in the one he has lost. As the relative does so, he slowly adjusts himself to an environment which no longer contains the lost one and can begin to extend other relationships and establish new relationships to fill the gap, to some degree. Thus, the period of mourning progresses to its end.

Grief is ordinarily more intense if the death occurs suddenly, if the survivor was particularly dependent on the dead person, if he was at all responsible for the death, or if he is particularly sensitive to separation as a result of previous experiences of separation early in his life. Although mixed feelings, or *ambivalence,* are present in all relationships, grief is more painful if the relative's feelings about the dead person are unusually ambivalent. Since for most people it seems difficult selectively to recognize one kind of feeling about something without recognizing other kinds, the grieving ambivalent relative must face his hostility as well as his affection. Society, however, has long-standing prohibitions against hostility or angry feelings about the departed. *De mortuis nihil nisi bonum* (speak nothing but good of the dead) is an ancient saying which still has currency. The ambivalent surviving relative, therefore, feels guilty, particularly if he has a rigid conscience. His feelings, put into words, might be: "Although I loved you, I also hated you; and when I hated you, I wished you were gone. Now that you are gone, it is almost as if my wish were the cause, so I feel responsible and guilty."

These feelings may be so disturbing to the relative that he conceals them from himself, or *represses* them. He thereby avoids facing the guilt about the hostile side of his feelings, but since the hostility and the affection are fused together, he also avoids facing his affectionate feelings associated with the loss. The process of mourning is thus delayed. The pressure of the unexpressed feeling continues, however, and later may form the basis of a depression (see page 242).

This man appeared to ignore or deny anything that did not support his hopes of recovery. He was well liked and happy in his work and family life and had a great deal to live for and a great deal to lose.

Neither high intelligence nor education is a bar to the use of denial.

> A brilliant and successful businessman whose two sons were physicians knew enough about medicine to realize the possibilities of metastasis at the time his carcinoma of the prostate was resected. When he later developed bony metastases, however, he convinced himself that he had arthritis. He exercised to keep his joints supple and interrupted any mention of his cancer with: "Oh, I had that all taken care of months ago."

Sometimes the denial takes the form of a conviction that the patient is a special case for whom the usual rules do not apply.

> Kaufman tells [12] of "... an intelligent young woman admitted for a second bout of acute disseminated lupus.... When she was asked what she knew of the nature of her illness, she disclosed an accurate knowledge of its name and nature. After her first admission, she had looked it up in a medical dictionary, where it was defined as a 'chronic, fatal disease.'
>
> "'You know,' she said brightly, 'a thing like that could scare you.' For herself, she managed not to believe that this definition could apply to her and thus succeeded in being sure she would get well."

The use of denial in these circumstances is by no means a sign of a neurotic or emotionally immature patient. The relationships of the mature individual are deeper and more extensive, and so he has more to lose by dying. With more to lose, he has a greater need for denial; on the other hand, a characteristic of maturity is the ability to meet unpleasant circumstances realistically. If he discovers that death is inevitable, he takes longer to build up the defense of denial, and meanwhile he suffers more intensely. The personality strength that makes him face facts also helps him put up a façade to conceal his grief from others. But although he struggles to hide his situation from those for whom it could cause pain, he cannot hide it from himself, and he may even find the answer in suicide.

A patient who is already depressed, however, may welcome death and need no defenses against recognizing it.

> An elderly retired farmer complained that his children were causing him needless discomfort and inconvenience in bringing him to the hospital. He maintained that he had known all along that his cancer would kill him and asked only to be allowed to die in peace.
>
> He had worked hard since the age of fourteen and had assiduously avoided vacations or any other situation in which he was not being productive. After arthritis forced him to retire, he became grouchy, glum, and depressed. He readily acknowledged that he had nothing to live for.

For this patient, cancer meant a welcome and acceptable substitute for suicide. Another example of this type of reaction occurred in a middle-aged woman who seemed unusally calm before an operation for a suspected malignancy. Instead of being relieved when the tumor was found to be benign, she became upset and refused to believe that she would ever get well. Her physician then discovered that she had been depressed about her personal and marital situation for some time before the tumor was discovered and that she had actually hoped that it would be malignant.

Acceptance of impending death is not necessarily due to depression. With increasing age, many people go through a period of *disengagement* [13] or withdrawal from outside contacts into themselves. As this process continues, they have progressively less to lose by dying and so become progressively more able to tolerate the idea of approaching death.

As their diseases progress, some patients who were not previously depressed may accept death rather than deny the evidence of approaching death. Late in the course of a fatal illness, particularly when severe pain causes a patient to center his emotions more and more on himself and to withdraw them from others, the discomfort of living may counterbalance his incentive to live. When he reaches this point, he drops his defenses; a patient who one day speaks hopefully of the future may the next day calmly tell his physician that he now realizes that he will not recover. Many patients, however, maintain their defenses until they die, unless outside interference breaks them down.

A cardinal rule in the management of emotional problems is that a patient's emotional defenses should be respected unless there is evidence that the advantages of breaking them down outweigh the advantages of supporting them. In supporting a patient's denial of evidence of impending death, the doctor may prevent a grief reaction which, added to the patient's misery, may hasten death, either through suicide or perhaps through loss of his will to live.

What are the advantages of breaking down denial? Perhaps the most frequently cited benefit is the chance to settle business affairs. If he has no warning of death, a man may jeopardize his family's economic security by undertaking expensive projects that require his presence to complete. On the other hand, a man who faces the imminent loss of all he holds dear may be too overwhelmed by grief to take appropriate steps, or he may avoid taking steps because their significance conflicts with his struggle to deny the evidence. Thus, a man who knows he is about to die may postpone drawing up a will because he equates his signature on the will to a signature on his own death sentence. When, however, a patient has been told that his illness is chronic and incapacitating and carries the *possibility* of death, he can usually put his affairs in order for retirement with more equanimity.

The same reasoning can apply to a second argument for informing a patient of his approaching death: that he should be told so that he can put his spiritual house in order. A patient may find it more possible to make his peace with God when he thinks death is a fair possibility than when he regards it as certain. Here a great deal depends on the patient's religious affiliations and on the lines of communication the doctor has established with the ministers, priests, and rabbis in his community.

A third argument for warning a patient is that he is entitled to know the truth and the doctor is obligated to tell it. The doctor is also obligated, however, to "Never do harm to anyone . . . nor give advice which may cause . . . death," * and he cannot wash his hands of the responsibility for precipitating a suicidal grief reaction simply by saying that he told the truth. Actually, no doctor is ever really sure that a patient will die until he is dead; he may know that ninety-nine out of a hundred persons with a specific condition die, but such statistics are meaningless when applied to an individual who will be either 100 percent alive or 100 percent dead.

> When a physician was informed that biopsy of his gland showed typical lymphosarcoma, he became extremely depressed, although he managed to conceal it from his family and his physicians. He was too realistic to deny the evidence, he was too considerate of his family to let them know how he was feeling, and he was too proud to let his physician know he was depressed. After weeks of loneliness and depression, he made a spontaneous recovery.

Even carefully substantiated diagnoses may be in error.

> A laboratory technician suffered deep depression when her diagnosis of leukemia was "confirmed." She was contemplating suicide when, two weeks later, her illness was found to be an atypical form of pernicious anemia.

When a physician makes a diagnosis of a presumably fatal illness, he probably should discuss it first with a responsible member of the patient's family. The relative will need privacy and plenty of time to express his own feelings and to prepare himself for discussing plans to meet the patient's physical and emotional needs. Any plan must have the cooperation of all close relatives in order to be successful. Either way—to protect the patient from depression or to deal with his depression—is difficult for

* The Hippocratic Oath.

members of the family, and they will need periodic opportunities to discuss their problems and feelings with the doctor.

As mentioned before, the patient may not ask for a prognosis, and the whole problem may be bypassed. On the other hand, the physician should be prepared to give his patient some kind of definite answer if he does ask, since obvious evasion or circumlocution in such cases only increases the patient's anxieties and distress. The unvarnished truth may be the easiest definite answer for the physician to give, but as the examples quoted above illustrate, it can be the hardest for the patient to receive. The other course requires the physician to shade the truth; misrepresentation of the facts is not easy, and the statements must be made with conviction in order to be effective. Although in almost any situation a physician helps his patient most by telling him the truth, impending death is possibly one of the few exceptions to the rule.

The following case example contrasts the implications of two approaches to the same problem. Dr. B. has just operated on his colleague, Dr. A., and has discovered a carcinoma of the stomach with extensive metastases to the liver. He might say:

> "I'm awfully sorry, Dr. A., but we found that your carcinoma has spread to involve your liver. As you know, this makes your future look bleak, but we can try some radiation to slow things down as much as possible. I hate to tell you this, but it seems only fair to let you know so you can arrange your personal and business affairs accordingly."

If Dr. A. has a great deal to lose by dying, he will begin to mourn his anticipated losses as soon as he has grasped the full significance of Dr. B.'s statement. He will then feel depressed and will either show or conceal his depression. He may attempt to relieve his depression by questioning the validity of the diagnosis, by deciding that his is a special case which does not follow the usual expectations, or by developing a blind and unrealistic faith in the therapeutic benefits of palliative treatment. Since these attempts at denial are difficult for a realistic individual to support and are easily torn down, the patient, apparently sensing their vulnerability, may keep them to himself. He then will give the impression of being resigned to his condition, while maintaining his own private reservations.

An alternative approach, calculated to protect the patient from depression and from the painful effort to build his defenses, might be:

> "As you anticipated, Dr. A., you had a carcinoma of the stomach. We did our best to remove all of it, but you know that we can never be absolutely sure. Although we are optimistic, we must of course consider the possibility of recurrence. For the time being, anyway, if you have not

already done so, I think you should arrange things so that you will be carrying little or no responsibility in your practice; you've had a good deal of surgical work done, and with the side effects of the radiation we will have to give you for your fullest protection, you'll need all your strength for some time to come to take care of your physical health."

An approach of this kind makes denial possible for the patient who needs to deny and at the same time paves the way for acceptance if, as in Zinsser's classic description of himself [14], he is prepared to accept. The patient who needs to deny can focus on the optimistic side of the surgeon's statement—"We did our best to remove all of it," and "We are optimistic"—and can still put his affairs in order on the basis of a prudent consideration for future misadventure, as he would before going into military combat. He can bring his will up to date and still reserve his own secret or open conviction that he is destined to survive. With this approach, the situation is recognized as serious by both patient and family, and so there is no need for the family and patient to pretend with each other that there is nothing whatsoever to worry about.

On the other hand, if Dr. A. is ready to accept death, he will not focus on the optimistic side but instead will probably respond with some such comment as: "Doctor, you're really telling me that things look bad, aren't you?" to which the surgeon might say: "That's right. Your condition is certainly very serious, but that does not mean that it is hopeless or that we are planning to give up our efforts to overcome it."

In the last analysis, the routine in these cases cannot be prescribed, since so many emotional implications for both doctor and patient must be considered in each individual case. If the physician feels, however, that he must tell his patient, it is both more humane and more realistic to permit him a little hope. In any event, he should resolve his own feelings so that he can maintain contact; a physician who studiously avoids a dying patient or bypasses him on rounds makes it obvious that he has abandoned him and thus withdraws his support at the very time it is most desperately needed.

A FRUSTRATING PATIENT

In the first three sections of this chapter, I discussed the significance of an understanding of personality to the physician in his management of physical illness in general and of fatal illness in particular. In this section, I will take up an example of a patient whose illness is primarily emotional in origin—more "psychiatric," if you will, than the patients mentioned earlier, yet a type of "psychiatric" patient that is encountered in substantial numbers by general practitioners, internists, surgeons, and other physicians. I will discuss her case, therefore, with particular emphasis on the problems and frustrations she presents to her physician.

When Dr. Wilson set up his practice in a small Midwestern town, he soon earned the reputation of being a warm and conscientious doctor who obviously enjoyed his patients. One of his first patients was Mrs. Helen Brown, a forty-five-year-old housewife who had suffered for three years from a succession of relatively vague headaches, backaches, and other pains and from attacks of bloating and miscellaneous complaints. Her previous physician had been an older man who was close to retirement and who no longer made house calls.

The nature and course of the symptoms and the absence of relevant physical or X-ray findings convinced Dr. Wilson that the episodes resulted chiefly from Mrs. Brown's emotions, although she was equally convinced that she had an organic disease. After several conversations, he learned that the first attack developed shortly after her discovery that her husband had been having an affair with another woman.

In the course of these conversations, Dr. Wilson learned a great deal about Mrs. Brown's background. As a girl, she had taken a lot of family responsibility, and while still in high school, she had frequently cared for her alcoholic father. She described her mother as a rather cold and self-pitying woman whose chief concern was to keep her furniture and possessions immaculate and who had delegated much of the care of the younger children to Helen. Although Helen had carried out her duties competently, her mother consistently showed her preference for a less conscientious daughter. Helen said that she had never been the type to complain or to indicate resentment. She recalled that as a child she had had frequent stomach upsets.

She had married an unambitious man who often drank to excess; many in the community felt that the occasional success he enjoyed was due more to his wife's efficient help than to his own efforts. Until the onset of the present illness, she had been active in community projects such as the church and PTA, and most of her neighbors had relied on her for advice and help. She had worked hard, had never taken a vacation, had never "given in" to minor illnesses, and had found it difficult to relax when she had the opportunity. Since her illness began, she had withdrawn from her friends and from outside activities and had even found it difficult to do her housework.

Dr. Wilson had been taught that most hypochondriacs tend to exaggerate and seem to enjoy their symptoms; but although he was convinced that Mrs. Brown's complaints were "functional," she did not seem to enjoy illness and she seemed genuinely unhappy at the necessity for calling him. He had also assumed that hypochondriacs would improve if they had a chance to talk over their troubles, but since he had encouraged Mrs. Brown to discuss some of her problems with him, her symptoms had become more frequent rather than less. He was perplexed by her failure to progress, and he found himself becoming more and more irritated with her, especially when her attacks of bloating routed him out of bed early in the morning. At such times he was tempted to tell her to struggle along without him, but realizing that she was suffering intensely and that her symptoms might be due to a new and dangerous condition, he would go out to see her. When he arrived, he invariably found no physical illness, so he would give her a sedative and sit down to talk with her until she felt better. These conversations had become longer and longer as time went on, and he was beginning to worry about her increasing use of sedatives. On two or three occasions when he had been unusually tired, he let his temper get the better of him and scolded her for inconsiderate behavior. He observed that this routine had always made her worse.

Dr. Wilson felt trapped; Mrs. Brown was taking up more and more of his time, and he was finding it harder and harder to control his irritation. He believed he must be handling the situation poorly, but there was no one in the community to consult and she had refused even to consider referral to a psychiatrist. He had given her medicine, and he had changed her diet; he had been sympathetic, and he had been angry; on some occasions he had advised her to rest, and on others he had advised her to resume her outside activities; and he had lectured her husband on his drinking. Nothing worked, and he became steadily more frustrated.

As I have described her, Mrs. Brown sounds like a most unsatisfactory patient, and one could hardly blame Dr. Wilson for wanting to get rid of her. There were several reasons why he did not get rid of her: first, he was a compassionate man and knew that she was suffering; second, he knew of no one to whom he could refer her; and third, in spite of her disagreement with his diagnosis, she seemed to be devoted to him, and he felt sure that she would not consider leaving him.

Dr. Wilson was concerned about the use of drugs in her case, because he knew that patients of this type often overuse drugs and may become addicted. He did not want to give in again to her insistence that he had "missed something" and that he arrange for more diagnostic procedures, because in the past the relief that followed his reassurance that a laboratory procedure showed no organic illness had always been temporary and was always followed by more insistence and more symptoms. Some patients of Mrs. Brown's type shop interminably from doctor to doctor; others drift away to chiropractors or naturopaths. A few improve, often without apparent reason. The question is, even though she refuses to consult a psychiatrist, can psychiatry help her doctor manage the problem?

Psychiatry's possible contribution can be demonstrated by a parallel between heart disease and emotional disturbance. For both, practical diagnosis requires more than a label such as "rheumatic heart disease" or "hypochondriasis." For proper handling of heart disease, the physician should know when it began, what caused it, how rapidly it has progressed, and how it has responded to stress and to treatment. He should know what valves or vessels or structures are damaged and what the nature of the damage is, what changes in function have taken place, what the likelihood is of response to either medical or surgical management, and what the prognosis is. The more the physician knows about all of these, the more intelligently he can plan his treatment.

Precisely the same considerations are relevant to proper management of emotional illness. The physician should know its duration, the precipitating factors, the nature of its progress and response to stress and treatment, the structural damage if any, the specific mechanics of symptom formation, the possible response to treatment of different kinds, and the prognosis. Here, too, the better the diagnosis, the better the treatment plan.

In both cases, the physician must understand normal development, structure, and function in order to evaluate the abnormal; in both cases, he must be familiar with the common abnormalities and their interrelationships and ranges of variation; and in both cases, knowledge of laboratory aids will simplify his diagnostic task.

Finally, there are similarities in the expectations of treatment. In either case, a complete and permanent cure is seldom accomplished; patients of both groups tend to carry scars or incapacities indefinitely. But as the physician can help most cardiac patients to improve and to return at least to limited function, so he can help a great many emotionally distressed patients to reach a better adjustment and to maintain their improvement indefinitely. In general, the prognosis in the neurotic is better than in the cardiac; age works against the cardiac, but it works as often for as against the neurotic.

There are differences, however, as well as similarities in the two approaches. The physician's evaluation of the emotional disturbance is derived primarily from his observations of the patient's behavior; in the case of heart disease, he has in addition more clear-cut physical findings, more highly developed laboratory findings, and corroborative evidence from postmortem studies. His evaluations can be described, therefore, in more definite and precise terms. His psychiatric evaluation is more likely to be in the form of generalizations and relatively tentative formulations, which he must continually test against his patient's specific problem. The principles of psychiatry provide, however, a framework within which to work, and they can give the physician practical help in the exercise of the art of medicine.

Practical psychiatry may also help the physician in handling his own feelings. If a better understanding of Mrs. Brown's emotional structure can help Dr. Wilson to treat her more effectively and at the same time to reduce the length and number of his house calls, he will be less irritated by her and will derive more satisfaction from her care. A great many rewards in the practice of medicine come from realizing therapeutic goals, and an understanding of dynamic psychiatry can help a physician set his goals more realistically and attain them more frequently with his emotionally distressed patients.

Although I can promise no magical solution to Dr. Wilson's problems with Mrs. Brown, I will refer to her case later in the book when discussing personality structures, diagnosis, and treatment, and I will use it as an example to illustrate the application of some of the theoretic concepts (see Index, Brown, Mrs., case of).

SUMMARY

Illness forces the patient to depend on others. In this dependence, he experiences feelings, often including anger, that he originally associated with childhood dependency. If these feelings are so frightening that they threaten to overwhelm him, he may attempt to deny the existence of his illness in an effort to avoid the feelings. In treating his patient, the physician can help him look at his illness realistically and so cooperate in rehabilitative efforts.

Grief is the reaction of the personality to the loss of someone or something dear. The individual who cannot express his grief usually becomes depressed. The physician often has the opportunity to forestall depression by encouraging the expression and consequent resolution of grief.

Patients who know they are going to die experience an emotional reaction analogous to severe grief. They may protect themselves from this reaction by denying that death is imminent. Before discussing prognosis with severely ill patients, therefore, the physician should carefully determine the relative importance to the patient of the information and of the protection offered by ignorance or denial.

REFERENCES

1. Rosen, V. H.: "The Role of Denial in Acute Postoperative Affective Reactions Following the Removal of Body Parts," *Psychosom. Med.*, 12:356, 1950.
   Weinstein, E. A., and R. L. Kahn: *Denial of Illness: Symbolic and Physiological Aspects,* Springfield, Ill. Charles C Thomas, Publisher, 1955.

2. Diamond, B. L., and Alice Ross: "Emotional Adjustment of Newly Blinded Soldiers," *Amer. J. Psychiat.*, 102:367, 1945.
3. Field, M.: *Patients Are People: A Medical-Social Approach to Prolonged Illness*, 2d ed., New York, Columbia University Press, 1958.
   Lewis, W. C., T. H. Lorenz, and G. Calden: "Irregular Discharge among Tuberculous Patients—A Major Unsolved Problem," *Psychosom. Med.*, 17:276, 1955.
4. Janis, I. L.: *Psychological Stress*, New York, John Wiley & Sons, Inc., 1958.
   Egbert, L. D., et al.: "Reduction of Postoperative Pain by Encouragement and Instruction of Patients," *New Eng. J. Med.*, 270:825, 1964.
   Titchener, J., and M. Levine: *Surgery, A Human Experience*, Fairlawn, N.J., Oxford University Press, 1960.
5. Long, R. T. and O. Cope: Emotional Problems of Burned Children. *New Eng. J. Med.*, 264:1121, 1961.
6. Coleman, L. L.: "The Psychologic Implications of Tonsillectomy," *New York J. Med.*, 50:1225, 1950.
   Levy, D. M.: "Psychic Trauma of Operations in Children," *Amer. J. Dis. Child.*, 69:7, 1945.
   Lipton, S. D.: "On the Psychology of Childhood Tonsillectomy," *Psychoanal. Stud. Child*, 17:363, New York, International Universities Press, Inc., 1962.
7. Bowlby, J., J. Robertson, and D. Rosenbluth: "A Two-year-old Goes to Hospital," *Psychoanal. Stud. Child*, 7:82, New York, International Universities Press, Inc., 1952.
   Jackson, Katherine: "Psychologic Preparation as a Method of Reducing the Emotional Trauma of Anesthesia in Children," *Anesthesiology*, 12:293, 1951.
   ————, Ruth Winkley, O. A. Faust, and Ethel G. Cermak: "Problem of Emotional Trauma in Hospital Treatment of Children," *J.A.M.A.*, 149:1536, 1952.
   Mason, E. A.: "The Hospitalized Child—His Emotional Needs," *New Eng. J. Med.*, 272:406, 1965.
   Prugh, D. G., et al.: "Study of Emotional Reactions of Children and Families to Hospitalization and Illness," *Amer. J. Orthopsychiat.*, 23:70, 1953.
   Visotsky, H. M., et al.: "Coping Behavior under Extreme Stress," *Arch. Gen. Psychiat.*, 5:423, 1961.
   Watson, E. J., and A. M. Johnson: "The Emotional Significance of Acquired Physical Disfigurement in Children," *Amer. J. Orthopsychiat.*, 28:85, 1958.
8. Pinner, M., and B. F. Miller: *When Doctors Are Patients*, New York, W. W. Norton & Company, Inc., 1952.
9. Engel, G. S.: "Is Grief a Disease?" *Psychosom. Med.*, 12:18, 1961.
   Lindemann, E.: "Symptomatology and Management of Acute Grief," *Amer. J. Psychiat.*, 101:141, 1944.
   Parkes, C. M.: "Bereavement and Mental Illness. Part 2. A Classification of Bereavement Reactions," *Brit. J. Med. Psychol.* 38:13, 1965.
   Solnit, A. J., and M. Green: "Psychologic Considerations in the Manage-

ment of Deaths on Pediatric Hospital Services. I. The Doctor and the Child's Family," *Pediatrics*, 24:106, 1959.
10. Kolb, L. C.: *The Painful Phantom: Psychology, Physiology, and Treatment,* Springfield, Ill., Charles C Thomas, Publisher, 1954.
11. Aldrich, C. K.: "The Dying Patient's Grief," *J.A.M.A.*, 184:329, 1963.
   Feifel, H. (ed.): *The Meaning of Death,* New York, McGraw-Hill Book Company, 1959.
   Solnit, A. J., and M. Green: "The Pediatric Management of the Dying Child," in A. J. Solnit and S. A. Provence (eds.): *Modern Perspectives in Child Development,* New York, International Universities Press, Inc., 1963.
12. Kaufman, M. R., A. F. Franzblau, and D. Kainys: "The Emotional Impact of Ward Rounds," *J. Mount Sinai Hosp.*, New York, 23:782, 1956.
13. Cummings, E., and W. E. Henry: *Growing Old: The Process of Disengagement,* New York, Basic Books, Inc., Publishers, 1961.
14. Zinsser, H.: *As I Remember Him,* Boston, Little, Brown and Company, 1940.

Chapter 2

PERSONALITY ORGANIZATION, FUNCTION, AND DEVELOPMENT

THE CAUSES OF PSYCHIATRIC ILLNESS

During the Middle Ages, mental illnesses were blamed on evil spirits or on possession by the Devil, and various dramatic ways of scaring away the spirits were undertaken [1]. Later, a more enlightened although perhaps more fatalistic viewpoint attributed mental illnesses to heredity or constitution, with the implication that nothing could be done about them. Although the mentally ill were presumably "born that way," it was paradoxically assumed that they could nevertheless modify their inborn characteristics by the exercise of willpower, and they were threatened or commanded to be more rational, less worried, more restrained, and so on. Still later, as the significance of physical, psychologic, and social factors in the environment became recognized, the heredity hypothesis was virtually abandoned for most mental illnesses. In the last few years, as the ancient medical tradition of seeking a single cause for each condition is being replaced by the realization that multiple causative factors coexist in almost every condition, the heredity hypothesis is being more scientifically reexamined (see pages 83–85). Although there is still much to learn about hereditary influences, it is probably safe to say that for the majority of mental illnesses, heredity is certainly not the only cause and for the relatively mild conditions, it is probably not the major cause. In any case, the hereditary factor is not susceptible to much modification, and from the viewpoint of treating the sick patient, more modifiable factors understandably receive more attention.

The possibility of an exclusively physical cause for psychiatric illness is appealing to both physician and patient. It keeps the physician in the area of medicine, in which the majority of his training has taken place, and it promises a tangible explanation and a tangible treatment program. It protects the patient's self-esteem, and it insulates him from having to look at submerged feelings and conflicts, many of which he is ashamed of and would rather not acknowledge. So far, however, the evidence for a physical cause or even a major physical causative factor is rather skimpy in most psychiatric illness and virtually nonexistent in many others.

The remaining alternatives in the search for the factors responsible for psychiatric illness require explorations of the patient's psychology and his social environment. In these explorations, human psychology is assumed to follow the rule basic to all science, which insists that phenomena must have causes. A dream, for example, is not an accident of nature and cannot be explained as "just a dream." Some chain of circumstances determines the form of a dream, just as a chain of circumstances determines the symptoms of smallpox. It may or may not be worth the effort to expose any part of the determining chain, and it may be impossible with our present knowledge to put together the whole chain; nevertheless, there is an explanation somewhere.

The explanation, however, is not always to be found in the usual kind of rational terms. The dreamer cannot be expected to give an answer when asked why he dreams; even if he gives a reason, its validity is suspect. This is also true for a daydream or a particular piece of absentmindedness or a patient's delusion. Even when the reason for the *occurrence* of a psychologic phenomenon is at least partly known, there are other reasons for the *content*. A complex chain of circumstances involving alcohol is responsible for the occurrence of delirium tremens, but it does not explain why one patient sees pink elephants and another is pestered by little green men. Yet another chain of circumstances accounts for a patient's drinking, and although the causes he suggests may have some relevance ("My wife doesn't understand me"), they are certainly not the whole story.

UNCONSCIOUS DETERMINANTS

Many of the phenomena of dreams, daydreams, absentmindedness, addictions, and hallucinations lead the observer to conclude that a part of man's psychologic function is out of his conscious control. This conclusion is perhaps most dramatically demonstrated by the phenomenon of posthypnotic suggestion [2]. A hypnotist tells his subject that after he is awakened from his trance, he will respond to a given signal by carrying out a specific action without knowing why he does it. He might suggest that when the hypnotist snaps his fingers, the subject will whistle. He then induces amnesia (forgetfulness) for all that has gone on during the trance, "awakens" the subject, and snaps his fingers, whereupon the subject whistles, even though the whistling embarrasses him and he has not the slightest idea why he is doing it.

Belief in the existence of unconscious mental processes, as generally demonstrated by dreams and experiments in hypnotism, led Freud and others to suspect that clues to the causes of apparently irrational and otherwise inexplicable psychologic phenomena would be found in that part of the working of the mind of which the subject was unaware [3]. Since conscious psychologic phenomena are the results of maturation or learning, there was reason to suspect that their unconscious counterparts were also based on maturation and learning. Many of the unconscious phenomena that seemed important in causing symptoms of psychiatric illness could be traced back to the emotions and experiences of early childhood—emotions and experiences that apparently had been forgotten but that continued to exert unconscious influences on the patient's behavior in a manner somewhat analogous to the influence of the posthypnotic suggestion on the whistling subject.

For some time after Freud began to publish his observations, psychiatrists were split into two camps: One group looked for virtually all the causes of human behavior in the workings of the unconscious mind; the other group paid little attention to unconscious factors. Although some still appear to cling doggedly to one absolute position or the other, most psychiatrists now recognize that behavior is the distillate of many interacting psychologic processes—conscious and unconscious, personal and social—superimposed on a complex physical substrate.

In this and succeeding chapters, the material on the structure and development of personality will emphasize social and psychologic causes. These causes should not be considered the sole causes but should be viewed as causative factors in a field of interacting causes of various kinds. The modern understanding of emotional illness, however, is based to a substantial degree on an understanding of the vicissitudes of emotional development.

STAGES OF DEVELOPMENT

Although a child's emotional development is a continuous process, several roughly defined, overlapping stages can be distinguished [4]. The determinants of these stages are related to biologic maturation and to the directions and foci of the child's instinctual urges, as well as to the events and attitudes he experiences in his environment. Emotional growth, like physical growth, has irregular spurts and plateaus and is much more rapid in the earliest years, so that the earlier stages are of shorter duration.

The seven ages of man, according to the chronology of emotional development, can be described approximately as follows:

1. Infancy—the period of dependency: the first few months
2. Training period—self-assertion and its control: from the end of infancy through the second and third years
3. Period of family identification and rivalry: approximately the fourth through the sixth years
4. School age: from about six through puberty
5. Adolescence: from puberty to the establishment of an adult orientation
6. Adulthood: from the end of adolescence to the usual retirement age
7. Old age: from retirement to death

FIXATION AND REGRESSION

Emotional growth, like physical growth, can be stunted. Malnutrition and disease are the chief deterrents to physical growth, although psychologic factors may play a part. In emotional stunting, the relative importance of these factors is reversed, with the major role attributable to parental, cultural, and group attitudes and a minor but definite role played by physical problems. When for any reason emotional growth fails to progress beyond a given stage toward maturity, the personality is said to be *fixated* at that stage [5].

In this book, the term "fixation" is used because it is the standard psychiatric term for a cessation of emotional development; however, a personality fixated at a particular level is not so rigidly anchored as the term suggests. *Suspension* or even *interruption* of development would, in most instances, describe the process more accurately, although when fixation becomes firmly established in character structure, it is very difficult to modify. Furthermore, the term "fixation," as used in psychiatric literature, usually does not mean that the total personality is involved but that the delay in development is limited to certain areas of interpersonal relationships. Thus, a man's personality is often said to be "fixated at the infantile level," even though he appears mature in his business and social life and the manifestations of his immaturity are revealed only at home.

The stages of emotional development are diagrammed in Figure 1.* In the diagram, the progress of emotional development is represented as a ladder leading step by step from birth to adulthood. The steps and the major developmental problems of each step are noted between the rungs,

* An alternative diagram of personality development can be found in Erik Erikson, *Childhood and Society*, 2d ed., New York, W. W. Norton & Company, Inc., 1963.

and one or two of the most significant personality results of favorable experiences at each step are listed at the left of the ladder.

Some of the personality characteristics which may result from fixation at a particular step are indicated to the right. The indicated characteristics by no means encompass all the interlocking and overlapping personal-

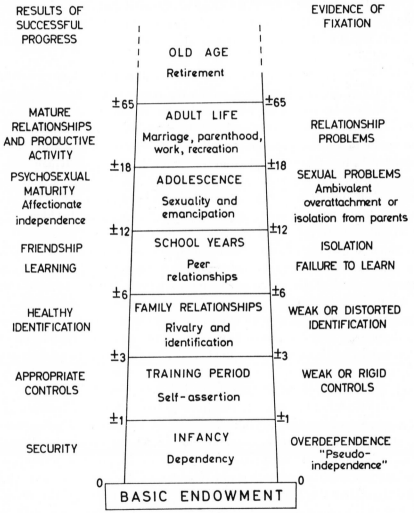

Figure 1. Stages of emotional development.

ity patterns to which fixation may contribute. However, they do give a general indication of some of the major adult character traits related to each developmental stage. Thus, failure of healthy emotional development in the stage of infancy, ordinarily brought about by failure of the infant to develop adequate security in the mother-child relationship, may be represented later either by an excess of dependent need (overdependence) or by an avoidance of dependency (pseudoindependence).

Failure to channel assertive and aggressive drives in a constructive manner during the training period, the initial stage of self-assertion, may affect character structure in different ways. It may result in overassertiveness and weak controls or, if the child has learned that to assert his individuality means seriously to threaten his security, in inhibition of any self-assertion and in rigid controls. It may also persist in such character traits as stubbornness and procrastination.

Several major types of disturbed emotional reaction stem primarily from distortions in relationships within the family circle. To a major degree, these relationships are established in the period (or step on the ladder) between the training period and the school years. As a consequence of failure to achieve a smooth resolution of the conflicts which arise as the child seeks to establish his place in the family, he later may remain overinvolved with his family or, perhaps to escape overinvolvement, may cut himself off entirely from family ties. Closely related to his ability to work out healthy relationships within the family is the quality of his identification and eventual perception of himself as an adult person.

The next two steps do not present new problems of adaptation so much as elaborations of problems that evolve from unsuccessful adaptation in previous areas. Thus, the capacity for friendship and the capacity for tolerating the give-and-take of competition with contemporaries, which are prerequisites for working with others, are first manifest to a major degree in the school years but primarily result from the successful completion of developmental processes in the previous stages. Similarly, the adolescent's capacity to integrate his sexual maturity with his attitudes toward family and friends depends on his past emotional development, as does his capacity to work out his emancipation from his family and his adjustment as a relatively independent individual.

Most people avoid undue fixation and, in spite of various handicaps, climb the ladder of emotional development to the point of securing a foothold at a fairly mature level of functioning. They may, however, be dislodged from this foothold and slip back to a previous step. This reversal of development is called *regression* and may be precipitated by a number of different types of stress [6]. In fatigue or illness, for example, temporary regression serves an adaptive function, but prolonged regression is usually a sign of failure of adaptation. Although enough external stress of any kind will break anyone's hold on mature functioning, each individual is most susceptible to stress related psychologically to his own most significant earlier conflicts. As in fixation, regression may involve the total personality but usually is restricted to a part. Total or nearly total regression is usually found in the more incapacitating emotional illnesses, or *psychotic reactions* (Chapter 11); partial regression is more often seen in the less incapacitating *psychoneurotic reactions,* or, as they are more commonly called, *neurotic reactions* (Chapter 10). Everyone, however, is subject to occasional, temporary, minor regressions which differ from neurotic reactions in degree and duration but not in kind.

Fixation and regression often occur in the same patient. One part of his personality may be fixated at an immature level, while another part can maintain itself at a more mature level under favorable circumstances but regresses under increased pressure. Adult life is full of situations which are related to earlier developmental stages and to which emotions and attitudes derived from the earlier stages may be generalized. Employees, parishioners, and patients are dependent on their employers, clergymen, and physicians in a manner similar to the child's dependence on his parent; many facets of marriage, work, and recreation stir up problems of self-assertion; parenthood recapitulates in reverse the family rivalry of the child; and adult recreation is to some extent a reenactment of the give-and-take of children's play. There are, therefore, many stimuli in ordinary life that can be specifically stressful to an individual with unfinished business at a particular level and that can precipitate or encourage regression.

Both fixation and regression can be demonstrated in the personality pattern of Dr. Wilson's patient, Mrs. Brown, the patient described at the end of the last chapter. In her case, the crisis precipitating regression—the external circumstance of the discovery of her husband's interest in another woman—appeared to be such a threat to her tenuous adaptation as an adult that she gave up the attempt to adjust in a mature manner and regressed to a more childlike approach to her problems. Regression, in turn, stirred up earlier conflicts which, although hidden from her awareness, led to her manifest neurotic symptoms by processes to be discussed later. Before she discovered her husband's wandering interests, however, she was suffering (and had suffered through all her adult life) from a partial fixation of personality structure at a dependent level.

The dependent fixation is not at first clear. Before her illness, Mrs. Brown seemed anything but dependent. She had carried successfully a great deal of responsibility early in her life and was a constructive leader in her community. She did not like to be ill; she did not enjoy vacations and always kept busy doing something "constructive." She seemed much more independent than dependent.

But if she were a truly independent woman, why did she have to carry independence to such extremes? Why could she not enjoy vacations? Why could she not relax? These questions suggest that Mrs. Brown was trying too hard not to be dependent—was *overcompensating* for dependency in much the same way as the woman with coronary disease described on page 9. Before her regression, Mrs. Brown had said she hated illness, never let it get her down if she could possibly help it, and was disgusted at chronic complainers. Others brought their problems to her, but she could not bring hers to anyone. Apparently there was no one she could trust with her problems and no one she could count on to take care of her needs, although she trusted herself to take care of others' needs.

This attitude suggests that she was afraid of being dependent—afraid that if anyone else took care of her, she somehow would be hurt. In her case, the fear apparently developed after her parents pushed her prematurely toward independence so that she took over responsibilities before she felt secure enough for them. The responsibilities frightened her, but she was more frightened of her mother's disapproval if she did not take them on. Rather than face her insecurity, she buried her needs for help and support below the level of her awareness and from that time on she acted as if she did not have them. To avoid reawakening these dependent yearnings, she denied herself any opportunity for dependence in illness, in vacations, or in sharing her problems with others. She was not aware of these needs, but they persisted. They finally made their presence evident through the disguise of symptoms when, as a result of her husband's extramarital affair, the pressure of current stresses caused her to regress and her need for dependency was increased to the point of outweighing her resistance to it.

Although fixation and regression are not always easy to distinguish, the proper planning of treatment requires a reasonably accurate appraisal of the relationship of the two processes. This appraisal, in turn, requires an understanding of the customary course of emotional growth and development and of the causes and manifestations of interrupted or reversed emotional growth. Before proceeding to a more detailed consideration of these subjects, however, the student should have in mind a framework of adult personality structure on which to attach developmental concepts. The next section is designed to provide this framework.

PERSONALITY ORGANIZATION

Man's survival as an individual and as a species depends on his ability to satisfy his inner needs within the context of his external environment.

Most animals—and, until relatively recently in the history of the world, man as well—spend most of their energy in the struggle for survival, and survival rewards those species and those individuals who have, through evolution, developed the most successful means of adaptation.

Personality reflects just one phase of man's adaptation to his inner needs and to his environment. Adaptation takes place on many levels, ranging from intracellular chemical mechanisms through simple reflexes to complex intellectual functions, with many intervening way stations. Generally, the simpler mechanisms respond automatically to stimuli, whereas the complex functions require that the individual choose between alternatives. The simple, *automatic adaptive mechanisms* may in themselves be enough to satisfy inner needs or to adjust to environmental stimuli. Thus, energy needs are at first automatically met by the mobilization of glycogen from the liver, and minor changes in outside temperature are met by vascular changes in the skin without requiring the individual to make a choice. However, as energy needs or outside temperature changes increase, the organism's automatic adaptive mechanisms become insufficient to neutralize them. They can, however, render these needs perceptible to the individual, who then *perceives* evidence of energy need as hunger and of temperature change as heat or cold.

At this point, civilized man has many more choices than have either animals or primitive man. The cold animal must exercise, find a natural shelter, find another animal who will consent to close physical contact, or endure the cold. Civilized man has, in addition to the animal's alternatives, an enormous range of possibilities, most of which represent adaptation *of* (rather than *to*) his environment. He can put on a coat, build a fire, turn on an electric stove, start an automobile motor, knock on someone's door and ask for help, and so on. He has rendered his environment infinitely more complicated and in so doing has made it possible to meet his basic survival needs more readily, so that he has energy left over for meeting less vital needs and for further complicating his environment. He can go to the concert or build a rocket to the moon without worrying about where the next meal is coming from; and although he has not solved the problems of population growth, distribution of resources, international tensions, or criminal behavior, these problems are much more complex and involve much more subtle and complicated relationships than their counterparts in the animal kingdom.

For man, the reconciliation of *conflict* is more complex than for animals, and the demands of civilization enormously increase the opportunities for the development of conflict. The domesticated animal's impulse to bite the hand that feeds him represents a conflict between aggression and dependency, if you will, that is usually solved by inhibition of the aggression; if inhibition fails and the pet dog nips his master's hand, he often tries to compensate by an exaggerated show of affection. In the human animal, an impulse to express aggression or dependency directly mobilizes conflict based on a complex amalgam of environmental expectations, guilt, shame, and past experience. Therefore, when aggression and dependency are simultaneously provoked in the human being, simple inhibitions or simple compensations seldom prove adequate to cope with the resulting conflict. The adaptational mechanism of the human personality bears about the same relationship to its animal counterpart as the digital computer bears to the abacus.

Man's personality, his most complex adaptational device, therefore has less in common with the personality of lower animals than, for example, his temperature-regulating mechanism has with the temperature-regulating mechanisms of lower animals. Consequently, the study of personality can have less reliance on analogies with animals than can the study of physiology [7]. Since personality characteristics are not customarily associated with specific anatomic findings, the postmortem has so far had little to offer in advancing man's understanding of his personality. He must rely for his understanding, therefore, on communication with his fellowman, but since successful adaptation requires him to conceal much of his true personality from his fellowman, most of the information about personality structure comes from the study of man's unsuccessful adaptation.

For this reason, less is known of the workings of the healthy personality than of the unhealthy personality, and the most fundamental parts of the personality are in many ways the most obscure. For example, there is little agreement about the number or nature of man's instincts. Even in the case of such a common human attribute as aggression, there is no unequivocal evidence to show either that man is born aggressive or that he learns to be aggressive in response to frustration.

Instincts, Drives, and Needs

Throughout the history of psychology, many different classifications of instincts have been developed. Freud, for example, used two classifications. In his first classification, he attempted to distinguish instincts of self-preservation from the *libido,* or instincts of race preservation [8]. Since the libido included most of the motivation for interpersonal relationships, it represented a much broader concept than is usually connoted by our term "sexual." (See page 96.) Later, as he found that he could not satisfactorily distinguish libido from self-preservation, he postulated another opposing pair of instincts: the constructive, or life-maintaining, instinct, including both libido and self-preservation; and the destructive, or death-seeking, instinct [9]. The exact nature of the libido and even the existence of a death instinct have remained controversial among psychoanalysts as well as among others.

The problem of differentiating instinctual from learned behavior is complicated by the late maturation of some apparently instinctual behavior—adult sexual and mothering patterns, for example—and by the fact that other apparently instinctual behavior, such as sucking, can become extinct or weakened, particularly if the organism lacks an opportunity for its expression. Furthermore, instincts, or at least their expression, can be modified or combined or in other ways rendered obscure. In the infant, extinction and modification have had a minimum of opportunity to modify the instinct expression, and so, although evidence of late-maturing instincts is absent, the infant is a favorite subject for the study of instincts [10].

A good deal of the waking infant's activity suggests that he is driven by a need for sensory stimulation. If he does not receive stimulation from external forces, he behaves as if he were attempting to manufacture his own, as by crying and restless activity. The techniques mothers learn to use to quiet their babies are stimulating to the senses: the sight of mother or of a moving object, the sound of mother's voice, the touch of her arms as he is cuddled, the warmth of her body, the movement of the rocking chair, the taste of food—all provide sensory stimulation. Even in the adult, sensory deprivation sufficiently protracted leads to severe restlessness and hallucinations [11].

Exactly how the search for sensory stimulation is translated into action is not clear. Some animals demonstrate the phenomenon of *imprinting* [12]—a newly hatched duckling, for example, becomes imprinted on, or attached to, the first moving object it sees, and apparently it instinctually follows that object. Under natural circumstances, this object ordinarily is its mother; following its mother serves a survival function, as the duckling stays close to its protector. Under laboratory conditions, however, a human investigator or even a moving mechanical device can be made the object of imprinting, and the laboratory duckling waddles along close to the heels of its human or mechanical foster-mother. In imprinting, the specific direction of a self-preservative drive is determined by the specific nature of the first visual stimulus.

The imprinted duckling instinctually follows the old sensory stimulus;

later another, related drive appears, which is, in its most elementary form, *curiosity*, or the drive to seek new stimuli. Curiosity in a way serves survival; unless the organism is motivated to investigate and comprehend its environment, it may overlook potential sources of danger. Curiosity also can lead to trouble, as the proverbial cat discovered; on the other hand, the search for new stimuli, translated into the more sophisticated search for new knowledge, has made man's civilization possible. How much of man's curiosity represents a sublimated search for the forbidden knowledge of good and evil or for forbidden sexual knowledge and how much is a derivative of the need for sensory stimulation is not clear—the proportions doubtless differ from one individual to another.

If the result of the stimulus-seeking behavior is gratifying or pleasurable or pain relieving, the organism tends to approach the stimulus; if the result is painful or pleasure destroying, the organism tends to withdraw from the stimulus. Approach or withdrawal depends, therefore, on the organism's evaluation of what is pleasurable and what is painful; so far, relatively little is known about the process of evaluation [13]. It is known, however, that experience modifies the basic pleasure-seeking, pain-avoiding orientation, sometimes to the point where pain appears to be sought and pleasure avoided (see page 134).

All these considerations complicate the task of understanding human instincts in pure culture. Since this task is far from completed, I will use sparingly the term "instinct," with its implication of a completely innate force, and instead use the less specific term "drive," which to my mind connotes innate forces as modified by as yet indistinguishable environmental influences. For the most part, I will use the term "impulse" to mean any episodic emergence of a drive. Thus, the patient had an *impulse* to attack his persecutor; the impulse was an episodic emergence of his aggressive *drive* to combat frustration; his drive, in turn, had its origins in self- or race-preservative *instincts*.

A comprehensive personality theory must take into consideration all human drives, from hunger and thirst to aggression and sexuality, as it seeks to establish their ultimate sources [14]; a book concerned primarily with practical applications, however, may be limited to the particular drives that have been implicated to a major degree in the causes of emotional illness. The most important of these drives appear in the forms of aggression and sexuality and usually require interpersonal relationships for their satisfaction. An equally significant manifestation, perhaps better described as a *need* than as a drive, appears in the form of a need to trust, to depend on, or to be loved or accepted by someone else; this is a need which seems closely related to a drive to give love and affection. Drives like hunger and thirst, which do not primarily require interpersonal relationships for their satisfaction, are of less practical significance, except in the specific circumsances when they appear to become fused with or to replace aggression, sexuality, or dependency.

Psychologic Adaptation

The psychologic adaptive mechanisms on which the student needs to focus his attention are those which integrate the expression of drives and the demands of the environment. As the human environment, particularly the interpersonal aspect of the environment, has become more complex, or more "civilized," it has developed complicated social systems of rewards and punishments. These systems vary considerably from one culture to another and among different social groups in the same culture, but in any social group, the immediate or direct expression of many drives is punished, while certain types of delayed or indirect expression may be rewarded or at least sanctioned. Other types of indirect expression are punished, and some types are rewarded or punished, depending on the circumstances.

The environment, therefore, is stressful to the human organism not only by making drive satisfaction difficult of attainment, but by penalizing many patterns of seeking satisfaction. Adaptation consists of the processes brought to bear by the organism to assess the environment's often obscure expectations, to delay or modify direct expression of drives so as to provide satisfaction with the maximum reward and the minimum punishment and to modify the environment so as to increase the possibility of drive satisfaction.

Exactly where in the brain and the rest of the body the processes of adaptation occur is still uncertain, although new techniques are gradually bringing neurophysiologists closer to the answers [15], and so for the time being, any representation of personality organization must be schematic.* Operationally, however, three major groups of psychological adap-

---

* In my earlier book, *Psychiatry for the Family Physician*, I interspersed diagrams throughout the text. I received two opposite types of comment from students and faculty colleagues: either the diagrams were helpful and clarified much of the text, or the diagrams were distracting and confusing, at the same time oversimplified and too complicated. No one was neutral, and although I find a visual framework helpful for myself, I can also see the opposition's point. For some time, therefore, while rewriting the book I was in a dilemma, and oscillated between leaving the diagrams in and leaving them out. I finally settled for the compromise solution of putting them all together in an appendix at the end. This solution makes more work for the pro-diagram people, but at least is less irritating to the anti's.

tive functions can be distinguished; one group evaluates the inner self and the environment, another inhibits or prevents the direct expression of drives, and a third provides substitute or indirect means of gaining satisfaction for drives. (For diagram, see Appendix B, Figure 6.)

The *evaluative* part of a man's capacity for adaptation tries to figure out what is going on in himself and in the outside world, what is its meaning in terms of his past experience, and what is currently expected of him by his family, by his social group, and by his culture, so that he can decide how he should react. His evaluation gives him the data for an internal decision among conflicting alternatives, such as whether to express or to inhibit a drive or which of two or more simultaneous but contradictory drives has priority. A satisfactory evaluation requires, besides sensory perception, memory, and reasoning, a function that Freud called *reality testing*. Reality testing is determining whether an idea or perception comes from within the personality or from the environment. When a man feels offended because a friend has ignored him, good reality testing first leads him to an accurate appraisal of the basis for the feeling and then leads him to a correct conclusion—either that the friend ignored him purposely and he has reason to feel offended or that the slight was unintentional and his offended feeling stemmed perhaps from his depreciation of himself, which for the moment he has attributed (*projected*) to his friend.

He customarily does not go through each step of the process of reality testing consciously; he simply "knows" that his friend passed by accidentally or passed by on purpose. The processes of reality testing and the rest of the evaluative functions are usually so rapid and take place so far below the level of his awareness, or consciousness, that he is not aware of having made an appraisal.

If he believes the friend's slight was an accident, there is no need to restrain or modify the impulse to shout at his friend and gain his attention. On the other hand, if he believes that it was deliberate affront, he may be tempted to swear at his friend or even to hit him. At this point, however, his moral standards or his fear of the consequences usually cause him to decide to control, or to *inhibit,* his aggressive, retaliatory drive, and the second group of psychologic adaptive functions is called into action. These functions also can be conscious or unconscious. If his inhibiting action is conscious, it is called *suppression;* if he is not aware of the inhibition, it is called *repression.* Repression in particular applies to emotionally tinged memories as well as to impulses; if you "forget" an event which you would remember if it were not for the disturbing emotional connotation, you have repressed the memory of the event. Repression is the internal counterpart of denial; a person *denies* an external circumstance that disturbs him but *represses* an internal drive, idea, or memory that disturbs him. (For diagram, see Appendix B, Figure 7.)

Terms such as "suppression," "repression," and "denial" do not represent entities that can be isolated for microscopic study but instead represent attempts to provide a working vocabulary by cataloging according to their function highly complex processes derived from the observation of even more highly complex behavior. Technically speaking, therefore, "repression" means the sum total of whatever it is that can account for the observation that some feelings and conflicts and memories do not appear in consciousness when, by ordinary laws of perception, learning, and memory, they would be expected to appear. To be strictly accurate, all statements about mechanisms probably should be prefaced by "appears to" or by "as if." Thus, repression *appears to* help inhibit the emergence into consciousness of a disturbing emotion *as if* to protect the individual from anxiety. Psychiatric writing is ponderous enough as it is, however, and I trust I can rely on the reader to supply his own "as if's."

When a drive is repressed, it does not just disappear. It may remain unexpressed, it may be held in abeyance for expression at a later, more opportune time, or the adaptive functions may provide substitute or indirect expression in a modified, less objectionable form. The indirect outlet generally permits the drive to be expressed in a way that conforms to the expectations of the environment, as the individual evaluates them, and to his own standards. When this process leads to socially acceptable and constructive behavior, it is called *sublimation.* Sublimation, as well as other types of indirect expression, may take place above or below the level of consciousness; thus, a man who indirectly expresses anger by participation in competitive sports may or may not realize that he is taking out his anger stirred up by his wife or by his boss on an innocent golf ball. The well-adjusted individual finds patterns which permit culturally and socially acceptable outlets for his drives and inhibits patterns leading to ineffective or socially disturbing outlets. He evaluates his environment correctly and directs his behavior accordingly. His personality is in balance, or in a condition of *emotional homeostasis.*

Freud used the term "id" to denote basic instinctual and biologic drives and the terms "ego" and "superego" to represent the adaptive functions [16]. According to his conceptual scheme, the *ego* evaluates both the environment and the *id* and uses a combination of repression, suppression, and various indirect techniques to arrive at methods of drive expression which can satisfy both the id and the environment. The *superego* acts as a censor of the ego's methods. To use a governmental analogy, the ego carries out executive functions, while the superego represents the supreme court which decides whether the ego's methods are constitutional, i.e., whether they conform to the individual's rules and standards.

Freud's terms are handy abbreviations for three *functional* parts of the personality. The terms become confusing and misleading, however, if they are equated with *anatomic* parts of the personality or if they are anthropomorphized to make them appear to be three distinct entities engaging in perpetual combat within the personality. Unfortunately, they are such convenient terms that they are occasionally used as substitutes for understanding. They often appear in books and articles on psychiatry, however, and the student should become familiar with their meanings.

RESPONSES TO STRESS

Under ordinary circumstances, most people have more than enough adaptive capacity to maintain emotional homeostasis and so have reserve strength to counterbalance unusual increases in inner drives or environmental pressures. If emergencies continue, however, and if the demands on the individual's personality increase, he will eventually arrive at the point where he has no more reserves to call on. (For diagram, see Appendix B, Figure 8.)

When the reserve is depleted—or when there was no reserve to begin with—any additional stress will destroy, overwhelm, or disrupt emotional homeostasis. For reasons not yet clear, the breakdown usually affects one function more than the others. Thus, if the ability to evaluate is primarily affected, the personality fails to assay external and internal demands and expectations correctly and, as a result, reacts inappropriately. In the last chapter, I pointed out that the threat of impending death may lead a patient to *deny the reality* of his illness. In this case, one part of the environment is not evaluated correctly, although adequate adaptation is maintained in other areas. More complete failure of evaluation leads to misinterpretation of a larger segment of the environment. When misinterpretation on this scale occurs, as in psychotic reactions (Chapter 11), inhibition and the capacity for constructive indirect expression are also disrupted.

If the breakdown of adaptation is chiefly limited to the inhibiting function, the individual cannot adequately restrain the direct expression of unacceptable impulses and drives. The result may be antisocial behavior or other conduct which is not consistent with the expectations of the environment. The inappropriate behavior may be generalized, or if the failure of inhibition applies to a limited number of drives, it may be restricted to one or more specific types of conduct (see Chapter 14).

Failure of the capacity for sublimation is the third possibility. In this situation, the individual correctly evaluates what is expected of him and inhibits the drives which are inappropriate but cannot find appropriate substitute channels for their expression. If time or circumstance increases the strength of the drive, the pressure on inhibition will increase and he will become *afraid* he might not be able to control the drive. An angry but timid employee might say: "Every time I see my boss, I want to hit him. I don't know what to do about this feeling, and I'm *afraid* someday he will aggravate me more than he usually does and I *will* hit him." (For diagram, see Appendix B, Figure 9.)

Ordinarily, it is easier to struggle against something when you know what it is you are struggling against. However, if identification of the adversary inspires a great deal of fear, shame, or other unpleasant emotion, it may be a relief not to know. In the previous example, the employee was not so ashamed of his impulse or drive to hit the boss that he could not acknowledge it, but he was afraid he might act on it. If, however, he was too ashamed of his hostility to acknowledge it to himself, he might inhibit it at a point below the level of consciousness, or repress it. This solution would work out very well as long as he could easily find an acceptable substitute outlet, or sublimation ("I'm not mad at anybody, but I sure like to chop wood"), or as long as the force of the drive was not stronger than his capacity to repress it.

If, however, no substitute outlets are available and if the drive is constantly stimulated, it builds up pressure until it threatens to break through the barrier of repression and erupt into consciousness. In this situation, the employee is not aware of a fear that he might hit his boss, because he is not aware of the nature of the drive; he is simply afraid and does not know what he is afraid of. He has a terrifying feeling of inner tension and impending disaster, with no idea of what to do about it. This feeling is *anxiety,* and anxiety is such an intolerable sensation that the personality shelves everything else to mobilize for an all-out effort to reduce its intensity. (For diagram, see Appendix B, Figure 10.)

The personality attempts to reduce anxiety by regrouping and realigning its adaptive functions. The employee first tries to strengthen his repression to the point of relieving his anxiety; but if he has no reserve strength, he can strengthen repression only by sacrificing either some of his ability to manage other drives or some of his capacity to evaluate his inner self and the environment. Only by narrowing the range of his evaluation of the environment or by limiting the number of substitute solutions he provides for drive expression can he increase the strength of repression.

He resembles the captain of a ship which has developed a serious leak; the repair of the leak takes priority over everything else, so he orders his lookouts and his firemen to drop whatever they are doing and help the repair crew. Meanwhile, the captain must reduce his speed, restrict the area he can observe, and devise the best possible contrivance to stop, confine, or pump out the leak. By analogy, the individual struggling to reinforce repression reduces his efficiency, restricts his interest span, and tries to work out a procedure to stop, confine, or "pump out" (i.e., find a substitute outlet for) the drive. The main difference is that the captain is aware of the whole process, while the personality carries on below the level of consciousness most of its attempts to counteract or adapt to a threatened collapse of repression.

Mental Mechanisms

The procedures used by all of us to stop, confine, or find substitute outlets for drives are called *mental mechanisms* [17]. They include direct manifestations of inhibition (suppression, repression), simple and socially acceptable substitute solutions (sublimation), or complex and devious indirect means of expression (e.g., projection, page 256; displacement, page 226). The use of some of these mechanisms, such as sublimation, is consistent with, and even a sign of, satisfactory emotional adjustment; others, such as projection, are considered pathologic, although they are used to a limited degree by everyone. The choice of mechanisms seems to be determined for the most part by early conditioning; for example, the child who is rewarded for suppressing rage generally grows up to suppress rage as an adult. The extent to which certain mechanisms are used varies in different circumstances; for example, the person who in the past has used denial to a limited degree may use denial extensively in anticipation of death.

Regression, or reversal of emotional development, may help a patient to repress more effectively. As he regresses, he gives up his adult independence and returns to more childlike, dependent relationships and attitudes. Since a child's environment is more limited and his drives less complex, a patient who regresses has less to evaluate and less to control and so can divert some of his adaptive forces to strengthen his repression. If the employee who is afraid he might strike his boss regresses and quits his job to stay home and act like one of the children, he no longer has to evaluate and adjust to the demands of the adult world or to behave as an adult at work and can thus avoid contact with the environmental stress produced by the boss. He can then concentrate more of his adaptive efforts on the task of repressing his aggressive drive.

Regression, however, brings new problems. His self-respect, his attitudes toward dependency, his obligation to his family now require integration. Each time he solves one of these problems, new ones turn up, so that by the time he gets to the physician, a superstructure of secondary or derivative problems has long since buried both the drive to hit his boss and its precipitating cause.

Before the personality's developmental patterns are traced in detail, one more characteristic of the adaptive functions should be examined. This characteristic is their tendency, under some conditions, to act apparently at cross-purposes. Occasionally, one function seems to be trying to outwit or deceive another function. This peculiar state of affairs will be somewhat clearer when the concepts of ego and superego are discussed; meanwhile, the examples of hunger, obesity, and pathologic loss of appetite may serve to illustrate it.

Ordinarily, as the time since the last meal lengthens, a person gradually becomes aware of hunger or the drive to eat. He usually integrates his drive to eat with his evaluation of environmental requirements by suppression (waiting until lunchtime, waiting until others are served, not taking food without paying for it, etc.). If the hunger is somewhat difficult to hold in check and environmental conditions still do not make full gratification convenient, a substitute solution may be found—smoking, for example. Unusual environmental pressures are met in the same way; when a sick patient comes into the office at lunchtime, the physician evaluates the situation, and if the patient is too sick to wait, the physician mobilizes more suppression of his hunger, and goes without lunch.

Although the delayed satisfaction of hunger as described in this context is all on a conscious level, the satisfaction of hunger is sometimes not such a simple procedure. Some people are chronically too hungry, eat more than they need, and become obese, while others are not hungry enough and eat too little. Most of the time, they do not understand why their appetites are distorted, but careful investigations of their personality structures show that most of them have, through early conditioning, unconsciously associated the legitimate hunger drive with some other drive whose direct expression is so disturbing that they have repressed it. This association or *fusion* of an unacceptable drive with an acceptable drive provides a substitute outlet—the unacceptable unknown drive is expressed in the guise of the acceptable hunger. (For diagram, see Appendix B, Figure 11.)

In obesity, since a great deal of the emotional energy of the repressed drive is expressed in the form of excess hunger, the remaining energy can be more easily repressed. In this sequence, one adaptive function, the ego's capacity to find a substitute method of expression, acts as if it were a separate force attempting to outmaneuver another adaptive function, the personality's inhibitory watchdog.

The inhibitory watchdog is not always outmaneuvered. Emotionally conditioned *anorexia,* or appetite loss, resembles overeating in its emotional structure because it, too, involves the attachment of the unacceptable drive to hunger. The patient may even temporarily express the emotional energy of the drive as hunger, but soon the process is reversed and the expression of both the disguised energy and the hunger is repressed. Here the repressing part of the ego acts as if it saw through the disguise and so represses not only the excess hunger but the original, now contaminated hunger as well. (For diagram, see Appendix B, Figure 12.)

DREAMS

Another approach to the understanding of unconscious processes is through the study of dreams. Since before the dawn of history, dreams have been considered significant; until the present century, however, their significance was thought to be predominantly supernatural. Freud first developed the idea that the significance of dreams lies in their relationship to the unconscious mind and that they serve both as a window and as a barrier to the understanding of unconscious mental processes [18]. He postulated that beneath the evident, or *manifest,* content of the dream lay a *latent wish,* usually so disguised as to be incomprehensible to the dreamer.

According to this theory, the latent wish represents an inner drive whose direct expression is unacceptable and so is repressed when the dreamer is awake. When asleep, however, his ego is resting and off guard, as it were, and consequently the unacceptable drive threatens to break through the barrier of repression into consciousness. Although unable to use repression as effectively as in the waking state, the sleeping, unconscious ego is able to disguise the true nature of the drive so that it is not readily recognizable as it appears in the hallucinatory form of the dream. [The dream serves the purpose of keeping the dreamer from awakening] —if successful, the partial, substitute expression of the drive that is pro-

vided by the dream relieves the pressure and the dreamer continues on in now dreamless sleep; if the dream fails to accomplish its purpose, the dreamer awakens and mobilizes his ego to repress the drive. His anxiety, aroused by the threatened failure of the dream to disguise the drive successfully, may remain with him after he awakens in the middle of a dream; but, typically, repression soon goes to work, and the dream which seemed so vivid and unforgettable at 4 in the morning is often hard to recapture a few hours later.

The following dream illustrates the maintenance-of-sleep function of the dream.

> A student was awakened by his roommate somewhat late for an early class and found that his alarm clock had rung earlier without disturbing him. He remembered dreaming that he had heard the alarm, turned it off, gotten up, dressed, had breakfast, and gone to class.

This dream seems to have permitted the student to ignore the call of duty and submit to the wish to sleep. Its transparency and lack of disguise suggest that the desire to sleep rather than to go to class was acceptable on a conscious level by the student. Except as it appears to illustrate one facet of dream theory, it is of little psychiatric concern. Of greater psychiatric interest would be the following dream.

> A woman awakened horrified at having dreamed that she had discovered the body of her mother, who had, in the dream, committed suicide by hanging. She was particularly horrified at her mother's expression of reproach toward her.

The context of the dreamer's life situation is necessary for accurate or constructive dream interpretation. In this case, the dreamer's mother was actually dying slowly and painfully of cancer. Her whole family, including the dreamer, had come to the point where they recognized that death would be a blessing for the mother. Nevertheless, the actual *wish* for her mother's death, under any circumstances, was basically unacceptable in principle to the dreamer's strong puritan conscience.

With the relative weakening of her repression in sleep, however, the forbidden death wish threatened to emerge. Her ego, in order to make it possible to stay asleep, attempted to disguise the wish. In this case, the disguise took the form of projection of the death wish from dreamer to mother. "*I* am not the one who wishes her dead; *she* is, and so she kills herself," the dream attempts to say. But the dream is not completely successful in its disguise of the guilty wish; the dead mother's expression is reproachful, as if the dreamer were really at fault. The dreamer is "horri-

fied," but warned that the death wish might be emerging despite the dream, awakens, thus strengthening her repression so she can reassure herself that she has no death wish. It is a "horrible" dream because in it she has lost her mother, not because she has wished her mother dead.

In this case, the emergence in sleep of an essentially altruistic wish met with strong opposition from the unconscious superego, or conscience. The ego's attempt to find a compromise solution resulted in carrying out the death wish but in a way which made the dreamer feel so guilty that, from the point of view of maintaining sleep, the dream failed and the dreamer awoke.

Dreams usually seem to have more than a single determinant, however, and further history revealed that in this dreamer's childhood, she had been firmly discouraged from expressing any kind of hostility toward her mother and had been taught that "evil" thoughts were as bad as "evil" deeds. In general, her mother had been affectionate and encouraging to her children, but there were frustrations, inevitable in any family. The anger that the child experienced in response to the frustrations had always been repressed. Lacking an outlet, the anger had remained dormant, so to speak, but was still there to add its impact, along with its associated guilt, to the conflict stirred up by the mother's illness.

A word of caution should be included at this point. The use of dream material in the treatment of patients requires a high degree of skill. The conflicts suggested by dreams are, for the most part, deeply unconscious, and their premature interpretation can lead to more anxiety than the patient is able to tolerate. In response to the anxiety resulting from a premature interpretation, the patient often mobilizes more effective means of disguise, with the result that he and the therapist are farther away from conflict resolution than they otherwise would have been. In psychoanalytic treatment, the patient's own associations to a dream are used in a painstaking and time-consuming process to help the patient work his way through to an interpretation that is more his own than the therapist's.

Since the discovery by Kleitman and his followers [19] of the cyclical nature of dreams, of their occurrence in virtually all subjects from four to seven times every night in the phases of lightest sleep, and of other characteristics disclosed by psychophysiologic studies, the way has been cleared for more comprehensive studies of dreams and for testing some of the Freudian hypotheses. These studies have shown that unless the dreamer awakens or is awakened during or immediately after the dream, the dream is not recalled at a later awakening. This observation suggests that the dreams customarily reported to psychoanalysts include a high

proportion of dreams which, theoretically speaking, have failed to accomplish the purpose of keeping the dreamer asleep. It is possible, therefore, that the average dream is a physiologic phenomenon unrelated, or very slightly related, to unconscious conflict, and it is only the "unsuccessful" dream, associated with the emergence of a conflict-loaded impulse, that has become available for the usual psychoanalytic study.] Thus, although the new findings cast some doubt on the applicability of dream theory to all dreams, its applicability to dreams that are accessible for use in the treatment of patients has been neither proved nor disproved.

A PSYCHODYNAMIC FORMULATION

The preceding paragraphs have suggested that, in attempting to understand the symptoms, behavior, and feelings of emotionally distressed patients, the student should pay particular attention to the following:

1. The drives most likely to be unacceptable, generally within the culture and specifically for the particular patient
2. The conscious and unconscious modification of these and associated drives
3. Suppression and repression, as they prevent the expression of unacceptable and associated drives
4. Substitute and indirect expression of drives, often in a disguised form
5. The environment, as the personality evaluates it and as it affects the first four factors

With these guideposts, the tentative, hypothetic reconstruction or formulation of the personality of Dr. Wilson's patient, Mrs. Brown, can be extended. As previously noted (page 35), there is reason to believe that her major unacceptable drive or need was to seek protection and a dependent relationship. Since seeking dependency directly had become unacceptable and frightening as a result of her conflicts with her mother, she attempted to inhibit expression of this need by repression and by avoiding vacations and other external circumstances which could tempt her to become dependent. Her overcompensatory concern for others represented to some extent an indirect or vicarious expression of her own dependency feelings (as well as a more mature wish to help others).

Her use of overcompensation had something to do with her selecting a husband whom she could outwardly control and take care of, thus disguising her dependency on him. However, when his interest in the other woman interfered with her control and with the maintenance of her overcompensation, her hidden dependency needs became mobilized. Clini-

cally, a partial regression took place, so that more of her personality resources became oriented toward seeking dependency, leaving less to function on a relatively mature level. Consequently, she no longer could sustain her previous adequate (although somewhat neurotic) adjustment.

Her mobilized dependency needs revived the fear or anxiety associated with the earlier conflicts, and her increased anxiety was accompanied by physiologic manifestations which took the form of headaches, backaches, and frequent attacks of bloating and abdominal pain. Why her anxiety appeared in the form of these specific symptoms is not clear; our understanding of the mechanics of symptom *production* is much more advanced than our understanding of symptom *choice*. As long as they were "physical" symptoms, however, they provided a medical rationalization for being cared for, and she began, secondarily and unconsciously, to exploit them in an effort to meet her dependency needs.

Even this limited and tentative understanding of her personality structure would help Dr. Wilson to plan her treatment. He would understand why she talked one way and acted another and why his sympathetic efforts to help were not being rewarded. He would see that he had been limiting his attempt to meet her dependency needs to times when she complained of physical symptoms and thus had unwittingly and indirectly encouraged her to continue her complaints. He would realize that it is impossible for a physician to supply to a patient of this kind all the love and security she had missed during her early childhood. He therefore would recognize that it was necessary to limit the focus of his treatment to her partial regression without attempting to alter the partial fixation, and he would see that to attempt too much not only would lead to disappointment but might even threaten the partial hold on maturity which she did retain.

Careful attention to the specific personality diagnosis, therefore, can protect both patient and physician from many frustrations in the management of emotional disturbance. In the next chapter, the last in Part 1, I will describe, from a more practical viewpoint, the procedure for obtaining the material needed for making a diagnosis. Part 3 of the book will demonstrate the ways in which the material can be used in the development of diagnoses, and Part 4 will outline its applicability to treatment.

SUMMARY

In this chapter, the rationale for the study of emotional growth and development was discussed. Emotional growth occurs in stages, and person-

ality structure is often determined by partial fixation at an immature stage. External stress, especially in vulnerable individuals, may produce regression to an earlier stage, with consequent symptom formation. The process is rendered obscure by the repression of unacceptable drives and conflicts.

The description of personality structure particularly emphasized the psychologic adaptive functions. In order to adapt his inner needs to the demands of his social milieu and maintain emotional homeostasis, an individual must evaluate his environment, inhibit some impulses, and find appropriate substitute expression of others. He carries on part of his adaptive activity consciously and the remainder unconsciously.

REFERENCES

1. Still the most comprehensive, although somewhat controversial, history of psychiatry is:
   Zilboorg, Gregory, and G. W. Henry: *History of Medical Psychology,* New York, W. W. Norton & Company, Inc., 1941.
2. Hypnotism is discussed at length in:
   Gill, M. M., and M. Brenman: *Hypnosis and Related States,* New York, International Universities Press, Inc., 1959.
   and more briefly in:
   Kubie, L. S.: "Hypnotism," *Arch. Gen. Psychiat. (Chicago),* 4:40, 1961.
3. Freud, S.: "A Note on the Unconscious in Psychoanalysis" (1912), in *Standard Edition,* 1958, vol. XII, p. 255.
4. The stages of development are discussed in:
   Josselyn, Irene M.: *Psychosocial Development of Children,* New York, Family Service Association of America, 1948.
   Brenner, Charles: *An Elementary Textbook of Psychoanalysis,* Garden City, N.Y., Doubleday & Company, Inc., 1957.
   In a somewhat modified form, they are discussed in:
   Erikson, Erik: *Childhood and Society,* 2d ed., New York, W. W. Norton & Company, Inc., 1963.
   Probably the basic Freudian contribution is:
   Freud, S.: "Three Essays on the Theory of Sexuality" (1905), in *Standard Edition,* 1953, vol. VII, p. 123.
5. The role of fixation in character formation is extensively explored in:
   Reich, W.: *Character Analysis,* 2d ed., New York, Orgone Institute Press, 1945.
6. Freud, A.: "The Role of Regression in Mental Development," in Solnit, A. J., and S. A. Provence (eds.): *Modern Perspectives in Child Development,* New York, International Universities Press, Inc., 1963.
7. See, however, Masserman, J. H.: *Behavior and Neurosis: An Experimental Psychoanalytic Approach to Psychobiologic Principles,* Chicago, The University of Chicago Press, 1943.

8. Freud's theory of the libido is outlined in:
Freud, S.: "Three Essays on the Theory of Sexuality" (1905), in *Standard Edition*, 1953, vol. VII, p. 123.
See also:
————: "Instincts and Their Vicissitudes" (1915), in *Standard Edition*, 1957, vol. XIV, p. 109.
9. ————: "Beyond the Pleasure Principle" (1920), in *Standard Edition*, 1955, vol. XVIII, p. 1.
10. See, for example: Bridger, W., and M. Reiser: "Psychophysiologic Studies of the Neonate," *Psychosom. Med.*, 21:265, 1959.
Engel, G. L., and F. Reichsman: "Spontaneous and Experimentally Induced Depressions in an Infant with a Gastric Fistula," *J. Amer. Psychoanal. Ass.*, 4:428, 1956.
Grossman, H., and N. Greenberg: "Psychosomatic Differentiation in Infancy," *Psychosom. Med.*, 19:293, 1957.
11. Solomon, P., et al. (eds.): *Sensory Deprivation*, Cambridge, Mass., Harvard University Press, 1961.
12. Hess, E. H. "Imprinting, *Science*, 130:133, 1959.
See also:
Lorenz, K.: *King Solomon's Ring*, New York, Thomas Y. Crowell Company, 1952.
————: *The Natural History of Aggression*, London, Methuen & Co., Ltd., 1964.
Tinbergen, N.: *Study of Instinct*, London, Oxford Univeristy Press, 1951.
13. See, for example:
Arnold, M. B.: *Emotion and Personality*, New York, Columbia University Press, 1960.
14. For a comprehensive summary of the concepts and terminology of drives, see: Cameron, N.: *Personality Development and Psychopathology*, Boston, Houghton Mifflin Company, 1963, p. 115.
15. Selye, H.: *The Stress of Life*, New York, McGraw-Hill Book Company, 1956.
16. For Freud's structural concept of personality, see:
Freud, S.: "The Ego and the Id" (1923), in *Standard Edition*, 1961, vol. XIX, p. 1.
17. For the classic work on the mechanisms of defense, see:
Freud, A.: *The Ego and the Mechanisms of Defense*, New York, International Universities Press, Inc., 1946.
See also:
Hartmann, H.: *Ego Psychology, and the Problem of Adaptation* (1939), New York, International Universities Press, Inc., 1958.
————: *Essays on Ego Psychology*, New York, International Universities Press, Inc., 1964.
18. Freud, S.: "The Interpretation of Dreams" (1900), *Standard Edition*, 1953, vols. IV and V.
19. The pioneer study of the psychophysiology of dreams is:
Aserinsky, E., and N. Kleitman: "Regularly Occurring Periods of Eye Mo-

tility and Concomitant Phenomena during Sleep," *Science*, 118:273, 1953. See also:

Fisher, C., and W. C. Dement: "Studies on the Psychopathology of Sleep and Dreams," *Amer. J. Psychiat.*, 119:1160, 1963.

Trosman, H.: "Dream Research and the Psychoanalytic Theory of Dreams," *Arch. Gen. Psychiat.*, 9:9, 1963.

Chapter 3

THE DIAGNOSTIC PROCESS

THE POSITIVE DIAGNOSIS OF EMOTIONAL ILLNESS

Appropriate treatment of any patient must always stem from a positive diagnosis. Treatment of emotional illness or emotional factors in illness is no exception to this rule. It requires positive diagnosis, and emotional illness cannot be diagnosed simply by the absence of pathologic findings in physical examinations or laboratory tests or by findings that are not sufficient to account for the symptoms. Diagnosing a neurosis by exclusion is just as inaccurate as diagnosing lung cancer solely because the physician cannot find evidence of tuberculosis, pneumonia, bronchiectasis, or anything he can think of except cancer that might be causing a cough. Until the physician finds positive evidence of the existence of cancer, he may suspect it, but he will not diagnose it; in the same way, until he finds positive evidence of the existence of neurosis, he may suspect it but not diagnose it.

Thus, the fact that Dr. Wilson could not find evidence of organic disease to explain Mrs. Brown's symptoms (page 22) did not in itself mean that her emotions caused her illness, although it naturally suggested that possibility to Dr. Wilson. No matter how many laboratory tests turn out to be negative, a patient remains a diagnostic problem until the doctor makes a positive diagnosis.

> A middle-aged man complained of precordial pain (pain over the heart). Physical examination and laboratory studies, including a conventional electrocardiogram, were within normal limits. He appeared to be reassured when his physician told him that his pains must be due to his "nerves."
>
> When his symptoms continued in spite of mild sedative medication, however, he was referred for psychiatric evaluation. The psychiatrist could find no emotional disturbance sufficient to account for his symptoms and sent him back to his physician. Serial electrocardiogram studies then showed evidence of a coronary infarction.

As in this case, diagnosis of emotional illness simply by the apparent exclusion of organic disease may delay definitive diagnosis and treatment.

In some cases, the delay jeopardizes a patient's chances for recovery. [The positive diagnosis of emotional illness depends primarily on an appropriate evaluation of three determinants: (1) the nature of the patient's symptoms and their resemblance to patterns found in emotional illness; (2) the synchronization of onset, increase, or decrease of symptoms to developmental or environmental crisis or stress or to changes in the patient's adaptive capacity; and (3) the influence of any coexisting or contributory conditions, such as organic illness. The ability to make a positive diagnosis depends, therefore, on skill in taking a history which gives proper emphasis to emotional factors and on familiarity with psychopathology as well as organic pathology. The last requirement, familiarity with organic pathology, makes a medical background virtually essential for the thorough-going diagnosis of emotional illness]

To reinforce a positive diagnosis, the doctor should understand the structure of the emotional illness. He should be able to recognize signs of disturbed equilibrium of psychologic forces—specifically, distorted evaluation of the environment, inadequate inhibition of drives, and failure to develop sublimation or other satisfactory outlets for indirect expression. He should have some knowledge of the specific strengths and weaknesses of the patient's adaptive functions, as demonstrated by his response to stress in the past. His diagnosis becomes more specific if he has traced the development of his patient's personality and has assessed his highest previous levels of adjustment. The physician should know what special meaning the specific developmental crisis or the external events that precipitated the illness had for the patient. He should also attempt to determine, in terms of past interpersonal relationships, the patient's capacity to respond to psychotherapy if psychotherapy should appear to be advisable.

The physician seldom can determine all the structural and developmental characteristics of an emotional illness from the first interview. His initial understanding is usually tentative and incomplete. His diagnosis becomes more accurate and more sharply defined as further interviews reveal new facets of the patient's personality, and he should expect to continue to enrich his understanding of his patient throughout their contacts.

Meanwhile, the physician must demonstrate the relationship of the emotional illness to the patient's symptoms. Neurotic patients are no more immune to organic disease than anyone else, and a doctor's assumption that all of a hypochondriac's complaints are due to his emotions may be disastrous. Complicating the diagnostic process is the hypochondriac's tendency to overreact to organic illness so as to obscure the underlying cause. Illness is a source of anxiety and perhaps of depression to many

patients, but in most cases, the sequence of events is quite clear. When the degree of emotional reaction is great, however, as it usually is in chronically psychoneurotic patients, it may overshadow the symptoms of the precipitating organic illness. For example, if Mrs. Brown should develop appendicitis, her reaction could so simulate her previous emotionally precipitated attacks that an unwary Dr. Wilson might conclude that no examination was necessary. The physician should therefore learn all he can about the onset of an illness and of any exacerbations, paying particular attention to the emotional as well as the physical milieu in which it originated. The precipitating event may be the key to the underlying problem; thus, although Dr. Wilson's diagnosis was not established by finding that Mrs. Brown's first attack followed her discovery of her husband's infidelity, this finding was an integral part of the diagnostic process.

Generally, in medicine, diagnosis should be the prelude to treatment, and formal treatment begun prematurely may obscure the diagnostic process. For the most part, this rule is violated only in an emergency, as when an antibiotic is given for an overwhelming infection before cultures can reveal the causative organism. Both diagnosis and treatment of emotional factors in illness, however, are carried out through the same medium—the doctor-patient relationship. Since the physician's attitude and comments during the history taking will inevitably reassure, encourage, frighten, antagonize, or in some other way affect his patient, the diagnostic and informal treatment processes tend to merge and cannot be completely separated. Whether or not the doctor wants to, he does influence the course of a patient's emotional illness by his diagnostic efforts.

He also influences the patient's attitude toward later, more specific treatment efforts. If, while making a diagnosis of emotional illness, he overemphasizes organic possibilities and particularly if he frightens the patient unnecessarily, he encourages the patient's preoccupation with organic illness and makes eventual psychologic therapy more difficult. On the other hand, if he conveys to the patient his attitude of understanding and respect for emotional illness, he gives him a head start toward treatment. The patient's attitudes are guided by the attitudes of his physician; if the physician shows interest in all aspects of his condition, including the emotional aspects, it is easier for the patient to overcome his own disinclination to look at his feelings. If the physician is interested only in organic conditions and particularly if he is somewhat contemptuous of patients with emotional illness, the patient will tend to reject any but an organic explanation.

The physician, therefore, should anticipate his patient's fear of feelings

and, whenever he suspects that emotional factors are present, should conduct his diagnostic process in a way that will establish the most favorable field possible for future treatment efforts. This approach requires him to keep in mind possible emotional causes as well as possible emotional effects from the time of his first encounter with any patient who presents a diagnostic problem. He should integrate an evaluation of emotional factors into any medical history he takes and should not put aside their evaluation until all possibilities of organic illness have been eliminated.

THE HISTORY

Since emotional factors frequently contribute to illness that is primarily organic and organic factors frequently contribute to illness that is primarily emotional, no clear a priori distinction should be made between a medical and a psychiatric history until the physician has found adequate reasons for believing that one or the other factor is of minor importance. Even then, he should keep in mind the possibility that he has underestimated the significance of a secondary emotional or organic component. In much of this section, therefore, no distinction is made between a "medical" and a "psychiatric" history, although the "psychiatric" elements are emphasized [1].

In obtaining a history from any patient, the physician should encourage him to describe his illness in his own words and in his own sequence. He should listen carefully and at the same time observe the patient's tone of voice, his facial expression, and any other signs of emotion. He should note for later exploration any pertinent relationships, events, or feelings which the patient appears to avoid or to overemphasize. Meanwhile, he should confine his own activity as far as possible to unobtrusive words or gestures which show his interest. To obtain the most accurate information in the shortest time, the physician should do his best to appear unhurried. He should restrict his own activity to the minimum consistent with keeping the patient's story going and with making sure that he understands the patient correctly. His attitude should come as close as possible to friendly but objective understanding.

Precipitating Factors

As the physician evaluates the symptom picture, he should look for precipitating factors. These may develop spontaneously: "I can remember what night it was—just after that awful row with my husband" or "I'd had pork chops and cabbage for dinner." On the other hand, uncovering

the precipitating factors may require later questioning. Direct questions, however, are not so effective in eliciting a history of emotionally charged events as they are in more neutral areas of investigation. A patient who will give a reliable answer to the question, "Had you been eating fried food or cabbage before the attack?" may dissemble or avoid a direct answer if the question is, "Had you been having trouble with your husband before the attack?" Fearing criticism, many patients hesitate to confide personal troubles even to their physicians and need to test the reception they will receive by exposing a small portion of the problem at a time. If the physician is in too much of a hurry or if he demands too much too soon, the patient who has a problem may retreat and deny its existence.

In the investigation of possible emotional components, relatively vague questions which permit the patient a choice of how much he will tell (if, of course, there is anything to tell) are best, such as, "What was going on in your life at the time your symptoms began?" The patient may then describe a significant stressful situation, or he may indicate that things were going along about as usual, or he may ask what the question means. At this point, "I mean how were you getting along with your husband?" may be too direct and limiting. "I mean how were things at home, at work, and so on?" is still general enough to encourage the patient to discuss sources of tension which he thinks are important. The answer to this question may give the physician the impression that emotional factors are not particularly significant in the patient's illness, or it may supply clues to possible areas of stress which he may decide to follow up then or later, depending on the patient's attitude. If the patient replies "Why do you ask?" the physician need not evade or apologize but should face the patient more directly with such a comment as, "Well, I was wondering if you felt that there was any nervous tension at home or at work which might be aggravating your symptoms." Some patients at first interpret a doctor's implication that emotions might be *causing* symptoms to mean that he thinks they are *imagining* them; however, patients seldom resent questions about the *effects* of tension or "nervousness" *on* their condition and often volunteer this information when the doctor asks what they have found that brings on attacks or aggravates symptoms.

The Patient's Concept of His Illness

Sometimes a patient's own concept of what is wrong with him can help the physician in diagnosis and later management. For instance, if the physician says, "This has troubled you for some time now; I wonder if there's anything in particular that you've worried about or what you've

thought your illness might be," he will be helped by any of the following answers:

"Doctor, I've been terribly afraid it might be cancer" warns him that he must be specifically reassuring if no cancer is found or that the presence of cancer would be an unusually threatening finding to this particular patient. The patient may have good reason to suspect cancer; if not, it is possible that he may be identifying himself with a relative who has suffered from cancer. The basis for some patients' unwarranted but persistent fear of cancer is a repressed guilty feeling about something else, a feeling that makes them inwardly believe that they deserve to have cancer, although outwardly they fear it.

"I've wondered if it couldn't be my nerves" indicates that emotional factors can be explored more freely than usual. An overenthusiastic acceptance of a diagnosis of emotional illness, however, may hide a deeper fear of organic disease.

"I've looked it up in my home medical book, and I think it's shingles" reminded one physician of a diagnosis he had not considered. When the characteristic eruption appeared the next day, he was glad he had asked the question.

"I think it's all due to the fall I had while working at the plant" may well be true, but it also should warn the physician of possible workmen's compensation considerations.

Even "You're the doctor; you're supposed to tell me" enlightens the physician regarding his patient's personality; if he knows the patient or the cultural pattern [2] well enough to anticipate this type of response, he should omit the question.

The patient's record of previous treatment is as important as his diagnostic ideas. This area of exploration may reveal significant information, → particularly in the detection of toxic factors.

A young man with paranoid symptoms was considered schizophrenic until a resident physician asked him about previous treatment and learned that he had been taking large quantities of amphetamine sulfate. After the drug had been taken away from him, his psychotic reaction gradually cleared up and the depressive reaction for which he had taken amphetamine became evident.

A sixty-year-old woman was admitted in a state of confusion, with a tentative diagnosis of cerebral arteriosclerosis. Her initial symptom had been insomnia, for which she had taken large quantities of a bromide preparation. A high blood-bromide level indicated that her confusion was the

result of a toxic reaction. When she had responded to treatment of her bromidism, the physician could evaluate the causes of her insomnia.

Questions about previous treatment may protect the physician from prescribing a course of action which has already proved inadequate. If an obese patient has failed to follow twenty previous diet prescriptions, for example, there is not much point in simply prescribing a twenty-first.

The physician also should know why the patient came to him at this particular time. Have his symptoms changed in character or increased in severity? Has he been disappointed in the results of previous treatment? Has he read an article in the paper which seemed applicable to his case and which frightened him? Is there a developmental or environmental crisis in his life which has mobilized anxiety about himself and everything concerned with himself, perhaps including symptoms whose significance he previously had minimized?

After the patient has completed his story, the physician systematically reviews the various organ systems in an effort to pick up information the patient may have overlooked. With each system, he should not neglect symptoms of possible emotional origin, such as palpitation, indigestion, headaches, tremors, faintness, and dizziness. In the more definite field of the emotions, fatigue; sleep disturbances and dreams; worries, fears, and tension; loneliness, depression, shyness, sensitivity, and indecision; and touchiness, irritability, and impulsiveness all require particular attention.

The Patient's Personality and Background

The physician will find that indirect questions or questions which open up discussion are more effective than questions which can be answered by "yes" or "no" in evaluating a patient's personality and background. Thus, "Are you irritable?" can be answered in a word, and the initiative is returned to the doctor, who must then think up other questions and try to form a picture of the patient's personality by assembling the pieces. He usually gets a more cohesive picture if he uses such words as, "I would like to know something about yourself and the kind of person you are." The patient should have some idea why he is being asked about his personality; usually a casual explanatory comment suffices, such as, "I'm particularly interested in knowing how an illness like this affects you." The doctor should not, however, disguise the reason for his interest in the patient's personality, family, and background if he suspects a significant emotional factor in the patient's illness and carries his exploration

further. Patients give more useful information if they know why it is wanted.

Patients who need help in initiating a self-description may find it easier to get started if the doctor suggests a comparison, as: "Perhaps it would be simpler just to tell me how you are like your sister (mother, daughter, etc.) and how you differ from her." Questions of this type may lead naturally into a discussion of the patient's background, and the physician may go on to suggest, "Now, I would like to hear something about your family." If the patient asks, "What do you want to know?" the physician may be a little more specific. "I'd like to know what your mother and father were like, and your brothers and sisters, and in general what went on in your earlier years" is still general enough to permit the patient to emphasize the elements of greatest importance to him and at the same time to gloss over, at least for the time being, material he does not wish to discuss. The physician can thus see the picture in the patient's perspective and still respect the patient's defenses.

Attitudes of relatives toward the patient are significant, specifically as they may contribute to his concept of himself.

> A capable and intelligent college student was extremely apprehensive about his ability to hold a job after graduation. He had no confidence in himself and was primarily interested in the amount of security he would have. He reported that his mother's characteristic reaction when she was annoyed with him was: "You're no good. You'll never amount to anything." He said that he had heard it so many times he had begun to believe it.

To fill in the gaps, the physician can extend his exploration by more specific suggestions, such as, "I would like to know something about your experiences at school," and finally, when necessary, by direct questions, such as, "When did your father remarry?" or "How old were you when you had rheumatic fever?" He should correlate significant events in the family history with the patient's development and with the present illness. It is at least as important to know how old the patient was when his mother died as to know how old she was. It is also important to know how he responded to the crises in his life. If his characteristic response has been depression, for example, or withdrawal, or physical symptoms, he is likely to react to current stress with the same kind of response.

The extent of the history taking necessary to make a diagnosis or to rule out significant emotional causes will vary from case to case and also will depend on the experience of the physician and on his familiarity with the patient and his family. The medical student goes through a long and de-

tailed routine in taking each history and performing each examination; eventually, he learns when to take short cuts, but when in doubt he can always fall back on a more extensive exploration. The experienced physician knows when to be selective and what to select in his search for significant causes. The family physician has the advantage of familiarity with the patient's personality, past history, and family background, although the closeness of his relationship to the family may in some ways strain his objectivity.

As the physician reads the chapters on personality development, the elements necessary to an adequate developmental diagnosis will become apparent. In general, he should be familiar with the relevant material in the medical history, the details of the patient's birth and early development, his school and work history, and significant aspects of his sexual and marital history. I have avoided the traditional listing of the specific subdivisions of these categories because it has seemed to me that lists too frequently encourage the physician to ask a series of questions whose relevance is not apparent to the patient. Although most patients passively comply, considering that the doctor must have his own reasons for his questions, they thereby miss the important opportunity the diagnostic process affords for learning about themselves and for participating actively in an important early phase of treatment. The resultant orderly collection of data looks well on the history sheet but may leave the physician with the false impression that, by relating the data to the list, he has completed the task. It is much more important, I believe, to obtain the data more slowly but in a way that encourages both physician and patient to relate the data to an understanding of the patient's development, particularly with respect to the development of his relationships with other people.

The physician's tact and his respect for the patient's feelings may suggest some omissions in the history. For example, a patient may say that she has been married for nine years and, at another point, give the age of her eldest child as eight and a half. Should the physician attempt to find out if the marriage was forced or if, instead, her arithmetic is faulty? The answer lies in the value of the information to the diagnostic process. If the illness is of short duration, there is ordinarily no need to risk embarrassing the patient at this time; on the other hand, if the illness has lasted nine years, the physician wants to know the emotional milieu in which it originated. Even so, he may find out more from indirect questions such as, "Did your symptoms start before or after your marriage?" or "I would like to know some more about your courtship and marriage"; whereas a blunt

"Was your marriage forced?" is likely to embarrass the patient if the answer is "yes" and may antagonize her if the answer is "no." If, in order to avoid possible criticism, she answers "no" when "yes" is the truth, the doctor has accumulated useless misinformation and the patient feels uneasy because she has misrepresented the facts and is in an embarrassing position if she wants to backtrack later. The advantages of completing the record by breaking down a patient's defenses are usually outweighed by the consequent loss of rapport and by the patient's increased resistance to further explorations. This is especially true of questions about sexual activity.

The physician should not assume, however, that the patient cannot tolerate a discussion of sexual material. By the time he first sees the physician, he may have related his symptoms to problems in the sexual area or he may be prepared to entertain the possibility; in either case, the patient may interpret the doctor's avoidance of this aspect of the history as evidence that the doctor is uneasy about discussing sexual subjects. This interpretation may indeed be true, as Lief and his coworkers [3] have observed; the doctor owes it to his patients to remove, by education or by treatment, barriers to his own objectivity in this area, so that he does not unnecessarily either inhibit the patient's expression of sexual material or increase his guilt or shame.

Historical material in general, particularly when it is highly charged with emotional significance, is most useful when the patient associates it spontaneously with events in his current experience. A patient who says, "You know, Doctor, when I walked in that man's office yesterday, I had the same feeling I used to have when I knew my father was going to punish me," has already begun to recognize a carry-over or transfer of feeling from one situation to the other. An isolated historical account of his earlier relationship with his father contributes much less to his understanding of its significance.

The patient's emotions may cause him to break into tears or tirades during the history taking. If a display of feeling makes the physician uncomfortable and he shows his discomfort or changes the subject or terminates the interview, he supports the patient's belief that emotions are dangerous and should be hidden. On the other hand, saying nothing and waiting quietly gives the patient a chance to get his feelings out of his system. As he composes himself, he customarily apologizes for his loss of control. A comment by the physician which indicates that he recognizes that the material under discussion is significant and upsetting to the patient makes him feel less embarrassed and more willing to continue

The Patient's Family

If the patient discloses a conflict with his wife, his boss, or others, the physician should be careful not to take sides. If he sides with or against the patient, he becomes directly involved in the controversy. He angers the patient if he sides against him and, if the patient is frightened of his own anger, may increase his anxiety if he sides with him. The patient needs neither an ally nor an adversary; he needs neutral, friendly help in understanding his conflicting feelings.

Nobody can take a completely objective view of himself or his family, and so the doctor should not assume that the details of a patient's history are necessarily accurate, particularly in emotionally charged areas. Members of the patient's family often can supplement the history by giving the doctor a picture of the kinds of problems the patient produces at home. At the same time, the doctor gets a chance to size up the people the patient lives with. Families are not necessarily any more objective than patients, however, and their contributions should be received with some reservations. In marital problems, for example, it is easy for each spouse to see the mote in his partner's eye and ignore the beam in his own. Since the physician is neither passing judgment nor arbitrating disputes, he does not have to track down each piece of evidence.

The patient, however, may interpret the doctor's request for permission to discuss his illness with relatives to mean that the doctor doesn't believe his story. It may take some tact on the doctor's part to convince the patient that this procedure is in the interests of obtaining a different perspective and that the results are likely to be helpful both in establishing a diagnosis and in treatment. If the patient still objects, the doctor may decide to postpone or even abandon the idea of talking with the family. Some patients are so ashamed of having an emotional illness that they will take great pains to conceal it from their families, at least until treatment has relieved some of their shame. If the patient is psychotic or suicidal or in other ways dangerous to himself or to others, however, the doctor must insist on the need to communicate with the family.

The family physician has a great advantage over the specialist in this phase of the diagnostic process insofar as he knows in advance the patient's personality, family, and background. His greater knowledge, however, may be counterbalanced by greater bias, as it is much more difficult to be objective in evaluating tensions in a family of old friends than in a family of relative strangers.

In psychiatric hospitals, family contacts are often made almost exclu-

sively by psychiatric social workers, while the psychiatrist devotes his attention to the patient. Provided that adequate communication is maintained between the physician and social worker, this procedure has the advantage of providing the family with a member of the professional team whose primary concern is with their problems. Since the social worker's professional orientation is more toward the family than toward the individual, he may be better equipped than the psychiatrist to help with the kinds of problems families of patients frequently present. If the division of labor is rigidly adhered to, however, and if the relatives see the social worker as a barrier interposed between them and the psychiatrist which keeps them from getting information from the horse's mouth, as it were, the advantages of the procedure may be seriously reduced.

The medical student identifying with the physician member of the team and observing the division of labor between social worker and psychiatrist in the effectively operating psychiatric ward may conclude that, as a physician, he will have no part in assisting the families of patients with emotional illness. However, although an increasing proportion of medical-practice groups now employ social workers, their numbers are still small, and the average physician will have to do his own social work as well as he can. He should take every opportunity, therefore, to observe competent social workers in action and to learn those aspects of social work practice which he can later apply.

Jackson, Ackerman, and others [4] have shown that a great deal of otherwise unavailable information can be obtained from interviewing a family together and paying close attention to the family interaction. This technique is unquestionably of great value in experienced hands, and it will be worth the time it takes to learn how to encourage spontaneity in people who usually have communication problems and to prevent a family session from deteriorating into a forum for mutual recrimination.

THE MENTAL STATUS

The assessment of a patient's intellectual and emotional functions—expressed in mood, activity, thought content, behavior, and appearance—is as important to the diagnostic process as the evaluation of the history. This assessment is called the *mental status,* a procedure that is approximately the psychiatric counterpart of the physical examination. For the most part, mental-status observations are made during the history taking, and the physician should be alert throughout the entire diagnostic process for verbal and nonverbal evidences of anxiety, depression, withdrawal, or other disturbances of thought or emotion.

The complete mental-status examination is usually mandatory for hospitalized psychiatric patients or patients in whom the physician suspects the presence of a psychotic reaction. Many of the items to be noted in the mental status refer to symptoms or signs found only in psychotic reactions; these items and their significance will be discussed at greater length, therefore, in Chapter 11 and are mentioned here only for the sake of completeness. Just as it is impractical for the general physician to give every patient a complete physical examination for each condition, so it is impractical for him to go through all the aspects of the mental status with every patient in whose condition an emotional component is suspected. But, as in the case of the physical examination, the physician who takes a shortcut in the mental status takes the responsibility for his assumption that the shortcut is justified.

A thorough mental-status examination includes a careful appraisal of the patient's appearance and behavior, his affect (feeling or emotional state), his verbal and nonverbal communication, the content and competence of his intellectual processes, and his sensorium. At the conclusion, the physician should have answers to the following questions:

1. The patient's *general appearance and behavior.* Is it consistent with his age and position in life? Or is there evidence of dilapidation, such as failure to bathe, shave, or take an interest in his clothes? Is he wearing inappropriate or bizarre clothing or adornment? Are his posture and mannerisms appropriate, or do they suggest depression, elation, or preoccupation? Does he have repetitive, stereotyped, or peculiar mannerisms? Does he feel compelled to perform certain rituals? What is the quality of his participation in the examination: for example, is he submissive, cooperative, suspicious, distant, or wary?

2. The patient's *affective state,* including both expressed and reported emotion. Is he angry and irritable, tense and anxious, withdrawn, or indifferent? Is he elated or depressed? If he is depressed, is he also retarded and apathetic, or is he agitated? Has he considered or attempted suicide? * Is his mood consistent, or does it vary, either predictably or unpredictably? Is his affect appropriate to his thoughts and to his situation?

3. The nature of the patient's *communication.* Is his speech spontaneous, logical, relevant, and appropriate? Are his words consistent with his gestures and other nonverbal cues? Does he talk too much or too little, too rapidly or too slowly, or not at all? Is he too easily distracted, or is he

---

* See the discussion on the merits and risks of asking a patient about suicidal thoughts, pages 255–256.

circumstantial (spinning out his story with unnecessary details)? Does he make up *neologisms,* or new words; does he show *verbigeration* (stereotyped repetition of apparently meaningless words or phrases)? Does he *perseverate* (repeat the same answer to different questions)? Does he have a *flight of ideas* (his thoughts seeming to come too fast for him to sort out), or does he seem to see associations between consecutive statements that are not evident to the doctor?

4. The patient's *thought content* and *perceptions,* aside from the material revealed in the history. Does he have *delusions* (false ideas) of *persecution,* of *grandeur,* or of *reference* (i.e., that others are referring to him in their conversation)? If delusions are present, are they *systematic* (interrelated)? Does he have *somatic delusions* (false convictions that a part of his body is destroyed or changed)? Does he have *hallucinations* (false perceptions of voices, visions, odors, or tastes)? Does he have feelings of *depersonalization* (i.e., that things are unreal or that he is somehow detached from himself)? Is he *hypochondriacal* (preoccupied with his health), or does he have *obsessions* (particular thoughts that persistently recur)? Does he have *phobias* (specific disproportionate fears)?

5. The patient's *sensorium* and *intellectual competence.* Although psychologic tests are required for an accurate appraisal of intellectual competence, the physician can get a rough estimate by asking a few questions, keeping in mind for comparison the patient's school and work record as revealed by the history. This information is particularly important in suspected organic brain disease. The physician should ascertain whether the patient is *oriented* to person, place, and time (does he know who he is, where he is, and the date?). Differences between the patient's *remote* memory for events in the past and his *memory for recent events,* such as the content of the last meal, are significant. *Retention* is commonly tested by asking the patient to repeat a series of three, four, five, or six numbers forward and in reverse order. *Recall* may be tested by giving the patient a name and address and asking him to repeat it after five minutes. The patient's grasp of *general information* and his ability to do *simple arithmetic* may be gauged; asking him to subtract serial 7s from 100 is a standard question. *Comprehension* and *capacity to abstract* are usually tested by asking the patient to give the meaning of such familiar proverbs as, "A rolling stone gathers no moss." *Judgment* is tested by asking the patient to indicate what he would do in certain social situations.

The physician should be tactful and restrained in his assessment of intellectual competence. In order not to impair rapport, he should not appear to depreciate his patient; abruptly asking an irritable, depressed,

but intellectually intact college professor to supply the name of the President of the United States is not likely to get things off to a flying start toward a helpful relationship. It may be wise to preface this part of the examination by a somewhat apologetic but firm statement that, although the subsequent questions may seem rather elementary, in the interests of thoroughness you would like to have him respond to some simple but standardized questions. The physician's evident understanding of the impact of the questions on him removes a good deal of the chill.

The reverse applies to the senile patient whose confidence in himself is already shaken. To be bombarded with questions whose simplicity he recognizes but whose answers he cannot find is a further blow to his self-esteem. Here again, an empathic preliminary approach is helpful. You might begin by asking him if he has had some trouble with his memory lately, then commiserate with him, and after that go on to ask him if you might ask him a few questions to understand better just how much trouble he is having. If he refuses, you can usually agree to postpone the questions until a little later on; eventually, you can usually persuade him to cooperate.

THE PHYSICAL AND NEUROLOGIC EXAMINATIONS

In any case of suspected emotional illness, the physical and neurologic examinations should be performed with particular care. Psychologic reactions due to acute or chronic brain disease, particularly in the early stages, frequently simulate reactions of emotional origin. Brain tumors are often difficult to discover in patients with psychotic reactions, metabolic disturbances such as porphyria may be detected only by specific laboratory procedures, and drug reactions often appear to be extensions of the condition for which the drug is taken. An exploration of the wide range of brain disease is beyond the scope of this book, but one must remember that any disease of the brain reduces the individual's adaptive capacity. When the ego is weak and on the brink of collapse, an almost imperceptible reduction in brain efficiency may produce a major emotional regression, with symptoms so dramatic that the evidence of brain damage is overlooked [5].

Whether the suspected condition is primarily emotional or primarily organic in origin, the patient will give the physician information about his emotional reactions during the physical examination. For example, a patient who complains of palpitation may show excessive apprehension, appropriate interest, or disproportionate unconcern when the physician examines his heart. If the doctor encourages him to talk at intervals

during the procedure, he may add significant material to his history; although this technique takes time, it may shorten the diagnostic process in the long run. Excessive modesty or inappropriate lack of concern for conventional coverings often indicates the patient's attitudes toward sexual subjects; and a patient who flinches at the first touch of the doctor's hand suggests, unless the doctor's hand is cold, that either consciously or unconsciously he is anticipating hostility.

The patient's particular reaction to such procedures as breast examination or blood-pressure reading may reveal specific anxieties, and he will often respond best to prompt explanation and reassurance. The doctor may not wish to reveal the blood-pressure figures, but he should be ready to explain why he believes it is not in the patient's best interest to know them. Patients are sensitive to the reactions of their physicians; the doctor not only distresses his patient by outward expressions of alarm or dismay ("Wow, what a blood-pressure!" or "Tch, tch, what an interesting murmur!") but may frighten him by unexplained lingering over a particular point in the examination or a whispered word to the intern or nurse. Briefly explaining any deviation from the ordinary routine usually reassures the patient.

The disturbing, unconscious significance to many adolescents of a pelvic examination will be discussed in Chapter 7. Pelvic examinations are disturbing to some older women as well. It is neither possible for the physician to modify these attitudes at the time of examination nor appropriate for him to attempt to do so, but an explanation of the reason for the examination and a sympathetic and gentle approach will at least reduce the patient's distress. Rectal examinations are equally disturbing to some patients and require the same consideration.

The physician should not explain everything he does in every case. Dependent personalities usually prefer not to take an active part in their medical care and may want the physician to take complete responsibility. When a patient is denying the significance of his symptoms, the physician's explanations may stir up anxiety or precipitate depression. On the other hand, patients who find dependency an anxious state appreciate full information. The importance of a selective use of explanation has been demonstrated by Fox and his coworkers in their study of patients undergoing cardiac surgery [6]. They observed that: "Quite a number of the patients were much reassured by the careful explanations they had received from the internist concerning the different tests that were being carried out, and they trusted his clear evaluation of their physiological status." In their cases, "... the surgeon allowed the patient to choose

whether or not he wanted to know the exact date of operation ahead of time. This allowed the patient to make use of his characteristic way of dealing with such situations. Some felt a reassuring sense of control when they possessed intellectual knowledge of what was ahead, and others with a strong need for denial preferred the protection of ignorance." The same type of individualization according to personality pattern is indicated when the physician discusses treatment.

THE PRELIMINARY DIAGNOSTIC STATEMENT

At the conclusion of the history taking and the physical examination, a patient expects his physician to have formed an opinion on the nature of his condition. The physician may or may not have arrived at a definite or tentative diagnosis by this time, but in either case he should have discovered the patient's attitude toward his illness and his specific areas of concern. Several possible procedures are now open to him.

1. When he has made a definite diagnosis which he believes will reassure the patient, he should simply state his diagnosis, prognosis, and treatment plan in terms consistent with the patient's understanding. If the illness is of emotional origin, the same rule holds; he explains it in reassuring terms, without minimizing the distress caused by the symptoms and without implying that they are imaginary or under voluntary control. Advising a patient to "Forget your troubles" or "Don't worry" will only demonstrate to him that his doctor does not understand him; if the patient could have forgotten them or put them aside by himself, he would not have come to the doctor. It is true that some patients are sufficiently relieved by the reassurance that organic disease does not exist that they can forget their symptoms and no longer need to worry. These patients, however, are responding to the reassurance implicit in the diagnosis and not to the subsequent advice.

2. In Chapter 1, I discussed some of the problems faced by the physician who has made a definite diagnosis which will disturb the patient. The patient must accept his illness or disability if he is to participate in rehabilitation, and the physician must spend enough time in explaining and in eliciting and answering questions for the patient to understand what he faces and what is expected of him. Intellectual acceptance will not be enough if the patient is denying his illness, and the physician will have to penetrate the patient's denial. In so doing, he will cause his patient to become depressed, as the patient mourns his lost health or capacity or body part. This type of grief, however, is a necessary prerequisite to rehabilitation, and attempts to prevent it by disguising the

real significance of the diagnosis or by letting the patient in on his problem gradually may jeopardize the patient's cooperation in treatment.

In illness which is generally fatal, when treatment in all probability will be at best palliative, there is usually no advantage in forcing the patient to face his prognosis, and in such cases the physician should respect his patient's defenses (see page 18).

3. When the physician suspects but has not definitely arrived at a diagnosis which will be disturbing to his patient, he usually does not need to frighten him with his suspicions unless they are confirmed by laboratory studies. The patient, however, generally expects that if the doctor had good news, he would say so, and therefore interprets the lack of any diagnostic statement to mean that the doctor suspects the worst. If the doctor states frankly that he is at present unable to make a diagnosis but that he expects the tests he is ordering will help him, the patient feels that his doctor is not avoiding confirmation of his fears and that a systematic investigation of his problem is under way.

4. When the diagnosis is tentative but reassuring, the physician usually says so, as: "I don't believe that you have anything more than a bad cold with some bronchitis, but to make absolutely sure, we'd better get a chest X-ray." The doctor thus lets the patient know he expects the X-ray to be negative; the patient is reassured if it is negative and respects the doctor's thoroughness if it is not.

The same procedure should follow the tentative diagnosis of an emotional disorder. Much of the therapeutic value of the physician's early diagnostic impression is lost if he does not communicate it to his patient. Walker, a cardiologist with a particular interest in emotional problems, describes in detail the technique he recommends and uses [7].

> If on completion of the history and physical examination, the patient is believed to be suffering primarily from an anxiety reaction or psychogenic cardiovascular reaction, he is informed somewhat as follows: "Mr. Jones, after a thorough examination I do not believe you have any serious heart disease, although you have suffered from distressing chest pain and are naturally concerned about it. The pounding and skipping of your heart, I believe, results from a nervous reaction rather than from disease in your heart. For instance, if you walked down a dark alley at night and a masked bandit suddenly stuck a gun in your ribs, I am sure your heart would beat very fast and hard—not because it was bad, but in response to the nerve impulse that went out because of the fear you were experiencing. Your breath would also come short and fast and your hands would be wet and shaking as they were when you came into the office. Prolonged worry, tension, anger or anxiety can produce the same nervous impulse as intense

fear. That this is probably a factor in your case is suggested by the appearance of your symptoms shortly after the arrival of the new foreman with whom you are having trouble . . . You are afraid that your heart is bad, and as a double check I suggest we get an electrocardiogram, chest X-ray, blood test and urinalysis as a part of a complete medical evaluation. I expect they will be normal and even if they aren't, I am sure most of your symptoms result from nervous causes since no form of heart trouble can completely explain your symptoms while a tension state readily can."

It is important that a positive diagnosis be made before doing the laboratory studies—the physician thus shows confidence in his diagnosis, and as each normal laboratory study is reported, the patient's confidence in the physician is increased. If he orders extensive laboratory studies without telling the patient he expects them to be negative, with each normal finding the patient's esteem for the physician will drop. The patient assumes the tests were ordered to find out what was wrong. When the physician finally tells the patient his symptoms are due to nervous factors, it appears he is saying this because he has been unable to find anything abnormal with the tests. To the patient, it looks like an alibi, his confidence in the doctor is shaken and the usual story is for him to consult a different physician who, too often, "does some different tests."

The problem of diagnosis is complicated when both emotional and organic causes contribute to the picture, and it is difficult, if not impossible, for the physician to determine exactly what proportion of the symptoms results from each cause. The patient benefits most from a frank approach, such as: "Considering what you have told me of these attacks and what I have found on examination, I believe that you do have some gallbladder disease. However, I believe that part of your reaction to these attacks, as well as the symptoms you have had between attacks, is caused by nervous tension. I can understand that such painful attacks would make you nervous, but I think the problem you are having with your child might also have something to do with it. In order to do a thorough job, we should investigate all possibilities, so I am going to order an X-ray and some blood tests to check on the gallbladder, and in the meanwhile I'd like you to tell me a little more about your child."

The concurrent investigation of both factors helps the patient to recognize that both play a part. If all her attention is directed to the gallbladder, she will expect that organic treatment will remove all her symptoms; if she then has a cholecystectomy and if the symptoms related to her emotional tension persist postoperatively, she is likely to resist any attempt to relate them to tension. She may even believe that the doctor who tries to persuade her of their emotional origin is making excuses for inadequate surgery.

PSYCHOLOGIC TESTS

The laboratory, besides helping to assess organic factors, may make positive contributions to the diagnosis of emotional illness through psychologic tests. Psychologic tests can be helpful in the assessment of intelligence, in the diagnosis of intellectual deterioration, and in refining personality diagnosis. The use of standardized intelligence tests in diagnosing mental retardation will be discussed in Chapter 13. Variations of the same tests plus certain special tests can give more objective evidence of intellectual deterioration than can the usual mental-status examination [8].

Questionnaire or card-sorting tests, such as the Minnesota Multiphasic Personality Inventory, can be helpful in personality diagnosis, but unless the physician has had special training or at least an unusual background of reading, he should send the tests to a psychologist for scoring and interpretation [9].

Another type of personality measurement is the projective test. In these tests, the patient is presented with a standardized set of either inkblots or pictures and is asked to tell what he sees in the blots or to tell a story suggested by each picture. Without realizing it, he projects his own personality characteristics into his descriptions or stories. His productions are then compared with the results of the same tests administered to patients with established diagnoses [10].

Valuable supplementary information often may be obtained from projective tests. They are not infallible, however, and their value is proportionate to the experience of the psychologist who administers and scores them. The confirmation by testing of a physician's diagnosis of emotional illness does not, of course, rule out organic disease any more than a shadow on the X-ray rules out a coexisting anxiety state.

A trial of treatment with a *placebo,* a substance without therapeutic value given with the suggestion that it will relieve symptoms, is not as good a diagnostic test as might at first appear. If the patient's symptoms respond to the placebo, it is an error to assume that they are psychologic in origin, just as, if they do not, it is an error to assume that their cause is organic. Placebos tend to relieve the symptoms of suggestible people; unfortunately, however, the relief comes without regard to the *cause* of the symptom. Pain of any type can respond to suggestion; dentists extract teeth under hypnosis, which is an extreme degree of suggestion, and (as will be discussed in Chapter 4) the labor pains of suggestible mothers may respond to similar procedures. Pain of organic origin, therefore, may be relieved by placebos in some people, while in other, less suggestible individuals, emotionally produced pain may not be relieved. Since the re-

sponse to placebos is often misleading and since the patient often finds out that he is being deceived, with consequent loss of trust in his physician, placebos should not be used in the diagnostic process. Placebos are almost equally unsatisfactory as treatment, but they do play an important role in research [11].

THE DIAGNOSTIC FORMULATION

As the physician accumulates material about his patient's illness, his past life, and his present adaptation, he begins to formulate a tentative diagnosis. As I pointed out before, diagnosis of emotional illness resembles diagnosis of heart disease more than it resembles diagnosis of infectious disease, but even the analogy of heart disease may be misleading. The clinical diagnosis of heart disease generally carries etiological implications ("coronary thrombosis," "arteriosclerotic heart disease"), whereas, for the most part, the clinical diagnosis of psychiatric disease is, except for organic conditions, simply a descriptive label ("phobic reaction," "manic-depressive reaction," "schizophrenia").

Furthermore, the diagnostic entities in psychiatry are not discrete but overlap each other to a considerable extent. Some psychiatrists find it useful to think of illness primarily caused by emotions as distributed along a series of continua, with the so-called "typical" symptom pictures located as landmarks at the ends or junction points. According to this conception, "typical" manic-depressive reactions are located at one end of a continuum at whose other end are several "typical" forms of schizophrenic reactions; other continua run from the depressive component of the manic-depressive to the neurotic-depressive reaction, from the paranoid component of the schizophrenic to the paranoid state, and so on. Usually, it becomes progressively harder to fit a patient into a typical symptom picture as more becomes known about him; a patient who on first impression seems to be typically schizophrenic may on further exploration reveal signs of other psychotic or even neurotic reactions. When careful and painstaking diagnostic techniques are used in psychiatry, "typical" almost becomes a synonym for "rare." As Fodéré said [12], almost 150 years ago, "When one has seen many insane people, one can recognize that there are as many (individual) differences among them as there are personalities among individuals whose minds are healthy.... It is therefore really difficult to make up classes of diseases which would not prove fictitious."

The clinical diagnosis has some usefulness as a reference point and for purposes of communication among professional personnel [13]. Its limitations should be kept in mind, however, and it should be supplemented by

a more comprehensive formulation that includes descriptions of the developmental, or "genetic," and the organizational, or "dynamic," factors involved, as outlined in Chapter 2. Even in illnesses with a substantial component of organic causative factors, it is well to keep the diagnosis of the emotional element open and to be ready to revise and to refine the diagnosis throughout the course of the illness as further significant information comes to light.

The advantages of incompleteness and of avoidance of closure in diagnosis in the area of emotional illness are in sharp contrast with the rest of medicine and contribute to making psychiatry unsatisfying for the student who likes to wrap up his diagnostic packages neatly and definitely. For other students, it offers the challenge of making each patient, in effect, a research project, unique and different from any other patient, and affording a never-ending supply of new material for greater understanding. Psychiatrists and others who work with psychiatric patients live with more uncertainty than their colleagues in other specialities and, if they are to take steps to help their patients, must act on incomplete formulations. A working formulation is necessary to give direction to treatment, but treatment should not be delayed until the formulation is complete, or it will never begin; on the other hand, treatment goals and methods must be open and subject to revision as new diagnostic evidence develops.

The next two parts of the book should help the physician make use of the material he has collected in his diagnostic survey. Part 2 places the major emphasis on the stages of personality development and the common vicissitudes at each stage that may encourage fixation. Part 3 focuses on the clinical manifestations of regression as they appear in specific emotional illnesses, on their classification, and on the personality dynamics behind them.

SUMMARY

In this chapter, I have emphasized the importance of a positive diagnosis of emotional factors in illness, rather than a diagnosis solely by exclusion of organic disease. The close relationship between the diagnosis and the treatment of emotional illness requires the consideration of emotional factors throughout the history taking and physical examination of any patient with a diagnostic problem.

REFERENCES

1. For a general discussion of interviewing, see:
   Bird, B.: *Talking with Patients*, Philadelphia, J. B. Lippincott Company, 1955.

For the integration of the medical and psychiatric history, see:

Gray, M.: "Principles of the Comprehensive Examination," *Arch. Gen. Psychiat. (Chicago)*, 10:370, 1964.

Stevenson, I.: *Medical History Taking*, New York, Paul B. Hoeber, Inc., 1960.

Whitman, R.: "Medical Interviewing," *Postgrad. Med.*, 21:191, 1957.

For a description of the associative anamnesis, see:

Deutsch, F., and F. Murphy: "The Associative Anamnesis," *Psychiat. Quart.*, 8:354, 1939.

————: *The Clinical Interview*, New York, International Universities Press, Inc., 1955.

For more material specifically on psychiatric interviewing, see:

Menninger, K. A.: *A Manual for Psychiatric Case Study*, 2d ed., New York, Grune & Stratton, Inc., 1962.

Redlich, F. C., R. Newman, and M. Gill: *The Initial Interview in Psychiatric Practice*, New York, International Universities Press, Inc., 1954 (book and records).

Sullivan, H. S.: *The Psychiatric Interview*, New York, W. W. Norton & Company, Inc., 1954.

Whitehorn, J. C.: "Guide to Interviewing and Clinical Personality Study," *Arch. Neurol. Psychiat.*, 52:197, 1944.

The diagnostic process in children is described in:

Group for the Advancement of Psychiatry. Report No. 38, *The Diagnostic Process in Child Psychiatry*, 1957.

2. For cultural aspects in the history, see:

Henry, J.: *Culture against Man*, New York, Random House, Inc., 1963.

3. Lief, H.: "What Medical Schools Teach about Sex," *Bull. Tulane Med. Fac.*, 22:161, 1963.

4. Ackerman, N. W.: *The Psychodynamics of Family Life*, New York, Basic Books, Inc., Publishers, 1959.

Jackson, D. D.: "The Question of Family Homeostasis,' *Psychiat. Quart. (Supp.)*, 31 (1):79, 1957.

5. Olin, H. S., and A. D. Weisman: "Psychiatric Misdiagnosis in Early Neurological Disease," *J.A.M.A.*, 189:533, 1964.

6. Fox, H. M., N. D. Rizzo, and S. Gifford: "Psychological Observations of Patients Undergoing Mitral Surgery: A Study of Stress," *Psychosom. Med.*, 16:186, 1954.

7. Walker, W. J.: "Neurocirculatory Asthenia," in F. C. Massey (ed.), *Clinical Cardiology*, Baltimore, The Williams & Wilkins Company, 1953, chap. 27.

8. Burgemeister, B. B.: *Psychological Techniques in Neurological Diagnosis*, New York, Paul B. Hoeber, Inc., 1962.

Schafer, R.: *Clinical Application of Psychological Tests*, New York, International Universities Press, Inc., 1948.

9. Hathaway, S. R., and P. E. Meehl: *An Atlas for the Clinical Use of the MMPI*, Minneapolis, The University of Minnesota Press, 1951.

10. Anderson, H. H., and G. L. Anderson (eds.): *An Introduction to Projective*

Techniques and Other Devices for Understanding the Dynamics of Human Behavior, Englewood Cliffs, N.J., Prentice-Hall, Inc., 1951.

11. Wolf, S.: "Effects of Suggestion and Conditioning on the Action of Chemical Agents in Human Subjects: The Pharmacology of Placebos," *J. Clin. Invest.,* 29:100, 1950.

12. Fodéré: *Traité du Délire,* Paris, 1817, p. 333, quoted by G. Zilboorg and G. W. Henry, *A History of Medical Psychology,* New York, W. W. Norton & Company, Inc., 1941, p. 392.

13. A helpful guide for the clarification of diagnosis is:
    Diagnostic and Statistical Manual of Mental Disorders, Washington, American Psychiatric Association, 1952.

Part Two

EMOTIONAL DEVELOPMENT
AND EMOTIONAL FIXATION

Chapter 4

FIRST STEPS, SECURITY,
AND DEPENDENCY

HEREDITY AND ENVIRONMENT

The influence of heredity in personality is still not definitely known in spite of a great deal of study. There are several reasons why research in genetics has failed to be as productive in the field of personality as in other fields. The study of animals, which has taught us so much about the human body, is of relatively little help here, for personality structure in animals cannot be well enough defined for this form of research to be precise. Almost as troublesome is the problem of distinguishing the effects of the child's earliest environment from the influence of his heredity, particularly since the influence of the environment during infancy and early childhood appears to be tremendous and since even the prenatal environment may be significant. Evidence from studies of twins has strengthened the case for heredity; for example, when schizophrenia is diagnosed in one twin, it is found in the other much more frequently when the twins are identical than when they are fraternal. Although this observation at first glance appears unequivocally to support a hereditary basis for schizophrenia, the evidence may be misleading. Identical twins are frequently confused with each other, even by relatives, and consequently they find it harder than fraternal twins to establish independent identities. This confusion may contribute to the formation of similar habit patterns, which in turn may have much to do with the parallel development of schizophrenia.

Even when identical twins are reared separately, there is a high mutual incidence of schizophrenia. This observation adds strength to the heredity hypothesis, although its opponents point out that the separate "rearing" in many of the quoted cases occurred after the time of the greatest emotional influence and, furthermore, that the mutual incidence in separated identical twins is considerably lower than the mutual incidence in identical twins raised together.

83

So the argument continues, without a definite answer as yet [1]. The argument is not entirely academic, however; although completely accurate assessments are not possible, estimates of the relative influence of heredity and environment can be helpful in the evaluation and treatment of emotional disturbances. Objectivity is particularly essential in making these estimates because the tedium and frustration of treating some emotional illnesses may lead a physician to abandon his efforts prematurely if he subjectively decides that the disturbance is totally hereditary and if he also assumes that nothing can be done to help a hereditary illness. In this way, he can rationalize therapeutic failure by blaming the germ plasm rather than the learned habit patterns, which, presumably, could be unlearned under proper guidance. Although this reasoning may console the frustrated therapist, an overemphasis on heredity delays or forestalls the investigation of psychologic factors. On the other hand, in conditions where environmental factors seem clearly present and easily modified, the physician may underrate the importance of heredity or constitution.

Most psychiatrists today believe that heredity sets limits to the potential development of a personality in any given direction but that the interaction of the individual and his environment determines how close to those limits the personality reaches. It is probably safe to say that the hereditary factor is greater in psychotic reactions than in neurotic reactions or personality disorders. Intellectual development follows a similar pattern; if cultural, educational, and emotional factors are optimal and if there is no organic brain damage, heredity determines intellectual capacity. If any of these factors are deficient, however, the influence of heredity is proportionately diminished.

In searching for the determinants of "temperament," psychiatrists have been particularly interested in studying the behavior of newborn babies. Just as individual infants have quantitative differences in their body characteristics and in their intellectual potentials, so they differ in their adaptive mechanisms and in the strength of their drives. For example, the quality of their automatic adaptation to energy deficit varies, so that some respond with a more immediate and urgent hunger drive. Their sensitivities to external stimuli also differ, so that some infants seem to perceive more intensely; apparently, there are individual differences in the range of automatic adaptation to visual, auditory, tactile, olfactory, or kinesthetic stimuli. Presumably, these differences in the infant's automatic adaptive mechanisms are, at least in part, hereditary and may account for many of the differences in "temperament" which newborn infants demonstrate [2].

PREGNANCY

At birth, the infant is catapulted into an environment in which the most significant emotional elements are his mother's attitudes toward him. These attitudes can range from all-out enthusiasm for a long-awaited first child to open rejection of a baby born out of wedlock or, occasionally, of the last of too long a succession of babies. Most expectant mothers, however, experience ambivalent feelings, a mixture of positive and negative reactions to the coming child. As a rule, the positive feelings present no problem; society expects a woman to be happy in anticipation of motherhood, and she is free to express her pleasure at the prospect. At the same time, she is less free to express any displeasure or, in some settings, even to acknowledge the existence of negative feelings. The negative feelings are varied and include many attitudes relatively close to the surface: fear of the pain of labor, fear of loss of attractiveness, resentment in anticipation of being tied down to the care of the baby, or concern at the increase in financial problems. Less conscious feelings also may be included, feelings such as anxiety at the prospect of the baby's helplessness and her own responsibilities as a mother. Previously unsatisfied dependency needs which have been repressed may be mobilized and brought to the surface during pregnancy. The anxiety of a prospective mother may result indirectly from rivalry with her own mother, while motherhood to a woman with an inner envy of men may mean the loss of opportunity to compete with men in business and social life.

Although we now know that babies are not visibly marked by frightening experiences of the pregnant mother, there is evidence that anxiety or emotional upset in the mother is accompanied by increased activity of the fetus [3]. Whether this increased physical activity is accompanied by any direct effect on the child's emotions is still a matter for speculation. In any case, ambivalent feelings may cause a mother to resent (or in a compensatory fashion, to overprotect) the newborn baby.

A pregnant woman may be aware of some of her negative feelings and through shame or guilt keep them to herself. She may consciously suppress, or try to forget, some of them, and she may repress others so that she becomes no longer aware of them at all. In either case, she conceals them, and whether suppressed or repressed, they tend to assume a proportionately greater role in her attitudes than they would if someone were to help her face them. As they accumulate, the feelings become magnified out of proportion to their significance and form the basis for an increase in the degree and duration of the depressed periods many women experience during or just after pregnancy. Severe depression immediately following delivery is so frequently encountered that it has been considered a separate disease entity, *postpartum depression,* and for many years was attributed exclusively to hormonal causes. In recent years, greater attention has been paid to psychologic causative factors, and postpartum depressions are now included in the general group of *depressive reactions.*

The physician is often in a strategic position to help the mother with her ambivalence. He can help her overcome some of her fears by explaining the process of pregnancy and childbirth to her in terms she can understand. He should be careful to avoid excessive technical material, particularly any unnecessary emphasis on pathologic aspects of pregnancy, an emphasis which will increase rather than decrease her anxiety. Some obstetricians have arranged group discussions for pregnant women so that beginners in particular can gain reassurance by sharing their problems with others. Sometimes a family interview helps to reassure both wife and husband that the wife's irritability, demanding attitude, and capricious sexual responses are temporary phenomena.

If the patient's ambivalence about her pregnancy has led her to attempt abortion, the opportunity to talk frankly with a physician who neither condones the attempt nor rejects the patient because of it is particularly important. Even if she has only gone so far as to consider or to fantasy abortion, the associated feelings of guilt may seriously affect her later relationship with the child unless she is helped to express and evaluate them in an atmosphere of understanding.

The woman whose physician has helped her with some of her ambivalent feelings about an anticipated baby is better able to cope with the emotional impact of miscarriage, spontaneous abortion, or stillbirth. If she feels too guilty to acknowledge that there are times when she wishes she were not pregnant, a miscarriage (which represents the fulfillment of the unacceptable side of her ambivalence) will make her feel even more guilty and will add depression to her grief at the frustration of her positive feelings. The depression may be obvious or it may be concealed in the guise of apparently unrelated symptoms.

There is some evidence to indicate that emotional factors may occasionally play a role in the incidence of both spontaneous abortion and infertility. Mann's program for treating patients with habitual spontaneous abortion, a program primarily oriented around supportive psychotherapy, reduced the frequency of abortions in his group from over 90 percent to 20 percent [4].

As mentioned before, a woman is more dependent and needs more emotional support when she becomes pregnant. Part of her increase in dependency appears to be hormonal in origin. Benedek [5] has demonstrated increased passivity and an increased need to receive love in women in the late, progesterone phase of the menstrual cycle, contrasted with a more active wish to give love in the early, estrogenic phase. When pregnancy interrupts the cycle, the progesterone phase continues and the emphasis on dependency remains. A reasonable amount of satisfaction of the mother's dependency needs during pregnancy helps prepare her for emotional "giving" to the child during infancy; since the husband is best situated to minister to her dependency, an interview or two with him can help him recognize the importance of his role.

If the pregnant woman cannot find added support in her environment or if past experiences make it difficult for her to accept dependency, she may seek a substitute source of dependent satisfaction. A frequent substitute is food; as a result, a pregnant woman often has a tendency to eat not only more than usual but more than enough to meet her increased metabolic demands. In the interest of health, this tendency requires curbing, and the doctor usually puts her on a diet. The diet, however, does not control her appetite; instead, it complicates the situation because she cannot eat to relieve her dependency needs and, at the same time, please her doctor by holding down her weight. She must jeopardize either one or the other source of dependency satisfactions, and the resulting dilemma may add to her negative feelings about the pregnancy and about the coming child. If the physician realizes the implications of the problem and adopts an understanding attitude about diet rather than an irritated and arbitrary one, he will have a better chance to help his patient reduce her food intake. Her recognition of his active sympathetic interest in her problems gives her a greater feeling of protection under his professional care and, in turn, diminishes her excessive appetite.

A relationship between emotional problems and the prolonged vomiting of pregnancy has been reported. Repressed ambivalent feelings apparently combine with a physiologic susceptibility to produce the symptoms, and psychologic support may be useful in preventing or alleviating them. The physician cannot afford to forget, however, that unconscious feelings do not respond to intellectual insight. The obstetrician who bluntly tells his miserably vomiting patient that her troubles are caused by her rejection of her unborn baby should not be surprised if she fails to see the connection.

Pseudocyesis

Perhaps the most dramatic demonstration of the relationship of emotional factors to bodily changes is false pregnancy, or *pseudocyesis* [6]. For every 250 pregnant patients accepted for prenatal care, there is one who, although demonstrating both signs and symptoms of pregnancy, nevertheless is not pregnant. The signs include the typical uterine, cervical, and breast changes; the symptoms include amenorrhea, morning nausea, weight gain, and, in patients who go to "term," "labor pains." Even laboratory tests may be positive, yet the pregnancy has only existed as a strong conviction in the patient's mind. The physician who is "taken in" by a patient with pseudocyesis is most unfair to the patient if he attempts to relieve his own frustration by accusing her of conscious deception. Her conviction is based on powerful unconscious forces, customarily resulting from deep ambivalent feelings about herself as a woman, and is supported by the physical "evidence" of pregnancy. First of all, she needs empathic recognition of the perplexity and embarrassment the diagnosis causes her; later, the underlying conflict may be explored.

The following case report is abstracted from the biography of a prominent historical figure of the sixteenth century.

> About four months after her marriage, the patient reported amenorrhea, morning nausea, breast changes, and other signs of pregnancy. Her "pregnancy" progressed in the customary way, although there were no reported fetal heart sounds and fetal movements were not at all characteristic. She refused categorically, with characteristic stubbornness, to consider the possibility that she was not pregnant or to undertake procedures that might clarify the situation. At "term," after one or two episodes of "false labor," her abdomen, which had the appearance of a full-term pregnancy, began to recede, the signs of pregnancy disappeared, and she became depressed.
>
> The patient was the only child of her father's first marriage who survived past infancy. Her father was wealthy, charming, and promiscuous; he was very attached to her during her childhood but obviously distressed at not having sons. When she was about twelve, her father's interest in other women led to estrangement from her mother and eventually to divorce. In the course of the divorce proceedings, her father left the Catholic church; and as his interest in his daughter dwindled, she sided militantly with her mother and became almost fanatic in her Catholicism.
>
> She grew up a rather plain girl, reasonably well educated but so pre-

occupied with her relentless and resentful feud with her father that she had little interest in other relationships. Her father meanwhile had a son by another marriage, but the son died shortly after he did, and the patient was left a lonely heiress at thirty-eight.

She soon fell in love with a younger man whose reciprocal interest in her was due to her possessions and not to her charms, a fact that was evident to everyone but the patient. She stubbornly refused to pay attention to her friends and married her suitor, only to discover almost immediately that his romantic interests were elsewhere.

Perhaps influenced by her father's preoccupation with his wish for sons, the patient believed that a child would bring her husband closer to her. During her "pregnancy," in fact, he was more attentive, although at its anticlimactic termination, he went abroad in disgust and irritation and did not return for a year and a half. Following his return, in spite of the previous fiasco, she again developed the signs and conviction of pregnancy, again was disappointed, and again became depressed.

She was a complex person, and no doubt many factors contributed to her pseudocyesis. One important factor probably was her feeling of inadequacy as a woman. Contributing to her feeling of inadequacy might well have been: (1) a conviction that her father would have continued to love her if she had been a boy; (2) an identification with her mother as a woman rejected by her father, leading to her inability to give up her involvement with him and her persistent struggle for revenge; (3) an acceptance of her father's belief that the only adequate woman is one that can produce a male heir; and (4) a realization of her husband's lack of interest, which she finally had to acknowledge. Keeping her husband at home, in spite of his lack of interest, may have been a secondary gain (see page 235).

"Natural Childbirth"

In the last few years, some physicians have emphasized the possible benefits to both mother and child of the mother's conscious and active participation in the delivery process. The concept stems in part from Read's belief that labor is naturally painless but is made painful through a state of emotional tension produced by fear of the experience [7]. He believes that pain can be removed by removing fear of pain, so that the mother will enjoy rather than dread the experience of childbirth and will thereby develop a closer, less ambivalent relationship with her child. With this goal, he has developed a prenatal routine, or preparation for childbirth, emphasizing education and relaxation. In many cases, this program is successful, but its importance in mother-child relationships is somewhat doubtful, and the role of suggestibility is so great that consid-

erable question has been raised about the universality of its applicability
[8]. There is an unfortunate trend among devotees of this method to
brand as "rejecting" those mothers who are not able to eliminate labor
pains. If the ability to deliver painlessly is a sign of responsiveness to suggestion (or to a modified form of hypnosis) rather than a sign of emotional health, it is certainly unjust to condemn mothers who do not respond. On the other hand, Read has performed a service in emphasizing
the emotional implications of labor.

INFANCY

No adaptation that man—or animal—has to make can compare in extent to that of being born. The newborn switches almost instantaneously
from fluid to gaseous surroundings, from darkness to light, from a constant surrounding temperature to a varying temperature usually a good
deal cooler, from a nutritional supply via the placental circulation to the
use of the alimentary canal, from predigested food to food needing digestion and excretion, and from a state in which all his needs are automatically supplied to one in which he must make his wants known. Immediately following the gratuitous use of his head as a battering ram, he has a
few seconds' grace in which to find out if he can breathe. Considered
from an adult point of view, such an abrupt change would make anyone
nervous, and much has been written on its presumed importance in the
production of emotional disturbance [9]. Yet even though the conditions
surrounding birth may have an influence on the development of neurotic
reactions, it is a little hard to believe that any process so universal in the
animal kingdom should be a major cause of emotional illness.

At the moment of childbirth, the mother's position automatically
changes from that of an involuntary supplier of fetal needs to that of a
voluntary supplier of food, warmth, and physical contact to her baby. She
now has a choice; she can give, withhold, give some but not all, or attempt to give more than is needed. Although her choice depends on many
considerations, an important factor is her capacity to relate to her child in
an empathic way. Benedek believes that, for the infant to obtain adequate security, his mother must permit herself partially to regress—
unconsciously—to a point where she can identify with her child as an infant and so provide him with the security and affection she received at an
analogous time in her life [10]. To accomplish this partial regression and
communication without self-consciousness, ambivalence, guilt, or com-
petitiveness requires a history of a reasonably comfortable relationship
with her own mother when she was an infant. If her own infancy left her

with too many dependency longings, she will lack enough security and will be too competitive with her infant for dependent gratification to share with him within the context of her partial regression. She will then either overtly reject the infant or, if she feels sufficiently guilty about her competitive and rejecting impulses, overprotect him. Benedek uses the term "symbiosis" to indicate the closeness of the reciprocating dependent relationship between mother and child, which appropriately lasts until the child can perceive himself as an independent entity.

The newborn infant, meanwhile, is helpless to do more than receive what is given or to express his reaction to discomfort by crying and aimless muscular activity. Throughout most of civilization and all that preceded civilization, mothers generally chose to supply their infants' needs as they became evident, to nurse their babies when and as long as they were hungry, and at the same time to provide close physical contact. These infants presumably associated food with the physical contact of cuddling and with the emotional experience of being loved. Most psychiatrists now believe that babies whose hunger cry is soon answered by food, physical contact, and love have the best opportunity to develop a fundamental sense of safety or security and to anticipate a helping response from the environment in time of need. A foundation of this type of security seems to prepare the child for gradual independence as his own powers mature. If infants go for any appreciable length of time while awake without food or cuddling, their personalities may be adversely affected and, as Bowlby, Spitz and others [11] have shown, continuing deprivation can lead to serious psychologic and physical illness.

Fortunately, in view of the frequency with which mothers or babies are ill and must be separated in the period immediately following childbirth, the newborn baby does not appear to discriminate between the source of supply. Grandmothers, nurses, or neighbors can then substitute for mothers, and provided that they supplement food with the other security-giving ingredients of manifest expression of affection, the infants do not appear to sense the difference. Far sooner than would be considered possible from a conventional appraisal of the infant's development, however, he in some way begins to discriminate between his accustomed source of security—usually his mother—and a substitute. This conclusion is derived from studies that show changes indicating an impairment of security when infants are separated from their mothers for any appreciable period at as early an age as <u>four months,</u> even when the mother is replaced by a competent substitute. After four months, therefore, the infant should not be separated from his mother except in emergencies. <u>For this reason,</u>

modern adoption agencies make every effort to place children in the first few weeks of life.

Even if an infant's mother is too sick to carry out household duties, her presence in the home maintains the kind of continuity that gives the child security, and although the physician may find it more convenient to treat the mother in the hospital, he should keep her at home if at all possible. The physician who is familiar with agencies in his community that provide homemaker or home-nursing services can direct the husband or other relative to sources of help in keeping the family together when the mother is ill. If the child requires hospital care, arrangements should be made for his mother to spend as much time as possible with him. To this effect, hospitals should be so arranged that a mother can live in the same room as her sick child whenever feasible. Hospitals that have initiated this experiment, usually reluctantly and with understandable skepticism, have been pleasantly surprised to discover that the mothers, far from being nuisances, have been helpful in providing care not only for their own child but for other children whose mothers have been unable to stay with them.

It is not clear whether the physical contact of cuddling or the actual nursing process is of greater importance in the development of the child's security. Although traditional psychoanalytic theory gives the nursing process priority, Harlow's experiments with baby monkeys and "mothers" made of terry cloth or wire suggest that cuddling is more crucial [12]. Harlow's findings, however, cannot be applied uncritically to human infants and live mothers. In either case, there is not much doubt that hunger usually arouses the infant from sleep and satiation of hunger encourages him to go back to sleep. The hungry baby shows every evidence of giving food a high priority in his current needs.

Scheduled or Demand Feeding

[In the early part of this century, a peculiar phenomenon occurred. A group of psychologists recommended that the infant's nutrition should be controlled by rigid scheduling of feeding times and amounts of food and that physical contact should be reduced to the minimum lest he be "spoiled." These recommendations were based on the erroneous concept that the child has no inner propulsion toward maturity and that he must be forced to grow up] They found extensive support in the contemporary concern with exact caloric requirements, and by limiting mother-child contacts to brief periods when the mother had no visitors and could be kept sterile—in the bacteriologic sense—the recommendations seemed to provide one solution for the problem of cross infection in hospital nurseries. They disregarded individual differences, however, and attempted to force all babies into the pattern of the mean. In this way, a great many babies whose individual hunger patterns did not conform to the statistical average went through many hours of helpless hunger—unfed, untouched, and uncomforted. Although there is no way to discover exactly how they felt about it, logic and observations of deprived children both suggest that their concept of the world was not so safe and satisfying as if their needs had been fulfilled.

Under this regime, the conscientious mother was torn between her wish to relieve the baby's discomfort and her obligation to follow the doctor's orders.

> In the course of giving background material to her son's psychiatrist, a mother stated that as an infant her child regularly awakened three hours after each feeding and began howling for food. She would pace the floor, alternately letting the baby cry in his crib and guiltily picking him up and holding him at arm's length. She never dared disobey the doctor's instructions by feeding him before the required four hours had passed.

Most women, more secure in their motherhood, either ignored or paid lip service to the rigid regime, and eventually some thoughtful pediatricians began to question its validity [13]. They knew that one would not attempt to toughen up a cold and shivering infant by withholding blankets, and they argued that there was not much more sense in applying the toughening-up procedure to food and affection, especially when the infant is totally helpless to do anything about it himself. Furthermore, rigid scheduling apparently had not produced psychologically healthier children; on the contrary, it seemed to increase insecurity when the child's individual hunger rhythm differed markedly from the schedule.

As a result of these criticisms, new rules were adopted; the infant was to be fed or comforted on demand or whenever he indicated his needs by crying. With relaxed mothers, who do not interpret every whimper as a hunger cry and who can be somewhat flexible in responding to the demand, this technique is successful. After an initial period of adjustment, babies fall into their own individual, widely differing patterns of feeding. They eventually give up feedings at peculiar hours and fall into a conventional schedule; even a baby who begins by sleeping all day and eating four times between 10 P.M. and 6 A.M. will work into the usual three meals a day. And if their feeding is consistently accompanied by cuddling and mothering, they develop a firm foundation of security on which they build a healthy, outgoing interest in growing up.

Some mothers, however, are too anxious or too inflexible to handle such an unstructured program. To this type of mother, every cry is a reproach, and an attack of colic (to which babies with overanxious mothers appear somewhat susceptible) can throw her into a panic. For example, if she cannot relax enough to learn to differentiate the hunger cry, the baby gets fed whenever he cries for any reason. If he is not particularly hungry, he takes a small amount, dozes awhile, then whimpers a bit and gets another sample, until he is being fed every fifteen minutes and the mother is frantic. Sometimes the physician can head off this process by helping the mother understand more about her baby, but usually she needs an authoritative routine as well, at least to begin with. The physician can be of greatest help by giving her an initial schedule, checking up frequently to see how the baby is adapting, and suggesting gradual alterations in the schedule until the three of them together—baby, mother, and doctor— arrive at the appropriate individual pattern.

Rooming-in

Individualized infant feeding and plenty of cuddling are hard to provide in the conventional obstetrical service, oriented as it is toward prevention of cross infection in the nursery. But if these measures are to give the infant security, they are most essential in the earliest days. Several hospitals, therefore, now permit the infant to remain in the mother's room, at least during the day. This procedure is called *rooming-in* [14]. It gives a mother, especially with her first child, a chance to get accustomed to baby care while trained help and instruction are available and while she is free from household duties. It also keeps the father from being completely left out; he has a chance to hold the baby and change its diapers occasionally, and he is not chased away when feeding time comes. He becomes more familiar with the baby and is better able to participate in his child's development when the family is reunited at home.

Rooming-in requires sympathetic nurses and other personnel, and special equipment, such as portable bassinets. The physician should not institute it before the mother feels ready for it, and ideally the baby should be removed at night so as not to interfere with his mother's rest. In places where these criteria are met, the plan works out well for mothers and infants alike and greatly eases the adjustment from hospital to home. But even under ideal hospital circumstances, rooming-in is not advisable for everyone. Many mothers, tired out after combining a hard pregnancy with housework and child care, feel with justification that they are entitled to a rest in the hospital. Attempts to deprive them of it will produce irritation with both baby and doctor, resulting in the loss of the program's advantages.

Breast Feeding

The rooming-in program also helps the mother to overcome the vicissitudes of beginning breast feeding. The first steps in breast feeding often discourage and frustrate her. Both infant and mother may take some time to adjust to this new method of giving and obtaining nourishment; meanwhile, the mother's milk supply is unpredictable, often either insufficient for the baby's needs or painfully overflowing. To add to her troubles, under conventional obstetrical routines with fixed feeding schedules, the baby may be brought in to nurse either half asleep and "lazy" or cranky and worn out after an hour's crying. So in addition to her other problems, she must attempt to awaken him and get him interested or try to soothe him enough to let him concentrate on nursing. Rooming-in, on the other hand, permits her to feed him when he is ready and reduces her problems accordingly.

Breast feeding has psychologic as well as physiologic advantages; the mother's fulfillment of her maternal role seems to strengthen the bond between her and her child, and the infant gains the security-giving benefits of close, intimate physical contact during nursing. Some mothers, however, find the procedure repugnant—perhaps a reflection of unsatisfactory nursing experiences in their own infancies. Others may find it impractical because of jobs, and the husbands of still others may strenuously object. Sometimes objections to nursing are due to misconceptions concerning the effects on the mother, which can be cleared up by the physician. He should be careful, however, not to shame the unwilling mother into breast feeding, since some of her antipathy to the procedure may then be transferred to the baby. A mother who gives in to this kind of pressure often finds it difficult to wean the child. She seems to feel so guilty about resenting the process that she tries to make it up to the baby by going on and on with it.

Sucking

In both breast and bottle feeding, the infant obtains satisfaction through the mouth by means of the sucking reflex. This reflex is quite strong in the infant, and unless permitted to die out through disuse, as with cup-fed babies, it remains strong throughout the nursing period. Even when no longer hungry, the child tends to suck on his thumb, his fingers, or whatever is handy. This prolongation of sucking activity suggests that it produces some type of gratification beyond that associated with food. The degree of resistance which a baby puts up to forcible interruption of sucking suggests further that this type of gratification is rather important.

Sucking seems to be the infant's first purposeful activity performed for nonutilitarian (as well as utilitarian) goals—or, in other words, for his own enjoyment. Freud believed that sucking was the precursor of other forms of pleasurable satisfaction and referred to the period of infantile dependency as the "oral phase of psychosexual development" [15]. His use of the term "sexual" distressed many who could not see the connection between nursing or thumb-sucking and conventional concepts of sexuality. Freud, however, used the term "sexual" in a much broader sense than we are accustomed to use it. His usage does not appear to be so far-fetched when the evident relationship to sucking of such a conventional sign of affection as the kiss is considered.

There are great individual differences among babies in the amount of energy available for sucking. Some placid types use it all in obtaining food and drift off to sleep after a short period of sucking; others work with desperate concentration on their thumbs or fingers even after their mothers try their best to prolong the feeding period. At present, it seems wisest for parents not to interfere with this means of releasing energy, although the physician may need to reassure some parents that most children eventually abandon the habit and that attempts to force them to give it up usually serve only to make it a point of contention and cause it to persist. It is probably better in the long run to permit a baby freely to fall back on this early source of gratification to let off steam or, later, to comfort himself when tired or upset. As he matures, he can reach out for sources of satisfaction outside of himself; he will then retreat to his thumb less and less frequently—in time, only when particularly tired or unhappy. On the other hand, a baby who is denied access to his thumb or to a reasonable facsimile may find it a little harder to develop enough internal security to risk reaching out for outside sources of protection. He thus is more apt to prolong his search for solace within himself.

Sucking, therefore, performs a triple function in infancy: It secures food, it releases surplus energy, and it comforts in adversity. In the weaning process, the first function is given up with varying degrees of reluctance in favor of spoon and cup. As the baby matures and discovers more about himself and the people about him, he finds more interesting ways of releasing surplus energy. Finally, as the infant learns through experience that when he needs comforting, he can get it from his mother, he will begin to trust and depend on her rather than on his thumb, the symbol of an earlier form of security. The mother or mother substitute who adequately satisfies the infant's dependency needs provides the foundation stone for all his later interpersonal relationships.

Postponement of Gratification

One of the first outward signs of security occurs when the baby can wait a little between his awareness of hunger and his insistence on food. He begins to tolerate delay at about three or four months of age, but the amount of delay he can tolerate varies greatly and depends on the strength of the particular infant's hunger drive and his developing ability to postpone its gratification. Postponing gratification depends in turn on the security he has developed—partly, at least, through conditioning. If his needs in the past customarily were satisfied before he became too miserable, he now feels safe in letting himself enjoy some sociability after he awakens. He can concentrate on what is going on around him instead of being tormented by the possibility that food will not be forthcoming. No one, of course, can be really sure what an infant is aware of, but observations of infants and later reconstructions make this a reasonable assumption.

All infants eventually learn to postpone gratification, but at different rates and to different degrees. The baby soon discovers that he is rewarded in rough proportion to his postponing ability; he discovers that sociability is pleasant, and he gradually finds other interesting things to do. He learns to tolerate frustration of his hunger needs, at first for a very short time, in order to maintain social contact and the approval of his parents.

This process represents the beginning of a change in the child's personality. A brake has been put on the infant's demands, not by his environment but by himself, in the interest of a more satisfactory adjustment. As the child grows up, he gradually develops a buffer zone of adaptive functions which mediate between his drives and the demands of his environment. These functions, as discussed in the preceding chapters, should include (1) the capacity to evaluate his inner needs and the expectations of the environment and to differentiate between them; (2) the capacity to postpone or inhibit gratification of dangerous, unacceptable, or untimely impulses and the consequent capacity to tolerate frustration; and (3) the capacity to discover and to use socially acceptable channels of expression of drives. In any child, the adaptive capacities develop at a rate proportionate to his security and his success in coping with his environment. They determine the quality of his relationship to reality and the degree of his resistance to the development of emotional illness.

CHRONIC DEPENDENCY

When the child, in the interest of social adjustment, begins to put a brake on his demands, they necessarily remain partially unfulfilled. For a while, these unfulfilled demands remain close to the surface and are easily mobilized whenever he encounters any obstacle in his attempt at a new adjustment. Once mobilized, they cause his temporary regression, or return to a more infantile search for security. At first, therefore, he will burst into tears at minor frustrations and turn to his mother for help; since the new techniques are not working, he goes back to the older, more familiar approach to problems. At this point, he needs acceptance of his regression, acceptance lasting long enough for him to rally his forces to return to the fray and followed by encouragement for him to persist in his attempt to make the new adjustment.

As his personality develops and as he experiences greater success with the new techniques, he can tolerate more and more frustration without regressing, and it requires more and more environmental stress to make him slip back. Meanwhile, he is learning more mature ways in which to meet his unfulfilled earlier needs. Eventually, he should be able to satisfy his dependency needs in an adult manner, within the reciprocal relationships of marriage and friendship, instead of eternally seeking the helpless, clinging dependency of infancy.

A mother who cannot give affection or who withholds affection, for whatever reason, deprives the infant of early gratification of his dependent needs when he is helpless and so threatens his foundation of security. Preoccupied with seeking or with maintaining his security, the child of a "rejecting" mother has less energy left over with which to adapt to new situations, and for the same reason he can tolerate less stress before he regresses. In a similar fashion, the overprotecting mother, who discourages the child's attempts at new adaptations, reduces his confidence in his ability to progress. Overprotection often, perhaps usually, represents the parent's attempt to compensate for his rejection. Although the parent is seldom conscious of either the rejection or the compensatory mechanism, the child may sense the nonverbal expression of the underlying rejection. The overprotected child, therefore, may combine insecurity with lack of self-confidence.

Dependent Personalities

The Passive-Dependent Personality. In the course of growing up, relatively minor life stresses will cause regression in the person without confidence in himself or the person with strong residual needs for security. In the most extreme cases, self-confidence is so small or unmet dependent needs are so great that the major part of the personality becomes *fixated* at the level of a search for the earliest gratifications. This type of fixation is often termed *oral fixation,* deriving its name from the importance of the mouth as a means of establishing human contact and receiving emotional gratification in the infantile stage of development [16]. Fixation at this level results in a character structure dominated by helpless, demanding, parasitic dependency, either obvious or masked. When obvious dependency persists into adult years, the individual appears completely unable to cope with the demands of his environment. He seldom tries to conceal his inadequacy and readily blames it on his earlier misfortunes.

When parental overprotection and overconcern are focused on the child's health, he learns that symptoms are keys that open the doors to the gratification of his dependent needs. Consequently, and usually without being aware of it, he begins to exaggerate and magnify relatively minor physical complaints. Unconsciously, but nevertheless effectively, he uses his symptoms as a lever to control his environment and to provide partial gratification of his insatiable dependent needs. Occasionally, his hypochondriacal symptoms dominate his life to the point of complete invalidism.

> A forty-five-year-old widow was wheeled to the clinic by her dutiful son. For fourteen years, she had been a helpless invalid, almost constantly in bed. Her childhood history revealed that her mother had not wanted her, had been doubly disappointed that she was not a boy, and had left her to the care of servants throughout her first few years, except when she was sick. Whenever she was sick, her mother attempted to compensate for her rejection by a flurry of overprotection which lasted until the child's return to normal health. Thus rewarded, the child, first consciously but later unconsciously, exaggerated and prolonged her symptoms.
>
> When she grew up, she married an extremely protective, solicitous man whose own neurotic needs led him to select a delicate wife willing to be completely dominated. Her symptoms became more severe during her only pregnancy, but she did not become a complete invalid until her husband's death. Her son gradually took over her husband's protective role, encouraged by her subtle references to the increase of symptoms during her pregnancy to believe that he was responsible for her invalidism.
>
> Although examination demonstrated that she was physically normal for

an inactive woman of her age, the patient and her son vigorously denied the possibility of an emotional factor in her illness.

The physician or, for that matter, the nurse or anyone else who works with hypochondriacal patients usually finds it difficult to be objective with them. A person who works long hours naturally resents an able-bodied adult who does not carry his share of the load. Furthermore, physicians and nurses are so busy taking care of others that they often ignore or deny the nucleus of residual but usually well-hidden dependency needs that persists in themselves as well as in everyone else. Hidden needs of this kind nevertheless may increase the irritation that arises when a patient appears to be "getting away with murder." But whatever the cause, the physician or nurse who shows his irritation intensifies rather than helps the problem, because his irritation means to the patient rejection by a person on whom he relies. It confirms the patient's opinion that he is not loved for himself but only protected because of his illness, and so his tendency to remain ill is strengthened.

On the other hand, the physician or nurse who is too sympathetic may have even more trouble. If, in his sympathy for the patient, he tries to supply all the lost dependent satisfaction, he will soon learn that he is attempting to fill a bottomless pit and that no one can compensate an adult for the deprivations of infancy. Trying to do so is as futile as giving an alcoholic enough whiskey to destroy his craving for it. Insatiably the patient demands more and more, until even the most devoted supplier tires of it and either withdraws his support or reveals his irritation.

The physician can be of great help to the passive-dependent patient by giving him psychologic support within definite limits. Limits are necessary to keep the patient's expectations of the relationship within realistic bounds and to preserve the physician's patience while he supports the patient's fragile capacity to deal with current problems and helps him gradually to improve his adaptation. An accurate diagnosis of the extent of the fixation warns the physician to keep his sights low as a protection from disappointment when the patient's overall improvement falls short of the spectacular.

The Pseudoindependent Personality. Western cultural attitudes discourage obvious dependent behavior in adults, particularly in males. The parallel premium for independent behavior encourages many people to conceal their unfulfilled dependency needs behind a façade of apparent independence. This group includes those who, instead of being deprived or overprotected, have been encouraged, shamed, or forced by circumstances to become relatively independent before they were ready. Although the baby is most helpless and hence most dependent during the first year, he does not shed all his dependency needs on his first birthday. Over a period of years, with some ups and downs along the way, he gradually loses his need for total reliance on someone else and replaces it with a mature interdependent relationship. But when his family pushes this process too rapidly for his dependent needs to be sufficiently satisfied (but not so fast that he is overwhelmed), he represses them and overcompensates for them, both to gain his family's approval and to protect himself from a painful awareness of his unresolved dependency.

Mrs. Brown, the patient discussed at length in Chapter 1, demonstrated this sequence of events. She might be called a *pseudoindependent personality;* that is, beneath an appearance of independence, she was a dependent person ashamed of her dependency. People like Mrs. Brown are outwardly full of aggressive independence—they find it difficult to work in a subordinate capacity; they are always on the go and find it hard to relax; they seldom take a vacation and, when they do, usually find a project with which to occupy all their time. Characteristically, they seek to solve other people's problems but find it difficult to seek help for their own. For them, illness means dangerous dependency. They tend to fight it every step of the way; they will not stay in bed or follow orders, and they usually exasperate their physicians. Retirement is a particularly bitter ordeal for them. A physician who recognizes this character trait in a patient often can get cooperation for his treatment regime by explaining its rationale and planning to his patient, informing him of developments, and taking care to avoid giving the impression of an authoritarian father.

> A sailor with a duodenal ulcer was about to go on pass. His physician gave him minute instructions concerning diet, intake of alcohol, and general behavior, warning him much as one would caution a child. In spite of his good intentions, the patient became involved in a series of dietary and other indiscretions and returned to the hospital with a severe exacerbation of symptoms.
>
> By the time the sailor was ready for another pass, however, the physician had recognized the patient's strong defenses against his dependent needs and realized that he would resent being treated as a child. Since the sailor had an intelligent grasp of the implications of his condition, he was sent off with a minimum of instructions from the physician and returned in reasonably good condition.

PSYCHOPHYSIOLOGIC MANIFESTATIONS

Many patients with peptic ulcer have pseudoindependent character structures, and there is some evidence that the personality pattern contributes to the cause of the ulcer. The close association between dependency and eating during infancy supports this hypothesis. If many dependency needs remain unsatisfied before the early association of food with the precursor of love has been replaced by an association of love with a specific human being, the *unconscious need for dependent love* may continue to be represented by *hunger for food*. The ulcer patient appears relatively unaware of this type of hunger—hunger over and above metabolic requirements—but his stomach keeps churning and secreting acid as if he were constantly hungry. Wolf and Wolff's studies [17] demonstrated the extreme sensitivity of the stomach to emotional stimuli, at least in certain predisposed subjects, and other studies suggest that the lining of an emotionally stimulated stomach is particularly susceptible to ulcer formation.

These experimental findings seem equally applicable to duodenal ulcer [18]. Moreover, evidence from intensive psychoanalytic study of patients with duodenal ulcer [19] and from observations of the effects of interrupting the cephalic phase of gastric secretion by vagotomy [20] indicates that conflicts in the dependency area may play a significant part in the production and course of duodenal ulcer in certain predisposed subjects. Not all conflicts in patients with duodenal ulcer are of the pseudo-independent type, however. An overtly dependent individual may develop symptoms after the loss of an important source of security.

> Two bachelor brothers in their sixties had lived together for years. One held a job; the other kept house, took care of the chickens, and played a more dependent role. Suddenly the working brother had an incapacitating stroke, and within three weeks the other brother developed a duodenal ulcer. Not only had he lost his protector, but the roles had been reversed; he now was forced to assume responsibility for which he was not prepared.

His discerning physician recognized that this ulcer patient not only could accept but badly needed paternal, protecting medical care which would relieve him temporarily of responsibility. He therefore gave him specific instructions for diet, activity, and medication in a fatherly manner without a great deal of physiologic explanation. He also referred him to the medical social worker, who was able to find a protected home situation for both brothers when they left the hospital. Even though the patient's personality problem was not attacked directly, the physician's understanding of his personality structure made it possible to carry out medical treatment in a psychologically helpful manner.

Hypermotility and hypersecretion secondary to emotional conflict do not inevitably lead to the development of an ulcer. More frequently, they result in chronic dyspepsia or other gastric disturbances classified as *psy-*

chophysiologic gastrointestinal reactions. For these patients as well as for ulcer patients, the effectiveness of treatment measures depends in large part on the physician's understanding of the personality characteristics of each individual patient.

Obesity

Another group of patients who associate food with dependency freely express their dependent needs as conscious hunger. They go right on eating past the point of satisfying their metabolic needs. The result is obesity, which often becomes a disheartening problem to both physician and patient. Differences in constitutional or metabolic requirements and in habit patterns influence a patient's hunger and the amount he eats, but with sufficient incentive, most people can modify their eating habits. In the chronically obese patient, however, whose history characteristically reveals many short-lived attempts to reduce, the emotional factor is inevitably present [21]. The nature of the emotional factor in obesity is not the same in every patient. Some patients apparently have received too little evidence of maternal love in infancy and early childhood and, at the same time, too much food as a substitute for love.

> An obese young man said: "I never felt that my family really wanted me around. All mother seemed interested in was getting enough food into me. Even when I was too fat, she continued to stuff me. I finally asked the doctor for a reducing diet, but he just told me I would outgrow it. I thought that if he gave me a diet, mother would quit stuffing me."

Bruch observes that a pattern of overprotection is more frequently reported than a pattern of gross neglect [22]. Overprotection, however, often represents a compensation for rejection, and the child may sense the underlying parental attitude. The mother is over concerned with having the child eat and avoid danger, almost as if she needed the resultant obesity and inactivity to convince herself that she is a "good" mother. Bruch suggests that, in his search for security, the obese child is so concerned with responding to his mother's needs that he abandons—or never develops—an awareness of his own needs. If he does not know when he is hungry or full, he takes his cues about eating from those around him and responds to parental cues rather than to his own. Bruch's conclusions do not necessarily apply to all obese patients; those that psychiatrists see usually have emotional components that are more severe than the average, and many of the obese patients seen by other physicians seem to be more aware of their hunger, although apparently powerless to control it, particularly when they feel lonely or criticized.

Once a child is fat, for whatever reason, the rest of the world joins in a conspiracy to convince him that he has no control over his appetite. Although he is laughed at for his weight, at the same time he is given the largest piece of cake and expected to eat it. Another complication arises when a child receives simultaneous but opposite parental messages. Often a mother is only conscious of sending one message, "Don't be a glutton," and is not aware that at the same time she is subtly encouraging the child to eat—so as to be "healthy" and to reflect credit on her ability as a mother. When a child enmeshed in this pattern tries to reduce, he gets little help; pediatricians are familiar with mothers who rationalize their sabotage of their children's reducing diets by asserting the importance of "keeping his strength up." The mother, vaguely uneasy or anxious about her inability to give affection, attempts to relieve her anxiety by giving food in excess. Meanwhile the child, deprived of affection but offered food as a substitute, responds both to his own need by increased appetite and to his mother's expectation by overeating.

> This reciprocal pattern may persist long after childhood, as in the case of a thirty-five-year-old married attorney with lifelong obesity who weighed a mountainous 300 pounds. His wife could not understand why her efforts to limit him to his reducing diet were so unsuccessful. She did not know, and he was too ashamed to tell her, that every day when he stopped by to see his mother on his way home from work, his mother would tell him that she was afraid his diet would weaken him and would ply him with sandwiches, ice cream, and cake, which he ate "so as not to hurt her feelings."

Most obese patients are ashamed of overeating and usually suppress or repress the memory of it. Typically, the obese patient protests plaintively that she (or, less often, he) eats "hardly enough to keep a bird alive." If accused of not telling the truth about her diet, she is genuinely hurt, feels more rejected, and seeks comfort in her usual way. Treatment by diet restriction with or without drugs, therefore, usually lasts just as long as the relationship with her physician supplies a prop to her loneliness. When an external circumstance increases her insecurity past the point of protection by the doctor's relationship, she relapses to overeating.

Unfortunately, many of the measures commonly undertaken in the treatment of obesity serve to convince the patient that he does not have the capacity to set limits to his impulse to overeat. The short-term success of these measures leads him to believe that he must look outside of himself for controls, and their eventual failure further diminishes his self-esteem. Medications and special foods fall into this category, as does hospitalization to "prove to the patient" that proper diet can control weight.

Even diets may backfire, unless they are provided only to give the patient information that he does not already have. The usual prescription of a diet with subsequent checking of weight at regular intervals treats the adult patient as a child. It encourages him to reenact childhood situations in which his mother—now the doctor—told him what he should and should not eat and in which he could please or displease his mother (doctor) by following or not following her suggestions. As he transfers his feeling in this area from mother to doctor, he also transfers feelings of resentment at his mother's domination and declares his independence by proving that the doctor cannot control his eating. The doctor, annoyed at the patient's failure to follow orders, becomes increasingly critical; the patient's transferred resentment is augmented by direct resentment, and the battle continues.

> In an interview with a medical student, a patient in a prenatal clinic complained that her obstetrician was always "bawling her out" because she gained so much weight. As she was talking, the student noticed that she was smiling. When he asked her what amused her about the situation, she confided that she had baked a chocolate cake and was going to eat it as soon as she had been weighed, had seen the obstetrician, and had returned home.

Sometimes a patient has little trouble in dieting but is so frightened by the new problems she encounters when her weight is normal that she eats her way back out of danger.

> On three or four occasions, an attractive young woman had lost and gained back over 80 pounds. When obese, she blamed all her troubles on her weight and believed that all she had to do was lose weight and she would be perfectly happy.
>
> Each time she reduced, she started dating and eventually became engaged. Each time, however, the engagement was broken, and she would resume gaining weight. At first she blamed this sequence on picking the wrong man, but after she had been encouraged to scrutinize carefully her tendency always to pick the wrong man, she began to realize that she was really frightened of the prospect of marriage. She discovered that when marriage and the associated obligation to play an adult sexual role became imminent, her dependent needs were mobilized and she retreated to the unhappy but familar problems of obesity.

If the doctor is critical or scornful of a patient's relapse, she feels doubly rejected and often gains back all that she has lost and more. The controlled study by Nicholson and his associates demonstrated the superiority in sustained results of a psychotherapeutic approach over conventional dietary admonitions and drug or hormone aids [23]. After a year, two-thirds of their patients given psychotherapeutic help had maintained a standard weight loss, while only one-fourth of those on diet alone had done so, and none of those on thyroid or amphetamine sulfate had been successful.

In spite of taking large doses of thyroid and amphetamine sulfate, an obese college girl complained of gaining weight, although allegedly on a 1200-calorie diet. There was no evidence of endocrine abnormality. Her doctor listened to her story without comment and then asked her whether there were specific situations in which she found her appetite unusually good. After some circumlocution, she revealed that she was hungriest when alone or when at parties and attributed her discomfort at parties to her appearance. Although her obesity did not begin until adolescence, she apparently had always felt unwanted and unloved, and these feelings were intensified when she was alone. However, she had been reasonably successful in concealing her periods of depression beneath a façade of superficial joviality.

When she realized that her doctor was genuinely interested in helping her overcome her periods of depression, she accepted his suggestion that she spend a half hour once a week in a joint attempt to understand them better. As she gradually grew more at ease in discussing her feelings with him, she became more aware of her tendency to eat her way out of her periods of depression. Her emerging trust in her physician made it possible for her to penetrate her repression of the distressing memory that when alone at night and sleepless because of the stimulants she was taking, she would make periodic raids on the refrigerator.

The doctor was careful not to be critical or accusing when she brought these repressed memories to the surface, although he pointed out that her recognition of this habit pattern represented an important step toward bringing it under voluntary control. She responded to this comment with a fatalistic statement implying that when it came to food she was constitutionally devoid of willpower. The doctor then helped her unearth the causes for this assumption, finding them in subtly conveyed parental expectations that she could not control her appetite, and helped her to modify her image of herself in this particular.

Meanwhile, through psychologic support (see Chapter 15), he helped her find new sources of security. He had discovered at the beginning that she knew the essentials of a reducing diet, and he carefully refrained from checking on her weight. (A dependent patient tends readily to give up responsibility for appetite control if the physician constantly keeps tab on her.) After fifteen or twenty weekly interviews, she became less depressed and better adjusted socially and appeared to be losing some weight. She stopped the use of medications, reported better appetite control, and voluntarily withdrew from treatment.

If the physician pays insufficient attention to the underlying dependency problem when a patient carries out a reducing program, loss of weight may be accompanied by depression as she is cut off from her means of handling dependent yearnings. Bruch observes that, for some patients, obesity is such an essential defense against overwhelming depression that attempts to reduce may be contraindicated. In other cases, successful weight reduction is followed by development of dyspepsia or a peptic ulcer, as the physiologic concomitants of hunger, chronic hypermotility, and hypersecretion continue but are now less frequently neutralized by food. As discussed earlier in this chapter, the problem of excessive weight gain during pregnancy appears to be closely related to the characteristic temporary increase in dependency needs.

Anorexia Nervosa

Although persistent loss of appetite, or *anorexia nervosa*, is symptomatically the opposite of obesity, its underlying emotional problems are often somewhat similar [24].

> A typical patient was a young woman who in spite of her emaciation was as active or even more active than the average. As a child, she had sought a substitute for security in overeating and was somewhat obese until adolescence. Unconsciously, however, she seemed to associate the pleasure of eating with sexual pleasure as well as with dependency, and with the adolescent intensification of sexual conflict, she began to attach a great deal of unconscious guilt to the eating process. The guilt was expressed consciously as a desire to reduce, which her family at first applauded. She went on a diet, worked at it valiantly, and appeared to be making great progress. Her family became alarmed, however, when she passed a reasonable point and went right on reducing. By the time she saw the physician, her weight had dropped to 70 pounds in spite of the threats and pleas of her relatives and in spite of her own expressed concern.

Amenorrhea, hair loss, and other signs of endocrine dysfunction accompany the appetite loss in anorexia nervosa, and it should be differentiated from the much more rare Simmonds' disease. In contradistinction to patients with Simmonds' disease, patients with anorexia nervosa tend to retain much of their physical vigor and show proportionately fewer signs of pituitary dysfunction. These patients respond poorly to forced feeding, since it intensifies their guilt and produces greater anxiety and depression, but some form of substitute feeding may be necessary as an emergency measure. The treatment and emotional rehabilitation of patients with anorexia nervosa require a psychiatrist's care, but relatively mild symptomatic appetite loss may occasionally respond to supportive measures.

A twenty-seven-year-old, childless married woman had been losing weight steadily for over a year in spite of the absence of significant physical illness. Although she weighed only 72 pounds, she continued to care for her home and to lead a reasonably active social life. The onset of her appetite loss followed a miscarriage. At the time of the miscarriage, her husband and his doting parents had been much upset, but the patient had carried on, comforting the others. In a few weeks, however, when the other members of the family had overcome their grief, the patient began to lose her appetite.

Her background revealed a great deal of early insecurity. She had been born during a period of parental discord and in effect had bound her somewhat cold and formal mother to an unhappy marriage. As a child, she had never enjoyed feminine activities as much as sports and was considered a tomboy. She had been successful at work, earned more than her husband, and had planned to return to work a month after the baby was born, when her mother could take over the child's care. Actually, she was very doubtful and anxious about her ability to be an adequate mother.

Although intensive psychotherapy was the treatment of choice to help the patient reorganize her handling of her femininity and dependency needs, geographic and financial conditions made it impractical. Since her adaptation in the past had been relatively adequate and since intensive treatment, even if available, might disturb the balance in her marriage (see Chapter 8), the psychiatric consultant suggested a trial period of supportive treatment.

By a program of psychologic support, with occasional careful clarification of her attitudes (Chapter 15), the family physician encouraged her to recognize a little of her ambivalence about the baby. As they discussed the fact that a baby would have produced major changes in her way of life, his accepting attitude helped her to acknowledge that she might have resented some of these changes even in anticipation. He let her know that he understood her resentment and did not condemn her for it, and as a result she became less guilty about it. With the relief of her guilt, she was able to express some of the grief she felt at the loss of the baby. After a period of expressing her grief, she found her appetite improved.

Her physician did not attempt to modify her character structure or to point out to her that she resented her femininity or to insist that she develop insight into her own dependency deprivation, which, although hidden, caused her to resent the prospective need to care for a dependent infant. To treat these unconscious problems effectively would have required intensive psychotherapy, which he was not trained to provide. His awareness of the dynamics of her illness, however, helped him to use supportive treatment wisely.

As this case illustrates, appetite loss is often a symptom of concealed depression and frequently part of an unresolved grief reaction. The physician must use caution in treating such a reaction to avoid bringing to the surface more previously repressed problems than the patient can handle.

He should limit himself to helping the patient restore the previous neurotic balance.

Not all emotional problems of diet are related to overeating or undereating. Adjustment to a rigid diet, as in diabetes, is often difficult. Diabetic children, particularly, find it hard to understand the necessary restrictions and may interpret them as a withholding of food—and love—by the parent. Adolescents may find the dietary restrictions a convenient battleground for expressing rebellion. Even adults with an intelligent understanding of the nature of diabetes may have unconscious dependent needs which make regulation a problem. The physician should not assume that poor control of diabetes is necessarily due to dietary indiscretion, however; as Hinkle has demonstrated, emotional upheavals in patients on a well-regulated diet may significantly alter blood-sugar levels as well as influence the production of ketones [25]. The frequency with which diabetics appear to have experienced early and chronic frustration of dependency needs has led to the hypothesis that this frustration may even have a part in the cause of diabetes. Food has such great emotional significance to so many people that the physician should evaluate the emotional setting in which any problems of diet regulation occur.

ALCOHOLISM AND ADDICTION

Alcoholism usually represents another neurotic attempt to relieve the anxiety and overcome the depression which result from chronic dependency frustration. The factors responsible for the preferential use of alcohol vary, but the alcoholic has the same kind of trouble controlling his drinking as the obese patient has controlling his eating.

Once the alcoholic begins to drink, the toxic effects of alcohol further weaken his adaptive functions—both his internal controls (particularly suppression and repression) and his capacity to evaluate. When the barriers to direct expression are down and judgment is blunted, the internal structure of his personality is exposed. Hidden hostility and aggressive sexuality may become evident in the customarily mild-mannered, and regressive dependency in the apparently independent. The specific symptoms shown by a particular person when drunk are usually characteristic and demonstrate the specific hidden drive that is closest to overt expression.

When the toxic effect of alcohol wears off and controls are reinstituted —on the "morning after"—the alcoholic, in common with nonalcoholics who occasionally overindulge, is usually repentant and promises himself that he will control his drinking. The difference is that the nonalcoholic controls it, at least temporarily, while the alcoholic either lacks the capacity to control or lacks confidence in his capacity to control. His best chance to avoid a repeat performance is to avoid the first drink, as the toxic effects of the first drink dissolve the last shreds of his resistance.

Alcoholism usually develops insidiously, with a gradual increase from ordinary social drinking, through excessive social drinking, then through a period in which blackouts and morning drinking begin, and finally to a stage in which drinking becomes the patient's major concern. There are variations in the patterns of drinking—some patients drink steadily and others confine their drinking to sprees interspersed with periods of abstention or of reduced intake [26]. Characteristic of most problem drinkers, unfortunately, is their tendency to repress memories of their drinking and its consequences and to deny their incapacity to control it. Since any kind of psychologic treatment requires the patient's active participation and since active participation requires acceptance of the existence of the problem, the first step in treatment is to help the patient "surrender" to the recognition that he has lost control of his drinking [27]. Pressure from relatives and threats of the consequences of continued drinking are usually ineffective, and helping a patient through the slow process of surrender requires a great deal of patience.

A typical alcoholic at first clings to his physician. He readily seeks advice and suggestions, flatters the physician by apparent confidence in whatever he says, and repeatedly and in all sincerity promises to reform. This initial stage of dependence on the physician is likely to produce optimism on both sides. The patient seems to feel, perhaps unconsciously, that he has at last found someone who really will take complete charge of him. But as he discovers that he will not receive such all-inclusive maternal care, he reacts by doubting the permanence of this new relationship and he begins to test the physician's interest in him.

The testing becomes evident when external pressures prove too much for his good resolutions and he relapses to the use of alcohol. If the physician then becomes hostile or critical, the patient generally interprets the hostility or criticism as rejection and either abandons the attempt to get well or becomes much more demanding of the doctor's time and interest. Unless the doctor can respond to the increased demands by setting friendly but consistent and objective limits to the time and attention he gives his patient, treatment is likely to collapse, with mutual disillusionment. If, on the other hand, the physician can overcome his irritation and treat the occasional relapse with kindness but without encouraging further relapses by condoning the drinking or by expecting it to continue, he may help the patient's controls grow stronger and the relapses become fewer. A hazard to successful treatment is the patient's assumption—often justified—that the physician feels superior to him. Much of the success of Alcoholics Anonymous and other group approaches seems to arise from the patient's recognition that those who help him have had similar problems and consequently are less likely to feel superior [28].

For cultural and perhaps other reasons, alcoholism usually occurs in males. Typically, they marry women of a specific personality type. Although their wives appear to be long-suffering martyrs, careful scrutiny often reveals them to be relatively dominating, aggressive women who belittle their husbands' accomplishments, foster their dependency, and often, with the best of conscious intentions, sabotage their attempts to overcome their alcoholism. They are women whose backgrounds have made it difficult for them to establish mature, interdependent relationships with men; instead, they seek out immature, dependent men whom they can mother. If for some reason the marriage becomes intolerable and breaks up, the wife is likely to marry another alcoholic and start the cycle over again (see Chapter 8).

Prolonged alcoholism may result in various types of acute and chronic psychotic reactions. The most common acute reaction is called delirium tremens, which will be discussed along with other deliriums in Chapter 12.

The abuse of barbiturates, amphetamines, and other drugs often occurs in alcoholics or in others with similar problems [29]. Although the barbiturates have a place in the symptomatic treatment of emotional illnesses, they are frequently overused or used without proper evaluation and treatment of the underlying disturbance (Chapter 15). Before prescribing them, the physician should discriminate between chronically dependent patients who are prone to develop addictions and the relatively mature patient who can be counted on not to misuse the drugs. Reduction of barbiturate intake in addicted patients should be undertaken slowly, as convulsive seizures and psychotic episodes frequently accompany rapid withdrawal. Insofar as it is primarily a psychologic phenomenon, addiction can occur to any substance, and there are no "nonaddictive" drugs. On the other hand, *physical dependence*, bodily changes resulting from a drug and requiring the same or a similar drug to counteract, varies greatly from one drug to another and is most pronounced in the opiates.

Narcotic Addiction

The abuse of narcotics resembles the abuse of other drugs in many characteristics [30]. There are three characteristics, however, which make narcotic addiction unique. First, physical dependence develops more rapidly and more intensely than with other drugs and makes a constant narcotic supply necessary to avoid the painful and serious withdrawal syndrome. Second, since the sale of narcotics to addicts is illegal in the United States, the user lives constantly in danger of arrest. Third, opiates chemically inhibit the sexual drive; they thus serve a double purpose for the dependent person who has an unconscious fear of expressing sexuality, temporarily relieving both the anxiety caused by his unexpressed hunger for love and the anxiety caused by his sexual drive.

The physician need not be so concerned about addiction in prescribing opiates for relief of pain if the patient is relatively mature as he should be if the patient is chronically dependent. Severe illness, however, particularly when accompanied by a great deal of pain, precipitates regression to dependency levels in any case, and the physician should not force a patient in this condition to carry the burden of decision in timing the relief of pain. When a patient is told, "You may have a hypo when the pain becomes too bad, but hold off as long as you can," he usually is caught in a continuous state of apprehension, suspended between his misery and his need for caution. The patient with relatively high dependency asks for relief prematurely, anticipating possible delays or a disinclination on the part of forewarned nursing personnel to give him help. His demands become more and more frequent, and soon a battle develops between the moaning, complaining patient and what appear to him to be hostile, rejecting nurses. He may be afraid to let himself sleep lest someone think he is too comfortable and withhold relief when he awakens. On the other hand, the man who rejects dependency may suffer undue pain as he fights off submission to this symbol of weakness. Patients in continuous pain, as well as addicts during the period of withdrawal from opiates, fare better if they are sure of receiving medication at definite intervals. The physician therefore should emphasize to the nursing staff the importance of giving such medication within a few minutes of the hour prescribed. He should leave unequivocal orders and not make the nurse responsible for deciding whether the patient should receive a scheduled injection.

Gradual withdrawal is indicated in narcotic addiction and always should be carried out in a hospital. Outpatient treatment of addiction that includes the administration of narcotics is not only likely to be unsuccessful but is against the law in the United States. After withdrawal, out-patient care, adapting the methods recommended for alcohol addiction, is worth trying.

The ready accessibility of narcotics to physicians, nurses, and pharmacists makes it easier for them to become addicted, and the incidence in these professions is substantially higher than the national average. A physician should never permit himself the rationalization that his knowledge of medicine or his knowledge of himself will in any way protect him from addiction [31]. Any physician, whether he does or does not recognize a dependency problem in himself, would be wise never to use a narcotic without examination and prescription by a fellow physician.

The patients discussed in this chapter have in common an unfulfilled longing for the protecting, unqualified love of a mother for her infant. The passive-dependent personalities express their longing openly; the majority of obese, alcoholic, and addicted patients seem to be seeking a substitute for love in food or drugs; the pseudoindependent personalities attempt to take care of all their needs by themselves. These types of patients by no means exhaust the possible outward manifestations of dependency yearnings. Both schizophrenic and manic-depressive reactions are at least in part results of frustrated dependency needs, but since the dramatic regression in these illnesses clinically overshadows the partial fixation, they are discussed in another chapter. Dependency problems are at the root of some antisocial reactions, in which the patient in effect tries to force from others some token of the love which was not freely given him as an infant or tries to get indirect revenge for his earlier deprivation (see Chapter 14).

Attempts to relive the past are doomed to inevitable failure; in the experience of growing up, adults have outgrown the capacity for the total surrender of their own independence which must take place in order for them to accept infantile dependency. Even if total dependency were available, they could not accept it. Therefore, as long as they seek a recapitulation of their infancy, they must either experience or cover up feelings of emptiness, loss, deprivation, or not belonging. These feelings are depressing, and many of the chronically dependent are chronically depressed. They adapt as best they can but never seem to be able to enjoy life and constantly expect the worst. One such patient expressed this empty pessimism by saying: "I should be happy—I have a wonderful husband and good children, but I can't enjoy them. I've never had any confidence in myself; I always look on the gloomy side of things and expect the worst. I plod on, but life seems terribly empty and unsatisfying."

The goal of treatment is to help the patient give up the fruitless search for infantile satisfactions and turn instead to current relationships in order to find meaning and significance in his life. This goal holds true whether the depression is evident or whether it is concealed by symptoms or symbols. Treatment of depressions hidden beneath such symptoms as obesity, alcoholism, ulcer, or synthetic independence does not inevitably require, and in many cases should not encourage, the exposure of the depression. Patients whose underlying depressions are overwhelming cannot tolerate the removal of their defenses; instead, their defenses should be buttressed and sustained by psychologic support (see Chapter 15). Before probing into psychologic defenses or interpreting hidden conflicts, therefore, a physician should be reasonably sure that the patient has enough strength to tolerate (and the physician enough background and experience to treat) the resulting anxiety or depression without the patient's collapse. Otherwise, the penetration of defenses will result in more harm than help.

SUMMARY

Prenatal factors in personality include developmental limits set by heredity and instincts or drives which make it possible for the child to survive. If prenatal care of the pregnant woman is carried out with concern for her emotional attitudes toward pregnancy and the baby, she may enter motherhood with more equanimity and give the infant greater security in the important months of infancy.

The helpless infant requires satisfaction of his needs for food and affection in order to develop the security prerequisite to optimal emotional development. Modern infant care emphasizes techniques which foster security but which consider the mother's needs as well.

Partial fixation at the infantile or dependency level appears to be the major cause of the passive-dependent and pseudoindependent personalities and of a substantial number of the chronically depressed. Many addicts to food, alcohol, and drugs, as well as many patients with appetite loss and psychophysiologic gastrointestinal reactions, demonstrate this type of personality problem. Finally, dependent fixations contribute to psychotic reactions and to some types of delinquent-behavior patterns.

REFERENCES

1. For more comprehensive discussions of the role of heredity in mental illness, see:

Benjamin, J. D.: "Some Comments on Twin Research in Psychiatry," in T. Tourlentes, et al. (eds.), *Research Approaches to Psychiatric Problems,* New York, Grune & Stratton, Inc., 1962.

Gregory, I.: "Genetic Factors in Schizophrenia," *Amer. J. Psychiat.,* 116: 961, 1960.

Ham, G. C.: "Genes and the Psyche: Perspectives in Human Development and Behavior," *Amer. J. Psychiat.,* 119:828, 1962.

Kallman, F. J.: "The Genetics of Mental Illness," in S. Arieti (ed.), *American Handbook of Psychiatry,* New York, Basic Books, Inc., Publishers, 1959, vol. I, chap. 8, p. 175.

Meehl, P. E.: "Schizotaxia, Schizotypy and Schizophrenia," *Amer. Psychol.,* 17:827, 1962.

Pollin, W., J. R. Stabenau, and J. Tupin: "Family Studies with Identical Twins Discordant for Schizophrenia," *Psychiatry,* 28:60, 1965.

Rosenthal, D. (ed.): *The Genain Quadruplets: A Case Study and Theoretical Analysis of Heredity and Environment in Schizophrenia,* New York, Basic Books, Inc., Publishers, 1963.

————: "Problems of Sampling and Diagnosis in the Major Twin Studies of Schizophrenia," *Psychiat. Res.,* 1:116, 1962.

2. Alpert, A., P. B. Neubauer, and A. Weil: "Unusual Variations in Drive Endowment," *Psychoanal. Stud. Child,* 11:125, New York, International Universities Press, Inc., 1956.

Bridger, W. H., and M. F. Reiser: "Psychophysiologic Studies of the Neonate," *Psychosom. Med.,* 21:265, 1959.

Grossman, H. F., and N. H. Greenberg: "Psychosomatic Differentiation in Infancy. I. Autonomic Activity in the Newborn," *Psychosom. Med.,* 19:293, 1957.

Thomas, A., et al.: *Behavioral Individuality in Early Childhood,* New York, New York University Press, 1963.

3. Montagu, M. F.A.: *Prenatal Influences,* Springfield, Ill., Charles C Thomas, Publisher, 1962.

Sontag, L. W.: "Differences in Modifiability of Fetal Behavior and Physiology," *Psychosom. Med.,* 6:151, 1944.

4. Mann, E. C.: "Psychiatric Investigation of Habitual Abortion," *Obstet. Gynec.,* 7:589, 1956.
See also:
Benedek, T., et al.: "Some Emotional Factors in Infertility," *Psychosom. Med.,* 15:485, 1953.

5. Benedek, T.: "An Investigation of the Sexual Cycle of Women," *Arch. Gen. Psychiat. (Chicago),* 8:311, 1963.

6. Barglow, P.: "Pseudocyesis and Psychiatric Sequelae of Sterilization," *Arch. Gen. Psychiat. (Chicago),* 11:571, 1964.

Greaves, D. C., P. E. Green, and L. J. West: "Psychodynamic and Psychophysiological Aspects of Pseudocyesis," *Psychosom. Med.,* 22:24, 1960.

7. Read, G. D.: *Childbirth without Fear,* New York, Harper & Row, Publishers, Inc. 1944.

Thoms, H.: *Training for Childbirth,* New York, McGraw-Hill Book Company, 1950.

8. Mandy, A. J., T. E. Mandy, R. Farkas, and E. Sher: "Is Natural Childbirth Natural?" *Psychosom. Med.,* 14:431, 1952.

9. Rank, Otto: *The Trauma of Birth,* New York, Harcourt, Brace and Company, Inc., 1929.

10. Benedek, Therese: "The Psychosomatic Implications of the Primary Unit, Mother-Child," *Amer. J. Orthopsychiat.,* 19:624, 1949.

———:"Psychobiological Aspects of Mothering," *Amer. J. Orthopsychiat.,* 26:272, 1956.

11. Some of the studies indicating the significance of maternal deprivation are: Bowlby, J.: *Maternal Care and Mental Health,* Geneva, World Health Organization, 1951.

———:"Grief and Mourning in Infancy and Early Childhood," *Psychoanal. Stud. Child,* 15:9, New York, International Universities Press, Inc., 1960.

———, M. Ainsworth, M. Boston, and D. Rosenbluth: "The Effects of Mother-Child Separation: A Follow-up Study," *Brit. J. Med. Psychol.,* 29:211, 1956.

Brody, S.: *Patterns of Mothering: Maternal Influences during Infancy,* New York, International Universities Press, Inc., 1956.

Garner, A., and C. Wenar: *The Mother-Child Interaction in Psychosomatic Disorders,* Urbana, Ill., The University of Illinois Press, 1959.

Goldfarb, W.: "Effects of Psychological Deprivation in Infancy and Subsequent Stimulation," *Amer. J. Psychiat.,* 102:18, 1945.

Provence, S., and R. C. Lipton: *Infants in Institutions,* New York, International Universities Press, Inc., 1963.

Spitz, R. A.: "Anaclitic Depression," *Psychoanal. Stud. Child,* 2:313, New York, International Universities Press, Inc., 1946.

———: "Hospitalization: An Inquiry into the Genesis of Psychiatric Conditions in Early Childhood," *Psychoanal. Stud. Child,* 1:53, New York, International Universities Press, Inc., 1945.

———: "Hospitalization: A Follow-up Report," *Psychoanal. Stud. Child,* 2:113, New York, International Universities Press, Inc., 1946.

12. Harlow, H. F., and R. R. Zimmerman: "Affectional Responses in the Infant Monkey," *Science,* 130:421, 1959.

———, and M. K. Harlowe: "A Study of Animal Affection," *J. Amer. Museum Natural Hist.,* vol. LXX (10), 1961.

13. Aldrich, C. A., and M. M. Aldrich: *Babies Are Human Beings,* 2d ed., New York, The Macmillan Company, 1955.

———, and Edith S. Hewitt: "A Self-regulating Feeding Program for Infants," *J.A.M.A.,* 135:340, 1947.

14. Bartemeier, L. H.: "Concerning the Cornelian Corner," *Amer. J. Orthopsychiat.* 27:594, 1947.

Montgomery, T. L., R. E. Steward, and E. P. Shenk: "Observations on Rooming-in Program of Baby with Mother in Ward and Private Service," *Amer. J. Obstet. Gynec.,* 57:176, 1949.

15. Freud, S.: "Three Essays on the Theory of Sexuality," in *Standard Edition,* 1953, vol. VII, p. 123.
See also:
Abraham, K.: "A Short Study of the Development of the Libido" (1924), in *Selected Papers on Psychoanalysis,* New York, Basic Books, Inc., Publishers, 1955.
16. Abraham, K.: "The Influence of Oral Erotism on Character Formation" (1924), in *Selected Papers on Psychoanalysis,* New York, Basic Books, Inc., Publishers, 1955.
17. Wolf, S., and H. G. Wolff: *Human Gastric Function,* 2d ed., Fairlawn, N.J., Oxford University Press, 1947.
18. Mirsky, I. A.: "Physiologic, Psychologic and Social Determinants in the Etiology of Duodenal Ulcer," *Amer. J. Dig. Dis.,* 3:285, 1958.
Weisman, A. D.: "A Study of the Psychodynamics of Duodenal Ulcer Exacerbations," *Psychosom. Med.,* 18:2, 1956.
19. See:
Alexander, F.: *Psychosomatic Medicine: Its Principles and Applications,* New York, W. W. Norton & Company, Inc., 1950.
————, T. M. French, et al.: *Studies in Psychosomatic Medicine,* New York, The Ronald Press Company, 1948.
20. Szasz, T.: "Psychiatric Aspects of Vagotomy," *Ann. Intern. Med.,* 28:279, 1948.
21. Aldrich, C. K.: "Mechanisms and Management of Obesity," *Med. Clin. N. Amer.,* 47:77, 1963.
Bruch, H.: *The Importance of Overweight,* New York, W. W. Norton & Company, Inc., 1957.
Frazier, S. H., et al.: "A Specific Factor in Symptom Choice," *Proc. Mayo Clin.,* 30:227, 1955.
Stunkard, A. J., and M. McLaren-Hume: "The Results of Treatment for Obesity," *AMA Arch. Intern. Med.,* 103:79, 1959.
22. Bruch, H.: "Disturbed Communication in Eating Disorders," *Amer. J. Orthopsychiat.,* 33:99, 1963.
23. Nicholson, W. M.: "Emotional Factors in Obesity," *Amer. J. Med. Sci.,* 211:443, 1946.
24. Bliss, E. L., and C. H. H. Branch: *Anorexia Nervosa,* New York, Paul B. Hoeber, Inc., 1960.
Nemiah, J. C.: "Anorexia Nervosa: Fact and Theory," *Amer. J. Dig. Dis.,* 3:249, 1958.
25. Hinkle, L. E., and S. Wolf: "Importance of Life Stress in Course and Management of Diabetes Mellitus," *J.A.M.A.,* 148:513, 1952.
26. Examples of the extensive literature on alcoholism include:
Manual on Alcoholism, Chicago, American Medical Association, 1962.
Pfeffer, A. Z.: *Alcoholism,* New York, Grune & Stratton, Inc., 1958.
Thompson, G. N. (ed.): *Alcoholism,* Springfield, Ill., Charles C Thomas, Publisher, 1953.
Wallerstein, R. S., et al.: *Hospital Treatment of Alcoholism,* New York, Basic Books, Inc., Publishers, 1957.

27. Tiebout, H. M.: "Surrender versus Compliance in Therapy with Special Reference to Alcoholism," *Quart. J. Stud. Alcohol,* 14:58, 1953.
    ———: "The Ego Factors in Surrender in Alcoholism," *Quart. J. Stud. Alcohol,* 15:610, 1954.
28. Ripley, H., and J. Jackson: "Therapeutic Factors in Alcoholics Anonymous," *Amer. J. Psychiat.,* 116:44, 1959.
29. Fraser, H. F., et al.: "Chronic Barbiturate Intoxication," *AMA Arch. Intern. Med.,* 94:34, 1954.
    Isbell, H.: "Abuse of Barbiturates," *J.A.M.A.,* 162:660, 1956.
    Knapp, P. J.: "Amphetamine and Addiction," *J. Nerv. Ment. Dis.,* 115:406, 1952.
30. Rado, Sandor: "Narcotic Bondage: A General Theory of the Dependence on Narcotic Drugs," *Amer. J. Psychiat.,* 114:165, 1957.
    "What to Do with a Drug Addict," report to Council on Pharmacy and Chemistry, *J.A.M.A.,* 149:1220, 1952.
    Wikler, A.: *Opiate Addiction: Psychological and Neurophysiological Aspects in Relation to Clinical Problems,* Springfield, Ill., Charles C. Thomas, Publisher, 1952.
31. Modlin, H. C., and A. Montes: "Narcotic Addiction in Physicians," *Amer. J. Psychiat.,* 121:358, 1964.

Chapter 5

SELF–ASSERTION AND
THE TRAINING PERIOD

Ordinarily, the first birthday is considered the end of infancy. There is, of course, no sharply delineated change in the child, but at about this time or a little earlier he begins gradually to be released from a parasitic existence of helpless dependency by his growing awareness of himself as an independently functioning organism. This transition takes about six months, and parallels further maturation of his central nervous system, which permits him to manipulate things, to walk, and, somewhat later, to use language. His new accomplishments not only provide him with new sources of satisfaction but also bring him into conflict with his environment as he struggles to establish his place in the scheme of things. In this chapter, I will discuss some of these conflicts as they are reflected in frequent but usually temporary problems of sleeping, feeding, toilet training, and the handling of anger. In the second half of the chapter, I will consider some of the more permanent effects of partial fixation at this emotional stage.

SLEEP AND SEPARATION ANXIETY

The year-old child appears a little anxious and overwhelmed by his new-found individuality; he seems not to feel strong enough to carry on all by himself. This weakness is reflected in the frequent occurrence of sleep problems within a month or so of the first birthday [1]. A baby who previously had no trouble going to sleep now cries when put to bed. Although he seems tired enough when a parent picks him up and rocks him awhile, he galvanizes into action again as soon as he is put down. This common problem may result from failure to adapt bedtime to the baby's needs. Babies differ in sleep requirements as much as they do in food requirements, and those who are not tired enough to welcome sleep appear to feel quite helpless, inadequate, and afraid when left alone. A few months earlier, the same baby may have cried himself to sleep on occasion, but he apparently was not sufficiently conscious of his own identity to realize that he had been deserted.

Ordinarily, parents can forestall sleep problems by watching for signs of fatigue and regression (such as thumb-sucking) before putting the child to bed. Also, in consideration of the baby's fragile ego and his progressively greater reliance on the mother *as an individual* (in contrast to his earlier concept of her as a relatively *nonspecific* source of dependency gratification), physicians should advise mothers to try to schedule any necessary trips away from the baby either before or after this period. Although realistic considerations may make it impossible, and the mother should not be made to feel guilty if she has to leave, it is best for the child if she can avoid being away for over a day or so in any instance from the time the child is four months old until he is a about three years old. Children do not have a clear sense of time until they are about five, and when they are younger, they may interpret a few days' absence of the mother as desertion. As a result, a year-old baby who is just getting a good start toward emotional security may develop *separation anxiety* and become clinging, fearful, and sleepless, as he apparently fears he is being deserted by the only person he has so far learned to trust. This early eruption of anxiety resembles the adult anxiety state discussed at length in Chapter 10. It is best treated before it becomes well established and before the child has a chance to exploit its attention-getting value. The mother may have to give up other evening activities for a while and sit in the baby's room until he learns that he can risk dozing off for a moment without losing his protector.

FEEDING PROBLEMS AND TOILET TRAINING

As the child gains confidence in his individuality, he begins to assert himself. His aggressive drives, which have been present all along but diffuse, can now be translated into definite action. A favorite site for his self-assertion is the dinner table, particularly in families in which there is a great deal of emphasis either on table manners or on appetite and weight as signs of health and good maternal care. The baby may decide to eat his cereal with his hands and, if that is forbidden or proves unsatisfactory, to declare his independence by not eating at all [2]. If his mother tries to force him to eat, he takes the offensive. Aided by the second-year slump in appetite, he refuses to eat, holds food in his mouth, or, as a last resort, vomits—demonstrating to one and all his ability to act independently. The mother's only successful stratagem is a graceful retreat accompanied by delaying action until hunger eventually stimulates the child's interest again. This procedure may sound simple, but in common with many mothers, she may find waiting difficult and may start the battle all over again before nature comes to her aid. She may believe that the baby's refusal to eat is a reflection on her care, she may simply be responding to an ill-advised overemphasis on the minimum daily caloric intake, or she may be overcompensating for ambivalent feelings and trying hard to protect herself from implications that she has any lack of enthusiasm for the baby; whatever the reason, she has a desperate need to get food into him. All the vitamins in the book are of no help here; the problem is the mother's need to find new techniques and to manage her own feelings. The physician should be patient and supportive with her and should anticipate a few relapses. One way to help is to inform her that a baby will normally lose his appetite at the first sign of a cold and that she should delay her efforts to encourage the baby to eat until either the cold develops or the appetite returns.

Another battleground for the baby's first struggles to establish his identity is the bathroom. Some time in the second year, the maturation process of the baby's central nervous system (*myelinization*) reaches the sacral segments and permits him to control his sphincters. So-called "toilet training" before this event is really training of the mother to observe the baby and place him in the appropriate position when he shows signs that the gastrocolic reflex is about to function. This alleged "training," if begun after the child can sit up comfortably by himself, seems relatively harmless as long as the mother recognizes it as simply demonstrating her awareness of an involuntary process and as long as she does not expect the child to take responsibility for control until later.

Whether or not the child controls his sphincters shortly after he has the ability to do so depends on several factors, the most significant of which are the attitudes of the parents—particularly the mother, who customarily takes the responsibility for toilet training. If she has an unusually strong need for cleanliness, if she is trying too hard to keep up with the neighbors, or if she is attempting to live up to her own mother's expectations— if, in short, she puts a lot of pressure on the child to conform—he is likely to react just as he does when someone tries to force him to eat, and with similar success. A struggle ensues, with the child parrying the mother's efforts by withholding, often to the point of constipation, or by producing at inconvenient times and places. Eventually the child gives in, but only after a prolonged round of irritation and impatience on both sides.

The child's resistance to external control appears to rise in a gradual crescendo as he gains in self-confidence until about the age of two and a half. If the problem of bowel control has not been solved reasonably soon after eighteen months, the physician may need to help the parents reduce their pressure on the child until after he reaches two and half in order to avoid the phase of greatest resistance. This recommendation may disturb a mother who emphasizes neatness, however, and the physician should gauge his suggestions by his evaluation of the mother's ability to accept them. In any case the nuisance of diaper changing and washing should not be taken lightly [3].

The consistency with which the struggle over bowel control appeared in late-nineteenth-century Viennese society led the early psychoanalysts to postulate it as a universal phenomenon. As a result of this and other considerations, they called the period covering roughly the second and third years the *anal period of development* and recorded evidence that much of the sensuous pleasure mediated through the mucous membranes of the mouth in infancy was transferred to the anus in the course of the toilet-training struggle [4]. Our national preoccupation with constipation and its remedies certainly suggests that in the United States this anatomic area has acquired a disproportionate significance, at least for a great many people; and even mothers whose emotions permit them to postpone toilet training until the child asks to go to the bathroom sometimes report problems. Whether or not a transfer of the site of pleasurable sensation from mouth to anus is universal remains to be determined by further investigation. At present, the term "training period" seems a more inclusive description of this developmental phase [5].

Daytime urinary control follows in general the same rules as bowel control. Automatic control of the sphincters, however, or control during sleep is a more complicated process than conscious control and usually requires a longer time to establish. The physician should recognize that there is a wide range of individual differences in the capacity for nocturnal regulation. Some babies have "dry nights" long before they establish daytime control, while others continue to wet their beds until the age of four or five with no apparent physical or psychologic abnormalities.

Enuresis

If bed-wetting continues after four or five, it is called *enuresis* [6]. Enuresis almost always is related to emotional tension, particularly when there is a history of occasional dry nights, and the physician should be careful not to increase the child's anxiety and concern about his genitourinary organs by unnecessary diagnostic procedures. A child with a congenitally small bladder will have diurnal frequency as well as

enuresis, and microscopic examination of the urine is usually enough to
determine the presence of urinary infection. When the child is under four,
the physician should reassure the parents and encourage them to ignore
the symptom. Even when the child is four or over, this advice may still be
the best, although the doctor should try to find out whether the child is
under tension. Sometimes the parents are too anxious about the child to
sit by and do nothing; in these cases, a system of minor rewards, such as
gold stars, may be helpful unless the child is made to feel that failure to
win the reward is a disgrace. The child often responds to reassurance that
he will overcome his problem in time; conversely, threats and punishment
increase both his anxiety and his enuresis and are manifestly unfair to
him. He cannot understand why he should be punished for something
that happens when he is asleep and therfore may interpret punishment as
evidence that he is not loved. Electrical conditioning devices, along with
efforts to limit fluids before retiring and medications calculated to
counteract spasm or reduce the depth of sleep, are all primarily directed
toward the symptom and not the cause and, if used at all, should supplement investigation and removal of sources of tension.

Sometimes the symptom persists because the parents do not permit the
child to take over his own control, or else the child reflects the parents'
expectations that the enuresis will continue.

> An eight-year-old girl consistently wet her bed in spite of the fact that
> her mother got her up to urinate every evening. She was usually dry when
> visiting away from home. Her mother had become very tense, distressed,
> and discouraged about it, although she tried earnestly to be sympathetic
> and not critical. She said, "I suppose she'll do just as I did and have 'acci-
> dents' until she's twelve."
>
> The physician discussed with the mother the importance of permitting
> her daughter to take over control of this function. He also spoke directly
> to the girl and indicated his confidence that she could overcome her prob-
> lem. Since she was convinced that awakening during the night was es-
> sential to success, the doctor suggested that she use an alarm clock to
> awaken herself. She was enthusiastic about the project and decided to
> start by setting the alarm for 11 P.M.
>
> A week later, the mother reported that "they" had been successful for
> two nights but that on the third night the alarm clock ran down and her
> daughter had not awakened. The mother felt it would be too bad if the
> new plan failed so soon and awakened her daughter, but the next morning
> she was wet again, and somehow things had gone back to the old routine.
>
> The physician patiently explained the value of letting the child take full
> responsibility and talked with the mother for a while to try to help her be
> a little less pessimistic and not assume that her daughter would repeat
> her own experience. The girl started the alarm-clock experiment all over

again, and this time the mother was able to let her daughter take complete charge of the procedure. After a good beginning, the girl had a few relapses which she discussed with her physician. He continued to let her know he was sure she would eventually overcome it. She began to remain dry even when she slept through the alarm, and soon she no longer needed the alarm at all.

As this child was permitted to take over her own controls, she overcame her enuresis. Ordinarily, however, the child begins to take over control of his urinary function during the training period. He also begins to take over control of his aggressive impulses, but before he develops internal controls, he must learn to adapt to external restrictions.

DISCIPLINE AND CONTROLS

In the training period, the child first encounters serious prohibitions by the parents. He is actively prevented from doing interesting things and going interesting places. Earlier (Chapter 2), the possibility was discussed that active resistance to frustration of self-assertion is an innate characteristic; whatever the cause, it can be clearly observed in action at this stage. Parental discipline frustrates the child's self-assertion, and the child expresses his resistance to frustration as anger. Instead of expressing diffuse infantile rage against the environment in general, the child now begins to focus his anger on a definite object, and that object is most frequently his mother, the person who is interfering with his plans. Since his mother is also the person on whom he is most dependent and from whom he receives the most love, his anger poses quite a frightening problem.

From all we can observe, his concepts of anger seem to follow the primitive law of retaliation—an eye for an eye and a tooth for a tooth—so he apparently anticipates equal anger in return. His expression of anger, although usually rather ineffectual, ordinarily has a destructive goal, as seen in the temper tantrums almost universal in this period or in the child who relieves his feelings on a toy or teddy bear. Finally, the child at this age functions on the principle of all or nothing; he either loves *or* hates, and for him, one excludes the other. The idea of ambivalence, of harboring simultaneous angry and affectionate feelings for the same person, is too complex for him to grasp as yet. His dilemma consists of having for the moment (although he may not realize that it is momentary) 100 percent destructive anger toward the stronger adult on whom he is dependent for love and security but who he expects will repay his anger by her own destructive anger and by withholding her love. The threat is increased by the immaturity of the child's personality. He still lacks enough buffering or adaptive capacity to keep his aggressive feelings under control for any length of time.

Under ordinary circumstances, most children eventually develop control of their aggressive feelings and thus protect themselves from their fear of the consequences of aggressive action. The specific pattern of control is determined primarily by parental attitudes. Fear of punishment is the basis for one pattern of control; however, the child whose early expressions of rebellion meet swift and severe punishment construes his parents and others in authority as jealous of their power and resentful of his attempts to take over in his own behalf. He sees discipline only as part of a combat to determine whose will shall prevail, a combat in which no holds are barred. With this attitude, he will conform when cornered, but if he is not overwhelmed by fear, he will do his best to outwit his adversaries. He tries to get away with as much as he can without getting caught; and if he *is* caught, he interprets punishment as an angry, vengeful attack upon him, not as an attempt to help him learn to conform to society's expectations. Such experiences in the training period determine in part his later attitudes toward authority [7]; if they are not counteracted, he grows up to believe that authorities are to be feared, evaded, hated, and outsmarted. Once his own authority is established, however, he assumes that it must be ruthlessly protected. This totalitarian concept of authority may be passed down from generation to generation within families and social groups and even within nations. In such a family, group, or nation, the policing function is important, since no one can be trusted to exercise his own controls. Each distrusts the other, and the only morality is that of force.

Not all parents with totalitarian family backgrounds carry on the same pattern. Some identify more closely with their children than with their own parents. They remember how intensely they feared and hated their parents, and they do not want their own children to fear them and to hate them with the same intensity. They may be particularly sensitive to these feelings if they are trying by overcompensation to disguise and conceal from themselves some ambivalence toward their children. These parents are among many who are so afraid to use discipline that they tolerate their children's unrestrained and often destructive behavior. Tyrannical children, rather than tyrannical parents, dominate the home. Although their behavior may antagonize the neighbors, the children appear reasonably content as long as their lives center around their homes. Later, however, when they want to adapt to others outside the family who are not willing to surrender personal and property rights, they find they must develop restraints in a hurry or lose friendships.

Some parents, and even some psychiatrists and psychologists, have interpreted the observation that repressed unconscious conflicts cause emotional illnesses to mean that emotional illnesses can be prevented by avoiding repression and therefore that any discipline is harmful to the child. This understandable but erroneous interpretation assumes that the child's adaptation to his inner drives and conflicts takes absolute precedence over, and is not affected by, his adaptation to his environment. It ignores the vital importance of repression for the integration of the child's drives and needs with the complex demands of the civilization he must live in. Children who have never learned to repress are at a serious disadvantage in social relationships because they have not developed internal controls strong enough to handle their impulses and to delay their gratifications in the interests of the rights and goodwill of others. Some of these children may act on impulses (which others repress) whenever the opportunity presents itself and the impulse is stimulated. If this type of character disturbance continues into adult life, especially if it is intensified by strong, unsatisfied dependency needs, it may lead to generalized antisocial behavior (see Chapter 14). Other children compensate for the lack of reasonable internal controls by imposing stringent external controls on themselves. Without confidence in their capacity automatically to control their impulses, they attempt to protect themselves by avoiding virtually any impulse expression and consequently live relatively restricted and impoverished lives. (See page 313.)

Parents who recognize that the child needs discipline to become civilized but who also recognize that discipline through fear of retribution has serious drawbacks are sometimes uncertain about how best to help the child establish his own controls and mature forms of expression in as comfortable a manner as possible. Tangible rewards, or bribes, can perhaps be quickly dismissed, as they put civilized behavior on a fee basis, open up unlimited possibilities for blackmail, and discourage the child from incorporating restraints into his own pattern of adaptation.

Intangible rewards are chiefly in the form of parental approval. Parental approval, however, can have several meanings to the child. It can mean, among other things, "I have pleased mother," "I am like mother," or "I am meeting mother's expectations." The first meaning, pleasing mother, is related to the child's beginning response to the receipt of love. The drive to love and to give to others seems to some extent to be an outgrowth of the earlier need to be loved. Successful development of the capacity to love requires a sense of security and the satisfaction of earlier dependency needs. When these needs have been met, the child's growing ability to give in return expedites his further emotional development. The child who *loves* his mother also wishes to make her happy, to please her by doing what she wants him to do. Although there are a few earlier signs of this process, ordinarily it is not strong enough to counteract the aggressive drive very adequately until around the middle of the third year. Even then, the wish to please needs help, and the child buoys it up by giving himself a pep talk. "No, no, mustn't touch," he tells himself when unobserved and tempted by an object he knows his mother does not want him to touch. His increasing ability to love thus helps him gradually to increase his ability to adapt.

The wish to please the loved person is not the same as love itself, however, nor is its presence in a given situation a measure of love. The child does not surrender his self-assertive drives when he develops the capacity to love, but it is easy to exploit his wish to please mother by demanding complete submission as the price of approval. Discipline by means of a child's wish to please his parents, therefore, is definitely not a *technique* to be exploited by the parents. The atmosphere engendered when the parents attempt to use it as a technique turns out to be one of fear, and the process—really an exploitation of the child's love—is likely to backfire. "If you love mother, you'll do as I say" has the implied threat of "If you don't do as I say, you don't love mother—*and then mother won't love you.*" Even a child who feels he *is* loved may become insecure if he is told—and believes—that his behavior can jeopardize that love.

The second meaning, "Mother approves of me because I am like her," is a somewhat sophisticated concept. It is a more significant force later in the child's development, as he becomes able to identify more closely with a parent, but it probably has some effect in the training period. It has a disadvantage similar to the wish to please; it may limit the child's independent strivings if the parent insists that the only acceptable identification is a complete identification. The concept of a complete identification is sometimes conveyed by the terms *introjection* and *incorporation,* although these terms are also used as synonyms for "identification." They imply a more uncritical, primitive, quasi-physical absorption of the parent and all his values than is usually implied by the term "identification."

Parental Expectations

The third meaning of parental approval is "I am meeting mother's expectations." Expectations by parents, and later by others, are most important determinants of a child's behavior. When the child is expected to please his mother by conformity or when he is expected to conform by identification with his mother, approval in the sense of living up to expectations overlaps the other meanings of approval. Expectations, however, cover a wider range of possibilities. They include the expectation that the child will be different from the parent ("Do as I say, not as I do") and the expectation that the child will displease as well as please the parent. Expectation is further complicated by parental unconscious attitudes which may be at variance with the conscious attitudes but which are often perceived by the child as contradictory and confusing expectations.

Contradictory parental expectations have been implicated by Bateson, Jackson, and their associates in the genesis of schizophrenia (Chapter 11, reference 4) and by Johnson, Szurek, and others in the genesis of some forms of delinquency (Chapter 14, reference 12). Implicit in these studies, however, is the great significance of parental expectations in the formation of behavior patterns in the average child. If the parent wants and expects the child to grow up, to adapt to new situations, to become more civilized, and to become more independent of the parent, the parent's expectations will be consistent with the child's drive toward maturity, the same drive that motivates him to "learn" to walk. In this situation, the child is more likely to regard parental approval and discipline as unequivocally in his long-term interests. However, if the parent inwardly needs or expects the child to be dependent or uncivilized; his outward approval of independent or civilized behavior may be given in a way that reflects his conflict. This inconsistency will be perceived by the child, and the double message will operate to reinforce his goal of immediate drive satisfaction as well as his long-term goal of mature adaptation.

The significance of expectation in the determination of behavior is not a new idea. Over a hundred years ago, Florence Nightingale advised nurses that "Patients do what they are expected to do." * A psychotic patient becomes more disturbed if the nurse is afraid of him and expects him to become more disturbed. Educators are familiar with this phenomenon; the capacity to maintain discipline in a classroom is a function not so much of the fear the teacher inspires as of the confidence he has in his ability to maintain discipline or, stated differently, of his relative lack of fear that he cannot maintain discipline and his consequent expectation that he can.

The expectation of control as a dynamic in producing control is not peculiar to the human animal. For years, or perhaps for centuries, it was

* Nightingale, Florence: *Notes on Nursing*, 1860.

recognized that lower animals can sense fear in a keeper or rider; the dog attacks the frightened postman but not the postman who is confident that he can manage the situation, the horse with an uncertain rider refuses the jump, and so on. Folklore attributes the difference to an odor of fear that the frightened person presumably emits and that the animal's sensitive olfactory apparatus picks up, but the absence of evidence for the odor makes it more reasonable to attribute the difference to the same kind of nonverbal communication that lets the child, the student, or the patient know that his parent, teacher, or nurse expects him not to conform.

Although intangible rewards are effective disciplinary measures in the long run, they lack effectiveness in the early stages of the training period and are often unsuitable for emergencies. The physician frequently can help parents to temper their expectations of discipline until the child is mature enough to profit by it. Meanwhile, modifying the environment often will forestall the development of tense situations. For example, if a child is too young to differentiate breakable ashtrays from unbreakable ones and if his impulse to investigate and manipulate his environment is not yet modulated by his desire for approval, his parents can prevent unnecessary trouble by putting breakables beyond reach until the child's controls are stronger. To restrain a child forcibly when he is running into a busy street or to slap his hand when he persists in playing with the light socket is an arbitrary action producing results by fear but an action often necessary in emergencies. Even the occasional explosive relief of tension by an overwrought mother may come under the heading of an emergency, although she runs the risk of rationalizing every situation into a call for instant action.

An occasional outburst from his mother may even reassure a child. He is often more aware of his own unreasonableness than his parents think and will feel less inadequate and guilty if he sees that his mother is not *always* the personification of reason. When he discovers that mother can be angry and still love him, he will find it easier to learn the important difference between *anger* and *rejection*. As he learns that mother's anger does not in itself mean rejection, he can tolerate anger better and see it in its proper perspective. Later on, he will be more likely to interpret someone's anger at him as the *consequence of his behavior* and not as a sign of rejection.

Conscience, Guilt, and Shame

As the child learns to control his feelings in much the same way that his parents control theirs, he also begins to assume their moral codes and standards. He forms the basis of his *conscience* by identifying with, or taking over as his own, the standards the loved parent sets and the behavior the parent expects of him. Later, his conscience is modified and elaborated by group standards and by standards of other individuals he comes to respect and admire, but the major component is ordinarily derived from the parents. Freud pointed out that although conscience is usually considered an exclusively conscious phenomenon, it contains both conscious and unconscious elements. He used the term "superego" to indicate the part of the personality which combines the conscious conscience and its unconscious counterpart [8].

Although Freud postulated that the superego is formed at about the age of six, when the Oedipus complex is resolved (see Chapter 6), many psychoanalysts now believe that its beginnings are found much earlier [9]. But whether or not the superego begins to be formed as early as the training period, parental attitudes in this period eventually determine the basic quality of the child's superego. The parents' standards, as incorporated in their own conscious and unconscious superegos, for the most part determine their expectations of their child; these expectations in turn determine the child's initial concept of himself and, secondarily, the basis for his own standards, sanctions, and prohibitions.

Children naturally do not always observe the prohibitions they have taken over from their parents. When they do transgress, they are frequently as critical of themselves as their parents would be—sometimes, in fact, they are more critical, since children usually interpret prohibitions literally and are more likely to equate thought and act than adults are. Self-criticism and the belief that punishment is deserved are defined as *guilt;* children and adults alike feel guilty if they violate, in fantasy or in fact, the prohibitions of their superegos, or consciences.

The parents expect the child not only to harness the expression of drives but to strive to attain goals and to live up to standards of accomplishment. The child incorporates the positive parental expectations in the form of an idealized image of himself, which is called the *ego ideal* and is usually considered part of the superego. When the child, or later the adult, fails to live up to his ego ideal, again either in fantasy or in fact, he suffers *shame* [10].

It is sometimes difficult to differentiate the prohibiting part of the superego from the ego ideal ("My conscience says I should share my toys with my friend, and I feel guilty if I don't" is close to "My ideal says I should be a person who shares, and I am ashamed if I don't"). Opposing parental messages confuse the child and weaken his conscience; for instance, if he is taught that "All cheating is prohibited, and I should feel guilty if I cheat in any way," he is bound to be confused if he is simultaneously encouraged to believe that "It is all right to cheat on the income tax."

In Chapter 14, I will discuss at greater length the effects of divergent, often unconscious parental standards in producing apparent discrepancies in the superegos of parent and child in some forms of delinquent behavior.

SIBLING RIVALRY

The arrival of a new brother or sister is particularly upsetting for children during the training period. No technique for adjusting the older child to the change in the family can circumvent the fact that the new arrival displaces the older child. He is forced to give up the primacy of his claim on mother's attentions and so loses part of his security just when he needs to face a new problem—the handling of his anger toward mother for having the newcomer [11]. From about the age of three, a secure child can identify well enough with the parent to welcome the baby to some extent and to join in the family enthusiasm, but before three, the threat to his security is too great for him to see any advantage. If the parents can accept the angry feelings of the older child (setting limits, of course, to the translation of these feelings into action against the baby) and do not immediately demand that he love and take care of his little brother, the child gradually may become genuinely fond of his brother as well as competitive with him. Too much pressure on a child to accept a new baby either prolongs the period of sullen resentment or encourages the child to conceal his angry feelings by a compensatory and specious protectiveness and overconcern.

A new sibling or a sibling who becomes ill can cause an older child to regress in the same way that environmental stress precipitates regression in neurosis. When the young child with residual dependency needs sees that the baby is not only given a great deal of dependency satisfaction but is also depriving him of his share, he may attempt to deal with the problem directly by telling his mother to take the baby back or by striking out at the intruder. If direct action does not produce results or if he fears that direct action will jeopardize further his weakened position, he tries to curb his mounting anxiety by regressing to an earlier level to look for more direct dependency satisfactions. Consequently, he may develop feeding problems, a relapse in toilet training, thumb-sucking, increased crying and temper outbursts, and so on. This behavior brings him into direct competition with the baby, and if he receives too much attention (if the regressive behavior is rewarded by too many secondary gains), it will persist. Ignoring the symptoms of regression while at the same time recognizing and responding to the child's need for security and helping him to accept his feelings about the baby usually suffices to counteract the regression.

CHRONIC HOSTILITY AND HOSTILE DEPENDENCY

A child's failure to develop satisfactory outlets and controls for his aggressive drives during the training period may result in an interruption of development or a partial fixation at that level of development. If not complicated by other factors, the fixation means that he grows up to become an *aggressive personality,* continually at odds with his environment as a result of his inability to control the hostile, angry component of his aggressive drive. As discussed in Chapter 4, the passive-dependent personality is characterized in the adult by outward helplessness, and angry feelings are seldom obvious. By contrast, in the aggressive personality the dependent feelings are hidden and the individual appears irritable, impatient, and cantankerous. He is so full of resentment that relatively insignificant frustrations in his environment cause him to boil over and strike out with inappropriate vehemence at whoever or whatever gets in his way.

Since children with dependent fixations are seriously handicapped in learning to handle their aggressive feelings, they are particularly susceptible to further fixation at the training-period level. Chronic dependency, therefore, is usually associated with chronic aggression in the *passive-aggressive personality* [12]. When an excess of both aggressive and dependent feelings are evident in the same person, he can be particularly frustrating to the physician or nurse. The passive-aggressive personality is constantly looking for someone who will compensate him for his earlier deprivation, but at the same time he openly resents the failure of those who help him to give enough to satisfy his needs. He unconsciously substitutes the doctor and the nurse for his parents and in a complaining, demanding fashion, insists on more and more help, at the same time sabotaging by passive resistance the help he does receive. He criticizes, either directly or by innuendo, the doctor's diagnosis, his treatment, and his attitude, but instead of finding another doctor, as dissatisfied patients usually do, he sticks like a leech to the doctor he seems to resent so much.

Not all passive-aggressive personalities show the same amount of hostility and dependency. The evident degrees of both range on a sliding scale from the passive-dependent, who appears dependent but not hostile, through the passive-aggressive, who is both hostile and dependent, to the aggressive personality, who appears hostile but not so dependent. The level of fixation appears to be more infantile as the patient approaches the passive-dependent end of the scale and to be closer to the training-period level as he approaches the aggressive end. The distinctions are not clear-cut, however, and the individual patient may vary from time to time in his behavioral manifestations.

Patients, particularly those with passive-aggressive personalities, transfer unconscious as well as conscious emotional significance from early dependent relationships to any treatment relationship. Thus, even if the doctor tries his best to restrict his therapeutic efforts to organic illness, he cannot avoid the emotional implications of acting as his patient's substitute parent. For the sake of effective treatment, therefore, and particularly to prevent the sudden unsuspected flowering of an intensely hostile dependent relationship, the physician should watch for signs of fixation in any of his patients. Just as his knowledge of the source of a fever gives him objective criteria for its treatment, his recognition of the source of a patient's hostile or dependent behavior helps him to limit dependency realistically and to neither counterattack nor capitulate in the face of the hostility.

Some aggressive or passive-aggressive personalities have so little inner control that they cannot keep from expressing their demands directly in the form of antisocial behavior. They insist on immediate fulfillment of their wishes; their urgency permits no consideration for the rights or feelings of others. They apparently think of other people only when they can use them to gain their ends. At one time, this characteristic was considered totally innate, and the clinical picture was called *constitutional psychopathic inferiority*. A later, somewhat less misleading term, *psychopathic personality*, was still too vague, and it has been superseded in the present classification by the more specific term, *antisocial reaction*. These people have suffered severe and long-continued deprivation of affection in childhood. Either they have been consistently denied parental warmth, or else permissiveness has been substituted for affection. Without a foundation of security, they grow up without any kind of meaningful relationship to others on which to base an adult identification, and they consequently never develop inner controls to divert or delay the immediate expression of their impulses. It is hardly surprising, therefore, that they appear frequently among professional criminals. All criminals, however, should by no means be dismissed as antisocial personalities (see Chapter 14). Furthermore, not all aggressive personalities who express their impulses directly are dangerous; both the strength of the hostile impulse and the ability to control it vary with the individual, so that some people of this type may act in a hostile manner rather infrequently. The greater the control and the more infrequent the hostile behavior, the better is the response to treatment.

Sadism and Masochism

In some people, hostile impulses eventually become associated with sexuality through a variety of conditioning called *erotization*. Erotization resembles the process described on page 47 in which dependent feelings which would cause anxiety if expressed directly are associated with hunger and expressed indirectly as a distortion of hunger. ("My hunger really isn't for love; it's for food.") When erotization takes place, a disturbing impulse is associated with the sexual drive and expressed indirectly as a distortion of sexuality. Thus, the erotization of direct hostility causes sexual feelings to be expressed cruelly, or *sadistically*. ("My wish to hurt you isn't because I want to destroy you; it's just my way of expressing sexual love.") This disguise is rather thin, and if the judicial function of the personality (the superego) is strong enough, it may inhibit sadistic expression and, with it, any other form of hostile or sexual expression. The analogy in this situation can be drawn to pathologic appetite loss (page 48), in which both hunger and dependency strivings are inhibited.

Under some circumstances, when sadistic expression is inhibited, the individual may erotize *receiving* punishment, so that sexual satisfaction is derived from cruel treatment by the partner instead of from cruelty to the partner; this turnabout is called *masochism* [13]. Masochism may develop in several ways. It may represent an overcompensation for sadism. It may be a way of suffering in advance and thus allaying sexual guilt sufficiently so that later gratification is possible. Some wives, for example, can only enjoy sexual relationships after they have provoked a "fight" with their husbands.

Masochism also may develop in the child who received practically no attention from the parents except punishment. Since he is too insecure to tolerate the absence of attention, he begins to behave in ways he knows will bring him punishment, to assure himself that his parents at least notice him. Eventually, he may begin to erotize (or to associate sexual satisfaction with) this situation, perhaps as a mechanism of defense against his hostility toward his rejecting parents or as a means of making his feeling of rejection bearable and even desirable.

The terms "sadism" and "masochism" are no longer used exclusively to refer to sexual deviations. They have been broadened to include attitudes of wider scope. For example, a hostile, depreciating attitude toward a spouse is often termed *sadistic*, and the complementary long-suffering acceptance of a spouse's sadism is called *masochistic.* These attitudes will be explored at greater length in the discussion of marital problems.

Masochism plays a role in some *hysterical* women (see page 232) who develop persistent abdominal pains of emotional origin. Although their pains are unconsciously determined, they seem calculated in their location, intensity, and response to examination to promote gynecologic surgery. As bit by bit the reproductive systems of these patients are removed without alleviation of their symptoms, their underlying sadism finds a sanctioned target in the surgeon who has failed to cure them. Psychiatric evaluation is a prudent antecedent step for the surgeon to take before scheduling exploratory surgery for women, particularly women with laparotomy scars, abdominal symptoms, and no other evidence of organic disease. Although more hypochondriacal than hysterical, Mrs. Brown, the patient discussed in Chapter 1, had some masochism in her makeup, and a less perceptive physician than Dr. Wilson might have been misled into undertaking surgery for her apparent gallbladder complaints.

Akin to masochism is *accident proneness*, a psychologic predisposition to accidents [14]. The interest in this condition was developed somewhat inadvertently. In the early days of the study of personality patterns of patients hospitalized with psychosomatic conditions, fracture patients seemed to be ideal controls. The "controls," however, turned out to be not at all representative of the general public. They included a high proportion of impulsive, somewhat depressed people who resented society's restrictions but who took their anger out on themselves. Subsequent statistical studies of taxi drivers showed that a relatively small number accounted for many more than their share of accidents. Since other possible contributing factors balanced out, personality factors were considered in all likelihood responsible for the high accident rate of the minority of drivers.

Speech and Learning Blocks

In some families, the child's attempts to explore and manipulate the world around him are rigidly rebuffed and treated as if they were hostile attacks on family possessions. The child then learns to associate his explorations with hostility, and since families of this type usually encourage the inhibition of aggressiveness, the child may give up or disguise his curiosity along with his aggression. Without curiosity, he has no incentive to learn new methods of understanding, and in this way, he may develop a learning block [15].

Learning blocks are not always evidence of inhibition of aggression. Some children, particularly in families that consider intellectual achievement very important, develop learning blocks as an indirect means of asserting themselves and resisting the family's pressures. With less family concern about brains and more about food or feces, these children might have developed feeding or toilet problems. A child with an emotionally conditioned learning block may appear to be mentally retarded, and since his status as a retarded child will permit him to regress and avoid conflict, the true nature of the problem may remain obscured for years. The physician or psychologist should be conservative when considering the diagnosis of mental retardation and should look for evidence in more than one or two areas. Learning blocks can be caused by defective sight or hearing or by neurologic lesions, as well as by hereditary or emotional causes (see Chapter 13).

The child not only may have trouble in learning to talk but may develop defects in his speech [16]. Many children, especially boys, go through a brief period of stuttering or stammering about the age of two and a half. In the majority of cases, the symptom has no abnormal significance and will disappear spontaneously if too much attention has not led to excessive secondary advantages. Some children, however, continue to stammer, almost as if they cannot decide whether to speak the word or not. Often they have associated language with forbidden aggression, as in the following case.

> A young man who had overcome his stammering to a considerable degree revealed that his mother had disciplined him exclusively and unsparingly by ridicule. As with most children, ridicule would make him terribly angry, and he wanted to strike back at her in the same way; but "talking back" was forbidden, and in any case, he was no match for her in either fluency or experience. He began to stammer, which made it impossible for him to talk back, and although he received more ridicule for his stammering, he also received more attention from his mother. Later, a competent speech therapist helped him to overcome his problem, so that he now speaks freely under ordinary circumstances. He seldom expresses anger to anyone, but he consistently signals the appearance of inner feelings of anger by the return of a mild stammer, and he always stammers when talking to his mother.

PSYCHOPHYSIOLOGIC MANIFESTATIONS

If aggressive feelings have not come under conscious control by the end of the training period, they may be unconsciously controlled, or repressed.

Repression of all hostility usually occurs in people who are so afraid of their anger that they dare not acknowledge to themselves that it exists. Their behavior with respect to anger resembles the pseudoindependent personality's behavior with respect to dependency. In some cases, the repression lasts indefinitely; in others, when external circumstances cause inner anger to increase, a breakthrough occurs, either directly or in disguised form. A patient who has repressed all his hostility will present a calm, friendly exterior, be ingratiating to his superiors, and tend to swallow petty irritations. The hidden hostility persists, however, and may underlie somatic symptoms which represent the physiologic concomitants of anger—the body's mobilization to fight. In different individuals different organ systems take the brunt of this expression; how much of the difference is due to constitutional variations in susceptibility and how much to variations in emotional development is not yet clear.

Essential hypertension, for example, frequently appears in patients who repress anger and who also have a family history of hypertension [17]. Overt anger is accompanied by short-term increases in blood pressure, and there is reason to believe that repressed anger is accompanied by long-term increases. Research workers, however, have not yet bridged the gap between demonstrating the short-term correlates and determining the possible role of long-continued repressed emotion in producing fixed hypertension. There is suggestive evidence in the relative consistency of personality structure in both labile and fixed types and in the frequency with which labile hypertension eventually becomes fixed. Psychiatric treatment in early cases may help to delay the transition to the fixed stage and may meanwhile contribute to the improvement of the patient's interpersonal relationships, as in the following case.

A young married intern sought psychiatric help after he was denied life insurance because of a mild, somewhat labile hypertension. He was an excellent intern who carried out his duties conscientiously and showed great deference to the attending physicians. After discussing his feelings over a period of time, however, he realized that he had developed several grievances against his superiors which he had not discussed with anyone and apparently had soon forgotten. He inwardly considered all his superiors, regardless of how mild-mannered they appeared, to be jealous of their positions, unable to tolerate disagreement, and eagerly awaiting an excuse to get rid of him.

The patient's father was an abusive alcoholic who intimidated the whole family. His mother had bent every effort to placate his father, strongly advising the children to do the same. The patient adapted himself to the situation by concealing his aggressiveness from his father and eventually even from himself, but although buried, it was stimulated whenever he found himself in contact with men in authority.

As his insight developed in treatment, he began to see and eventually to react to the attending men as they really were and not as if they were carbon copies of his father. He became more aware of his hidden resentment against his father. He also discovered that he had displaced some of this resentment to his wife and consequently had remained somewhat cold and aloof in his relationships with her.

After several hours of psychotherapy, his blood pressure returned to normal levels. It is hard to demonstrate whether his treatment forestalled, postponed, or had any effect on the development of permanent vascular changes, but it unquestionably contributed to the improvement of his marital adjustments. As an intern, he became less servile and obsequious and more willing to express an opinion of his own.

Not all hypertensives fit into this patient's overt pattern of surface friendliness. Some, in fact, are apparently the opposite and tend to be quarrelsome and argumentative. A careful evaluation, however, may disclose that the anger is directed at individuals who are not too important to the patient; it represents a release of pent-up anger redirected from a focus of dependent needs toward a substitute target. In psychologic terms, although these patients repress most of their anger, they *displace* some of it from the real focus to a substitutue focus and then *act it out* by showing open irritation. The relief that such a release may give is temporary, since the fundamental problem has not been resolved.

Chronic repressed hostility appears in the personality structure of patients who suffer from other psychosomatic disturbances. There are several possible points of contact between psychologic and physiologic factors in these conditions. For example, the vascular phenomena of many migraine headaches appear to be physiologic responses to hidden hostility, occurring episodically when compulsive mechanisms (see page 139) are not sufficient to absorb the patient's repressed anger [18]. Attacks of some skin disorders, such as giant urticaria, appear to be precipitated by a threatened breakthrough of previously concealed, unacceptable hostile feelings [19]. Some dependent personalities, who apparently are predisposed by having unusually sensitive gastrocolic reflexes, suffer from attacks of diarrhea when they mobilize but cannot express anger against parents or people in authority. Similar personality factors, along with other, undiscovered elements, have been implicated in the development of chronic ulcerative colitis [20]. The physician should be careful, however, not to assume an invariably consistent relationship between specific personality patterns and psychosomatic disease. (See page 229–230.)

OBSESSIVE–COMPULSIVE MANIFESTATIONS

When hostility is not permitted overt expression but is too strong to be repressed, substitute outlets by means of mental mechanisms may be found. One such mechanism is _reaction formation._ By means of reaction formation, any unacceptable drive or its symbolic equivalent is associated with its opposite. The conscious expression, therefore, is the opposite of the patient's inner feeling—black becomes white, and hate becomes love. Thus, a person who unconsciously hates a parent may express great conscious devotion for the parent and thereby try to convince himself and others that his inner hostility does not exist. He must continue to affirm his love indefinitely, since the cause of the hidden hostility is not removed, and the pressure continues to build up. The repetitive nature of his protestations soon arouses the suspicion of others; as Hamlet's mother observed when the murderous player queen overstated her love for her intended victim: "The lady doth protest too much." (For diagram, see Appendix B, Figure 13.)

In reaction formation, the individual appears to seek the support of the environment in strengthening his ability to repress. He seems to be saying: "If I show you so much love and no anger at all, perhaps you will believe that I have no anger inside me, and if you believe it and treat me that way, perhaps I can convince myself."

Reaction formation is one of the typical mechanisms of the *compulsive personality.* Reaction formation alone, however, does not provide enough protection for the compulsive, who attempts to strengthen his defense against the unacceptable drive by using additional unconscious disguises. Instead of dealing directly with hostile feelings, a compulsive person will unconsciously substitute a *symbolically* hostile activity, such as soiling, for direct hostility. In other words, he unconsciously associates or attaches his hostile feelings to an activity which is not in itself destructive but which he has found by past experience is irritating to his parents and therefore indirectly hostile. He may then continually counteract his supercharged wish to soil by a second unconscious mechanism (reaction formation) and express the now thoroughly disguised hostility in the form of a perfectionistic preoccupation with cleanliness [21].

This method of controlling hostility is usually encouraged by parental example, as illustrated by a docile and obedient four-year-old girl, dressed in a starched pinafore, who stood aloof from the sandbox in which her overall-clad friends were playing. "*My* mommy," she commented smugly, "says there are *germs* in that dirty old sand." As in this case, the mothers of compulsive children often are themselves compulsive, greatly concerned about dirt, germs, feces, and general disorder. They disapprove of expressions of aggression and reward conformity, so that their children tend to follow the parental pattern of reaction formation in order to protect their security. [They become overclean, overcontrolled, overconcerned about germs, preoccupied with bowel regularity, and extremely devoted to order and detail. So much emphasis is put on the sanctity of possessions that they substitute possessions for the human security their hostile feelings threaten. They become ardent collectors and find it difficult to get rid of anything, including their money and their ideas, so that they are customarily parsimonious and stubborn. Freud pointed out that they may even have trouble getting rid of feces, with a resultant tendency to constipation. Mild compulsive traits may in part determine vocational choice and are useful (if not carried too far) for the bookkeeper, the accountant, the surgical nurse, or the pharmacist.]

A person's compulsive manifestations vary from time to time, apparently in relation to the amount of hostility mobilized by circumstances. In some cases, the outward signs are minimal and the basically compulsive personality appears to operate at a fairly mature level unless an increase in external stress puts so much strain on him that some of the more mature part of his personality regresses to the level of his partial fixation. With this regression, his heretofore repressed aggression is stirred up, and he calls additional compulsive defense mechanisms into play to help counteract it. If the amount of stress is great, the resulting symptoms take the form of rituals repeated over and over in apparently meaningless, stereotyped thoughts (obsessions) or acts (compulsions). The patient is usually aware of their irrationality, but no matter how hard he tries, he cannot keep from thinking or performing what amount to almost magical protective measures.

This condition is called an *obsessive-compulsive* reaction, and is considered a form of *psychoneurotic disorder* (see Chapter 10). It can be extremely incapacitating, as demonstrated by one patient whose efficiency was markedly cut down because he felt compelled to do everything three times or by a student who failed because she felt compelled to count the leaves on the tree outside her window before beginning to study or by a diabetic who went through such a long and complicated ritual before she could administer her insulin that by the time she finished one injection it was almost time to begin preparations for the next. As in most obsessive or compulsive rituals, if something interfered with her routine, she had to start all over again.

A patient may attempt to wipe out a past sin by a symbolic *undoing,* as dramatically illustrated by Lady Macbeth's hand washing. The symbolic undoing does not solve the problem because, as she says, "What's done cannot be undone," but she nevertheless persists in the attempt. One patient was so obsessed with cleanliness and her attempt to "undo" the hostility of which she was unaware that she spent all day in the bathroom, alternately washing her hands and waiting for the inevitable speck of dust to contaminate them. The water continually ran from the tap because if she touched the faucet to turn it off, she would have to turn it on again immediately to repeat her cleansing ritual.

Some obsessive-compulsive patients indicate their mixed feelings by paradoxical combinations, as did the patient who was extremely careful to wear spotless outer garments but seldom changed her underclothing. The underlying background of hostility is usually more obvious in obsessive thoughts, which may even involve murder. "What if I should kill my children?" is a fairly common and extremely distressing obsession. The compulsive often indirectly reveals his hostile feelings when he tells what he secretly fears will happen if he does not carry out his compulsion. The secret fear usually involves a catastrophe to himself or to a member of his family; the compulsion serves to counteract the destructive thought, but the thought persists, so he must repeat the compulsion—and so on indefinitely. Many obsessive neurotics suggest their conflict over self-assertion by indecision over apparently trivial matters; one spends hours deciding which necktie to wear, while another is practically immobilized by the choices on a menu.

Although the obsessive-compulsive person usually recognizes the unrealistic nature of his symptoms, he may struggle to rationalize them—for example, by pointing out that germs do cause disease and therefore are to be avoided. A physician or anyone else who advises a patient to forget his obsessions or to stop his compulsions, implying that such a solution is within his patient's power, is making an impossible request. Unable to deal with his irritation at being expected to do the impossible, the patient usually responds with further symptoms or with more rationalizations.

Incapacitating obsessive-compulsive reactions present difficult therapeutic problems. Their point of fixation is so early that the interpersonal relationship necessary for treatment is hard to form and, even if formed, is hard to work with because it is so dominated by hostile and ambivalent feelings. Furthermore, even in treatment, the patient uses the same techniques he uses in other situations to avoid facing his hostility. These factors combine to make treatment of an obsessive-compulsive reaction by insight development an extremely long and tedious process. Favorable results are so difficult to obtain that a few investigators go so far as to recommend the drastic and irreversible surgical procedure of lobotomy in completely incapacitated cases of long duration. In mild cases, when the regression and the development of the reaction are recent or not well established, supportive treatment (Chapter 15) may produce a reduction in symptoms. Compulsive personalities may be helped to function more efficiently by psychologic support of constructive patterns of reaction.

Most children of school age go through a period with mild compulsive overtones, as reflected in their preoccupation with the rules rather than the game or in their careful avoidance of hypothetically dangerous acts such as stepping on sidewalk cracks. The jingle, "Step on a crack, break your mother's back," intimates that one function of this activity is to counteract hostility. Many (perhaps most) adults continue to use these mechanisms occasionally in performing compulsive eating or dressing routines or in thinking private little obsessional thoughts under certain circumstances. They should not be considered neurotic in the sense of being ill, however, unless their symptoms interfere substantially with their daily lives.

Symptomatically, obsessive-compulsive reactions may resemble *phobias* (persistent but irrational fears—see Chapter 10). It may be difficult to distinguish a fear of knives, for example, from obsessive thoughts about knives. The patient with a phobia, however, reacts with obvious anxiety when he perceives a knife; the patient with an obsession thinks about knives with less obvious anxiety whether or not he perceives one.

Occasionally, an obsessive-compulsive patient becomes convinced that his obsessions are based on fact. For example, a man who continually has washed his hands because he fears that they *might be* dirty may begin to believe that they actually *are* when they are not. For him, the process of regression is continuing; he is distorting reality and slipping into a psychotic reaction (see Chapter 11).

Distorting reality is not the only solution to the breakdown of defenses which are based on reaction formation. The abundance of prohibitions and regulations in the family pattern provides the obsessive-compulsive patient with a rigid, uncompromising, and punishing superego. Whenever an unacceptable drive comes too close to consciousness, his conscience leads him to punish himself by a redirection of hostility toward himself. The patient condemns, punishes, and hates himself instead of the one he really hates, and he becomes clinically *depressed*.

SUMMARY

The period from one year to three gives the child a broader field for the assertion of his individuality and the expression of his aggressive drive.

Sleep problems, feeding problems, and toilet problems often occur. Parents play important roles in strengthening the child's developing ego by their use of discipline. Discipline helps the child establish impulse control more effectively when it makes use of rewards than when it uses fear alone. The beginnings of the superego development, or the development of conscience, may also appear in this period.

Fixation at the training-period level causes the adaptive functions to be absorbed with problems of the expression of aggression. Repressed aggression may be associated with learning and speech problems and with certain psychosomatic disturbances. Aggression may be acted out in delinquent behavior or erotized as sadistic behavior. Aggression modified by isolation and by reaction formation may appear as obsessions or compulsions. With excessive guilt, aggression may be internalized and may appear as a form of depression.

REFERENCES

1. Fraiberg, S.: "On the Sleep Disturbances of Early Childhood," *Psychoanal. Stud. Child*, 5:285, New York, International Universities Press, Inc., 1950. Shirley, H. F., and J. P. Kahn: "Sleep Disturbances in Children," *Pediat. Clin. N. Amer.*, 5:629, 1958.
2. Freud, A.: "The Psychoanalytic Study of Infantile Feeding Disturbances," *Psychoanal. Stud. Child*, 3–4:119, New York, International Universities Press, Inc., 1947. Schwartz, A. S.: "Eating Problems," *Pediat. Clin. N. Amer.*, 5:595, 1958.
3. Spock, B., and M. Bergen: "Parents' Fear of Conflict in Toilet Training," *Pediatrics*, 34:112, 1964.
4. For a discussion of the anal period, see: Freud, S.: "Character and Anal Erotism" (1908), in *Standard Edition*, 1959, vol. IX, p. 167.
5. Josselyn, I. M.: *Psychosocial Development of Children*, New York, Family Service Association of America, 1948.
6. Breger, E.: "Etiologic Factors in Enuresis: A Psychobiologic Approach," *J. Child Psychol. Psychiat.*, 2:667, 1963.
7. Freud, A.: "Aggression in Relation to Emotional Development, Normal and Pathological," *Psychoanal. Stud. Child*, 3–4:37, New York, International Universities Press, Inc., 1947. Szurek, S. A.: "Emotional Factors in the Use of Authority," in Ethel L. Ginsburg, *Public Health Is People*, New York, The Commonwealth Fund, 1950, p. 206.
8. Freud, S.: "The Ego and the Id" (1923), in *Standard Edition*, 1961, vol. XIX, p. 1.
9. Klein, M.: *Contributions to Psychoanalysis*, London, The Hogarth Press, Ltd., 1948.
10. Piers, G., and M. Singer: *Shame and Guilt*, Springfield, Ill., Charles C Thomas, Publisher, 1953.

11. Levy, David: *Studies in Sibling Rivalry,* research monograph, New York, American Orthopsychiatric Association, 1937.
12. Whitman, R., H. Trosman, and R. Koenig: "Clinical Assessment of Passive-Aggressive Personality," *AMA Arch. Neurol. Psychiat.,* 72:540, 1954.
13. Freud, S.: "Beyond the Pleasure Principle" (1920), in *Standard Edition,* 1955, vol. XVIII, p. 1.
    ————: "The Economic Problem of Masochism" (1924), in *Standard Edition,* 1961, vol. XIX, p. 157.
    ————: "Three Essays on the Theory of Sexuality" (1905), in *Standard Edition,* 1953, vol. VII, p. 123.
    Stekel, W.: *Sadism and Masochism: The Psychology of Hatred and Cruelty,* New York, Grove Press, Inc., 1964.
14. Dunbar, H. F.: *Mind and Body: Psychosomatic Medicine,* New York, Random House, Inc., 1947.
    Hirschfeld, A. H., and R. C. Behan: "The Accident Process: 1. Etiological Considerations of Industrial Injuries," *J.A.M.A.,* 186:193, 1963.
15. Piaget, J., and B. Inhelder: *The Growth of Logical Thinking from Childhood to Adolescence,* New York, Basic Books, Inc., Publishers, 1958.
    Rabinovitch, R. D.: "Reading and Learning Disabilities," in S. Arieti (ed.), *American Handbook of Psychiatry,* New York, Basic Books, Inc., Publishers, 1959, chap. 43, p. 857.
    Staver, Nancy: "The Child's Learning Difficulty as Related to the Emotional Problem of the Mother," *Amer. J. Orthopsychiat.,* 23:131, 1953.
16. Dominick, B.: "Stuttering," in S. Arieti (ed.), *American Handbook of Psychiatry,* New York, Basic Books, Inc., Publishers, 1959, p. 950.
17. Reiser, M. F., et al.: "Psychologic Mechanisms in Malignant Hypertension," *Psychosom. Med.,* 13:147, 1951.
    Wolf, S., et al.: *Life Stress and Essential Hypertension,* Baltimore, The Williams & Wilkins Company, 1955.
18. Wolff, H. G.: *Headache and Other Head Pain,* Fairlawn, N.J., Oxford University Press, 1948.
19. Kerwin, L.: "Emotional Factors in Urticaria," *Psychosom. Med.,* 9:131, 1947.
20. Daniels, G. E., et al.: "Three Decades in the Observation and Treatment of Ulcerative Colitis," *Psychosom. Med.,* 24:85, 1962.
    Engel, G. L.: "Studies in Ulcerative Colitis, III. The Nature of the Psychological Process," *Amer. J. Med.,* 19:231, 1955.
    Grace, W. J., and H. G. Wolff: "Treatment of Ulcerative Colitis," *J.A.M.A.,* 146:981, 1951.
21. Abraham, K.: "Contribution to the Theory of the Anal Character," in *Selected Papers on Psychoanalysis,* London, The Hogarth Press, Ltd., 1927, p. 370.
    Freud, S.: "Character and Anal Erotism" (1908), in *Standard Edition,* 1959, vol. IX, p. 167.

Chapter 6

POWER POLITICS WITHIN THE FAMILY

FAMILY RIVALRY

Just as there is no clear-cut termination of infancy, so there is no definite end to the training period. Ordinarily, however, by the beginning of the fourth year the child has received enough unambivalent love to give him a modicum of security in relation to others and has developed enough confidence in his controls to keep him reasonably comfortable in relation to himself. All his problems of dependency and hostility are by no means solved, but at least part of the time he is free enough from the earlier pressures to be able to use his developing capacity to give love as well as to continue to receive it. Before this period, his affection, gratitude, and desire to be with specific people have been largely an expression of his own needs for love. Now, provided the degree of fixation at earlier levels is not too great, the child begins to give love. He still is primarily concerned with himself, and at first there is a period in which he seems to try out his new ability to give love by directing it toward himself. Soon, however, he begins to experiment in directing his love toward others [1]. He begins to modify "I want to be loved" to "I still want to be loved, but I also want to love you."

At about the same time, he becomes aware of the significance of sexual differences. Before this period, he has observed and probably wondered about them, but they had no special meaning. Cars were sedans or convertibles, weather was sunny or rainy, people were men or women; all were inexplicable variations in a world too complex to begin to understand. But now, as he develops more understanding of the world about him and as he begins to give love, he also notices the pattern of love-giving among others.* In his daily routine, he sees his mother and father ex-

* The question of whether the emotional problems of this period are intrinsic and universal or conditioned by the culture is still controversial. The question is intriguing but somewhat academic for consideration in a book focused on practical psychiatric problems in Western, monogamous, patriarchal culture.

pressing affection for each other; even if his home is broken, he realizes that this pattern customarily exists between mothers and fathers. He also begins to relate the social roles of mother and father to their sex. As he discovers the significance of sexual differences in those about him, he becomes more concerned with his own sex, so that he thinks of himself more as a boy or a girl than simply as a child.

A third development in this period is a beginning capacity to think in abstract terms. Heretofore, the child has thought only in concrete tangible terms; for example, Christmas meant Santa Claus and presents rather than the spirit of giving. Time is an abstract concept which the smaller child finds hard to comprehend, and until he comprehends time, growth remains a mystery; the child thinks of himself as perennially a child, and adults who talk about "when you grow up" only mystify him. When he matures to the point of understanding time, he can begin to understand growth and can then think of himself as a boy who will become a man or as a girl who will become a woman.

Identification

The capacity to think of what he will be, and not only of what he is, is a step toward *identification,* or the wish to be like someone else [2]. Since the boy thinks of himself as eventually a man, he usually identifies with or wants to be like the man closest to him—his father. Finally, since the capacity to give love is developing concurrently, the boy wants to give love as his father does—to his mother, who is also the person from whom he has received most love. For the girl, the process is analogous, starting with identification with her mother as the woman on whom she has been most dependent. She then wants to give love to the man her mother loves, who is also the man closest to her—her father.

The theoretic reconstruction of the first events of this developmental phase is based on the summation of a great many small bits of evidence from psychoanalytic studies and from observations of children as they go through this stage [3]. Casual observation, however, gives us an inkling of the development of identification; for example, while children at this age often clump around in their parents' shoes, girls practically always use their mothers' shoes and boys their fathers'.

The child's search for identification is more complicated when his home has been broken by the loss of the parent of his sex. Often a boy in this situation may identify with a grandparent, an uncle, or a male friend of his mother's. Even if no substitute is available, he may identify with a fantasied ideal who represents his father or someone he would like to have as a stepfather. The attitude of the remaining parent is important in the development of the ideal. If a mother thinks and speaks of her departed husband with affection and respect, her son is more likely to make a strong masculine identification than if her attitude toward her husband is hostile and contemptuous.

Another type of identification may result when a child is frightened of the parent of the same sex and sees him as hostile and destructive. He

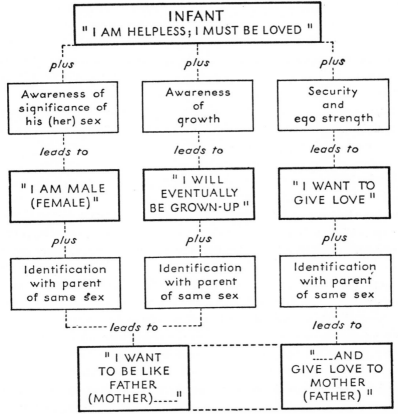

FIGURE 2. Identification and the development of family rivalry.

may still identify with the parent, but out of self-defense instead of love, as if to say, "Don't hit me; I'm on your side." He thus acquires a *hostile identification* with the parent, sometimes called *identification with the aggressor*. Instead of growing up to give love, he grows up to be like his parent, hostile and destructive.

Psychoanalysts usually interpret this process in a slightly different manner, placing identification at a later stage. They believe that an inner sexual urge developing at this time directs the giving of love to the parent of the opposite sex and that identification with the parent of the same sex only appears as a mechanism of defense against the conflicts stirred up by this focus of love. Although a sexual urge can be understood as one factor in the close relationship between a boy and his mother, some have questioned whether it is strong enough at the age of three or four to cause the girl to give her love not to the mother, who has been closest to her, but to the father, who is a comparative stranger. The physician, who often wishes to understand this period without going too deeply into psychoanalytic theory, may find it simpler to think of identification both as a step in development at this point and as a later defense mechanism in the resolution of consequent conflicts.

Identification alone seldom produces conflict in a reasonably well-knit family; on the contrary, the parents, if they are comfortable in their own roles, are delighted to see their children imitate them and will strengthen the identification by their approval. The child, however, has since infancy made evident his wish to monopolize both parents. The little girl, for example, wants to monopolize mother when she is available and father when he is at hand. As she begins to comprehend something of the nature of the intense relationship between mother and father, she begins dimly to realize that her wish to monopolize father brings her into a special kind of competition with mother. It is not just the same as elbowing brother or sister out of the way to see who gets in mother's lap first. It is not the same as wanting to be mother's favorite girl, because that would not be replacing anybody of major significance. To be father's favorite girl would mean replacing mother. Although she has learned something about sharing love, she still finds it difficult, and she still is somewhat afraid of her own and her parents' anger. So when she competes with her mother for first place in her father's affections, she assumes that her mother thinks in the same way she does. She fears that her mother will be jealous and angry at her and will punish her either by hurting her or by withdrawing her love.

Close observation of the girl's behavior through this period may disclose some intimations of this conflict. The three-year-old daughter often is coquettish with her father, who is customarily pleased and responsive. Her mother usually thinks her behavior is cute and pays little attention to it, but the little girl watches her mother carefully to note its effect. Then for a period the girl seems particularly anxious to remain in the good graces of her mother. Mothers often wonder what brings about this urge to placate, but since it results in relatively good behavior, they are seldom very much concerned. The coquetry and placation continue, with varying intensity, until at around age six, the girl acts as if she realized that she is fighting a losing battle and can never really be first in her father's affection. She seems to give up the struggle and makes peace with her mother, who often is quite unaware that there is a war on.

Part of the peacemaking consists of reinforcing her identification with her mother, which in turn helps to strengthen both her ego and her superego. Released from preoccupation with family relationships, she now can turn to friends and playmates for the satisfaction of part of her needs to love and be loved. She becomes less attentive to her father and less competitive with her mother, and although she still invests a great deal of love in the family, she is less intensely involved. Part of the conflict remains, but she is able to repress it for the time being, until adolescence stirs it up again (see Chapter 7).

Unsupported observations of this type would not in themselves justify the great emphasis that dynamic psychiatry places on this conflict situation. Studies of the fantasy lives of both healthy and disturbed children, however, have indicated the great significance of the intrafamily relationship in the inner thoughts of the child. Early investigations of unconscious factors in adult neurosis so consistently implicated this conflict that it was at first thought to be the basis for all neurosis. Although later psychoanalytic investigators have found evidence that conflicts around dependency and aggression are significant [4], there is still reason to believe that family rivalry plays a major part in the production of many emotional disturbances. A good deal of this evidence comes from memories of adult patients undergoing treatment, as in the following incident.

> A mother customarily had a cocktail with her husband in his study before dinner, excluding her young daughter with the statement that father was tired and needed to relax. When the daughter came to treatment years later, she recalled that she had interpreted the exclusion as evidence of the mother's fear that her daughter would threaten her priority in her husband's affections.

Such memories are often subject to distortion, but they appear with sufficient consistency to justify taking them seriously.

Boys, especially in our urban culture, usually have fewer opportunities to strengthen their identifications with their fathers than girls have with their mothers. Even though fathers are out of the home during most of their children's playtime, however, there is ample evidence of identification in the quality of boys' play. Boys usually mimic either their fathers' vocational activity or their fathers' secret ambitions, at least to the degree that they can comprehend them.

The boy's apparent conflict with his father over rivalry for first place in his mother's affections is usually more intense than the girl's. Part of this is

FIGURE 3. Copyright C 1962, The Hall Syndicate, Inc.

due to the family structure; the boy, along with his siblings, has his mother to himself all day but then must give her up to father in the evening (Fig. 3). He is alternately encouraged at his temporary daytime success and defeated as he is sent to bed in the evening. He thus is more stimulated toward hope of success than the girl and may in turn be more apprehensive of the consequences, especially if his father plays the traditional role of the parent who does the punishing.

But although it is a greater struggle, he, too, eventually concludes that he cannot really win and abandons the fight as the girl does. He cements his identification with his father and in so doing, strengthens his ego and superego. He is able to turn part of his attention and affection to his schoolmates, and since his ego has grown stronger, he can repress much of the remaining conflicted feeling.

The Oedipus Complex

In this way, the *Oedipus complex,* as Freud termed it, is resolved. The term is derived from the Greek legend of King Oedipus who, unaware of his ancestry, killed his father and married his mother. When he realized he had committed both patricide and incest, his guilt was so great that he blinded himself. Freud used this dramatic analogy to point out the unconscious desire of the boy to eliminate the father and have the mother to himself and to emphasize the drastic consequences.

The fear of these consequences he termed *castration anxiety,* or fear that the father would revenge himself on the boy by removing his genitals, according to the primitive concept of making the punishment fit the crime. If this part of the psychoanalytic theory is taken symbolically rather than literally, i.e., that the son fears that his father might prevent him from growing up and being a man, it is not so disturbing. Taken literally, however, it is difficult for many people to accept, chiefly because there seems to be so little external evidence to support it. Actually, much of the evidence for the existence of castration anxiety comes from glimpses into unconscious fears provided by the dreams, fantasies, and symptoms of adults. The extreme importance attached to this type of anxiety may be somewhat related to the family patterns of Freud's day, two aspects of which are of considerable significance.

One aspect was the high cultural value placed on males and male children. With this attitude firmly embedded in the boy's mind, the possession of external genitals became of crucial importance to him as soon as he discovered the physical difference between boys and girls. Freud believed he had evidence to justify concluding that the boy's initial interpretation of his first sight of female genitals was that the woman once had possessed external genitals but lost them (and with them the preferred place in the family hierarchy). The boy's hypothetical reasoning continued: If she lost them, someone must have removed them, and that someone was probably father, who administered the rest of the corporal punishment. Next came the disconcerting thought that if it could happen to her, it also could happen to him; but that was such a horrible thought that he repressed it and never dared bring it back into consciousness to check on the reality of the danger, so that it continued indefinitely to influence his behavior.

The second significant aspect of the family pattern in the rationale for castration anxiety arose from the strength of the taboo against masturbation. All babies and small children tend to explore and manipulate their bodies, but the manipulation of nose, ears, fingers, or toes does not precipitate much parental distress. When the boy, finally freed from diapers, begins to play with his penis, the parents are often extremely upset. They may attempt to scare the child by telling him of the hazards of such procedures, hoping that he will abandon them through fear of the consequences. Apparently, in Freud's day, the threats were more universally drastic than they are now and customarily involved the possibility of losing the genitalia if the genital manipulation continued. Whether or not the child continued his manipulation, the idea was implanted that castration was possible as a punishment. Thus, both the family preference for boys and the masturbation taboo intensified the anxiety related to castration.

As cultural patterns have changed, the status of women has risen; and as sexual education has become more general, masturbation has become less alarming. Yet even in families where women and men are equally esteemed and where masturbation is tolerated, children show evidence in their play, conversation, and fantasies of some castration anxiety. The family rivalry is still there, and although the paternal anger may be anticipated in more diffuse form, the characteristic first reaction of any suddenly frightened four-year-old boy is still to grab and protect his genitals.

The female manifestation of castration anxiety is called *penis envy*, also produced by awareness of the physical difference between the sexes. Freud believed that penis envy, which actually involved the wish to be a boy instead of a girl, was universal among girls, but others have suggested that it is more significant in families where boys are held in greater esteem [5]. Although this pattern still prevails, it seems not to be so universal as it was in Freud's day, and in families where each parent considers the other of equal value, there is much less evidence of penis envy in the daughters. As the cultural pattern changes, castration anxiety, in the literal sense, also may be becoming relatively less significant as a basis for neurotic conflict.

Whether there is always an actual conscious erotic or sexual component in the child's feelings toward the parent during this period is open to question. Psychologically, however, the future sexual orientation appears to be profoundly affected by the events of this period. The next section of this chapter will describe some of the clinical pictures resulting from fixation and regression secondary to conflict in the family area and will perhaps clarify to some extent the theoretic concepts of this section.

PROLONGATION OF FAMILY RIVALRIES

Certain parental attitudes during the three- to six-year-old period play a major role in interrupting emotional development at this point and in setting the stage for later regression. Three attitudes—dissatisfaction, hostility, and seductiveness—are most likely to interfere with a child's successful solution of the problems of identification and family rivalry.

The Dissatisfied Parent

Any unwanted, rejected, or disliked child finds it difficult to identify with his parent, and as discussed in Chapters 4 and 5, he may retain in-

definitely an immature emotional orientation. But even a reasonably secure child may find identification difficult if his parent is basically dissatisfied with his own role as male or female. For example, if a mother is
unusually envious, either overtly or unconsciously, of male prerogatives,
her daughter may feel that it is a major misfortune to be a girl. She may
then try her best to emulate a presumably more desirable boy. This is one
reason why a girl becomes a tomboy, an adaptation which is often quite
satisfactory until bodily changes and cultural demands at adolescence
make it difficult to continue the disguise.

Paradoxically, the tomboy pattern seems to have appeared more frequently as women have come closer to achieving social and vocational
equality. Although previously women may have envied men, they envied
them from a much greater distance, for they then had no choice but to
accept their position. The passive acceptance of their presumably inferior
femininity was perpetuated as each generation of daughters identified
with mothers who passively accepted their lot. As women gradually began to establish their equality and as acceptance of an inferior role became no longer inevitable, society began to sanction direct competition of
women with men. Some women now see evidence of equality only in the
sharing of *masculine* prerogatives and still consider the roles of housewife
and mother inferior. Their rebellion against woman's role becomes a rebellion against femininity, and so they tend to foster an analogous rejection of femininity in their daughters. Perhaps the pendulum will swing
away from this tendency as more and more women develop a feeling of
equality to men within roles as housewives and mothers [6].

Woman's envy of man receives greater social acceptance than man's
envy of woman and is therefore less likely to be repressed. Most men at
times envy women's relatively dependent role in the marital partnership,
her more intimate contact with children, and her greater social sanctions
for self-adornment. They also envy women's creative role, forgetting or
underrating their own contributions to it. Although a father may repress
his envy of women so that he is unaware of its existence, he may, by pro-
testing too much or by other subtle communications, convey his dissatisfaction to his son with enough emphasis to influence the son's attitudes
toward the masculine role.

Even with a father secure in his manhood, the boy in our society may
find masculine identification difficult. Since his waking hours coincide
with his father's hours of work, they see relatively little of each other. Except on a farm, the boy has few chances to see at first hand the satisfaction his father derives from his work. The husband's familiar gambit of

complaining each evening of a hard day at the office as insurance against being asked to help with the dishes even when his job satisfactions are great, may give the son a false conception of the rewards of being an adult male.

The Hostile Parent *

A father who punishes with great severity may appear to be such a dangerous adversary that his son dares not risk incurring his anger. If a boy discovers that rivalry and competition expose him to overwhelming counterattack, he may retreat from competition with his father for his mother's affection either by regressing to a dependent relationship with her or, in some cases, by abandoning women altogether as objects of love.

A hostile mother may frighten a boy in another way. If he sees his father helplessly controlled by his belittling or contemptuous mother, he may interpret his father's capitulation to mean that heterosexual relationships are traps in which women ensnare men and men lose their strength or manhood. This symbolic castration anxiety may be enough to cause him to avoid heterosexuality altogether. If the threat he perceives is not quite enough to cause him to renounce heterosexuality, he may instead repress the entire problem and its dangers and keep it out of consciousness until later social situations reactivate it.

The child's limited capacity to evaluate his environment may cause him to jump to a conclusion about the relationships between men and women before he is mature enough to understand the total situation. If his conclusion is so frightening that he represses it, he loses the chance to reevaluate it as his capacities increase. In this predicament, he continues to respond to the repressed idea in terms of his early view of the environment although he can respond to other related ideas in terms of a later view. This point is illustrated in the following case.

> A twenty-four-year-old man sought help because he found himself so frightened at any demonstration of affection by a girl that he began to fear he never would marry. His mother was a competent but very aggressive professional woman who made the family decisions. She was short-tempered and often blew up over minor problems. Whenever an explosion occurred, her easygoing husband gave in to keep the peace. The patient grew up with the inner conviction that his father was so afraid of his mother's hostile outbursts that he was helpless to take any action. He felt that in succumbing to affection for his mother, his father had in effect lost his manhood as well as his individuality. Consciously he knew that his

---

* In this section, the effect of a hostile parent on the boy is considered; similar considerations with the opposite parent apply to the girl.

father was not so vulnerable and that not all girls resembled his mother, but inwardly he feared that marriage would disable him as he believed it had disabled his father.

During the course of treatment, his attention was drawn to the inconsistency in his attitudes toward his father. He was encouraged to get to know his father better. His father was a successful professional man with a great many civic and intellectual interests, and the patient discovered that his surrender of authority in the home was voluntary rather than a sign of defeat. He began to realize that his father was capable of taking a firm stand with his mother in matters he considered important.

As treatment continued and as the patient began to see that his father had retained his strength in spite of marriage, he lost his fear of an affectionate tie with a girl and terminated treatment. A few months later he married, and still later he reported a successful marital adjustment.

In this case, the father was actually more adequate and a more satisfactory person with whom to identify than the patient had fantasied. The treatment problem is much more difficult when the patient's inner appraisal of the parent of the same sex is more accurate. Under these conditions, the patient ordinarily must go through a long and tedious process of disengaging himself from his identification with the weak and helpless parent and of developing a new identification with a stronger substitute parent—usually the therapist.

The "Seductive" Parent

Often a parent who has lost, or is at odds with, the wife or husband turns to a child for comfort. Particularly when the child is of the opposite sex, there may be seductive implications in the relationship which neither parent nor child recognizes. A mother, for instance, may confide the problems of an unhappy marriage to her son. Her son takes this opportunity to strengthen his tie to his mother, but in the process he pushes his father further out of competition. His sympathetic response encourages his mother to be more confidential, and the bond between them becomes still stronger.

Although the actual exchange of confidences is likely to occur later than the three-to-six-year-old period, the attitudes which encourage this mutual interchange often are established at this time. The serious problem comes in adolescence when the son begins to associate conscious heterosexual feelings with feelings of affection. At this point, he must either give up his mother as his "best girl" or give up his heterosexual feelings, the choice depending to some extent on the closeness of the maternal tie.

Occasionally, the relationship has physical as well as verbal components which make it even harder for the child to give up his parent and which tend to discourage a heterosexual orientation. Some young men with homosexual problems report that their mothers arranged to sleep with them, often in an acknowledged or poorly concealed attempt to discourage their husbands from seeking sexual relations. Such experiences indicate to the boy that sexual relationships are abhorrent to women, at least to "good" women like his mother. They also foster the boy's hope that his mother prefers him to his father.

Contact between father and daughter is usually more subtle in its manifestations than is contact between mother and son, although excessive fondling and caressing may occur between them with similar results. In either case, the child develops a great deal of fear, conscious or unconscious, as a result of his fantasy that the displaced parent is contemplating a drastic form of retaliation.

In common with most classifications in psychiatry, the classification into dissatisfied, hostile, and seductive groups of parents who make a child's identification difficult is an oversimplification. To some degree, there is usually an overlap; the predominantly seductive parent customarily exhibits elements of hostility and dissatisfaction, and other characteristics—partial dependent fixations, for example—may also contribute. These elements also vary in time, so that the degree of a parent's dissatisfaction may be greater during the period in which one child is seeking to establish his identification than it is when his sibling is going through the same period. Finally, for various reasons, one child in a family may be unconsciously selected by the parent as a target for seduction. A term such as "hostile parent," therefore, should be read as shorthand for the "parent who at a crucial time in that particular child's life is perceived by the child as predominantly hostile."

SEXUAL ABERRATIONS

Failure to develop strong identification with the parent of the same sex does not inevitably mean that a child will identify with the opposite sex or become homosexual. There are several possible pathologic solutions to the problem of family rivalry, and it is not always easy to understand why a particular pattern is adopted by a particular individual. Patterns of personality fixation and disturbed character structure are discussed in this section and, to some extent, in the chapter on marital problems (Chapter 8); problems of regression, which produce more acute clinical disturbances, are discussed in Chapter 10. Here again, it is important to recognize that an individual patient may utilize a combination of patterns at varying times and to varying degrees.

Narcissism

The term *narcissism* is derived from the Greek legend of the beautiful youth Narcissus, who fell in love with his own image reflected in a pool. The psychologic concept of narcissism, however, is not completely synonymous with vanity. It means the lack (or relative lack, since there are degrees of narcissism) of an object of love outside oneself. A narcissistic girl, for example, usually has progressed just far enough in her rivalry with her mother to cut herself off from a dependent relationship but never has taken the next step to resolve the conflict or to make a satisfying identification which would help her to give and receive a more mature love. Her fear of her mother's anger stops her at the threshold of a meaningful relationship with her father, and she avoids the rivalry problem by abandoning all external objects of love and by indefinitely prolonging her early orientation of love toward herself. When we speak of narcissistic people, therefore, we usually mean those whose emotional orientation has become fixated to a considerable degree at the level of self-love. They may be vain (and beauty facilitates narcissistic fixation), but they also may be lonely and unhappy.

> An unusually attractive girl had many beaux during her adolescent years. She appeared poised and at ease with them and enjoyed their attentions but never developed any lasting attachments. She married twice, but each marriage broke up over relatively minor differences. As she grew older and less sought after for her beauty, she became depressed over her inability to form a sustained relationship with anybody.

This patient did not cling to anyone in a dependent, childlike fashion, although there were indications that strong dependency needs were present. She had never developed the capacity for more mature relationships and had nothing to fall back on when she could no longer rely for emotional satisfaction on the superficial adulation her physical attractiveness had brought her.

Dissociation of Love and Sex

One way in which the adolescent boy can keep his mother in first place in his affections, avoid conflict with his father, and still retain his heterosexuality is to dissociate love from sexual feeling or to prevent their association. If he can consciously and unconsciously keep the two separate, he can preserve his pure love for his mother and confine his sexual desires to his sexual partner. He uses the cultural attitude that sex is dirty or bad, at least as far as children are concerned, to rationalize that the love between his mother and himself is on a higher plane than that between his mother and father. Unconsciously, he divides women into two groups: respectable, nonsexual, mother types (madonnas) and depreciated, sexual women of the world (prostitutes). Consciously, the categories are not so dramatically differentiated, but boys and men who use this mechanism tend to place their mothers and women identified with their mothers on a pedestal and to develop contempt for any woman who shows evidence of sexual feeling. They either deny the obvious existence of their mothers' sexual activity or assume, often correctly, that their mothers unwillingly submitted.

All their efforts to minimize or to ignore the significance of the parental sexual relationship do not protect them completely from anger at their mothers for participating in an intimacy from which they are excluded. To acknowledge this anger, however, is to acknowledge their mothers' sexuality, and in order to protect their defenses against this awareness, they displace their hostility to the "sexual" woman. A man who dissociates love and sex is apt to choose a marital (sexual) partner whom he considers beneath him socially or intellectually and then to spend his married life criticizing her. For example:

> An extremely wealthy son of a possessive, widowed mother married an attractive daughter of a laborer. Shortly after their honeymoon, she became depressed, stating that he criticized her manners, her clothes, her grammar, her interests, and her failure to respond to his incessant sexual demands. She attempted to change to conform to his wishes but never could satisfy him. She had been aware of his critical tendencies during their courtship but had felt that the security he offered was worth the criticism and that she could conform to his expectations. But whatever she did failed to satisfy him, and the marriage ended in divorce.

There are several other variations of the madonna-prostitute theme. Some men with similar patterns marry motherly women, whom they unconsciously endow with the characteristics they attribute to their own mothers. If they keep their wives on the pedestal, they usually have sexual problems (impotence or premature ejaculation) in marriage, although in extramarital affairs they may be sexually adequate.

> A married man stated that whenever his wife showed any sign of passion, he became "chilled" and could not perform intercourse. On the following day, however, he would pick up a girl at a bar and have relations with her successfully. He rationalized the whole sequence by stating that he needed a sexual outlet and that his wife disgusted him when she—a lady—acted like one of the bar girls.

Some men respect their fiancées and treat them as women beyond reproach as long as they are virgins, but after consummation of the marriage, the wife is virginal no longer and so, more or less unconsciously, is transferred to the prostitute category. Typically, the wife will be sadly perplexed by the switch, complaining: "Before we were married, nothing was too good for me, but since then he treats me like dirt under his feet."

In a case of this type, the wife's motivation for the marriage should be carefully explored. Frequently, it appears that the woman's unconscious conflicts played a significant part in determining her choice of a husband. For example, she may feel so guilty about her attachment to her father that she unconsciously sought as punishment a marriage in which she would be devalued. Or she may be so narcissistic that she took her fiancé's adulation as her due, while her own inability to give love prevented her from properly evaluating her partner. She may even have developed her own dissociation of love and sex in the same way as her husband, a dissociation which permits her to identify with her mother as a mother but not as a wife. Therefore, she relates to all men in a maternal way and is attracted to those who unconsciously are seeking mother substitutes. Whenever there is an emotional disturbance in one marital partner, there is likely to be a complementary disturbance in the spouse. In Chapter 8, I will elaborate on this theme and point out some of the opportunities physicians, social workers and other counselors have to be of help in marital problems.

Sexual Deviations

Homosexuality. There are several possible bases for homosexuality. For example, the surrender of heterosexual goals in favor of homosexual goals is one defense against the seductiveness of the parent of the opposite sex and the anticipated consequent hostility of the parent of the same sex. Since fear of retaliation usually causes this surrender—as if the boy were saying to his father, "Don't hurt me; I don't love mother (or women), I love you (or men)"—it is not surprising that homosexual relationships tend to be jealous and stormy.

Homosexual tendencies in a boy may also result from fear of a hostile mother who sadistically dominates her husband. A homosexual of this type appears to believe, unconsciously, that all women treat men as his mother treats his father, and so, to protect himself, he redirects his sexual impulses toward less dangerous males. He is likely to become an active homosexual partner, whereas those who use homosexuality as a means of placating men tend to become passive partners. A mother may be hostile and seductive at the same time, however, as indicated in the following excerpts from the history given by a twenty-one-year-old soldier who found it hard to keep his homosexual tendencies under control in the intimate living conditions of barracks life.

"Everybody at home gives in to Mother.... She dislikes being alone and always wants me to be with her.... She wants to control me and everyone else. It's perfectly evident she isn't in love with Father.... She has never been affectionate with him; she is much more affectionate to me in front of him.... She wants me to kiss her all the time. It embarrasses me—it isn't natural—it's indecent. I freeze up.... I get the same feeling when I'm out with girls.

"Father is a pretty submissive fellow until he gets riled up; then he can be brutal.... Mother dominates and ridicules him; she is sharp and cruel to him; she really breaks him down. I don't understand why he takes it; I guess he's afraid to leave.... I don't like him; I don't dislike him either, I just feel sorry for him."

A mother may be so hostile toward men that she repudiates the thought of bearing a male child. If she has a boy, she treats him as a girl from infancy. She approves of any feminine interests or manners he shows and often goes so far as to dress him in girls' clothes and braid his hair. It is obvious to the child that his mother expects him to act like a girl and he can only assume either that his father also expects feminine behavior from him or that his father is powerless to interfere with his mother. Both parents thus give him a head start toward identifying with women, and if they also intimate to him that they suspect him of abnormal inclinations or activities, the boy is apt to develop homosexual tendencies.

Homosexuals often rationalize their orientation. Once they have convinced themselves that the homosexual relationship is somehow better than the heterosexual, they lose their incentive for treatment. Those who do not rationalize remain anxious and unhappy. Their homosexual orientation is seldom obvious; they do their best to conceal or suppress it. Often they repress the problem, so that it is not apparent to themselves or to others although it may appear in disguise in dreams or symptoms. In most cases, it is more accurate to speak of the degree of homosexual orientation rather than of its absolute presence or absence; for example, it may appear only under stress situations, as in the following case.

An apparently happily married man complained of infrequent temporary homosexual impulses. Further study revealed that these occurred when the patient was in open conflict with male authoritative figures and disappeared when the conflict was resolved. Although supportive treatment did not remove the basis for the problem, it helped him keep it more completely repressed.

Sometimes, the sexual aspect of the homosexual element may be repressed or latent, although the nonsexual aspects are permitted expression.

> A wife complained that her husband treated her coldly, perfunctorily carrying out the sexual act and in other ways acting as if she were a hired housekeeper. He spent a great deal of his spare time at his club with the "boys" and had developed a confidential relationship with one particular man. The wife had observed that her husband consistently went out of his way to note and condemn behavior in others that might conceivably be considered unmasculine, and she wondered whether he could be protesting too much.

Fleeting, usually disguised, but occasionally conscious evidences of regression to homosexual thoughts or fantasies are so common that they can hardly be considered pathologic. They usually are not too disturbing to men who are secure in their masculinity, but they can precipitate panic in a man who is finding it difficult to maintain repression of homosexual impulses.

For a long time, it was assumed that homosexuality had an endocrine origin. This assumption was fostered by the effeminate appearance of many male homosexuals. There is, however, no evidence whatsoever that endocrine factors cause homosexuality. This conclusion is reinforced by studies of hermaphrodites, whose sexual orientation is determined not by their gonads but by the direction of their upbringing [7]. Hermaphrodites who are brought up as boys usually acquire a male sexual orientation, and if they are brought up as girls, they usually acquire a female sexual orientation. The association of homosexuality with an appearance of effeminacy may be explained by the tendency of fathers who are apprehensive about latent homosexual inclinations in themselves to indirectly encourage homosexual behavior in a delicate, effeminate-appearing son by signaling his expectations [8]. The impact of parental expectations in encouraging other unconventional behavior will be further discussed in Chapter 14.

Since homosexuality does not have an endocrine basis, it is not surprising that it does not respond to substitutive endocrine therapy. In fact, treatment with hormones, if it has any effect at all on the sexual drive, is likely to increase the intensity of the sexual urge without changing its direction. Patients who are not content with a homosexual orientation should be encouraged to discuss their problems with a psychiatrist. Some patients (those with relatively good ego strength and with strong motivation to change their basic homosexual orientation) respond to intensive psychiatric treatment, although it is at best a long and difficult process.

It is sometimes difficult, however, to determine whether a patient who complains of homosexual tendencies should be reassured that his manifestations are within normal limits or whether he should be encouraged to undertake psychiatric treatment. Most people, including physicians who have not had a good deal of clinical experience with homosexuals, find serious discussion of the subject somewhat distasteful and may be tempted to make a premature decision in order to extricate themselves from the situation. As the physician's understanding of the problem in general deepens, he will become more comfortable in postponing an individual decision until he can accumulate enough information to make an appropriate recommendation.

In this section, the discussion has been limited to the consideration of homosexuality in males. Female homosexuality is perhaps almost as common, although in some ways its manifestations are less obvious to others, and perhaps for that reason it is culturally somewhat more acceptable. The dynamics of the development of homosexuality in women resemble in general its development in men, substituting "male" for "female" and "female" for "male."

Other Forms of Deviation.   Other sexual aberrations may result from similar dynamics, although the patient uses different mechanisms. *Fetishism*, for example, represents the displacement of sexual interest from the woman to a part of her clothing or to some object which represents her.

> A young man sought psychiatric help under pressure from his wife, who complained because their year-old marriage had never been consummated. The patient stated that he became panicky at the thought of intercourse. He somewhat shamefacedly admitted that he was sexually stimulated by his wife's shoes but not by her. His earlier history indicated a retreat from adequate heterosexuality, arising from fear of both his seductive mother and his hostile father. The shoe symbolized woman (and mother) but was safer because other men (father) would not be jealous of his affection for it.

In this case, the partial but safer satisfaction of the sexual drive by means of the fetish is substituted for the complete but dangerous total satisfaction of intercourse. Partial satisfaction is also obtained by the peeping tom (voyeur) or by those who seek relationships with children. *Exhibitionism* often seems to represent a symbolic search for reassurance of male adequacy, and other types of sexual perversion generally represent variations on similar themes. The treatment of any well-established perversion requires prolonged psychiatric care.

The fears resulting from family rivalries may not be sufficient to cause a child to retreat from heterosexuality, but they may be so threatening that he uses all his available ego strength to repress them and does not have enough left over with which to work out a satisfactory solution of the conflict. Repressed intrafamily conflicts become potential sources of anxiety which later may be stirred up by relationships with the opposite sex or differences with the same sex. The school child ordinarily can keep them under control, however, until his sexual impulses are biologically stimulated at puberty. Even then, if his ego is strong and if the conflicts are not too intense, he usually can continue to repress the anxiety successfully and can maintain emotional homeostasis in most situations.

If, however, the unconscious conflicts later increase in strength to the point where he can no longer repress them, they threaten to erupt into consciousness. Their threatened eruption forms the basis for many of the neurotic reactions (see Chapter 10).

SUMMARY

In the developmental stage which runs from about three to about six, the child becomes more definitely aware of sexual differences and begins to identify with the parent of his own sex. At the same time, he is learning to give as well as to receive affection. As he gives affection to the parent of the opposite sex, he runs into competition with the parent with whom he identifies. The nature of the resolution of this competitive struggle has a great deal to do with determining the quality of the child's future attitudes and interpersonal relationships.

The most common causes of fixation at the period of family rivalry can be traced primarily to dissatisfied, hostile, or seductive parents. Fixation takes a variety of forms, including homosexuality and other sexual deviations, narcissism, and the dissociation of love and sexuality.

REFERENCES

1. Freud, S.: "On Narcissism: An Introduction" (1914), in *Standard Edition,* 1957, vol. XIV, p. 67.
2. Erikson, E.: "The Problem of Ego Identity," *J. Amer. Psychoanal. Ass.,* 4:56, 1956.
   Freud, S.: "The Ego and the Id" (1923), in *Standard Edition,* 1961, vol. XIX, p. 1.
3. Material on the Oedipus complex and its vicissitudes can be found in:

Brenner, Charles: *An Elementary Textbook of Psychoanalysis,* Garden City, N.Y., Doubleday & Company, Inc., 1957.

Fenichel, O.: *The Psychoanalytic Theory of Neurosis,* New York, W. W. Norton & Company, Inc., 1945.

Freud, S.: *A General Introduction to Psychoanalysis,* New York, Garden City Books, 1938.

————: "Three Essays on the Theory of Sexuality" (1905), in *Standard Edition,* 1953, vol. VII, p. 123.

4. Guntrip, H.: *Personality Structure and Human Interaction,* New York, International Universities Press, Inc., 1961.

5. Freud, S.: "Female Sexuality" (1931), in *Standard Edition,* 1961, vol. XXI, p. 223.

   Thompson, Clara: *Psychoanalysis: Evolution and Development,* Baltimore, The Williams & Wilkins Company, 1950.

6. Friedan, Betty: *The Feminine Mystique,* New York, W. W. Norton & Company, Inc., 1963.

   Parsons, T., and R. F. Bales: *Family, Socialization and Interaction Process,* New York, The Free Press of Glencoe, 1955.

7. Hampson, J. G., J. Money, and J. L. Hampson: "Hermaphroditism: Recommendations Concerning Case Management," *J. Clin. Endocr.,* 16:547, 1956.

8. Johnson, A. M., and D. B. Robinson: "The Sexual Deviant (Sexual Psychopath): Causes, Treatment and Prevention," *J.A.M.A.,* 164:1559, 1957.

Chapter 7

LATER CHILDHOOD, ADOLESCENCE, AND MATURITY

THE SCHOOL CHILD

When a child has succeeded reasonably well in working out the problems presented by family rivalry, he can begin to invest some of his drive to love and be loved in his contemporaries, repressing most of the remaining conflicts about his parents. The ease of this transition depends on the quality of his experiences in earlier stages. Reaching out to others is easier for him if his earlier dependency needs have been satisfied so that he does not have to cling too tightly to his parents. If his experience in the training period has taught him to handle his aggressive feelings comfortably, he can face and overcome his anxiety without regression when others—parents and schoolmates—show their aggressive feelings. Genuine affection and an evident close bond between his parents will help him to resign part of his involvement in the intrafamily struggle. He finally seems to recognize that the odds against him are too great—for the moment, at least—and he gives up the fight. A strong identification with the parent of the same sex encourages this process, and in turn the cessation of hostilities strengthens the identification. He still loves his parents and seeks love from them but in a somewhat less intense manner.

Not all of the conflict is resolved, even under the most favorable circumstances; part of it is deeply repressed, and another part, although controlled, remains close to the surface. In Freud's day, apparently, most of the conflict was hidden in one way or another until adolescence; Freud therefore called the developmental phase between the resolution of the Oedipus complex and the onset of adolescence the *latency period* [1]. During this developmental period, children of both sexes strengthen their relationships with others like themselves. A part of the drive to love and be loved is diverted to strengthening these relationships, and friendships with school children of the same sex gradually become a major interest. Children of this age appear to grow more and more independent of their parents, who note (often with some regret) that the children now prefer to stay and play with their friends than to spend time with their mothers or fathers.

Friendship

To establish satisfying relationships with other children, a child must subordinate in some degree his own needs to the needs of the group. He must be secure enough to share and even to give up some of his individual wants without fear of losing his identity. He must have enough control of his aggressive impulses to be able to assert himself without unduly antagonizing his playmates. Finally, he must be free enough from intrafamilial emotional ties to invest real affection in the friends with whom he identifies and competes.

Brothers or sisters give a child an opportunity for a head start toward friendship. If in earlier years he has learned to share both possessions and family affection and if he has learned to manage his aggressive impulses toward his siblings, the transition to the school milieu is not so difficult. Brothers or sisters, however, by no means provide assurance of an easy transition, and under some circumstances the opposite is true. An insecure older child, for example, may remain partially fixated at the dependency level through competition with a younger child. Since the younger child gets more attention and presumably more love because he is more helpless, the older child remains helpless in an attempt to gain the same love and attention. By contrast, a younger child may feel that he must put up a continuous battle against his older sibling's priority in age and position. These considerations may account for the frequency with which the older child in a two-child family is more dependent and the younger more aggressive. In some families, however, the opposite may occur; the younger child apparently feels that the competition is too tough and remains dependent, while the older fights to keep his place in the family. Middle children often show evidences of both problems, alternating aggressive behavior to catch up with the older and regressive dependency to compete with the younger. There is no position in the family group that guarantees immunity from problems nor any that makes the development of problems inevitable.

Seeing a child begin to move away from his family and form outside friendships is especially difficult for a parent who has turned to his child, usually without realizing it, to satisfy his own dependency needs. In this case, a parent often indirectly attempts to prolong his child's preference for his company.

A seven-year-old girl had trouble making friends at school. Her mother, who had experienced an extremely insecure childhood, discouraged her play with neighbor children. She had rationalizations for excluding each neighbor child; one used bad language, another had inferior standards of cleanliness, a third was from a wealthy family and would give her daughter feelings of inferiority. The mother hoped to move to an isolated home in the country, since neighbors made her "nervous." Although her conscious interest was only in her daughter's well-being, in reality she was unconsciously so dependent that she could not share her daughter's affections with anyone else.

Homesickness and School Phobia

It is so natural to think of the child as dependent on the parent that it is hard to recognize how often the opposite relationship exists concurrently. Adults who unconsciously seek undue dependent satisfactions from their children usually were deprived in infancy by their own parents. Often a dependent parent, by more or less subtle signals, communicates to the child his need for his child to stay at home. The child may then respond to the parent's wish or expectation that he will prefer to stay home by becoming afraid of school (*school phobia*) [2] or homesick.

A nine-year-old boy who had not previously been away from home looked forward enthusiastically to spending four weeks in a summer camp. His mother, although encouraging him to go, warned him about the possibility of homesickness and reassured him so often that he would not be homesick that the boy sensed her expectation. She wrote to the camp explaining that although she had reassured her son, he probably would be homesick and giving elaborate instructions for reaching her at any time by telephone.

When the time arrived, he was the most homesick boy in camp. His earnest and conscientious counselor, however, worked hard and with considerable success to help him adjust. On visitors' day, two weeks later, the parents arrived. As his mother came to meet him, tears in her eyes and arms outstretched, he shouted, "Hi, Mom! See you later; I've got to play ball," and ran off with his friends.

This was too much for the mother. As soon as she could corral him, she took her son off to a corner and described all that he was missing at home, his dog's loneliness, and his friends' new interests. At the end of this recital, she said, "You certainly don't seem to be missing me up here," in a tone of voice that implied, "which you would if you loved me." He was reduced to tears, and with outward reluctance but with evident inner triumph, she packed his clothes and took him home.

It is easy to become critical of this kind of performance. If the physician is overtly critical, however, he only succeeds in antagonizing the mother, which results either in increasing her self-justification or in making her feel inadequate. Thus her dependency is intensified and, with it, her pressure for her boy to meet her needs. Enlisting the mother as an ally in a joint attempt to understand the child's problem, on the other hand, bolsters her self-esteem and, tactfully managed, encourages her to recognize for herself the child's need for independence and the altruistic surrender she must undertake to help him.

Not all homesickness and school phobia can be accounted for by a parent's need to hold on to his child and by his maneuvers to make the child feel guilty if he wants to leave home. Sometimes the child is simply responding to being pushed prematurely to camp or to boarding school. The insecure, dependent child may interpret the event, often correctly, as evidence that his parent wants to get rid of him. Although mild homesickness and school phobia often respond to relatively brief psychotherapeutic efforts by the physician or school counselor, prolonged or recurrent fear of school usually is evidence of a reasonably serious disturbance, and the family should be referred to a child-guidance clinic.

Limits and the Superego

The apparent independence and confidence of most children as they approach puberty may lead parents to overestimate their maturity. In this period, the child is still immature and needs parental comforting to help him counteract external pressures or disappointments. He also needs help with internal pressures, as in the training period he needed limits set by adults to prevent his impulses from getting him into trouble with his environment. If these limits are set too narrowly, the child will not have room to maneuver, to learn from his mistakes, and so to develop judgment. On the other hand, if the child finds it easy to modify the parental limits, he may become anxious because he fears that his impulses will get him into trouble and that no one will step in to protect him. He then may look for a firmer set of limits outside the family circle and perhaps exaggerate their rigidity in order to reassure himself (see page 313).

> An example of this problem was an eight-year-old girl who was troubled with nightmares. Her parents treated her as a miniature adult, always carefully explaining their reasons for a request or a prohibition. If she did not accept their reasoning, they were likely to give in. Although she exploited the situation to get her way, her nightmares frequently followed. By contrast, at school she was unnecessarily compliant, never questioning the most trivial suggestion of her teacher. With help, the parents learned to accept their privilege and obligation to exert authority when necessary; the child eagerly accepted their guidance, and the nightmares ceased. Si-

multaneously, she became less submissive at school, since she no longer needed to go outside her home to search for limits.

As discussed in Chapter 5, some parents who find it hard to set limits are attempting to compensate for ambivalent feelings toward the child. Others are seeking to offset their own childhood experiences with excessively strict parents. In either case, they usually have a genuine desire to do their jobs as parents and generally respond to the physician's support of their good intentions when he helps them to clarify the problem the child is facing. Ordinarily, it is neither necessary nor advisable for the physician without specialized training to attempt to develop parents' insight into their own ambivalence.

The parents' standards continue to be patterns for the child's developing superego. The superego, roughly the equivalent of the conscience, originated in earlier years from the child's identification with his parents and from his incorporation of their standards and their expectations of him (Chapter 5). The standards he incorporates in this way concern chiefly what *not* to do, as contrasted with the ego identification which helps him determine what *to* do. (The superego may, however, exert permissive as well as restrictive influence on behavior, as mentioned before and as further discussed in Chapter 14.)

In the school-age period, the superego is still in a fairly early phase of development. And just as a novice schoolteacher tends to clamp down hard on borderline student behavior, which he later will tolerate, so the child at this point exerts a more rigid, uncompromising control than he will in later years. The rules of the game, whatever it may be, become complex and important, sometimes more important than the game itself. This rigidity is not a sign of strength; rather it conceals the youthful weakness both of repression and of the capacity to find acceptable substitute outlets. The intricate structure of rules, therefore, is susceptible of complete dissolution when someone with weaker controls enters the game. As the intruder takes over without regard for the pattern, the players gradually desert the game or abandon the rules until it ends in a free-for-all. The child's lack of confidence in his ability to control his impulses thus causes him to exert rigid control when he can, compensating for his weakness by extreme rigidity. His behavior resembles that of a compulsive personality who compensates for his weakness in controlling soiling impulses by demanding excessive cleanliness. As the child matures and gains more confidence in his ability to exert controls, he can afford to be more flexible.

Adaptation to School

The behavior and attitudes of school-age children reflect a gradually increasing ego strength, which gives them a greater capacity to coordinate internal drives and external problems. Most of them are able to adapt themselves reasonably well to the extremely complex intellectual and emotional demands made upon them by the modern educational process. The intellectual demands, however, are for the most part scaled to the average student and therefore present problems to children with either more intelligence or less intelligence than the average, as well as to children with specific blocks in learning. This subject will be discussed further in Chapter 13.

In school, the child is expected to adapt himself to teachers and school officials and to establish relationships with other children (the *peer group*). Heretofore, he generally has recognized as authorities only his parents and (occasionally) other relatives, who usually take their cues from the parents. Now, for a large part of the day, the teacher replaces the parent as the authority. Since the teacher's concept of appropriate behavior may differ considerably from that of the parent, the child must adjust to changes in the rules. Every day, as he goes from home to school and home again, the rules change, often confusing him and sometimes encouraging him to set one authority against the other. Children may seek at school what they lack at home; some, like the girl with nightmares just discussed, seek limits at school, while others, rigidly restricted at home, express their independence vigorously in the more lenient atmosphere of school.

Many parents of children who misbehave at school assume that the school is at fault. The school psychologist or social worker or the physician who attempts to handle such problems should keep in mind the possibility that the child is really rebelling against parental authority but can do so only in the schoolroom, where the teacher is too busy to exert individual control. The school is an easy scapegoat for parents; but if the majority of pupils in a group are adjusting adequately, the chances are that the source of problems in one or two members of the group will be found in their homes.

> A nine-year-old boy's consistently unruly behavior culminated in his kicking his teacher. Although there were no similar problems in the class, the boy's mother insisted that the school was entirely at fault for its lack of discipline. She reported that her son was always docile and well behaved at home, which was fortunate because her husband was nervous and ir-

ritable and would strap the children severely if they stepped out of line. She would not consider the possibility that her son was too frightened to express himself at home and was taking out his pent-up aggressiveness against the teacher. She sent the boy to a private school, and when similar problems developed, she found a school with military discipline.

Teachers are naturally more aware of the child who has a behavior problem than of the child who is extremely shy or withdrawn, although excessive shyness may indicate a more severe personality disturbance. Some shy children cling to their mothers, regressing to a preoccupation with the search for dependency, while others remain at the periphery of the group, frightened of the aggressive action demanded by the competitive struggle. Many of these children, if given reassurance and help by their parents, make a reasonably adequate adaptation as they become accustomed to the new situation. Severe degrees of shyness or withdrawal, however, deserve psychiatric evaluation.

Some insecure children, who are not afraid to express aggression but who are unable to subordinate their own wishes, try to get their own way by bullying others. This pattern may be established by the child's identifying with a parent who bullies his child to assert his own fragile identity. In this manner, the struggle for control and authority can be passed down from generation to generation.

ADOLESCENCE

In the period just before puberty, the average child experiences relative emotional comfort. His ego has developed enough to master most of the usual internal and external pressures. He pushes ahead boldly to establish new relationships with friends and to develop new skills. He is reasonably independent and responsible. Confident of his ability to accomplish his goals and to make his decisions, he begins to seek a life more separate from his parents. Until now, his identification has been primarily with his parents; in the process of beginning separation, he reaches out for new objects of identification beyond his parents. By the end of adolescence, in order to be ready for the tasks of adulthood, he must have achieved his own identity, or a firm sense of self, by means of a successful synthesis of his early identifications or part identifications with the unique elements that he alone has contributed [3].

The new objects of identification cover a wide range. For the boy, an older brother, the father of a friend, or the high school athletic hero are possible transitional substitutes for the parents. Sometimes he may choose a more remote object—a television star, perhaps, or a professional athlete, but in any case he begins to draw comparisons between the new and the old objects, with emphasis on the deficiencies of the old. He becomes more critical of his father, and although he by no means discards his earlier identification, he uses criticism as a testing ground for his independence. The success of his tests depends to some extent on his father's tolerance; if the father rigidly clamps down on any sign of rebellion, his son may give up his attempts, at least for a while. If, on the other hand, the father takes criticism so seriously that his feelings are hurt by the unfavorable comparisons, the boy may inhibit his independent strivings, feeling that he may be jeopardizing his own basic security by threatening his father. The father who is secure in his role has helped his son feel secure enough to make the challenge and is prepared to welcome the challenge when it comes.

The girl goes through an analogous period of challenge. Hers is both more intense and less intense than the boy's—more intense because she is in closer contact with her mother, less intense because of the girl's greater subtlety in expressing aggression.

So begins, at a reasonably modulated pace, the child's effort to break away from family protection and to establish his own identity. Just as the process is getting under way, however, the balance between ego and drives is upset. Until puberty the ego (in a child who is relatively secure) has increased in strength faster than the drives, thus exerting an ever-increasing degree of control. Now, within a short time, the strength of the drives increases tremendously, leaving the ego in a relatively much weaker position.

The relative ego weakness generally becomes evident as the familiar phenomena of adolescence. In adolescence, smooth and predictable behavior is ordinarily replaced by clumsy and unpredictable behavior, relative responsibility by relative irresponsibility, and smooth development of maturity and independence by a spasmodic oscillation between demands for equal rights and regression into helpless dependency. The phases of the oscillation are often so irregular that no parent, however astute, can keep up with them.

The average adolescent, halfway between boy and man, wants desperately to be grown up but is appalled at adult responsibilities. Typically, when he looks at what is ahead of him, he retreats into the safety of his home; once safely ensconced under the protective wings of his parents, he feels more secure, his adult strivings take over, he becomes enraged at the failure of his parents to give him the recognition he believes he deserves, and once again he returns to try to master simultaneously both his drives and his environment. Eventually, as he accumulates some successes and particularly if he is able to fall back on the security of parental understanding without too much loss of self-esteem when he fails, his ego begins to catch up with the adolescent surge of instinctual drive. As he discovers that he can identify with his father and still be an individual, he reduces the intensity of his rebellion and moves on into maturity.

Although falling back on parental understanding can give him security when things get tough in his struggle for emancipation, it also represents regression, and he tries to avoid it if he can. Instead of turning to the adversary, therefore, he turns when possible to someone who is on the same side in the struggle. His peers, and often one particular peer, replace the parents as confidants, in person or on the telephone, and the friendships of the school age become intensified.

Meanwhile, he has used several techniques to help him in his struggle for emancipation. One technique is daydreaming, in which he may picture himself in heroic or romantic roles defending the underdog. Daydreaming permits him to structure an adult role and test out its potentialities, to balance a fantasied success against the inevitable buffeting the adolescent encounters in his attempts to be an adult, and to sublimate some of the anger he feels at the frustration of his independent strivings. It also gives him a chance to explore the prospect of adult heterosexual activities and ties without actual involvement. Daydreaming helps him toward maturity, therefore, as long as he recognizes it for what it is and does not confuse it with reality and as long as he does not invest so much of his energy in it that he avoids the realistic problems of adolescence.

The adolescent's idealism is not only expressed in daydreams; he also expresses it in political, religious, or artistic activities through which he attempts intellectually to break away from parental standards and control by building a better world. This dramatization of rebellion has led in the past to the fairly consistent adolescent support of world-remodeling movements, with the older generation—the parents—cast as old-fashioned reactionaries. Psychologic dissections of its origins should not be used, however, to discount adolescent idealism as no more than a symptom; particularly when channeled into constructive efforts for the improvement of mankind, it contributes both to individual maturity and to the betterment of the world we live in. It is no more and no less a symptom than the middle-aged conservatism that opposes it. Adolescents and the middle-aged usually agree on the principle expressed in the last two sentences and only disagree, occasionally with some heat, about which efforts should properly be labeled "constructive."

Rebellion against parental viewpoints, manners, and customs is almost universal in the adolescent's struggle for independence. The conventions of the peer group with which he associates now become significant determinants of his behavior; although a radical in his departure from his old patterns, he remains a conservative in his need to conform to the group mores. The group customs change rapidly and without notice, but adherence to their current pattern is a matter of considerable importance to the adolescent.

The extent of his rebellion against his parents chiefly depends on the adequacy of his superego; if it is strong, he rebels mainly through unconventionality in ideas, dress, table manners, or language. On the other hand, if he enters adolescence with a weak superego, he is not protected against antisocial expression of his impulses and may express his defiance by delinquent behavior (see Chapter 14). But no matter how adequate his superego, he still is much more comfortable if external limits are set for him. He seems to realize that he is not quite ready to carry out his boasts, and he needs the protective assurance that he will not be permitted to go too far. He therefore wants the limits so set up that he can feel free to attack them without the fear that he will overthrow them. The ambiguity of his approach can confuse even the most secure parents, who at times find it disconcerting to be asked subtly for protection and then berated for providing it.

> A high school girl at a party telephoned her mother for permission to accompany her friends on an excursion after the party. The hour would be late, the distance considerable, and the destination not familiar. The mother detected a note of real anxiety in her daughter's voice as she asked: "I *suppose* you won't let me go, will you, Mother?" The mother said she thought it might be wisest for the daughter to come home right after the party. The response came back in a voice now resonant with confidence and loud enough to proclaim to the party the martyrdom its owner suffered: "Oh, Mother, you're so old-fashioned! You never let me do anything that's fun!"

Adolescents do not always check with parents in the hope of receiving a negative answer. But in this case, the limits set by the mother protected the daughter both from going to a party for which she felt unready and apprehensive and from incurring the scorn of her associates for not wishing to conform.

Implications of Sexual Maturation

The increase in the strength of the drives is related to the endocrine changes accompanying puberty. As a child who has resolved most of the problems of family rivalry reaches sexual maturity, his feelings of love

the other hand, those with the weakest egos may give up the fight completely, as will be discussed in Chapter 11.

Occasionally, the progress made in earlier periods toward solving the family-rivalry problem is reversed in the school-age period by ego-weakening circumstances. A long illness will stimulate dependency needs and bring the patient into more intimate contact with his parents and less close contact with his contemporaries. The death of the parent with whom the child identifies may bring him so close to the remaining parent that he withdraws from the search for a contemporary love object. Organic brain damage may weaken the ego and should always be considered as a possible contributing cause to regression. Any of these conditions decreases the adolescent's capacity to handle the recurrence of the family-rivalry problem and may halt or slow down his progress toward maturity.

The illness or death of the mother of an adolescent girl not only permits her to replace her mother in many aspects of family life, thus contributing to the prolongation of her family rivalries, but pushes her prematurely into an adult role. Even when the mother's health is good, the oldest girl in a large family often is given a great deal of responsibility for the care of her younger siblings. Some girls in this position, in spite of backgrounds of early insecurity and unmet dependency needs, appear to grow up very rapidly and seem well able to take care both of themselves and of others at an early age. Closer observation, however, suggests that they use the care of others as an indirect, compensatory method of satisfying their own needs to be cared for. In some ways, their pattern resembles the pseudoindependent personality structure often associated with peptic ulcer (Chapter 4). Predisposed individuals with this personality pattern may develop thyrotoxicosis when circumstances interfere with their opportunities to care for others [5]. The nature of the predisposition which leads to thyrotoxicosis in this situation is not clear, but the evidence is strong that these emotional factors play a definite role in many cases, although the disease does occur in other emotional settings.

Often the physician, and perhaps even more often the clergyman, become involved directly or indirectly in the problems of adolescence. Parents at first may hesitate to ask directly for help with their child's problems. Ashamed of their inability to prevent or to solve the problems and sensitive to anticipated criticism, they bring the adolescent to the physician for a checkup or for a minor complaint. If the physician is patient and postpones definite action until he knows what the parents really are seeking, he can gently help them to reveal their concerns. The physician then is in a strategic position to help them understand their child's erratic and rebellious behavior, and by supporting and reassuring them, he can lighten the child's load.

Sex Education

Occasionally—perhaps less frequently now than in the past—an anxious and harassed parent calls on the physician for help in telling a child the "facts of life." The simplest and best approach to sex education is for the parents to answer the child's questions in a matter-of-fact fashion as they arise, neither postponing the discussion nor telling him more than he wants to know at the time, until by the age of nine or ten the child has accumulated a reasonably satisfactory background of information. This ideal sequence of events is unfortunately more the exception than the rule. So when parents look to the physician for help in this process, it is safe to assume that the parents themselves have problems in the sexual area which keep them from talking to their children about sexual subjects without embarrassment.

The reasons for parents' inability to tell their children about sex or for their attitudes which, conveyed to the children, have discouraged questions about sex are usually complex. They are related not only to cultural taboos against free communication about sexual matters but to self-consciousness arising from the parents' emotional involvement with their children. If the physician attempts to shame the parents into discussing such topics with their child, they either will drop the whole project or will carry it out with such an embarrassed manner that the child becomes more confused than ever. Even when he recognizes the futility of such an approach, however, a physician may continue to unload the responsibility onto the parents in order to protect himself from the same embarrassing situation that frightens the parents.

A physician who is comfortable in his own attitudes about sex can best help such a family by first determining from the parents whether there is any real necessity for a discussion with the child. Often parents become panicky when their children start dating and feel obligated to deliver some sort of lecture; usually by this time the children have been reasonably well informed through other sources, and the physician can help the parents bypass any educational efforts. A reassuring and supportive attitude, however, may open the door to a discussion of parental problems, such as a fear that their child will misbehave sexually. The physician should evaluate these problems carefully and either help the parents or make an appropriate referral (see Chapter 15). In such a situation, he should remember that the parents' primary concern is not their own problem but their child's, and he should avoid being too aggressive in confronting them with problems to which they have made an adequate adaptation. For example, in discussing her embarrassment in talking about sex to her high school daughter, a woman may acknowledge that she has been frigid throughout her twenty years of married life. The enthusiastic doctor should not seek to modify this symptom unless the patient is distressed enough by her frigidity to justify upsetting the rationalizations and other defenses she has established over the years.

If, after talking with the parents, the physician feels that the child needs some sexual education and that the parents are too tense about the subject to do an adequate job, he may suggest that they tell the child frankly that there are some problems connected with growing up which they feel the doctor is in a better position to discuss than they are. All children should know why they are being sent to the doctor, and in a case like this, they should have the privilege of declining to go. If the child does go, the doctor should restrain himself from launching immediately into a lecture on anatomy. He can spend the time more profitably by finding out the child's feelings about the visit and its object; he may discover that no lecture is needed. If the child has some special concerns about which he wishes help, they can decide together on a single interview, a series of interviews, or a referral.

Even when a parent has been extremely conscientious in answering questions, some information may so upset the child that he represses it. For example, a mother carefully explained menstruation to her eight-year-old daughter, but when the daughter started to menstruate at twelve, she accused her mother of failing to prepare her for the event. Usually such girls have associated sexuality with sin or with hostility, and they may interpret menstruation unconsciously as either punishment or injury. Similar conflicts, as well as ambivalent feelings about the role of an adult woman, may contribute to the development of functional dysmenorrhea.

Physical maturity is disturbing to girls whose families have shown a marked preference for boys, to girls who have been trained to be ashamed of any evidence of sexuality or sexual attractiveness, and to girls whose emotional involvement with their fathers is still unusually close. Some of them are so ashamed of their development that they attempt to conceal their menstruation, particularly from their parents, or they bind their breasts tightly to try to hide their figure changes.

Attempts to deny sexual maturity are often more pronounced when puberty arrives early, since the additional problem of nonconformity plagues the child who begins to look, feel, and think in a new way while his contemporaries continue in their old patterns [6]. A child who matures late has similar psychologic problems, which are often intensified if his parents become alarmed over his failure to develop. In such cases, if the physician finds no developmental defects, he can assure the parents of the rather wide variations in the normal age of puberty; he will thus help release the pressure on the child and restore some of the child's essential self-esteem. For girls with this problem—and, for that matter, for any adolescent girl—pelvic examinations should be limited to the minimum consistent with good medicine. Even when a girl consciously recognizes the nature and rationale of a pelvic examination, she frequently equates it unconsciously to an attack, hostile or sexual or both. In all dealings with adolescents, but particularly when sex is involved, a physician is most helpful if he recognizes and respects the child as a proud and sensitive individual who wants to grow up but who is well aware of his limitations.

Warranted reassurance helps the boy whose late maturity makes him feel inferior to his friends. The physician should realize, however, that genital examination may be outwardly embarrassing as well as inwardly threatening to the adolescent boy.

Acne is a serious problem to a great many adolescents, handicapping their already uneasy approaches to companionship with the opposite sex. Surrounded by a composite of fact and legend relating it to sexual development, acne makes the adolescent feel more unlovable than ever. The doctor who attempts to reassure a patient with acne simply by telling him he will outgrow it may reassure his parents but gives small comfort to the patient. He is miserable about it right now and deserves the best available therapy.

Masturbation

Often the physician's acceptance of the seriousness of the problem of acne will open the door to a relationship which is productive in other areas of concern. For example, some adolescents will confide to the doctor their fear that acne is due to *masturbation*. Here again, simple reassurance that there is no relationship between masturbation and acne will not necessarily relieve their fears about masturbation. Since physiologic sexual expression apparently reaches its peak frequency in adolescence, when opportunities for heterosexual relations are customarily limited, it is not surprising that masturbation is an almost universal practice. Religious and cultural considerations combine to produce guilty feelings about masturbation, and the guilt is intensified if the act is accompanied by fantasies of a forbidden or disturbing character. Once more, the physician should not underestimate the significance of the problem to the patient. He can be most helpful, in the average case, if he listens to the patient's concept of his problem, corrects his misconceptions without ridicule, respects the viewpoint of his religion, permits him to keep his fantasies secret if he wishes, and creates an atmosphere of nonjudgmental understanding to which the patient can feel free to return for support as he works out his solutions. A physician who tells an adolescent that masturbation is not physically harmful counteracts his reassurances if he goes on to advise limiting its frequency or to suggest various sublimations which as a rule fail to accomplish their purpose.

Limiting the frequency of masturbation may be important to the adolescent, however, either for religious reasons or to bolster his self-esteem. Adolescents who masturbate more than they wish to are particularly depressed by their apparent inability to exert conscious control over the impulse. The depression is heightened by advice to "use your willpower"; when the advice fails to produce results, they can only assume that they are basically deficient in a vital commodity, and with diminishing self-esteem, their fatalistic attitude about the habit increases. One approach to treatment starts with a joint search by patient and physician for the basis for the patient's initial loss of confidence in his capacity to control. As they explore the background of the problem together, the physician's consistent optimism that the goal of conscious control can and eventually will be attained begins to counteract the patient's pessimism, even though the pessimism has been substantially reinforced by repeated failure and by implicit expectations of failure on the part of parents and others.

For some adolescent patients, concern about masturbation screens more serious problems. Peculiar or bizarre concepts of masturbation or its consequences may signal an incipient schizophrenic reaction (Chapter 11), and here, as elsewhere, a treatment regime should not be undertaken until the symptom has been evaluated in the context of the total personality.

MATURITY

It is difficult to say exactly when adolescence ends. Physically, the adolescent growth spurt levels off at about eighteen years in girls and twenty in boys, but the end of emotional adolescence is more variable and is closely related to social and economic factors. Thus, a high school graduate who goes to work is given a greater environmental push toward adult responsiblity than one who goes to college, and a man who goes to work as soon as he finishes college must adapt to responsibility sooner than one who continues on to graduate school. A long educational process such as that of a physician usually prolongs dependency on the family, and a student unconsciously may undertake it for that reason; on the other hand, since a long period of preparation permits a more gradual assumption of responsibility, it should lead to the exercise of better judgment when full responsibility is finally assumed.

The goal of an adolescent is to attain a sense of identity as an adult, and, with it, the ability necessary for assuming the responsibilities expected of adults [7]. How well an individual assumes these responsibilities and the judgment he uses in carrying them out depend on his experiences in earlier stages of emotional development. If he has been successful in mastering earlier problems and in effecting realistic compromises between his drives and the environment's demands and expectations, he will be free to direct most of his adult energy and attention to current rather than past challenges. The greater the partial fixation at earlier levels, the more energy he directs away from the solution of current problems. And when partial fixations have materially weakened his capacity to meet current problems, he is more likely to give up the struggle and to regress to one fixation point or another. Some of the results of fixation have already been mentioned; in Chapter 10, milder manifestations of regression will be discussed, and in Chapter 11, more catastrophic forms will be described.

In order to be free to focus on current challenges, the adult should have developed a healthy superego, one which is firmly enough entrenched to operate almost automatically. An adult should not have to weigh ordinary decisions consciously in terms of their rightness or wrongness; his superego should automatically and unconsciously eliminate from his choice any solutions which are definitely contrary to his and to society's standards. On the other hand, a superego which is too rigid, so that every decision is dominated by considerations found in the fine print of the code, unduly restricts both freedom of action and adaptability.

The major new responsibilities for which the adolescent prepares as he becomes an adult are those of marriage, parenthood, and vocation. In many ways, the most exacting test in our culture of adult interpersonal relationships is marriage. The success of married life depends not only on the capacity to incorporate adult sexual feelings into intimate relationships but on the ability to give and take within a close and continued personal relationship. Such intimacy contains many potential sources of troubles, and when trouble occurs, the family physician or the minister is usually among the first to hear about it. Their roles in the diagnosis and treatment of marital discord will be explored in the next chapter.

Parenthood also brings problems, particularly when a parent sees his child pass through developmental stages in which unsolved problems of his own occurred [8]. Here again, the family physician or the pediatrician is the logical first source of help for the distressed parent, and in previous chapters some of the ways in which he may give this help have been pointed out.

Although the physician's advice is often sought in problems of vocational choice, his qualifications in this area are limited. He knows a good deal about medicine, but from such a personal point of view that he seldom can be objective, and he knows little about other lines of endeavor. Psychologists trained in vocational counseling are usually available, and their tests, background information, and experience place them in a much better position to give proper guidance and assistance.

The adolescent's experiences in developing satisfactory interdependent, interpersonal relationships, however, contribute a great deal to his satisfaction in any vocation. He usually begins his working years at the low end of a hierarchy, subordinate to a good many superiors, and much of his success depends on his capacity gracefully to accept advice, guidance, and direction. He can do this best if he has learned to associate dependency on others with security and the encouragement of his own development.

Later, his ability to assume leadership becomes equally important and is usually more obvious than his ability to permit others to lead. His conception of leadership, however, also is related to his childhood experience with his parents. As Szurek has pointed out [9], *authoritarian* leadership is quite different from mature and *authoritative* leadership. The authoritarian leader, parent, or supervisor uses his authority to bolster his insecurity through maintaining his control of his subordinates. Since he cannot relinquish leadership without threatening his security, he finds it difficult to recognize or to foster leadership talents in the people he needs to control.

The authoritative leader, parent, or supervisor, on the other hand, is confident of his qualifications for leadership and does not require external trappings to bolster his confidence. He also does not need to hold on to leadership indefinitely to maintain his identity. He can enjoy the prospect of growth in his children and subordinates. He can look forward with pride and realism to the time when their capacities for leadership exceed his, and he can willingly turn over the reins to a competent successor. The authoritative parent, therefore, is not personally threatened by his child's development and so can encourage unlimited growth in his child without ambivalence.

When an adult is relatively free from fixation at earlier developmental stages, he can give as well as receive affection and fit into an interdependent family unit characterized by mutual respect. Although his primary objects of affection are his spouse and his children, he can also invest affection in friends, relatives, and associates, permitting his family to do the same. He has channeled most of his aggressive drive into constructive accomplishment and competition in work and recreation, and he is able to lose as well as to win gracefully. He can appropriately postpone both the satisfaction of his needs and the expression of his irritation according to the demands of his culture. Content with his own role as homemaker or provider, he neither envies nor depreciates the role of his partner. Although parenthood is not essential to a satisfactory adult adjustment, it is a goal of most adults, and they regret (although they also adjust to) any circumstances which prevent its attainment.

SUMMARY

The years from about six to the onset of puberty give the child an opportunity for ego and superego strengthening with some respite from intense emotional involvement. The child establishes relationships outside the family and develops the techniques of friendship. He builds up some reserve strength with which to face the adolescent onslaught of instinctual and environmental pressures.

The adolescent deals with two major interrelated problems: the urge for emancipation from his family and sexual maturity. He needs both encouragement and limits as he struggles to establish himself as an adult and as he endeavors to gain control of his stimulated drives. He needs to work out his relationships with his parents, particularly with the parent of the opposite sex, before freeing himself sufficiently to set up patterns for mature heterosexuality. An understanding of the particular areas of stress in adolescence permits the physician, clergyman, or other counselor to be of considerable help to both parents and child in this difficult period.

REFERENCES

1. Freud, A.: "The Latency Period," in *Introduction to Psychoanalysis for Teachers*, London, George Allen & Unwin, Ltd., 1931.
2. Eisenberg, L.: "School Phobia: A Study in the Communication of Anxiety," *Amer. J. Psychiat.*, 114:712, 1958.

3. Blos, Peter: *On Adolescence,* New York, The Free Press of Glencoe, 1962.
Erikson, Erik H.: "The Problem of Ego Identity," *J. Amer. Psychoanal. Ass.,*
4:56, 1956.
Freud, A.: "Adolescence," *Psychoanal. Stud. Child,* 13:255, New York,
International Universities Press, Inc., 1958.
Gardner, G. E.: "Present-day Society and the Adolescent," *Amer. J. Ortho-
psychiat.,* 27:508, 1957.

4. Freud, S.: "Three Essays on the Theory of Sexuality," in *Standard Edition,*
1954, vol. VII, p. 123.

5. Ham, G. C., F. Alexander, and H. T. Carmichael: "A Psychosomatic Theory
of Thyrotoxicosis," *Psychosom. Med.,* 13:18, 1951.

6. Rafferty, F. T., and E. S. Stein: "A Study of the Relationship of Early Me-
narche to Ego Development," *Amer. J. Orthopsychiat.,* 28:170, 1958.
Schonfeld, W. A.: "Body-image Disturbances in Adolescents with Inappropriate Sexual Development," *Amer. J. Orthopsychiat.,* 34:493, 1964.

7. Whitehorn, J. C.: "A Working Concept of Maturity of Personality," *Amer.
J. Psychiat.,* 119:197, 1962.

8. Benedek, T.: "Parenthood as a Developmental Phase," *J. Amer. Psychoanal.
Ass.,* 1:389, 1959.

9. Szurek, S. A.: "Emotional Factors in the Use of Authority," in Ethel L.
Ginsburg, *Public Health Is People,* New York, The Commonwealth Fund,
1950, p. 206.

Chapter 8

MARRIAGE AND MARITAL PROBLEMS

Harmonious marriage requires that two people share their problems and responsibilities. To respect, trust, and protect each other, to work together and at the same time to retain separate identities calls for maturity in a man and in a woman. If each is to rely on as well as to protect the other, they must be interdependent; that is, each must have the capacity to be dependent, to be independent, and to accept the partner's dependency as the situation requires. As some of the examples in Chapter 4 have shown, it is not always easy for an adult to permit himself dependency. If as a child a man could not trust those he depended on, as an adult he will find it hard to permit his wife to take responsibility, make household decisions, handle money, or care for him when he is ill.

Mutual respect usually accompanies mutual trust. Superior or envious attitudes toward the opposite sex or toward the significance of the spouse's role in the marriage interfere with respect. Mutual respect, when both partners are free of major unsolved fixations in the area of family relationships, makes it possible for a husband and wife comfortably and maturely to express their love for each other in all terms, including the sexual.

A satisfactory preparation for marriage, therefore, requires a satisfactory childhood; if there are serious deficiencies in emotional development, they are not likely to be corrected by two or three sessions of premarital counseling. On the other hand, marriage itself is a growth experience; few couples enter marriage fully equipped to relate maturely to each other, but most couples are not so handicapped by their fixations that they cannot learn and develop through the give and take of marriage. Counseling, however, often can help them make faster progress than otherwise might be the case.

187

PREMARITAL COUNSELING

Couples planning marriage are often advised to have a talk with their physicians to develop a better understanding of the psychology and the physiology of sex. An informative chat, with or without diagrams, suffices for some. Others will have specific concerns which they may be too embarrassed to reveal without some help. Here, as in the case of the adolescent who is referred by his parents for sex education, the physician may lose the chance to discover the basis of the trouble if he launches prematurely into a discourse on physiology. Medical training prepares a doctor to speak in anatomic terms which many laymen consider vulgar, and his attempts to educate may further embarrass a patient already too embarrassed to express his concerns. Ordinarily, by the time they plan marriage, a couple has acquired sexual information in one way or another, even though they may be too diffident to discuss easily what they already know.

The physician's first step, therefore, may be to make it easier for them to tell him specifically where they need help. This requires privacy (fiancés are ordinarily best interviewed separately, at least for initial interviews) and an unhurried willingness to listen and to let the patient beat around the bush awhile before coming to the point. He wants and needs to be taken seriously, and a physician who conceals his own discomfort in this situation by facetiousness or an off-color remark may cause the patient to abandon altogether the effort to solve problems which may interfere with the harmony of the marriage.

Once the patient does get to the point, his questions may cover a wide range, including various combinations of anatomic, physiologic, psychologic, and moral problems. Generally, direct answers suffice when the physician is qualified to give an answer, but occasionally an apparently simple question conceals a major problem. For instance, a young woman may seek reassurance that she has no anatomic limitations to painless intercourse. In such a case, reassurance based on a physical examination and the explanation that the vagina is a highly muscular passageway with a considerable range of painless dilation and contraction (as demonstrated in the birth process) may be enough. On the other hand, the doctor should be alert to the possibility that her fear that the penis is too large or the vagina too small may be an outward sign of an inner belief that any act of intercourse is the same as rape—inevitably a hostile or destructive act. If anatomic reassurance seems to be insufficient, he should encourage her to express her concern about other aspects of the marital relationship. Painful intercourse (*dyspareunia*) usually results from a woman's unconscious association of hostility and sexuality. This association stirs up anxiety during intercourse, producing painful vaginal muscular spasm (*vaginismus*). The patient with dyspareunia generally needs treatment of her emotional problem rather than treatment directed exclusively to the symptom.

Premarital problems may be introduced by questions concerning contraception. Patients asking such questions also may be embarrassed, and may need time and encouragement to express their underlying anxieties. On the other hand, some patients want and are entitled to examination, technical advice, and prescriptions or fitting of contraceptive devices with a minimum of discussion. The physician who is sensitive to the nuances of the patient's communication of her request can usually discern if the patient is really asking for more help than simple clinical information. In the area of contraception the physician should be familiar with the points of view of churches other than his own in order to work within the patient's religious restrictions as well as within his own.

A patient, most often a woman, who feels guilty about an earlier affair may confess it to her physician during a premarital visit. The doctor can help her most if he listens to her seriously and with forbearance, neither condemning her nor cutting her off with glib reassurance. If the doctor identifies too strongly, consciously or otherwise, with the prospective husband, he may be tempted to encourage her to tell her fiancé. A case can be made for the ideal of withholding no secrets from a mate; revealing an earlier, intimate, presumably affectionate relationship with someone else, however, may not be essential for marital harmony, may be motivated by ambivalent feelings, and may provide ammunition which one partner can use against the other in later quarrels. On the other hand, if the doctor takes the initiative in encouraging her not to tell her fiancé, he may by implication reinforce her guilt.

A patient who, because of emotional problems, seeks help prior to marriage may be concerned about his readiness for marriage or his choice of a partner. As the time for the wedding approaches, he may develop mild anxiety or depressive reactions or may even demonstrate conversion symptoms. Premature advice, either to go ahead and forget his worries or to call the marriage off, may influence the decision of a suggestible individual, but his basic problem remains untouched. Many patients of this type will talk themselves out of their fears if given an opportunity; those who are too immature to accept the type of responsibility marriage demands or whose choice of a partner is determined mainly by neurotic considerations may, by talking their problems over with a physician, develop enough understanding of themselves to decide to postpone the wedding until they have worked out their emotional difficulties. The physician should avoid making decisions for his patient, particularly in areas in which his own bias plays a significant part, but he need not remain completely silent; by objective clarification of the issues involved (see Chapter 15), he can help the patient to make his own decision.

APPROACHES TO MARITAL PROBLEMS

Adjustment problems during or just after the honeymoon often can be dealt with in the same way as premarital problems, but later marital problems are usually more difficult and require considerable diagnostic and therapeutic skill. Social workers in family agencies, psychologists trained as marriage counselors, and ministers probably see more marital problems defined as such than do physicians. The physician's patient seldom presents a marital problem directly; instead, he may mention it during the course of a visit for a physical illness, or he may acknowledge its existence while the doctor is searching for corroborative evidence to back up a tentative diagnosis of emotional illness.

> While a gynecologist was taking the history of a twenty-six-year-old housewife who complained of dysmenorrhea, his patient revealed that her marriage was not very satisfactory. Although she had a college education, her husband treated her as a housekeeper, never discussing his intellectual interests with her. When the physician explored her background, he learned that her husband was still dependent on his parents and frequently compared his wife unfavorably with his mother.
>
> The patient later revealed that she was not receiving satisfaction from sexual intercourse. She explained that her husband's perfunctory approach made her feel that she was simply being used to provide satisfaction for him without regard to her needs.

In a situation like this, a physician may be tempted to see the whole problem as a result of the husband's sexual attitude and to call him in for a talk on techniques of lovemaking, accompanied perhaps by some fatherly advice on the importance to a marriage of loosening parental ties. If the husband is somewhat passive, he may docilely accept the lecture, express his thanks, and leave. He feels chastened but slightly resentful that he has not had a chance to defend himself, his wife feels justified in considering her husband exclusively to blame, and the doctor believes that the problem is solved. In fact, both the sexual manifestations and the unfavorable comparisons to his mother in such a case represent symptoms rather than basic causes of his problem. And although symptomatic treat-

ment may produce temporary improvement, it seldom prevents later re-
currences of the same problem.

In the example given above, however, the physician gave the husband
a chance to discuss the marriage.

> He complained that his wife nagged him over trifles, that she belittled
> his business accomplishments, and that whenever he attempted to discuss
> things logically, she would get angry and bring up past incidents as evi-
> dence of his incompetence. Since he never could recall these incidents as
> well as she could, he felt unable to cope with her, so that he had gradually
> given up trying and had turned more and more to his own family for
> support and encouragement. He attributed their sexual problem to his
> wife's martyrlike attitude, by which he meant that she made him feel
> intercourse was an unpleasant chore for her, to be endured as briefly and
> as infrequently as possible.

At this point in a case, where such clear evidence of misunderstanding
exists, a doctor, an attorney, a minister, or whoever is attempting to provide counsel may decide to get both parties in his office and arbitrate the
dispute. Admonishing them both on their respective roles and sending
them off with mild chastisements may produce a brief illusion of success,
but the illusion is soon dispelled. When the next point of contention
arises, each accuses the other of ignoring the counselor's advice, and the
old battle lines are re-formed.

The counselor also may have temporary success if he listens to both
sides and attempts to judge each argument on its merits. This technique,
however, will eventually get him into trouble. By deciding each issue, he
implies that the couple cannot make such decisions for themselves, and he
encourages their dependency on him. Instead of a running start toward a
more mature relationship, he fosters regression and more immature means
of arriving at answers. The result is the same as when a parent always
settles conflicts among his children without permitting them the growth
experience of finding their own answers; they bring more and more problems to the parent, and the losers—in this type of arbitration, both parties usually consider themselves losers—develop the feeling that the decisions are based on prejudice in favor of the opponent, so that bitterness is
engendered all around.

When a counselor plays the role of a referee, more often than not he
eventually gets angry at both principals, feels that his efforts are unappreciated, and withdraws from the field of battle. He can protect himself
from this unfortunate and unproductive sequence of events if he treats
individual quarrels and grievances as symptoms of an underlying disturbance. The counselor can never settle all differences of opinion in a mar-

riage, but he may be able to help each partner eliminate the emotional blocks which keep the couple from working out solutions together. Grievances and quarrels develop in most, if not all, marriages; they become problems only when the husband and wife lack the capacity to resolve them.

It is, therefore, more constructive to look at any marital problem from the point of view of each partner's personality rather than to attempt to classify the problem according to its sexual, financial, or religious manifestations. Since mature individuals are seldom sufficiently attracted to the immature to marry them, accurate family diagnosis requires an understanding of both partners. The counselor should also know that people with certain types of personality makeup often seek complementary types of spouses. They thus establish in marriage a *neurotic balance,* or *neurotic complementarity,* which, although vulnerable to external pressures, tends to keep the marriage together. An overzealous attack on one partner's neurosis without taking the other's into account may upset the balance and with it the marriage [1].

In the next few pages, I shall discuss the effects on marriage of partial fixation at early developmental levels, indicating as I go along some of the neurotic balances which may result.

NEUROTIC BALANCES IN MARRIAGE

Chronic Dependency

A man or woman with considerable dependency fixation seeks to receive love from his spouse but cannot give love in return except, perhaps, synthetically as a device to receive more love. If he or she marries someone whose own emotional needs lead him to take the place of a parent instead of a spouse, the couple may achieve a *parent-child balance,* often encountered in cases where alcoholic men have married long-suffering maternal women (see Chapter 4). This balance is always somewhat delicate. Illness or pregnancy of the wife, for example, may be seriously disrupting, since it reverses the direction of the dependency relationship so that the husband is forced to take responsibility and the wife is forced into the dependent position she has been struggling to avoid.

Husbands do not always play the child role in parent-child balances, and it is usually easier to maintain a stable balance if the wife plays the child. However, if she is too much of a child—like Dora, for example, in Charles Dickens's *David Copperfield*—or if a baby provides too much competition, the balance will be upset.

If both husband and wife suffer from uncompensated dependency fixations, a balance is difficult to establish, since each seeks only to receive love from the other. Both give up easily in the face of conflict, and each may return to his parents, projecting the blame for the separation on the other. However, if both partners can invest their dependency needs in an external parental substitute, a balance may be established. Occasionally, the church becomes the major source of emotional support for both, reducing the pressure on each to give to the other and allowing the balance to be maintained.

Some dependent couples move into the parental home of one or the other and act almost as brother and sister, competing and quarreling for parental attention and showing little sexual interest in each other. The balance in this situation may be upset when a parent dies or when circumstances force the couple to move. Although living with in-laws is generally an unsatisfactory expedient in a marriage, there are some marriages that cannot survive in independent quarters.

Chronic Hostile Dependency

Some of the examples in Chapter 5 illustrated how children who have been deprived of security satisfactions resent their deprivation either consciously or unconsciously and carry over their hostility as well as their unmet dependency needs into adult life. They often attract each other, apparently because they share the same attitudes toward people, but once married, they take turns controlling and punishing each other. This apparently unstable equilibrium can produce a *hostile-dependent*, or *sadomasochistic*, balance, in which the wife usually appears to observers to be consistently helpless or masochistic and the husband hostile or sadistic. The apparently one-sided character of the relationship gains credibility when the husband acts out his sadism: it is difficult to consider sadistic a wife who frequently shows signs of physical beatings. A closer view, however, often discloses that between his explosions, she nags, needles, and prods her husband unmercifully and that the neurotic teeter-totter is more frequently weighted by her subtle sadism than by his more overt hostility. Although the aggressive element in this type of marriage is more spectacular, the couple's mutual dependency is frequently enough to keep them together in spite of the constant atmosphere of attack and counterattack.

Prolonged Family Rivalries

Partial fixations at the period of family rivalry set the stage for later marital conflicts by causing intense, unresolved ambivalent feelings toward parents to continue into adult life. Their specific effects on marriage vary, but all marriages between partners with unresolved family rivalries are subject to in-law troubles. Many possible combinations can lead to friction; a few of the most frequent patterns are described below.

"Housekeeper" Marriage.   A man overattached to his mother has little affection to give his wife. He marries her primarily for sexual reasons; he is often scornful of her intellectual, cultural, and social attributes, compares her unfavorably with his mother, and considers her qualified only for menial work (see Chapter 6). The wife feels devalued and resents the primacy of his mother in her husband's affections, and trouble between the two women ensues, with the husband taking his mother's part. Hostile feelings toward his idealized mother are displaced to his wife, who finds herself on the receiving end of a lot of apparently unprovoked hostility.

If, as often happens, he marries a woman who feels insecure about her femininity or who feels guilty about her own attachment to her father, she may be willing to accept a depreciated role. The balance is maintained unless he carries his hostile displacements too far or unless for some reason she becomes aware of and dissatisfied with her role. In the opposite picture, a girl who keeps her love for her father inviolate is often attracted to a man guilty enough about his own involvement with his mother to accept a servile position in the family.

Role Reversal.   If a man's unresolved conflicts with his father have made it hard for him to play the role of a husband, he either does not marry at all or finds a mate who cannot identify as a wife and who has a strong need to compete with men. This produces a marriage in which the customary masculine and feminine roles are reversed, the wife wearing the pants while the husband wears the apron. A reasonably satisfactory neurotic balance may be maintained in this situation unless something happens to intensify the husband's need to assert his masculinity or the wife's need to assert her femininity. Pregnancy, by forcing the wife into a more passive position and again reversing the roles in the marriage, usually stirs up conflicts, since both partners are deprived of their previous neurotic satisfactions.

Readjustment of roles within a marriage is difficult no matter what circumstances bring it about; thus the balance in a marriage begun when the husband is a student and the wife a wage earner may be seriously upset when the husband graduates and takes over income-producing responsibilities and the wife stays home to take care of the children.

Narcissistic Marriages.   Individuals who are partially fixated at the stage of self-love have never developed the capacity to invest their love in others. They seek admiration from others rather than the opportunity to share affection, and when they marry (if they do marry), their marriage ties are brittle. Admiration cannot always be forthcoming, and when it is not, they accuse their wives (or husbands) of not appreciating them and often look elsewhere to find support for their narcissism. This factor often has been implicated in speculations about possible causes of the fragility of some marriages among actors and actresses.

These categories are useful only as points of departure in understanding individual marriages and not as definite diagnostic entities. There is even more overlap in the classification of family patterns than there is in personality diagnosis. For example, the marriage of the gynecologist's patient discussed in the previous section has elements of the housekeeper marriage on the husband's part and of role reversal on the wife's.

Disturbances of the Neurotic Balance

If, in the course of a precariously balanced marriage, life experiences foster substantially greater psychologic growth in one partner than in the other, the balance may be disturbed. This phenomenon may account in part for the high divorce rate among early marriages and represents an argument against contracting marriage in adolescence or before the emotional growth curve has begun to level off. Rapid change in social or economic status also may upset the balance if one partner is better prepared for the change.

The fact that divorces are more frequent in childless families should not be interpreted to mean that a marriage can be saved by having a child. Actually, the addition of a child almost inevitably complicates a marital problem, and although the couple may decide not to separate for the sake of the child, the conflict persists and the child is brought up in an atmosphere of hostility and insecurity. The child usually becomes a pawn in the struggle and seldom can disengage himself enough to mature emotionally beyond the stage of family relationships.

The birth of a child may precipitate a marital problem, particularly when a somewhat passive-dependent husband or wife resents the infant's priority in competing for dependency satisfaction. A mother who has trouble identifying sufficiently with her own mother to accept a feminine role may find motherhood a difficult adjustment. Many of these women repress their ambivalence toward the child and displace their resentment to the child's father, with resulting marital discord. Having a baby on medical recommendation does not make a woman who resents her role more feminine but merely confronts her with problems which she is not prepared to overcome. The same rationale applies to the adoption of a child; it should never be prescribed to solve a marital problem or to make a woman more feminine.

MARITAL COUNSELING

The Marital History

The physician, clergyman, social worker, marriage counselor, or attorney, therefore, should always look beneath the symptoms of marital conflict to the underlying personality problems. It is also important, in the exploratory stage, for him to evaluate the history of the marriage. Was this match impulsive or was it well considered? Was there a period of time when the marriage was successful, when each partner met the other's needs? Could they ever communicate their needs and feelings to each other, or has there been a breakdown of communication between them? What were the circumstances surrounding the onset of the problems? The answers to these questions provide important prognostic information. For example, a forced marriage between two casual acquaintances who never have communicated or adjusted to each other has an extremely remote chance of developing into a mutually satisfying relationship. On the other hand, a couple who were in love for some time before marriage and who spent several happy years before environmental stress touched off their conflict have a much better chance of working out their difficulties.

For many years, it has been customary to diagnose and treat the partners in a marriage conflict separately, preferably with a separate therapist for each partner. This procedure has been standard in most family- and marriage-counseling agencies and was based on the theory that in evaluating a marital problem, one should be more concerned with the two combatants than with the combat [2]. Lately, some doubt has been cast on the necessity or even the desirability of rigid adherence to this policy, and some investigators believe that the goal of restoration of a disturbed marital balance can often be better achieved when the marital couple is seen together [3]. In either case, as each partner tells his story, he usually tends to project the blame on to the other. A premature attempt to overcome the projection antagonizes him; the counselor often must listen for some time to the projection with an attitude of interested neutrality before he gets an opportunity to relate the problem to the circumstances of its onset and thus lead up to the earlier history of the marriage. In exploring its history, he can bring out the strengths as well as the weaknesses of the marriage, and he can try gradually to make the sessions into cooperative investigations of the causes of the trouble rather than struggles to enlist the counselor as an ally against the spouse. The goal is not to get the facts and deliver a judgment but to help each partner look at his own role objectively. It is therefore important for the counselor to be objective from the beginning, not to take sides, and not to become a weapon in the hands of either contestant.

Goals and Techniques

A husband and wife usually come for help because they want to save their marriage, but in most cases, they have considered separation. Although the counselor will want to improve the marriage, he should recognize that the final decision to work it out or to separate is theirs. If he feels that they must remain together, he may unwittingly push them in the opposite direction. As he begins to represent to them an authoritarian, parental figure, forcing them to behave as he wants them to, they may feel under pressure to separate simply to prove their independence.

The goal of marital counseling is to help each partner look at the marriage objectively and then, if he feels it is worth working for, modify his own attitudes and behavior so as to restore the previous balance or to arrive at a new, more satisfactory balance. The usual method is psychologic support of each partner, individually or together, with the occasional judicious and conservative use of environmental modification. Each is helped toward more satisfactory communication with the other, so that they can eventually work out compromise solutions to their problems as they arise. Compromise is difficult to accomplish unless both partners voluntarily participate, and it requires both tact and patience to gain the cooperation of the partner—usually the husband—who is not the original complainant. His cooperation is worth waiting for, however, because in the long run better compromises and adaptations can be made if each partner either shares in the procedure or knows that the other is going through a similar process of self-evaluation [4].

The gynecologist mentioned earlier in this chapter might use the techniques of marital counseling in approaching the problem brought up by the wife with dysmenorrhea. He might feel, however, that this technique required more time than he could give or that he was temperamentally unsuited to carry it out. His best move in that case would be to refer the couple to a family agency or a professionally qualified marriage counselor or any other suitable community resource.

Still other patients involved in marital problems suffer from neurotic reactions which may benefit more from intensive psychotherapy on the level of insight development than from marital counseling. Since a couple's incentive to seek professional help for marital problems is weakened by multiple referrals, it is important for the physician or clergyman to investigate any marital problem that comes to his attention thoroughly enough to make an appropriate referral if referral is indicated.

Postmarital counseling is also important, although perhaps not a separate category of counseling. The significance to a widow or widower of expressing grief was discussed in Chapter 1; following divorce or separation, it may be less difficult to mobilize ambivalent feelings, but problems of loss of self-esteem and shame at failure to make a success of marriage are complicating factors. Occasionally, a severe set of environmental stresses mobilizes the conflicts of one partner, usually the husband, to such a degree that he precipitately deserts his family, leaving the wife to cope with her grief, anger, and shame, as well as with the whole burden of the environmental stress. The family physician or clergyman is usually the first professional person to whom the deserted wife turns, and his support may be crucial to her success in maintaining her own and her children's stability through the period of immediate crisis.

SEXUAL PROBLEMS

Sexual difficulties often accompany marital problems, but they are usually the result rather than the cause of disturbed interpersonal relationships and are symptomatic of more extensive personality troubles. The few that appear in isolated form may respond to educational techniques, usually directed toward helping the husband recognize the importance of foreplay in preparing his wife for the act of intercourse. Some marital problems, on the other hand, occur without gross sexual incompatibility; a husband who compares his wife unfavorably to his mother in everything else may be able to demonstrate a modicum of synthetic affection toward her in connection with the sexual act. He dissociates love and sex, reserving his real affection for his mother and sex for his devalued wife.

Perhaps the most common sexual complaint the doctor hears is a wife's objection to her husband's demands. She may preface her complaint by asking the apparently casual question: "How frequently should a couple have intercourse?" The doctor is wise to defer answering this question and should instead attempt to discover what is back of it, for she may be looking for ammunition against her husband in a conflict involving scheduling of intercourse. In this case, any answer he gives will align him with one side or the other without his knowledge.

Husband and wife often give discrepant estimates of the frequency with which they have intercourse. This discrepancy results from the difficulty (Kinsey et al. to the contrary notwithstanding [5]) that most people have in recalling accurately this particular type of statistic and possibly also from differences in interpretation. For example, a wife may interpret nightly caresses, endearments, or even facial expressions as invitations and say, "He *wants* intercourse every night," while her husband complains, "We only *have* intercourse once a month." Although there are great individual differences in sexual desire, mature couples ordinarily arrive at satisfactory compromises. When no compromise has been reached, the physician should direct his attention to the basis for their failure to work it out.

Frigidity

A complaint of frigidity should be evaluated in relation to its degree and to its course. Ordinarily, *frigidity* is defined as a complete lack of sexual response. *Relative frigidity,* in which the woman is somewhat responsive although she fails to attain orgasm, is more common. When frigidity develops during marriage, it is usually a symptom of a neurotic regression, often precipitated by marital conflict [6]. Resolution of the conflict frequently leads to removal of the symptom. On the other hand, women who have always been frigid usually are suffering from a partial fixation at the level of family relationships and are likely to require more intensive psychiatric treatment. In these women, affectionate relationships are unconsciously so closely tied to family relationships that enjoyment of sexual satisfaction produces more guilt than they can tolerate.

Another type of frigidity occurs selectively in marital relations or in relations with men who are respected and loved. These women resemble the men described earlier who unconsciously separate affection and sex. They can experience sexual satisfaction only in casual or clandestine contacts or with depreciated men. Sometimes a woman who experiences sexual satisfaction in premarital contacts with her fiancé becomes frigid as soon as they are married; apparently she must stop enjoying sexual relationships when they become respectable. This possibility is one of the factors that makes premarital testing of sexual compatibility an unreliable procedure. Such testing is equally unreliable for a woman with a strong superego who can adjust well within the marital relationship but who may feel too guilty about premarital relationships to respond.

Impotence

Relative impotence in the man may develop under similar circumstances and for the same reasons as frigidity in the female. Relative impotence occurs only under conditions of intercourse and does not interfere with morning erections, nocturnal emissions, or (usually) masturbation. Absolute impotence, or impotence under any conditions, is rarer. Although absolute impotence also may be caused by emotional factors, neurologic lesions or endocrine dysfunction must first be considered. In relative impotence, an erection may occur prior to intercourse but is lost just before intromission, almost as if the man were afraid that his penis would injure or be injured by the woman's genitals. Impotence is less common than frigidity but is usually a source of greater concern to the patient, perhaps because it is less easy in our culture for a man to rationalize impotence than for a woman to rationalize frigidity. Early recognition of the emotional causes of impotence is important in order to help the patient receive psychiatric treatment at the optimal time [7].

> A forty-three-year-old man was referred for treatment of impotence of five years' duration. Although physical and neurologic examinations had been negative and although a capacity for erectile activity was present, as revealed by a history of frequent morning erections, he had been treated for five years by testosterone injections, prostatic massages, and vitamins, while no attention had been paid to the precipitating marital problem. The severity of the marital problem had increased, partly as the result of his impotence, and over the five years so much bitterness had developed on both sides that the marriage ended in divorce before psychiatric treatment could get under way.

Psychiatric treatment does not, of course, guarantee a cure for impotence, but its chances of success are greatest when the duration of the symptoms is short. Endocrine treatment is contraindicated in most cases of relative impotence due to emotional conflict; if it intensifies the sexual drive, it only increases the conflict and the consequent anxiety. When it is apparently successful, the success is likely to be the result of suggestion rather than of the specific replacement substance and usually occurs only in cases of "failure anxiety," in which an initial episode of failure, due perhaps to fatigue or alcohol, has sensitized the patient to the anticipation of continuing failure. The resultant anxiety at the time of the next attempt absorbs all his attention; he has none left over for the sexual act itself, and the vicious circle continues. If he is convinced that the endocrine treatment is the answer, he may overcome his anxiety to the point where he can concentrate his energies on his performance. Under these circumstances, however, it may be difficult to persuade him to give up the endocrine "crutch," and continued endocrine treatment not medically indicated may have undesirable repercussions. Furthermore, if the strength of the suggestion is not sufficient to overcome his anxiety, his confidence in his physician will be reduced and the size of the therapeutic job increased.

Premature ejaculation is more frequent than impotence; it has similar dynamics but represents a slightly less intense fear of the woman or of the patient's own destructiveness. The patient is not so frightened that he cannot penetrate the woman's genitals, but he acts as if he were frightened enough to want to get away as soon as possible. Here, too, treatment depends on the duration of the problem; if it is of recent development, it may respond to adjustment of conflicts in the marriage, but if it is of long duration or if it persists despite successful marital counseling, psychiatric care is indicated.

Variations in sexual technique are numerous and of complex psychodynamic origin and significance. When one partner insists on technical maneuvers which the other finds distasteful or repulsive, these may become the focus of marital conflict. Treatment should be directed toward the emotional problems producing the demands; mature couples, respecting each other's feelings and free from intense neurotic drives demanding a specific type of satisfaction, can control impulses or experimental designs that are not mutually acceptable.

SUMMARY

Marital problems customarily develop in marriages between partners with complementary emotional disturbances. When circumstances upset the neurotic balance between them, they develop grievances against each other which they cannot solve by themselves. Many of these respond to supportive treatment, with the relatively limited goal of restoring the neurotic balance.

Early evaluation of prognosis is important in helping the physician or clergyman decide whether treatment is indicated and, if so, whether he should undertake treatment or should refer the couple to a family social agency, marriage counselor, psychiatrist, or other resource.

REFERENCES

1. Cleveland, E. J., and W. D. Longaker: "Neurotic Patterns in the Family," in A. H. Leighton, et al. (eds.), *Explorations in Social Psychiatry*, New York, Basic Books, Inc., Publishers, 1957.
   Eisenstein, V. W. (ed.): *Neurotic Interaction in Marriage*, New York, Basic Books, Inc., Publishers, 1956.
   Hollis, Florence: *Women in Marital Conflict*, New York, Family Service Association of America, 1949.
   Spiegel, J.: "The Resolution of Role Conflict within the Family," *Psychiatry*, 20:1, 1957.

2. Bird, H. W., and P. A. Martin: "Countertransference in the Psychotherapy of Marital Partners," *Psychiatry,* 19:353, 1956.
3. Hallowitz, D., et al.: "The Treatment Process with Both Parents Together," *Amer. J. Orthopsychiat.,* 27:587, 1957.
   Reding, G. R., and B. Ennis: "Treatment of the Couple by a Couple," *Brit. J. Med. Psychol.,* 37:325, 1964.
   Thomas, A.: "Simultaneous Psychotherapy with Marital Partners," *Amer. J. Psychotherapy,* 10:716, 1956.
4. Greene, B. L. (ed.): *Psychotherapies of Marital Disharmony,* New York, The Free Press of Glencoe, 1965.
   Klemer, R. H. (ed.): *Counseling in Marital and Sexual Problems,* Baltimore, The Williams & Wilkins Company, 1965.
   Nash, E. M., L. Jessner, and D. W. Abse (eds.): *Marriage Counseling in Medical Practice,* Chapel Hill, N.C., The University of North Carolina Press, 1964.
   Goode, W.: *After Divorce,* Glencoe, Ill., Free Press, 1956.
5. Kinsey, A. C., et al.: *Sexual Behavior in the Human Male,* Philadelphia, W. B. Saunders Company, 1948.
   ———, et al.: *Sexual Behavior in the Human Female,* Philadelphia, W. B. Saunders Company, 1953.
6. Benedek, T.: *Psychosexual Functions in Women,* New York, The Ronald Press Company, 1952.
   Marmor, J.: "Some Considerations Concerning Orgasm in the Female," *Psychosom. Med.,* 16:240, 1954.
7. Hastings, D. W.: *Impotence and Frigidity,* Boston, Little, Brown and Company, 1963.

Chapter 9

LATER YEARS

THE MENOPAUSE

The end of the period of maximum productivity confronts the adult with new problems, and his ability to make a satisfactory adjustment to them is measured largely by his reserve capacity to adapt. For a woman, the menopause is dramatic and clear-cut evidence that she has lost her ability to reproduce, and its significance depends on the relative importance of this ability to her self-esteem. The extensive hormonal changes at the menopause are, in general, the opposite of the changes at puberty. The menopause is often accompanied by signs of autonomic imbalance, such as hot flushes, palpitation, sweating, and attacks of nausea, and by symptoms of emotional instability, anxiety, depression, and insomnia. For a long time, physicians assumed that all the signs and symptoms associated with menopause were caused solely by the endocrine changes and consequently treated them exclusively by attempts to supply the hormonal deficiencies. Often the results were temporarily encouraging, but carefully controlled investigations indicate that many of the favorable results of endocrine treatment on symptoms in the emotional sphere are due to the effects of suggestion or to the physician's unwitting psychologic support of his patient as he takes an interest in her symptoms and problems. Other studies have shown that the severity of emotional disturbance in menopausal women is not in proportion to the degree of estrogen deficiency. Anxiety and depressive reactions at this time, therefore, appear to be related more to the psychologic significance of the menopause than to physiologic changes, although estrogen deficiency as a contributing cause to autonomic imbalance should not be disregarded, and post-menopausal maintenance estrogen treatment may delay some of the effects of aging.

The psychologic significance of the menopause, however, varies greatly with the individual personality. A woman's grief for her lost youth will be proportionate to the particular significance youth has for her. The menopause particularly threatens a woman whose security depends on her ability to control others, since it means she can no longer produce children and the children she has produced and controlled are growing up and need her less. Most women have a need to be needed, but not all are so insecure that they must control the recipients of their help. Their security makes it easier for them to permit their children to grow up and away from them and to shift their helping interests to friends and community activities. These women can make the menopause an opportunity for further emotional development [1].

Many women have an exaggerated idea of the extent of menopausal changes, as well as of changes after a hysterectomy or other pelvic surgery, expecting a dramatic loss of their feminine attributes and the disappearance of their capacity for sexual response. This idea is particularly disturbing to women who attach unusual significance to physical attractiveness and youthful appearance, often as a result of a narcissistic fixation (see Chapter 6) which is fostered by the cultural emphasis on the value of youth. The physician who takes the time to help these women express their fears, to answer their questions, and to reassure them can relieve much of their apprehension. The same technique may be at least partially effective in helping a woman who mistakenly believes that because her mother suffered an involutional depression, it is inevitable that she also will become psychotic during her menopause.

Most menopausal emotional disturbances, however, require more extensive psychologic support than simple educational reassurance. Many women need an opportunity to express their grief over their lost youth in a setting in which they are neither ridiculed for their concerns nor prematurely reassured. In the following example, a family physician was able to effectively diagnose and treat a mild reaction of this type.

> A forty-eight-year-old woman complained of anxiety, palpitations, depression, and apathy of about six months' duration. Her menopause had begun about a year before, and although she still suffered from mild vasomotor instability, most of her signs of autonomic imbalance had disappeared. Hormone treatment had been prescribed when she first became anxious and depressed, but she had not improved.
>
> She was a shy, intelligent woman whose husband worked long hours and was preoccupied with his job. She had always found it difficult to make friends and had devoted herself to her two children. Recognizing that she was inclined to overprotect them, she had conscientiously tried to permit them their independence. The onset of her distress coincided with her daughter's engagement announcement and followed closely her son's departure for college.
>
> The doctor knew that her husband was fairly set in his devotion to business and realized that since his patient had always been too shy to make

social contacts before she became depressed, she could not be expected to do so now.

After making sure that she was not suffering from a psychotic or suicidal depression, he invited her to come in for a brief conference at a stated time each week and prescribed mild sedation as an adjunct to his psychologic support. At these conferences they discussed her marriage, her family, and her interests, and he encouraged her to express her loneliness for her children and her feeling of futility and uselessness. Although it was evident that she did not have enough to keep her busy, the doctor did not try to redirect her interests into channels of his choice but helped her to discuss possibilities of her own. Eventually, she brought out, rather self-consciously, that she had once been interested in painting. The doctor then gently and patiently encouraged her until she enrolled in a course at the art museum. There she gradually enlarged her circle of acquaintances, and as her interest developed, her symptoms subsided.

A surgical menopause brought on by a hysterectomy, which frequently has almost the same psychologic significance as a normal menopause, is more often than not a serious psychologic threat to a woman, particularly a young woman [2]. Even if she has not been exposed to misleading folklore, the realization that her childbearing years have been foreshortened increases any feelings of inferiority as a woman she may have harbored. "I feel empty, useless, unattractive," said one patient. "How can I respond sexually when I am only half a woman?" She also may consciously or unconsciously equate the loss of her reproductive organs with punishment for past sins, particularly sexual sins.

Not all of the emotional response to surgical menopause can be prevented. The physician, however, has an opportunity to reduce its impact by affording the patient preoperatively the chance to express her feelings —including any resentment, however unwarranted, at the doctor who is about to remove her reproductive organs.

A thirty-nine-year-old woman who suffered from many hypochondriacal complaints was at first categoried by her irritated physicians as a "hostile, difficult patient." When one physician finally recognized the depression beneath her symptoms, he encouraged her to express her hostility to him, and did not meet it with counter-hostility. She then related her depression to a hysterectomy following an ectopic pregnancy at the age of twenty-two. She had not been told of the extent of her surgery until she was about to leave the hospital. Her physician then prefaced his explanation by telling her how bad *he* felt about the necessity for the surgery.

"He told me that nothing in his practice had ever made him feel so miserable," she said. "I ended up consoling *him*, when it was *my* uterus he had removed. Oh, whenever I think of it, I could kill that man."

The physician clearly had protected himself against the patient's overt resentment by anticipating it and, in effect, exonerating himself. Without the opportunity to express her grief, she still suffered from a prolonged, somewhat disguised grief reaction and still was taking out her anger at the original doctor on the rest of the medical profession.

INVOLUTIONAL REACTIONS

Since the ability to adapt to new situations is so important in adjusting to the menopause, it is not surprising that women with rigid, compulsive personalities have a difficult time. They are particularly susceptible to the severe depressions, or *involutional psychotic reactions,* so often encountered in this age group. Although the reasons for this susceptibility are complex, current thinking usually implicates two major factors. In the first place, the involutional period signals the end of major productivity— literally, with respect to childbearing, and also symbolically, with respect to other personal accomplishments. If the patient has not attained her goals of personal accomplishment by this time, she is not likely to in the future. Since compulsive personalities set their personal standards high and are particularly critical of themselves, as well as of others, they are especially depressed by the recognition that the likelihood of further productivity is limited.

The other factor concerns *aggression.* The woman with a compulsive personality started at an early age to use reaction formation to keep any evidence of aggression or hostility in check. As a result, she has never learned to distinguish between hostility and less destructive forms of aggression. So much of her ego strength is devoted to defending herself against her aggression that she lacks enough margin of safety and flexibility to deal with the new problems presented by the menopause.

Overwhelmed by the new problems, she seems no longer able to contain her aggression by the reaction formation she learned to use in the training period and has continued to use all her life. Since she has avoided rather than mastered aggression, she must marshal all her psychologic resources in an effort to establish control when the protective mechanism which made avoidance possible breaks down. Emotionally, she recapitulates the problem she could not solve as a child, the problem of finding appropriate outlets for aggression. In psychologic terms, she regresses to the point of her partial fixation.

As the aggression begins to emerge into consciousness, however, it runs into a roadblock in the form of her conscience. Her compulsive personality's rigid and punishing conscience, or superego, turns the mobilized hostile, aggressive impulses back at her so that she hates herself instead of others. Hating herself and feeling unloved, she becomes depressed and agitated. She loses her appetite and finds it impossible to sleep. Her superego makes her feel guilty, although since the angry impulses have been turned back before reaching awareness, she does not know why she feels guilty. She may rationalize her guilt, insisting that she has committed an unpardonable sin whose exact nature is never quite clear. She may suffer from somatic delusions, the false belief that part of her body has been damaged or destroyed, as if in symbolic retribution. The ultimate expression of hostility turned inwards is suicide, which was common in involutional depressions before the advent of modern methods of treatment and which is still a risk requiring serious consideration.

The involutional patient may also *project* hostility, with the consequent development of *paranoid* symptoms—particularly delusions of persecution, in which the patient's hostility is still directed against herself but through the agency of a nonexistent persecutor. The paranoid symptoms usually appear to be secondary in significance to the symptoms of depression, although some patients develop *paranoid reactions* at this time in life without observable depression (see Chapter 11). These patients seem to have been conditioned in earlier years to project the source of hostility on to others rather than to turn it directly on themselves.

The psychodynamic explanations of involutional psychotic reactions are not completely satisfactory [3]. For example, they do not explain why paranoid symptoms are so frequently a part of involutional psychotic reactions and are seldom if ever encountered in neurotic-depressive reactions. They also do not account for the response to electric shock treatments in involutional reactions.

Formerly, hormone deficiency was thought to account for the differences between involutional and neurotic depressions or even to be the chief cause of involutional reactions, since they occur much more frequently in women and bear such a close relationship to their endocrinologic reorganization at the menopause. Estrogens were therefore used to replace the lost natural ovarian function. Carefully controlled studies, however, have shown that they do not relieve the symptoms of involutional reactions, and the treatment has been generally abandoned. Although endocrine factors still may play a part, no one as yet has provided a completely satisfactory explanation of the factors which supplement psychologic causes in the development of involutional reactions.

RETIREMENT

Involutional reactions occur less frequently in men, possibly because men do not experience such a marked or abrupt physiologic change as the menopause. In the absence of an analogous clear-cut termination of reproductive capacity, the dramatic event which gives a man unmistakable evidence that his powers are waning is retirement. The age of retirement is subject to much more individual variation than the menopause—a professional athlete is an old man at thirty-five, but a physician at thirty-five is just beginning his career—and it is subject to more modification by individual choice or external circumstance. Even so, the observed reactions of men to retirement or to the threat of retirement and of women to the menopause have enough in common to justify our considering them events of similar psychologic significance.

No matter how much economic security a man has in the form of pensions, insurance, or savings, he still must face at retirement the realization that he is no longer considered as capable as he was and that a younger man is taking his place. Psychologically, retirement represents a reverse adolescence, in which the transition is made from independence back to dependency, with a corresponding reawakening of whatever dependency problems have remained unsolved and repressed.

Thus, overtly dependent personalities, whether men or women, may welcome retirement, since it gives them a rationalization for being dependent. Others, who are afraid of dependency, may find retirement a serious threat to the security they have built for themselves by adopting pseudoindependent attitudes in early childhood and maintaining them all their lives (see Chapter 4). People who have never taken vacations and who do not enjoy days off postpone retirement as long as possible because they feel secure only when on the production line and are lost without their work. Typically, when they are honored for their years of service and are told that they have earned their leisure, they already recognize that they will be unable to enjoy it. They often become depressed and may deteriorate rapidly in their physical and intellectual capacities. They need help from a physician or other counselor who understands their problems, one who will not simply recommend unproductive hobbies but will consistently give them psychologic support over the period of time they need to make their adjustment.

Another type of man who finds retirement particularly difficult is the authoritarian leader who is jealous of his position and sees the accomplishments of his children or his subordinates as threats to his security. He, too, resists giving up the reins as long as possible; when at last he reluctantly surrenders, he becomes even more destructively critical than before. His boasting and his hostile attitude are often hard to take, but they represent his protection against anxiety, and the doctor usually can tolerate them in divided doses as he helps his patient face and eventually accept his new status.

For some men, anxiety or depression in response to the threat of retirement is expressed in the guise of neurotic symptoms. The specific nature of a man's hypochondriacal or conversion symptoms usually indicates the specific areas of his greatest bodily concern. Concern about sexual competence, for example, is frequent among men of retirement age, and the rapid onset of impotence at this time is usually more closely related to psychologic factors than to endocrine disturbance.

Retirement does not have to be a period of psychologic upheaval. Just as women can make the menopause a developmental stage, men who have enough flexibility and reserve ego strength can adapt themselves to retirement by developing new interests and relationships and by obtaining vicarious satisfaction from observing the accomplishments of their children and their former subordinates. To the individual, the stress of retirement is somewhat related to the significance of his work. If he has thought of his job as drudgery, a necessary evil to be tolerated, he usually will welcome retirement. Studies of men who have retired from relatively mundane and uninteresting jobs reveal a surprisingly high proportion of contentment among them [4]. Physicians, teachers, executives, and others who have invested more of themselves in their work are more likely to mourn the loss.

AGING

The borderline between late maturity and old age is variable and indistinct. Gradually, with increased physical infirmity and diminished capacity for accomplishment, the elderly individual is forced into greater dependency on others. Intellectually, his capacities diminish, particularly in areas involving speed, memory, and adaptability [5]. For many years, psychiatrists assumed that elderly people inevitably marched on toward intellectual and personality deterioration at a pace exactly proportionate to the senile changes in the brain. The relationship between symptoms and pathology, however, is inconsistent, and in most cases personality factors play a significant part in the development rate of senility [6]. While changes in the brain do produce a progressive weakening of the ego and gradually encroach on the ego's reserve, the individual's personality pattern determines the amount of this reserve, and hence his resistance to the development of symptoms. The mental hygiene of old age, therefore, begins in childhood; an adult who has developed superior adaptive capacity as a child can adapt to new areas of productivity when the physical, social, and economic constrictions of old age shut off his previous outlets.

Delirium and the Response to Surgery

As the years go by and the ego reserve becomes depleted by changes in the brain, the elderly individual becomes susceptible to sudden deterioration. A fractured hip or a major surgical procedure may be enough to transform rapidly and permanently an apparently well-integrated man into a confused and dilapidated senile. The process is not always irreversible, however. Illness of any kind, particularly when it requires hospitalization or harasses an already depleted ego with toxins, may cause enough of a change to overwhelm the ego temporarily and produce the agitated, confused state called *delirium* [7]. Elderly patients in the hospital are most susceptible to delirium at night, in a manner somewhat reminiscent of the separation anxiety in the year-old child discussed on page 120. The child who is just learning to relate to his environment is frightened by the absence of familiar people and voices and by darkness, with its distortion or blotting out of familiar sights. In the same way, the elderly patient in the hospital, whose ego has become weakened to the threshold of collapse by a combination of toxic effects secondary to his illness and the physical and emotional changes of age, is frightened when darkness intensifies the strangeness and unfamiliarity of his environment. He may become panic-stricken and confused, forget where he is, and misinterpret or reconstruct his surroundings by means of delusions and hallucinations. As he seeks to reestablish contact with his environment, he tries to eliminate anything that is strange; he pulls out catheters and other attachments and may endanger his life in attempting to find safety.

Although most frequent in children and the elderly, delirium can occur at any age whenever toxins, injury, or lack of oxygen seriously weakens the ego. The prevention and treatment of delirium should not be limited to measures calculated to improve the oxygen supply to the brain or to counteract toxicity, but should include nursing instructions which emphasize the importance of reassurance and explanation at the first signs of anxiety. Often the presence at night of an understanding relative or friend will reassure the patient; the somewhat maligned old custom of "sitting up with a sick friend" has actual validity. A night-light may be helpful if it is placed so that it does not merely add frightening shadows, and a warm tub bath may produce relaxation and induce sleep more effectively than sedation for sleepless patients. Sedation adds another element of toxicity and, if it is not sufficient to put the patient to sleep, may frighten him more than it helps him, by further clouding his capacity to evaluate his environment.

The emotional significance that the elderly patient attaches to a surgical procedure may contribute more to his anxiety than the physician realizes [8]. This is particularly true when surgery causes the loss of a part of the body which symbolizes femininity or masculinity, such as a breast, uterus, or prostate gland. An elderly widower with a hypertrophied prostate may appear to have everything to gain and nothing to lose by an operation which will relieve his discomfort. Yet he may exasperate his doctor by stalling and postponing surgery in spite of a dangerous degree of urinary retention. He may be hesitant, through fear of the doctor's ridicule, to express his real concern, which frequently is that he will lose his sexual powers. He may misunderstand the nature of the operation—physicians are so accustomed to anatomic understanding that they sometimes fail to realize that even intelligent and well-educated laymen often confuse prostatectomy and castration—or he may have the misconception common among elderly men that prostatectomy inevitably causes impotence. This misconception is carried on by the rationalizations of his contemporaries. A man whose sexual powers have already waned to the vanishing point often uses the prostatectomy as an external justification in protecting his self-esteem from recognition of his weakness. He thus says to himself and perhaps to his friends: "If it were not for the surgery, I would be as good a man as ever."

Neurotic Reactions

The elderly individual not only uses neurotic mechanisms but may demonstrate clinical neurotic reactions with or without accompanying organic brain disease [9]. The doctor should be careful to differentiate evidence of neurotic and depressive reactions from signs of senility or cerebral arteriosclerosis; physicians too frequently assume that any sign of emotional disturbance in the elderly patient is due to physical effects of aging. It is important to make this differentiation in order to give the patient the benefit of early appropriate treatment, as in the following case.

> A seventy-two-year-old woman complained of weakness of her right arm, a weakness of a year's duration. Her physician at first believed that a cerebral vascular lesion was responsible for her symptoms, but he could not find substantiating evidence on physical or neurologic examination.

He then recalled that her husband had suffered a right hemiplegia before his death, which had occurred a few weeks before the onset of the patient's symptoms. He discovered that she had not been on good terms with her husband at the time of his death, that she had not expressed much grief at that time, and that she had then moved in with her son and daughter-in-law. Her symptoms began when she had been frustrated in her attempts to take over their household. The physician noted that her weakness was not consistently present in the same degree and that it did not follow lines of anatomic distribution. In addition, she seemed somewhat indifferent to her disability.

From this evidence, the physician made a diagnosis of a concealed and prolonged grief reaction, manifested by conversion symptoms (see Chapter 10). He encouraged her to come to his office for a series of weekly half-hour interviews, and after an introductory phase, in which she found to her satisfaction that he was honestly interested in her personal life, they discussed her problems in her son's home, her feelings at the time of her husband's death, and finally, her earlier marital problems.

As she began to face her feelings and share them with her doctor, she was able to free herself somewhat from her emotional bondage to her dead husband. She then took more interest in her appearance, her friends, and her former church and community activities. Meanwhile the physician had prescribed massage and exercises for her arm, both for their suggestive effect and to help her save face. He realized that as long as she was willing to talk about her emotional problems, he need not force her to acknowledge that her symptoms had no physical basis. After ten interviews, she had improved, symptomatically and emotionally, to the point where she took a part-time job at her church. As she found interests of her own, she no longer tried to run her daughter-in-law's household.

Family Conflicts

Living arrangements for elderly people present an increasing social problem. With every forward step in medicine, more people are able to live longer, and census officials now estimate that in 1980 there will be more than 25 million Americans over sixty-five years old. Our increasing sociologic and economic accent on youth, however, has caused the prestige of older people to drop as their numbers have increased. More intimate living conditions and smaller homes have contributed to the tendency of modern families to think of making a place for grandmother as a burden, not a privilege. The weight of the burden depends to a great extent on such personality factors as the amount of the grandparent's dependency or need to control or the amount of security the younger couple have as parents and in their marriage.

In any case, the presence of grandparents in the home probably represents at least an inconvenience to the majority of families. Some families openly resent and seek to avoid this inconvenience, while others are so overconscientious or so guilty about their ambivalent attitudes toward their parents that they tolerate the presence of a disturbed and disturbing older person long after hospitalization is indicated, much to the detriment of their own and their children's personal and social adjustments.

The physician, clergyman, or social worker is often called on for advice in such problems and as often finds his objectivity strained. His relationships, whatever they are, with his own parents and children make it hard for him not to overidentify either with the children, saddled with an intolerable burden, or with the parent, about to be cast out by ungrateful children. If he can retain a dispassionate interest in the problems of all members of the family, he may be able to help them work out a satisfactory solution, as in the following case.

A college student who lived with his widowed mother and his grandfather complained that he could not concentrate on his studies. His crotchety grandfather had not adjusted well to retirement and spent much of his time complaining that he was lonesome and that no one cared enough about him to listen to what he had to say. This was true, chiefly because the old man talked almost exclusively either about his complaints or about minor events in the remote past. The patient's mother worked hard to support the family and tried to appease her father by spending all her free time with him, but in spite of her efforts, he continued to be critical and dissatisfied.

The patient said that the atmosphere at home was depressing, but he felt so obligated to his mother for financing his college education that he did not feel justified in spending time and money on social life or on extracurricular activities. He had wanted to take a part-time job, but he was having so much trouble concentrating that his grades were dangerously low.

Thus the son's unhappiness was secondary to the mother's and the mother's secondary to the grandfather's. The grandfather was eligible for admission to a sectarian old people's home, but the mother felt that to suggest such a move would reflect unfavorably on her family loyalty. By this time, she was so guilty about the anger she had built up in response to her father's attitude and about her wish to get rid of him that she could not initiate any plan which would relieve her of her responsibility.

With the youth's permission, the doctor discussed the situation with the mother. He did not attempt to force the issue but gave her plenty of opportunity to express her feelings. He avoided appearing to side with her against her father but let her see that he was as interested in him as in the rest of the family. He then gradually introduced the possibility of the home for the aged and talked over her fears that the old man would be mistreated or that she would be criticized. After observing that much of her father's irritability might be due to his lack of congenial companions, he helped her arrange a visit to the home. Fortified by his psychologic support, she decided to arrange for her father's care at the home and was able to discuss the move with him.

When her father had settled down in his new environment and had overcome the resistance to change characteristic of elderly people, he brightened considerably, found friends with mutual interests in the past, and showed an obvious preference for his new location. His daughter began to make new friends of her own and to participate in social activities outside her home. Her son no longer felt obligated to stay at home and give her moral support, and as his tension left him, he found he could study more effectively and still keep up outside activities and part-time work.

Three prerequisities to the success of this case are not always present in similar cases. In the first place, although the mother felt guilty, she did not feel so guilty about her ambivalent feelings toward her father that she resisted any objective consideration of the problem. Otherwise, the physician would have been forced to limit his help to psychologic support of the son in his efforts to adapt to the situation.

Second, the doctor was willing to devote a good deal of time to the patient and his mother. In some communities, family-service agencies have developed programs to help resolve the problems of older people and their families; in other situations, the church may help; but in any case, the family cannot be rushed into such a decision, or their later regrets are likely to interfere with its success.

Finally, and most important since this grandfather's personality was not well suited to independent living, there was a satisfactory home available. The quality of adequate facilities for the aged varies enormously, and the supply lags far behind the demand. Physicians cannot avoid being aware of this problem; they can contribute to its solution by stimulating and participating in community projects for care of the elderly. These projects include, besides construction and improvement of housing for independent living and of homes for the aged, foster-home programs, provision of vocational and recreational facilities, and day-care centers.

Until the recent past, the older person's alternatives to living with his children have been virtually limited to hospital or nursing-home care or permanent care in a home for the aged. These alternatives deprived the elderly person of much of his independence, but until recently it was generally assumed that he did not especially value his independence. Now, particularly as older people have become more confident of financial support and of the availability of facilities for them if they become incapacitated, the preference of most older people for independent or quasi-independent living, as compared with institutional care, has become evident. As facilities for independent living become more available, the functions of homes for the aged are becoming progressively more similar to the functions of nursing homes.

The sensitivity, complaints, and preoccupation with the past of the elderly man in the last case illustration are evidence of a progressive personality change which eventually, if he lives long enough, will produce so much deterioration that he will require hospital care. His rate of progress toward senility, however, will be determined by his previous personality and by his medical care, as well as by senile changes in his brain.

SUMMARY

In this chapter, the psychology of the menopause, of retirement, and of old age was discussed. In all these situations, maturity and flexibility expedite the patient's adjustment, while partial fixations at immature levels make adaptations more difficult. The same factors help the individual resist the psychologic breakdowns, temporary or permanent, which are associated with aging.

REFERENCES

1. Benedek, Theresa: "Climacterium: A Developmental Phase," *Psychoanal. Quart.*, 19:1, 1950.
2. Menzer, D., et al.: "Patterns of Emotional Recovery from Hysterectomy," *Psychosom. Med.*, 19:379, 1957.
3. See, however: Barrett, J., A. Lefford, and D. Pushman: "Involutional Melancholia," *Psychiat. Quart.*, 27:654, 1953.
4. Palmore, E.: *"Retirement Patterns among Men and Women,"* paper presented at American Gerontological Society, Minneapolis, November, 1964.
5. Birren, J. E. (ed.): *Handbook of Aging and the Individual,* Chicago, The University of Chicago Press, 1959.
   Cumming, E., and W. E.. Henry: *Growing Old: The Process of Disengagement,* New York, Basic Books, Inc., Publishers, 1961.
6. Rothschild, D.: "Pathological Changes in Senile Psychoses and Their Psychobiologic Significance," *Amer. J. Psychiat.*, 93:757, 1937.
   Sands, S. L., and D. Rothschild: "Sociopsychiatric Foundations for a Theory of Reactions to Aging," *J. Nerv. Ment. Dis.*, 116:233, 1952.
7. Doty, E. J., "Incidence and Treatment of Delirious Reactions in Later Life," *Geriatrics*, 1:21, 1946.
8. Titchener, J., I. Zwerling, L. Gottschalk, and M. Levine: "Psychological Reaction of the Aged in Surgery," *AMA Arch. Neurol. Psychiat.*, 79:63, 1958.
9. Birren, J. E., et al. (eds.): *Human Aging: A Biological and Behavioral Study,* Washington, U.S. Department of Health, Education and Welfare, 1963.
   Goldfarb, A. I.: "Psychiatric Problems of Old Age," *New York J. Med.*, 55:494, 1955.
   Zinberg, N. E., and I. Kaufman (eds.): *Normal Psychology of the Aging Process,* New York, International Universities Press, Inc., 1963.

Part Three

PSYCHIATRIC ILLNESS

Chapter 10

NEUROTIC REACTIONS

In the last few chapters, personality was explored primarily from the longitudinal, or developmental, point of view. Included in this discussion were descriptions of the psychodynamics of several conditions that are uniquely associated with one or another stage of personality development.

In the next four chapters, the exploration of personality will be continued from the cross-sectional viewpoint, with primary emphasis on the mechanisms of symptom formation rather than on personality development and with more emphasis on conditions that are not clearly associated with a particular developmental stage. Across this unavoidably artificial division (developmental versus cross-sectional viewpoints), there inevitably is some overlap, usually indicated by cross-references. And although certain *conditions* may be covered in the sections devoted to only one of the viewpoints, the physician should attempt to understand each of his *patients* according to both his developmental history and his personality structure.

The symptoms of neurotic reactions include both the clinical manifestations of *anxiety* and the results of some of the attempts patients make to protect themselves from anxiety [1]. Anxiety, as defined on page 45, is a state of tension in which the individual is afraid but does not know what he fears. It is usually the result of conflict between repressed, presumably dangerous drives which threaten to break into consciousness and the internal forces that find them unacceptable. As a child, the individual repressed these drives because he was afraid of them or of their implications or because he felt guilty or ashamed of them or because he felt incapable of expressing them appropriately; as an adult, he can continue to avoid facing them as long as he maintains repression. If for any reason the relative strength of the accumulated drives increases past his reserve capacity to repress, however, he must either face them or find new ways to control them or he must disguise their expression. Since he has never looked at these drives in the light of adult understanding, he has never been desensitized to the fear he felt when originally confronted with them, and so he does everything possible to keep them buried or disguised.

In some cases, an indirect or substitute expression of a presumably dangerous drive is possible if the patient can unconsciously tie or fuse it to another drive which is more acceptable (see page 47). Thus, if a child has become conditioned to believe that expression of the wish to be loved is dangerous, perhaps because of repeated experiences of feeling abandoned early in his life, he may repress this drive and unconsciously associate it with the safer hunger drive, producing symptoms related to appetite and gastrointestinal function. Indirect expression of a repressed drive by associating it with an antisocial impulse which then can be acted out will be discussed in Chapter 14. Through this process, a presumably dangerous yearning for love, for example, can be expressed symbolically in the form of stealing.

Another type of indirect expression by unconscious association is carried out through the mechanism of reaction formation. In reaction formation, the expression of the potentially dangerous drive is concealed beneath its opposite. Thus a child who is afraid of his aggressive drive and has found that his parents consider dirt and disorder to be signs of aggression may conceal and at the same time indirectly express his aggression by an intense, "aggressive" drive toward cleanliness and order (see obsessive-compulsive reactions, Chapter 5).

These substitute expressions represent attempts, by people whose capacity to evaluate the environment remains relatively intact, to find indirect outlets for drives that threaten to break through the barrier of repression. In each case, direct expression of the drive is blocked for one reason or another. In each case, the personality undergoes partial regression, so that part of the ego's efforts are deflected from current adaptations in order to attempt to resolve unfinished problems of childhood adaptation. The particular indirect or substitute solution chosen in any individual case depends on a combination of external circumstances, the patient's personality structure, his past patterns of reaction to anxiety, and treatment.

The various symptomatic manifestations of the ego's attempts to channel anxiety are called *neurotic* or *psychoneurotic reactions* when the manifestations are not accompanied by distorted evaluation of the environment [2]. In contrast, conditions where regression is more complete and where failure of adequate adaptation to the underlying drive is accompanied by distorted evaluation of the environment are called *psychotic reactions*. Although this distinction between neurotic and psychotic reactions holds for the majority of instances and will suffice for the present, it is not completely satisfactory. In the next chapter, I will enlarge somewhat on the problems of differentiation between these two groups.

ANXIETY REACTIONS

An anxiety reaction is a neurotic reaction in which no form of direct or indirect expression relieves the pressure of repressed drives [3]. In an anxiety reaction, an unacceptable drive or conflict is stirred up, usually in response to an external stimulus, and although the patient attempts to repress it, he is not able to keep it completely under control. The drive or conflict, therefore, continues to exert pressure for expression until it threatens to erupt into consciousness. The patient is not aware of the cause of his anxiety but is aware of its symptoms—symptoms which reflect his inner fear that if he faces the drive or conflict within him, he will not be able to cope with it. (For diagram, see Appendix B, Figure 14.)

The symptoms of anxiety are similar to the symptoms of fear. After a narrow escape from an accident, for example, fear produces physical symptoms. Palpitation, rapid heart rate, shortness of breath, dizziness, fainting, loss of appetite, nausea, diarrhea, sweating, pallor, urinary frequency, abdominal cramps, tremors, sleeplessness—all, to different degrees and in various combinations depending on the individual constitution or conditioning, may result from fear. The same symptoms indicate anxiety; but in fear the cause is evident, while in anxiety it is hidden.

The original purpose of the physiologic response to fear was to prepare for attack or retreat—in Cannon's words, for "fight or flight" [4]—and many of the symptoms of fear are caused by the mobilization for emergency action at the temporary expense of digestion and other body functions. Primitive man needed such emergency mobilization for survival, and although the fears of civilized man are more complex, he still responds to them physiologically in the primitive manner. Man also seeks to identify and to remove the causes of his fears, but in anxiety, his wish to get at the cause is opposed by his original intent to repress the cause. The following case illustrates the symptoms of anxiety and the type of problem which often produces them.

> A twenty-six-year-old unmarried accountant complained of apparently unprovoked attacks of palpitation, tachycardia, weakness, sweating, diarrhea, urinary frequency, and a feeling that he was going to die. Although the attacks at first had appeared to occur at random, a careful history revealed that they often developed after a date with his fiancée. He observed that the dates which customarily led to attacks were characterized either by passionate embraces or by heated arguments.

His physician made a definite diagnosis of anxiety reaction. He could find no complicating physical illness and referred the patient for psychiatric evaluation.

The psychiatrist learned that when the patient was four, his father had deserted the family, leaving his mother angry and helpless. She used her son both as a source of affection and as a substitute outlet for her anger at her husband. Alternately seductive and hostile, she expected him to take his father's place and ridiculed him as an incompetent child. The boy was equally frightened of her expectations and of her ridicule but felt helpless to protect himself.

As time went on, however, she found other emotional outlets and learned to control her feelings. An uncle became an acceptable father substitute for the boy, who gradually developed an ego strong enough under ordinary circumstances to repress his conflicts with his mother. He remained essentially symptom-free until he fell in love, and began to suffer anxiety attacks.

With the help of the psychiatrist, he gradually gained enough confidence to allow him to lift the barrier of repression and face some of the conflicting feelings he harbored. He then could see that embraces or arguments with his fiancée in a way recapitulated his childhood experiences. Arguments with the girl he loved best stirred up his old fears of his mother's ridicule, and their embraces reminded him of his earlier fear in the face of his mother's demands for affection. His anxiety attacks, therefore, resulted when a situation with a specific connotation in terms of his past experience mobilized such strong conflicting feelings associated with his past that they threatened to break through into consciousness. As a result, he regressed from a primary concern with current problems to a preoccupation with establishing control over the earlier conflict.

His recognition of the source of his anxiety helped him use constructively the corrective emotional experience of intensive psychotherapy. As he understood and became less frightened of the earlier conflict, he became relatively free of anxiety attacks.

As I mentioned in Chapter 6, Freud felt that intrafamily rivalries and their ramifications constitute the central conflict in all neuroses, and subsequent experience has shown that they play a significant part in a large share of them. Other types of conflict, however—related to variations in cultural patterns—also play parts of varying significance.

In the following case, unresolved grief proved to be the major cause of an anxiety reaction.

A fifty-year-old executive appeared to accept the hardly unexpected death of his ninety-four-year-old father with equanimity. When two years later he developed an anxiety reaction, his physician at first assumed that it was due to business reverses, but when the anxiety persisted after the business had improved, he began to look further.

The physician, interested in the office treatment of the milder forms of emotional illness and with enough experience to be comfortable in undertaking it, suggested a series of weekly interviews with his patient. At first, the patient painted an idyllic picture of his earlier relationship with his father. The doctor, thinking his story sounded a little too perfect, carefully steered the conversation around to the circumstances of the father's death. He became more convinced that he was dealing with delayed grief when the patient became disproportionately upset while describing his remorse at having been out of town when his father had his fatal heart attack.

Later the patient recalled that years before he had planned to go into business with his father but that at the last moment his father had decided that he did not have enough experience. The patient had started a different business on his own and had been successful, although his father had predicted he would fail. The patient told this without rancor and as if it had been a good joke on his father. But when the doctor said, "Although you can laugh at it now, I wonder if you didn't resent your father's attitude at the time it happened," the patient stopped, caught his breath for a moment, and then began to pour out his pent-up anger at his father, whom he now pictured as an insecure, belittling authoritarian who could never countenance anger, rebellion, or competition.

The patient had accumulated so much hostility and so much consequent guilt about his hostility that he could not face his feelings when his father died. He had repressed them successfully for two years, but the business reverses—evidence to him that his father's prediction was coming true—put so much strain on his ego that his repression began to give way. The threatened breakthrough of his angry feelings and the fear of their consequences frightened him. Since he did not know what was frightening him—the hostility and guilt had not yet come into his consciousness—he became anxious.

Before the doctor interpreted the patient's inner resentment, he had made certain that the patient had a strong ego and could tolerate the removal of his defenses. His social and vocational success and his ability to use repression successfully for two years were evidence of his ego strength. Once the patient understood and experienced his angry feelings and related them to their cause, the doctor was able to help him express his grief and free himself from his ambivalent emotional tie to his father enough so that his symptoms disappeared.

Severe anxiety attacks do not usually last long, although they are likely to recur. Since the symptoms and feelings associated with anxiety are extremely unpleasant, the individual tries to eliminate them as soon as possible by increasing the strength of repression. When the attack responds, as it often does, to medication, to a change in environment, or to techniques which support and strengthen the ego, both patient and doctor may be content to let well enough alone and not seek more intensive treatment. If the factors responsible for stirring up the patient's anxiety cannot be modified sufficiently to forestall future trouble, however, the physician should consider psychiatric treatment to develop the patient's insight into his unconscious drives and conflicts and their associated or component guilt, shame, or fears. These drives and conflicts are more accessible to exploration at this point than they will be later if the patient calls other mechanisms into action to provide more effective disguises.

Rationalization of Anxiety Symptoms

A mechanism commonly used to disguise the cause of anxiety is *rationalization,* or the development of an apparently reasonable and acceptable justification for an action or feeling. The nature of anxiety symptoms makes it relatively easy for the patient to explain them on the basis of physical illness rather than unconscious conflict. The particular illness he selects as a rationale may depend in part on the organ or organ system most affected, but it also may be determined by an illness that is significant in the history of the patient or his family. The fifty-year-old executive in the previous case illustration, for example, emphasized his palpitation and tachycardia and to some extent rationalized that his symptoms of anxiety were due to heart trouble. On the other hand, an anxious patient whose father died of a stomach cancer may emphasize his nausea, anorexia, and abdominal cramps and may believe that he, too, has cancer. The tenacity with which the patient persists in a well-established rationalization despite reassurance gives a clue to the importance of concealing the conflict. Although it would seem that anyone who wants to live would prefer to explain his symptoms on an emotional basis rather than on an organic basis (presumably he can live indefinitely with palpitations due to anxiety, but he is faced with the imminent possibility of death if they are caused by a coronary thrombosis), patients with anxiety tend to keep searching for organic explanations. As long as they can rationalize that the anxiety arising from inadequate repression is due to organic disease, they can avoid the greater fear of facing their inner conflicts.

Since rationalization makes treatment of anxiety more difficult, it is important that physicians not encourage this mechanism unnecessarily by suggesting or supporting organic explanations during the patient's work-up.

> A fifty-four-year-old widow came to the psychiatric clinic reluctantly, convinced that she had heart trouble. She had been well until two years before her clinic visit, when she suffered an "attack" of weakness, pain over her heart, and palpitation. This attack occurred shortly after her only

son received his draft notice. His departure would confront her with the prospect of remaining on the farm alone with her grouchy, uncommunicative husband, who had recently been treated for mild heart disease.

Her physician at first told her she had a coronary thrombosis, but after a thorough work-up, he revised his diagnosis to "nervous heart." She was not convinced, however, that her symptoms were of emotional origin, and she began to interpret normal physiologic phenomena such as breathlessness from exertion as signs of heart disease. In spite of her symptoms, she was able to carry on until her husband suffered a heart attack during a heavy snowstorm. The roads were blocked, and before she could get out for help, her husband died. The experience was extremely frightening, and her palpitations, weakness, and pain recurred. She again thought she had heart disease, but this time, even after her symptoms improved, she was afraid to exert herself in any way and eventually became completely incapacitated. Her physician still could find no evidence of heart disease, but she could not accept reassurance and was referred to the clinic.

She told the clinic doctor that she had married at seventeen to get away from her home, which was dominated by her cold and unloving mother. She idealized her father and recalled that he often complained to her about his unhappiness and her mother's lack of understanding. She had never felt close to her husband and compared him unfavorably both to her warm and sympathetic father and to her son, whom she described in the same terms as her father.

At this point in his exploration of a problem of this kind, the doctor should develop a tentative formulation to serve as a working hypothesis to guide him in further diagnostic exploration and in planning treatment. His formulation should include many of the following elements, virtually all of which would be subject to modification as more historical material comes to light.

Although she had married early, presumably to get away from home, the patient's history suggests that she had carried with her a strong, unresolved attachment to her father which she had repressed, presumably because she felt too guilty or was too afraid to face it. Her overattachment to her father prevented her from developing a mature love for another man, and her marriage to a man she did not love protected her from a disturbing closeness to her father. She had successfully repressed her conflicting feelings about her father until she encountered the new, external threat of the departure of her son, to whom she had transferred many of the feelings which she had originally directed toward her father. Since she lacked enough ego strength to deal with the new threat and at the same time maintain adequate repression, some of the frightening early feelings about her father began to push their way toward consciousness. Apparently conditioned by her husband's illness, she rationalized that the consequent signs of anxiety were signs of a heart attack. Her rationalization was strengthened by the doctor's original diagnosis of coronary disease.

The subsequent death of her husband, about whom her feelings were ambivalent, increased the environmental stress and further drained her reserve adaptive capacity while mobilizing still more disturbing feelings. Although she resented him, she also had depended on him, and his death took away a source of her security while at the same time it caused her to feel guilty because of her hostility. As she became more anxious, she found it still more difficult to contend in an adult fashion with both internal and external pressures. Since the internal pressures were more threatening, she gave up the struggle with her current environment and regressed to almost total preoccupation with her attempt to repress the conflicts of the past. Even so, they threatened to erupt, and in order to avoid facing them, she persisted in her rationalization, so that the anxiety arising from the conflicts appeared in her consciousness disguised as fear of illness and of death. Her husband's death from heart disease firmly convinced her that she too was about to die of a coronary attack.

Since, with rationalization, the apparent cause of anxiety is one step removed from its true source, the patient is usually more difficult to treat than the patient with an uncomplicated anxiety state. Instead of complaining of anxiety and requesting help in finding the cause, he inaccurately claims to know the cause and requests help in treatment of the heart, gallbladder, colon, or whatever part of the body he has implicated. The patient interprets his anxiety as evidence of physical illness rather than as fear of an unconscious conflict breaking through repression and stubbornly resists any attempt to expose this disguise. Therefore, if the doctor confines his treatment to a vigorous attack by logic, persuasion, or ridicule, he usually loses the patient to another physician, and if the process is repeated, eventually the patient goes to charlatans outside the medical profession who will support and live off the patient's belief that he has an organic disease.

Rationalization of the symptoms of anxiety is not the only mechanism that causes a patient to be preoccupied with his health. Rationalization explains anxiety *after* it develops. It does not protect a patient so much as would a mechanism which would permit him to anticipate and explain anxiety *before* it develops. When a patient is so threatened by possible exposure of his conflicts that he cannot tolerate the period of unexplained anxiety before rationalization sets in, he may unconsciously *displace* or attach the anxiety to a particular object, situation, organ, or organ system chosen in advance to explain the symptoms. Displacement to an object or situation results in *phobias*, which will be discussed later in this chapter. Displacement to organ, organ system, or disease is a special type of phobia used most frequently by patients who, as children, were encouraged by their parents or learned by their parents' example to worry about their health. When this type of displacement occurs, the organ appears to him to be the source of all his anxiety; even when he is not experiencing physiologic evidences of anxiety, he worries about his body. Although the organ he chooses is a part of him, he talks and acts as if it were somehow separated from his inner self. The source of the anxiety therefore seems to come from outside of him and not from within. The patient is still afraid but is now afraid of the tangible and relatively less threatening possibility of organic disease rather than of the possibility of his unacceptable impulse breaking through. (For diagram, see Appendix B, Figure 15.)

Treatment ideally begins before rationalization or displacement has obscured the nature and causes of the basic anxiety. Even if one of these mechanisms has become active, the physician is often able to help his patient focus on causes rather than on symptoms.

Sometimes, however, a process such as rationalization is so well established and so strongly fortified by secondary gains of sympathy, relief of responsibility, and financial reward that the direct approach is not effective. In such cases, the physician may give supportive treatment "within the neurosis," that is, by neither supporting nor attacking the rationalization. To be successful with this technique, he does not argue with the patient; instead he allows the patient his own interpretation, although if questioned he indicates his position in a matter-of-fact way without insisting that the patient conform. He does not respond to the patient's pressure to perform unnecessary laboratory tests, but since he realizes that a positive diagnosis of an anxiety reaction does not exclude the possibility of coexisting or subsequent organic illness, he schedules laboratory tests and physical examinations as he (and not the patient) sees their indications. Above all, he has performed his initial work-up with sufficient care so that he can be firm in his own convictions both that an anxiety reaction exists and that organic illness either does not exist or does not account for all the patient's symptoms. If the physician makes a diagnosis of a neurotic reaction simply by ruling out organic illness, both he and the patient will be continually concerned with the possibility that something has been missed, and so treatment of the emotional problem will be avoided.

Many patients with organic illness exaggerate their symptoms. They have latent tendencies toward rationalization of anxiety which are readily mobilized by organic illness. Thus, they suffer from two conditions at the same time: the organic disease and the superimposed anxiety reaction. It is both difficult and important to assess the relative significance of these two conditions. If the doctor does not recognize the neurotic element, he may overestimate the seriousness of the organic disease and thus make the patient more of an invalid than is necessary; if he does not recognize the organic element, the patient's condition may deteriorate unnecessarily or his illness may be prolonged.

The development of anxiety reactions may be recapitulated as follows:
1. An adult who is apparently healthy but who is finding some difficulty in repressing childhood conflicts encounters:
2. A precipitating factor, such as
   a. Increased environmental stress,
   b. Mobilization of repressed conflicts, or
   c. Weakening of his adaptive capacity. All these threaten to upset his emotional homeostasis by undermining the adequacy of his repression of unresolved, conflict-laden drives and so stir up:
3. *Anxiety,* which produces symptoms of autonomic dysfunction and also produces:
4. *Regression,* in the sense of diversion of the focus of his adaptive efforts from current problems to earlier childhood conflicts. In the ensuing struggle to forestall the presumably greater anxiety which he seems to believe would result from direct dealings with the earlier conflicts, he unconsciously may call other mechanisms into play. If he is predisposed by experience or by parental precept to excessive concern about his health, the mechanism may be:
5. *Rationalization* that the anxiety produced by the conflict is due to physical illness. He then says, "I am naturally afraid, because I *have* heart trouble." But if rationalization *after* anxiety is not safe enough, he may use:
6. *Displacement* of anxiety to an organ or organ system *before* he is aware of the anxiety. He then says, "I am worried and afraid that I *might develop* heart trouble."

PSYCHOPHYSIOLOGIC AND PSYCHOSOMATIC REACTIONS

The symptoms of the fifty-four-year-old widow in the last case illustration were primarily referable to her heart and cardiovascular system, and her doctor had thought of her as suffering from a "nervous heart," or "cardiac neurosis." Various terms have been used to indicate anxiety symptoms referable to the digestive system: gastric neurosis, functional bowel disease, and the like. In the current nomenclature, subgroups of anxiety reactions in which symptoms are relatively limited to one "target organ" or organ system are called *psychophysiologic reactions*—e.g., psychophysiologic cardiovascular reaction, psychophysiologic skin reaction, psychophysiologic musculoskeletal reaction. It is not completely clear why one system is more susceptible than another or why some psychophysiologic reactions seem to lead on to *psychosomatic* conditions associated with structural body changes. The most common conditions considered "psychosomatic" include peptic ulcer, chronic ulcerative colitis, hyperthyroidism, bronchial asthma, essential hypertension, neurodermatitis, and rheumatoid arthritis. Psychosomatic conditions are sometimes classified among the psychophysiologic reactions, but they are more often classified according to pathology [5].

In Chapter 4, some of the reasons were given for suspecting that certain specific constellations of emotions are likely to be present in cases of dyspepsia due to emotional causes, a form of psychophysiologic gastrointestinal reaction, and in cases of peptic ulcer in which emotions are significant contributors to the cause. In Chapter 5, hypertension, ulcerative colitis, and some other "physical" illnesses were discussed from the same point of view.

The pioneering work of Dunbar [6] and others in the 1930s encouraged the hope that eventually one discrete group of personality patterns or characteristics would be found to be exclusively associated with each type of psychosomatic illness and therefore would presumably be the major contributor to its cause. Later, the enthusiasm for this type of specificity waned, as it became evident that there were many exceptions to the profiles as well as a good deal of overlap. Furthermore, some patients develop a series of different conditions. For example, a woman with an invalid mother developed hyperthyroidism when the last of her younger siblings no longer needed her care, bronchial asthma when she married and left home, a peptic ulcer when her husband went into military service, and neurodermatitis when some of her resentments came close to the surface during treatment.

Considerations of this kind have encouraged investigators to look more closely for specific situations in which psychosomatic conditions develop, rather than for specific personality profiles [7]. In spite of some contradictions and inconsistencies, however, there is evidence that the personalities of sufferers from a psychosomatic condition such as chronic ulcerative colitis generally have more in common with each other than they do with patients who have rheumatoid arthritis or neurodermatitis or peptic ulcer. There is also evidence that their personality characteristics antedate their illnesses and so cannot be adequately explained as the results of their illness.

As research in psychosomatic medicine has become more comprehensive, the vast complexity of the human mind and its physiologic relationships has become more evident than ever before. Specific personality determinants are still considered significant, but they are viewed as part of a complex field of interacting variables [8]. According to this concept, multiple factors in various combinations can lead to a single symptom picture. Thus, some cases of bronchial asthma seem almost completely understandable in terms of a specific allergy and others in terms of a characteristic personality pattern, but for still others, perhaps the majority, neither explanation is sufficient in itself. It may be that, with a high but not quite sufficient titer of a specific allergy factor, the additional personality factor needed to produce symptoms can be less specific than would be necessary if the titer of the allergy factor were lower.

Psychosomatic conditions are more easily studied than psychophysiologic reactions. Psychosomatic conditions can be more definitively diagnosed; they leave their mark, and they are less likely to shift from system to system. Psychophysiologic reactions, on the other hand, are more transitory, shifting, and evanescent—so much so that it would be a mistake to assume, at least in the present state of our knowledge, that the various types of psychophysiologic reactions represent discrete disease entities. The concept of psychophysiologic reactions is nevertheless useful to classify patients whose expression of anxiety is manifest primarily through one or another major target organ or system. As compared to the generalized symptoms of an anxiety reaction, the concentration of symptoms on one organ or system in a psychophysiologic reaction makes it easier for the patient to rationalize his condition as organic disease.

CONVERSION REACTIONS

Although rationalization or displacement of anxiety represents an effort to conceal its true source, it does not eliminate the patient's discomfort. He still is worried and afraid. Some patients, however, can eliminate or at least reduce anxiety by a mechanism called *conversion,* which produces the neurotic picture of a *conversion reaction* (formerly called *conversion hysteria*). Conversion produces an apparently physical impairment which the patient seems to develop specifically to protect himself from the unconscious drive causing the anxiety by making it impossible for him to act it out. Thus, it paralyzes the hand that might strike, blinds the eyes that might peep, silences the voice that might talk out of turn. In conversion, the physical symptom counteracts the anxiety, permitting the patient to be consciously comfortable, while in rationalization or displacement, the patient continues to be anxious but interprets the symptom as the cause of his anxiety. In general, the symptoms of conversion *simulate* disturbances in the *voluntary* nervous system or in the organs of special sense; the symptoms of anxiety *reflect* disturbances of the *autonomic* nervous system or the endocrine system. (For diagram, see Appendix B, Figure 16.)

Although many symptoms may result from conversion, disturbances of sensation and motion are the most common. The disturbances of sensation include anesthesia, or absence of sensation; paresthesia, or distorted sensation; and pain. Superficial or deep sensation, or the special senses may be affected. The disturbances of motion include paralyses, usually of limbs, digits, or the speech mechanism, and uncontrolled movements, as in specific types of tics or convulsions. Although the symptom generally bears some kind of relationship to the underlying emotional problem, the relationship may not be at all evident but may instead be concealed by a complex symbolic disguise which may be difficult or impossible to unravel.

Conversion reactions may resemble practically any neurologic disturbance, and the differential diagnosis is often difficult. The patient with a conversion reaction usually demonstrates the following characteristics:

1. The onset of a conversion reaction is customarily, although not always, more acute than would be expected in a corresponding organic condition.

2. The neurologic signs follow the patient's ideas of anatomic distribution. For example, hysterical anesthesia after an injury does not follow segmental or peripheral nerve distributions but involves areas such as the entire hand or foot (the so-called *glove* or *stocking anesthesia*). Physiologically impossible combinations and inconsistent variations are also seen.

3. The conversion symptoms have a symbolic relationship to the unconscious conflict or to the precipitating situation. Thus, a rifleman may develop a hysterical paralysis of the trigger finger, or a patient with a conflict over his impulse to look at sexual activity may develop an hysterical blindness. Conversely, the symbolically significant area may be spared, as in a hysterical hemianesthesia (loss of sensation of one half of the body), which customarily in males spares the genital area.

4. The patient shows *less* anxiety than an organic illness producing the same degree of disability would be expected to produce. Since the conversion mechanism protects the patient from dealing with his conflict, it *relieves* inner tension—in contrast to rationalization or displacement,

which respectively *explain* and *shift the focus of* anxiety but do not relieve it. The conversion patient's characteristic lack of concern about his symptoms was called *la belle indifférence* by Janet, one of the first who described this condition in detail [9].

5. Patients who use the conversion mechanism effectively have a characteristic group of personality traits. These *hysterical personalities* have learned through past experience and identifications easily to put aside, ignore, or deny external unpleasantness. If they cannot pay their bills, they file them away without thinking of them; if there are troubles at home, they can slip off to a movie and forget them. They are also inclined to be histrionic, dramatizing everyday events as an alternative to denial and enjoying the limelight in an exhibitionistic fashion. They are suggestible, often masochistic, and prone to develop dissociative reactions (see page 237) as well as conversion reactions. On the surface, they appear seductive, but they are usually inhibited sexually, often to the point of frigidity.

6. Conversion reactions usually respond, temporarily, to therapeutic suggestion; faith cures, electric spark machines, spine adjustments, and placebos can remove conversion signs or symptoms. A favorable response to suggestion is by no means diagnostic of a conversion reaction, however, since suggestion can also relieve pain of organic origin in suggestible individuals.

The effect of suggestion is short-lived unless the underlying problems have been solved or unless repression has been substantially reinforced, and hysterical patients characteristically develop new symptoms in different areas as the old symptoms respond to suggestion. For this reason, treatment of conversion symptoms by suggestion alone has fallen into disrepute, although it may still be indicated when judiciously combined with methods calculated to restore the emotional balance. These methods may include modifying the environment, supporting the ego to strengthen repression, or developing insight as a step toward freeing the patient from the burden of earlier unresolved problems.

At one time, a seventh characteristic would have been added to this list: that conversion reactions occurred exclusively in women, particularly young women. The derivation of the original term for conversion reaction—hysteria—reflects the ancient belief that the condition resulted when the uterus somehow broke loose from its moorings, and even in the early twentieth century, the exertion of manual pressure over the ovarian region was advocated as a treatment measure. Later, more sophisticated theories attempted to explain the predisposing causes of conversion reactions by implicating sexual conflicts, particularly conflicts surrounding the relationship between a patient and the parent of opposite sex that appeared to stem from the Oedipal or family-rivalry period of development [10].

By World War I, it had become evident that males as well as females were susceptible to conversion reactions, and a substantial proportion of American psychiatric casualties suffered from this condition. The precipitating factor in men was more likely to be a threat to life than a clear-cut sexual conflict; financial compensation as a secondary gain was more evident, and the susceptible personality was more dependent than hysterical.

For this and other reasons, some investigators have questioned the psychodynamic specificity that assumes a consistent predisposing pattern of Oedipal developmental conflict in conversion reactions and have placed proportionately greater emphasis on oral or dependency conflicts [11]. These questions parallel to some extent the questions that have been raised about the specificity of personality patterns in psychosomatic conditions. As in psychosomatic conditions, the failure of traditional psychodynamic formulas adequately to account for all aspects of conversion reactions does not mean that the traditional formulas are valueless. It does suggest, however, that the psychodynamic patterns may better be considered not as exclusive causes but as contributing causes of varying although usually major significance in a field of multiple interrelated factors, including cultural factors, psychologic factors, and (very likely) others as yet not clearly delineated.

Cultural factors have been given increased consideration in recent years, particularly in the light of the experience of World War II, in which the relative incidence of conversion reactions among psychiatric casualties was substantially reduced from the World War I incidence. Conversion reactions, at least in their more dramatic manifestations, seem now to be more characteristic of patients in lower socioeconomic groups than of the more educated and sophisticated population segments [12].

The impact of unconscious conflicts is not always obvious to the physician in a case of conversion reaction. In the following case, the basis for the conversion reaction appeared deceptively simple.

> A twenty-four-year-old infantryman prepared to go out on patrol. A shell landed nearby, and he was knocked over by the concussion. He did not lose consciousness but discovered that he could not move his right arm. He was willing to be examined by a physician, who found that the paralysis of his arm did not follow either segmental or peripheral patterns and that the patient was quite unconcerned about his injury. No findings consistent with organic disease or injury were discovered during physical and neurologic examinations.

At first glance, this reaction appears to represent an obvious compromise solution of a conflict between the patient's fear of being injured or killed on patrol and his self-respect, which would not permit him to evade his duty.

This explanation is true as far as it goes, but since many other soldiers go through similar frightening experiences either without symptoms or with different symptoms, there must be more to the problem than a simple escape. Why was this particular soldier so sensitive to danger? And why, once the danger was over, did he not get well again?

An extended psychiatric examination was necessary to discover some tenable answers to these questions. The psychiatrist found evidence of an earlier unresolved conflict in the area of family rivalries that appeared to explain why he did not combat his fear of injury or death more realistically. The psychiatrist's reconstruction of the development of this reaction was as follows.

> As a child, the patient had resented his father's cruel treatment of his mother and had wanted to defend her. He had felt sure, however, that if he had tried to defend her, his father would have treated him with equal cruelty, and he had felt so helpless that he believed his father would have killed him. This possibility was so frightening that he had repressed everything involved in the situation: his fear, his resentment, and his wish to defend his mother. All of these, as well as his conviction that he had saved himself by withholding his defiance of his father, remained below the surface of his awareness for many years until he was knocked over by the concussion of the shell. This evidence of danger from the aggressive action of an enemy stirred up his repressed fear of death from the aggressive action of his earlier "enemy," his father. It also stirred up the associated impulse to defend his mother, the impulse which had apparently endangered him. As a soldier with a gun in his hand, he was now expected to attack in spite of his inner belief that to attack assured his destruction.
>
> By unconsciously converting his childhood fear to a paralyzed striking arm, however, he avoided the earlier danger. He said, in effect: "I am now powerless to strike at the enemy, and therefore he will not kill me, just as my father spared me when I did not attack him."

He thus relieved his anxiety, and his symptoms persisted at first in order to prevent the return of the anxiety. Once the adequacy of his repression had been threatened, the possibility of a return to the situation in which his aggressive drive had been mobilized was too dangerous to risk. The first function of the symptom—the primary gain—was the relief from intolerable anxiety.

Secondary Gains and Malingering

One important consequence of his conversion reaction was his removal from combat. This was a *secondary gain,* or a secondary advantage which the patient derived from his illness. It would be a mistake to confuse the secondary gain with the precipitating cause, or primary gain, of the reaction. He did not become ill in order to get out of combat but in order to reduce the anxiety about taking aggressive action. The symptom reduced this anxiety, at least for the time being, but it also led, secondarily, to his removal from combat. The fact that the symptom both accomplished its primary purpose and produced a secondary gain added to the difficulties of treatment. Treatment of any neurosis is much more difficult when secondary gains are great or cannot be modified, and the problem is intensified in a conversion reaction in which the symptom has so effectively served to reduce anxiety.

The secondary gains of illness may be financial, in the form of a pension or compensation, or they may be emotional, as in the gratification of dependency needs stirred up by the regression. Their modification should be approached tactfully, however, since the patient is not aware that they influence his symptoms or stand in the way of his improvement. Thus it is neither fair nor helpful to a patient with a conversion reaction to accuse him of producing symptoms in order to avoid duty or gain a pension. Since the patient perceives that this accusation is untrue, he can only assume that it stems from the physician's hostility to him. Whether it is real or apparent, hostility on the part of someone on whom the patient is dependent will increase his insecurity and make it more difficult than ever for him to risk exploring his underlying conflicts.

When a conversion reaction allows a patient to avoid work or danger or when it permits him to receive a pension, the physician may find it difficult to believe that the mechanism is entirely unconscious. It is true that an occasional patient consciously simulates illness, or *malingers.* The malingerer, however, generally fears consciously that his deception will be detected and either evades examination or is tense and apprehensive during examination procedures. On the other hand, since the patient with a conversion reaction is misleading himself as well as others, he either welcomes or is indifferent to standard examination procedures.

Treatment

Occasionally, a patient with a conversion reaction improves after direct and aggressive confrontation with the psychodynamic forces which apparently are producing his symptoms. With few exceptions, however, this technique does not lead to sustained improvement and may lead to more severe and incapacitating symptoms. In these cases, the aggressive interpretation seems to strip the defenses from the underlying conflict, abruptly exposing the patient to the overwhelming anxiety he has been at such pains to conceal from himself. He responds as if the confrontation had demonstrated to him that the conversion mechanism was inadequate to control his dangerous impulse, and so he must find an alternative solution that is more impermeable to frontal assault. If the alternative solution is a psychosis, the patient's goal of conflict protection is indeed attained, as he is much more insulated from treatment by a psychosis than by a conversion reaction, but his chances of rehabilitation are seriously impaired. Fortunately, most patients with conversion reactions respond to premature confrontation by simply rejecting the interpretation and not by a retreat into psychosis, and an increase in the patient's resistance to a latter, better-timed interpretation is usually the only damage that is done.

The appropriate role of the physician in the management of conversion reactions does not differ materially from his role in the management of other neurotic reactions. This role is discussed in some detail in Chapter 15. If psychologic supportive measures and efforts to reduce secondary gains are not effective in a reasonably short time, the physician should refer the patient for a more intensive form of psychotherapy, aimed at uncovering the causes of his anxiety and desensitizing him to them. When the soldier in the case discussed above can break through the barrier of repression and bring into consciousness the childhood reasons for his fear of aggression, he can reappraise his fear in the light of current adult realities. This reappraisal represents an important step toward reducing the impact of past problems on the patient's response to present stresses.

Differential Diagnosis of Neurotic Reactions with Physical Symptoms

In this part of the chapter, I discussed two general types of neurotic reaction resulting in physical symptoms: (1) anxiety reactions and psychophysiologic reactions, whose symptoms represent physiologic accompaniments of anxiety, often rationalized as organic illness; and (2) conversion reactions, or physical manifestations which protect the patient against anxiety.

Also mentioned were the group of phobic reactions in which the apparent source of anxiety is displaced to a part of the body. Unwarranted preoccupation with health is by no means limited to these three conditions; it is probably the most frequent single symptom of emotional illness. Many dependent personalities are chronically hypochondriacal. Patients with schizophrenia, particularly early schizophrenia, and depressed patients often complain of physical symptoms, and the content of some obsessions may be related to health. The beginning failings of the patient with organic mental disease may be rationalized as illness in other body areas. In short, there is virtually no psychiatric illness which is not accompanied by concerns about health.

Sometimes the nature of the symptom can be a key to its classification. For example, the tension headache in anxiety reactions is generally described as "bandlike." It is usually bilateral and accompanied by other signs of muscular tension. The headache of the hypochondriacal dependent personality is usually vague and poorly defined. The phobic patient expresses an inordinate concern about the possible origin of a relatively mild headache; he is preoccupied with the possibility that it is due to a brain tumor. The headache in a conversion reaction is described in dramatic terms, but the patient shows a disproportionate lack of concern about it. The depressed patient's headache is likely to be described in fatalistic terms, and there is usually a bizarre quality about the schizophrenic's headache. A specific type of headache which appears to result at least in part from a localized psychophysiologic vascular reaction is called *migraine.* Migraine is commonly unilateral, preceded by an aura, intense in degree, and limited in duration. It occurs most often in somewhat compulsive personalities when under unusual stress or, in some patients, at the end of a stressful period.

Complicating the differential diagnosis is the fact that patients do not always restrict themselves to the use of one mechanism; the same individual may use rationalization, displacement, and conversion either sequentially or all at the same time. Finally, there is always the possibility that a neurotic patient may also suffer from organic illness; a patient's headache may be due to a brain tumor, whereas his other symptoms may be due to his neurosis.

DISSOCIATIVE REACTIONS

Conversion and dissociative reactions, although using different major mechanisms, usually occur in hysterical personalities and often have been reported sequentially in the same patient. Both conditions are problem solving, in that they relieve rather than divert anxiety.

In a dissociative reaction, the patient combines denial and repression to disavow an anxiety-laden aspect of his personality, usually by means of *amnesia,* or loss of memory. The disavowed aspect frequently but not always has a sexual connotation. Repression is a universal phenomenon; the patient who dissociates differs from the average person in the degree to which he uses repression and in his extensive use of denial. He also differs from the average young or middle-aged person because his amnesia or forgetfulness primarily includes recent or relatively recent rather than remote events. Patients with dissociative reactions are often young women who come to the attention of police or physicians after wandering around in strange cities, unable to tell who they are or what they are supposed to be doing and failing to recognize their names or addresses. Their information and opinions about subjects without special relevance to their personal lives customarily remain intact. The condition is relatively easily differentiated from organic memory defects by its more sudden and dramatic onset, by the specific and total amnesia for conflict-laden material as contrasted with the absence of any defect in other areas, and by the absence of pathologic findings on neurologic examination.

Hypnosis or sodium amytal interviews are often effective in helping the patient to remember the repressed or denied material, although, as in any emotional illness, the physician should recognize that the defense mechanisms serve a purpose and that their precipitate removal may mobilize so much anxiety that the patient may retreat behind the protection of new and more impenetrable defenses.

The dissociative reaction and the hysterical personality are not limited to women, as shown by the following case.

> An enlisted man in the Air Corps had some previous experience as a private pilot. After a disagreement with his wife, he decided to punish her by committing suicide. Choosing the most dramatic method he could think of, he took off in a large, unattended aircraft and made several passes at the local river, each time pulling up before he plunged in. Very soon, all other aircraft were diverted to other cities, and the local control tower was concentrating on trying to persuade him to change his mind. He finally agreed, but then he discovered that although he knew how to take off, he did not know how to land the unfamiliar plane. After some tense interchanges with the control tower, however, he managed to get the plane down. When the welcoming party of military police arrived at the plane, he found himself unable to remember his name or anything about his identity, his present situation, or the events leading up to it.

Not all cases of dissociative reaction are so dramatic or so evidently related to precipitating factors. In the case described above, the solution was so apposite that it was natural to suspect that the patient was malingering, or consciously simulating amnesia. However, his willingness, in fact his eagerness, to submit to procedures such as hypnosis that were intended to restore his memory and to prepare him, as it were, for court-martial made unlikely the diagnosis of malingering.

Amnesia is not the only symptom of the dissociative reaction. The multiple personality as described by Prince and others [13] is the most spectacular manifestation. Some patients have disturbances of consciousness that may be difficult to distinguish from organic stupors and deliriums, and other patients have episodes of depersonalization that symptomatically resemble schizophrenia, although the course is likely to be shorter and more dramatic.

PHOBIC REACTIONS

In phobias, or neurotic fears, anxiety is displaced to objects or situations outside the body or, as briefly mentioned in the first part of this chapter, to an organ or organ system within the body. The object or situation chosen is symbolic of the conflict, either obviously, as in a phobia of knives, or subtly, as in a phobia of mice, where the significance of the mouse can only be discovered through the patient's associations [14]. The extent of the disability in phobias varies greatly; for example, someone who suffers from a mild fear of high places can protect himself with little inconvenience by staying away from parapets and the like. On the other hand, a patient with a severe phobia of open places may be forced to remain a virtual prisoner in his own house in order to avoid the feared situation. (For diagram, see Appendix B, Figure 17.)

If a patient can displace his anxiety to something he can avoid, he can be comfortable most of the time. This has been called the *economic function* of the mental mechanism, clearly seen in the phobia. For example, in *The Locomotive God*, Professor William Ellery Leonard describes the phobia of locomotives that kept him from crossing railroad tracks and so confined him to his campus for over twenty years [15]. As long as he stayed away from railroad tracks, the professor was comfortable; without such a pattern of defense, he presumably never would be free from anxiety. It follows, then, that a well-established mechanism of defense, such as displacement, makes the inner conflicts difficult to treat; a patient who has developed a phobia resists efforts to break down the mechanism he has built up, efforts which would reconstitute a situation in which he could not escape his anxiety. He is usually much more receptive to treatment of the symptom than to treatment of the conflicts and often makes attempts on his own to counteract his fears. These so-called *counterphobic* attempts lead him to climb mountains if he is afraid of heights, go to zoos if he fears animals, and so on. He seems to feel that if he overcomes the symptoms, he can control the conflict without having to contend with it directly.

Encouragement of and assistance to the patient's counterphobic efforts are the major distinguishing features of "behavior therapy," based on the concept that the phobia is a conditioned response that is best approached by "deconditioning" [16]. This technique appears to be most successful under two conditions: (1) when it represents a part, or adjunct, of a more comprehensive treatment approach; and (2) when the phobia has, psychodynamically speaking, outlived its usefulness. The phobia has outlived its usefulness when it continues as an habitual pattern after emotional homeostasis has been restored in one way or another. However, when the phobia continues to represent a significant protection to the patient, the therapist should be careful when encouraging the patient's counterphobic efforts not to overstretch his ability to tolerate his fears, or new mechanisms will be called into action and new symptoms will develop.

The following fairly typical case illustrates the development of a phobia and its treatment by a physician with a particular interest in emotional illness.

> A university student complained to his physician of fear which assailed him whenever he attended class. He was so preoccupied by his fear that he could not pay attention to the lectures and so concerned about his problem that he could not concentrate on his studies. His academic future was seriously threatened because he was on probation following a poor performance in his previous term's examinations, although he had had a good record in earlier years.
>
> The patient was the younger of two siblings. His older sister, described as headstrong, self-centered, and "spoiled," had married during high school, much against her family's wishes. During the previous term she had returned home, pregnant and with two small children, after a particularly severe outbreak of marital conflict.
>
> When the sister arrived with her family, the house became crowded; the patient's study space was preempted for a nursery, and when he could find a place to study, he was frequently disturbed by the noisy babies. The sister seemed to be using her pregnancy and her misfortune to justify avoiding all of the housework, while his mother attempted to care for the small children as well as to do her own work. His mother was frequently exhausted and, at first apologetically but later routinely, asked the patient to do the shopping and other chores when he came home from class. On one or two occasions, he begged off because of the pressure of studies; his mother did not complain, but he felt too guilty about the extra work it was causing her to get any studying done. His mother met his suggestion that his sister do the shopping with reproving looks and

patient reiteration of his sister's unfortunate predicament. His father, burdened by additional financial problems, seemed oblivious of the patient's distress.

Characteristically, he kept his feelings to himself, but when his poor examination results arrived and he realized how little his needs had been considered, he was angry enough at all of them to be ready to break through his reserve and tell them how he felt. Before he found the right opportunity, however, his parents took the wind out of his sails by accepting the responsibility for the poor results, borrowing the money to make it possible for him to live elsewhere, and insisting that he should not take a job but should devote his full attention to his studies.

Their reaction made him feel so ashamed of his anger that he repressed it. He still inwardly resented his sister for her selfishness and impulsiveness, but outwardly he excused her because she was unhappy; he still inwardly resented his mother for her overprotection of his sister, although consciously he was sympathetic because she was overworked; he inwardly resented his father for his passivity and failure to perceive his problem, but he rationalized that he was doing all he could. Finally, the room his parents rented for him turned out to be uncomfortable and not conducive to study; meanwhile, with the birth of his sister's latest baby, her family absorbed the only beachhead he retained at home, so he could not even go home on weekends.

Ingrained in his personality structure as a result of early experience was a strong prohibition against expressing any anger that did not have a clear-cut justification. Although in this case he could not justify it, the accumulation of inner resentment became so great that it threatened to break out into overt hostility. Instead of experiencing the consequent anxiety as an unknown, terrifying, internal force from which he could not escape, he was able to localize and identify it—erroneously but effectively—as fear of the classroom. The cramped quarters of the classroom and his inability to leave without becoming conspicuous represented a trap, symbolizing the trap he was in with his family. By displacing his anxiety from a concern about the breakthrough of hostility to anxiety about the close quarters of the classroom, he had diverted the focus of attention from the "real" and apparently inescapable danger to an intrinsically harmless substitute from which he could escape by leaving the room, if his fears justified the embarrassment of leaving.

By the time his physician had arrived at this formulation, he considered that the relationship he had established with the patient justified his undertaking a trial of treatment before considering psychiatric referral. Recognizing that, although handicapped, the patient was not overwhelmed by his classroom fears, the physician encouraged him to continue his counterphobic efforts by continuing to attend classes and, in a series of interviews, gently explored his feelings about his home situation. Gradually, the patient became less frightened of his anger, and as he felt more at ease in sharing it with his doctor, he found he could be more objective about the family and about himself. He realized that he had contributed substantially to constructing his own trap by taking the line of least resistance each time another problem came up and by expecting his family to recognize his needs without his expressing them.

By the end of five or six interviews, he was able to remain in class with no more than an occasional twinge of anxiety. He was studying effectively, and he had taken the initiative in changing his room. He also discovered that, with some effort on his part, he could communicate better with his father and that his sister responded surprisingly well to the occasional mild suggestion he offered when he stopped by at home. His basic personality was essentially the same; he still avoided anger if possible, he still felt guilty whenever he thought he was burdening his mother, it still required an effort for him to assert himself, and he still became anxious under stress.

He felt well enough, however, to be confident of his ability to complete his education. The rapid progress he had made encouraged him to believe that he would continue to progress without further treatment, although he recognized that he might later decide on more intensive psychiatric treatment if he ran into more trouble.

Early in its course, a phobia responds well to intensive psychotherapy, but if the phobia is well established, a less intensive, supportive type of treatment may be indicated in an effort to improve defenses rather than to remove the conflict. The closer the phobia resembles an obsession or compulsion, the more difficult it is to treat, and in some cases the difference is hard to detect. A phobia of dirt, for instance, may be the forerunner of a washing compulsion; a phobia of knives may gradually develop into an obsessive fear of killing someone, as the patient's regression spreads to require more of his concern. Here, as in the neurosis with physical symptoms, patients with clear-cut clinical entities are seen less frequently than patients who use several mechanisms in varying degrees at different times in their clinical courses.

DEPRESSIVE REACTIONS

Feelings of depression may be associated with a variety of emotional disorders. As discussed in Chapter 1, depression can result when grief is not directly expressed and remains buried in the patient's unconscious. Ambivalent feelings toward someone who dies make it difficult for the survivor to express grief at his loss. If his ability to inhibit is strong enough, he may repress these feelings indefinitely. The effort of repression, however, immobilizes part of his adaptive capacity, leaving his personality more vulnerable to internal or external pressure. Often the bereaved person tries to avoid any circumstances which might stir up his feelings about the deceased; for example, a widower forbade his children to mention their mother's name and insisted that all her pictures and possessions must be kept out of sight. If failure of repression becomes imminent, the patient may express his grief in a disguised form. Since his disguise will follow the same pattern as the symptoms of a clinical psychoneurosis, the dynamic significance of the grief may be missed. Conversion, phobic and psychophysiologic patterns, and anxiety reactions are common disguises of grief.

In some patients, the expression of grief is simply exaggerated and prolonged. Long after his loss, the patient continues to look downcast and fatigued, with the corners of his mouth turned down, his posture bent, and his movements, his speech, and most of his body functions slowed. He sighs frequently and loses appetite, weight, and sleep. He is concerned primarily with himself, and it is often his concern about his physical health that brings him to the physician. Some patients report only the physical symptoms—constipation and anorexia, perhaps—and the presence of an underlying depression may not be evident [17]. One clue is the patient's attitude—he usually comes without much hope that anything can be done, and his whole demeanor expresses pessimism. In severe cases, his symptoms may be accompanied by agitation, severe insomnia, feelings of worthlessness, and a need for punishment which can result in suicide.

This condition, formerly called *reactive depression* and now renamed *depressive reaction*, resembles concealed grief in that it also results from ambivalent feelings toward the deceased, but although the *hostility* is repressed, the *guilt* is not. Usually, people with this condition have grown up in families which did not permit the outward expression of hostility. When they incorporated their families' attitudes and prohibitions, they developed strict superegos which made them feel particularly guilty about their hostile feelings [18]. Their guilt makes them feel deserving of punishment, and they appear to deflect the target of their angry feelings from others to themselves. Instead of saying, "I hate him," they seem to be saying, "I don't hate him; I hate myself instead. I am unworthy and do not deserve any consideration from anybody." Since they are not aware of their hostility, they do not understand explanations of the basis for their depressions, and since their guilt makes them believe they should be punished, sympathy or cheering up or anything that gives them special consideration makes them feel more undeserving and more depressed. (For diagram, see Appendix B, Figure 18.)

It is often difficult to determine where appropriate grief ends and depression begins. The determinants are essentially quantitative: how long the symptoms last, how much self-accusation is present, how complete is the patient's withdrawal from other contacts. The same criteria for differentiation apply when an event other than death is the precipitating factor. Although the death of someone for whom the patient has ambivalent feelings is the usual precipitating event in this type of depression, it also may be set off by other circumstances which mobilize his ambivalence. In these cases, however, the diagnosis of depression is less complicated; for example, it is easier to identify depression as contrasted to grief in a mother whose son had just gone into the Army than in a mother whose son has just been killed in action, because appropriate grief in the second case is greater and its manifestations more closely resemble depression.

Although a strong element of ambivalence is customarily present in delayed or disguised grief reactions, the assumption of its presence cannot be made on the basis of the diagnosis alone without confirming evidence. A depressive reaction may also result if the patient's relationship to the deceased was unusually dependent or if it was complicated by sexual feelings which were unacceptable to the patient.

Unacceptable sexual feelings may be enough in themselves to precipitate a depression where there has been no death or other loss.

> A fifty-two-year-old executive complained of constipation and vague abdominal pains. His physician noted his downcast and pessimistic demeanor and discovered that, although not seriously incapacitated, he had been staying home from work, remaining for the most part in bed and responding to his family's concern about him with unaccustomed irritability. At first he could not think of any recent change in his life circumstances, but he finally remarked, "I did hire a new secretary six weeks ago." He acknowledged that he had developed sexual feelings for his new secretary and that he found these feelings frightening and unacceptable. "After all, she's young enough to be my daughter."
>
> He recalled that in twenty-nine years of a happy marriage, there had been one extramarital episode. Twenty years earlier, he had had sexual intercourse with a fellow employee on one occasion. He had felt guilty and had broken off the relation without really coming to grips with his feelings about it, and ever since then he had tried to forget it. Although he had not acted on his feelings toward his new secretary, he nevertheless felt he deserved punishment because he had transgressed in the past [19].

This man felt guilty about his past transgression but also ashamed of his inability to control his current sexual feelings. Shame, guilt, or both together, therefore, as well as grief and guilt, can cause depressive reactions, and sometimes all three of these elements are present.

The therapeutic approach varies with the cause. If the expression of grief has been inhibited by repressed anger, the doctor must help his patient to face his repressed, angry feelings. Facing his anger is less difficult when the precipitating factor is not a death; it is easier to express anger at a doctor who has amputated a leg or at a son who has left home than to acknowledge anger at someone who is dead and can neither retaliate nor forgive. In any case, before he faces his anger, the patient needs help in mitigating the severity of his superego with respect to hostility; otherwise, as he begins to comprehend the extent of his hostility, his guilt will overwhelm him.

If the doctor's attitude is too sympathetic, the patient feels even more guilty because the doctor is so nice to him. On the other hand, if the doctor is firm and a bit stern with the patient so that his attitude toward the patient is not completely different from the patient's attitude toward himself, the patient can permit the doctor in a way to represent his conscience for a while and so can be somewhat less self-punitive. The doctor might insist that the patient remain out of bed and that, if he continues for a while to stay home from work, he should clean out the basement and take care of some of the other chores around the house. By making realistic demands, the doctor becomes a benevolent taskmaster who helps the patient expiate some of his guilt.

The doctor's course is on another tack when the patient's major problem is shame. The patient who is depressed because he is ashamed needs bolstering of his self-esteem, and the assignment of drudgery is not calculated to raise his self-esteem. Instead, in combating low self-esteem, the doctor searches for and supports the patient's emotional strengths. With the patient who is both guilty and ashamed, the doctor requires considerable skill to adapt his approach to the particular facet of the problem that currently predominates [19].

The differential diagnosis of neurotic and psychotic depression (p. 264) is often very difficult to make, and whenever the physician has any doubts about the diagnosis, the suicide risk, or the appropriate treatment of a depressed patient, he should obtain psychiatric consultation.

Although psychotherapy is the treatment of choice, antidepressant drugs or, in very severe cases, electric shock treatments occasionally are used for this type of depression. Electric shock treatment usually produces at least temporary improvement and may be necessary when the suicide risk is great. Ordinarily, however, the symptoms of a neurotic depression return as the immediate effects of the treatment wear off, and the patient is then more difficult to treat psychotherapeutically. This sequel is particularly true when, as often happens, the patient interprets the shock treatment as punishment and its administration as evidence that the doctor believes he *is* guilty and deserving of retribution.

A number of drugs have been developed to elevate the mood of depressed patients. Although none of them is a panacea, they can in many cases be helpful adjuncts to treatment, provided that a psychotherapeutic approach is carried out concurrently (see Table III, p. 345).

The prognosis for a depressive reaction is usually good, although if a long span of time has elapsed since the crucial loss, it may be difficult to recover the memories and their associated feelings.

OBSESSIVE-COMPULSIVE REACTIONS

One other important type of neurotic reaction will only be mentioned here for the sake of completeness. The obsessive-compulsive reaction is seldom seen in patients who are not compulsive personalities, and so it is discussed together with the personality disorder (Chapter 5).

SUMMARY

Anxiety results when repressed drives or conflicts threaten to break into consciousness. If a patient cannot strengthen repression, reduce or find satisfactory substitute outlets for the drives, or resolve the conflicts, his anxiety persists and forms an anxiety reaction, characterized by generalized autonomic nervous-system dysfunction or by a psychophysiologic reaction (when the autonomic dysfunction is primarily manifest in one organ system). These reactions are often rationalized as organic disease. Various forms of substitute expression or resolution of anxiety may be undertaken, either by association with acceptable drives or by the use of defense mechanisms such as displacement to an organ, object, or situation; conversion to a physical disability; denial and dissociation; or reaction formation.

A general discussion of the office treatment of neurotic reactions will be found in Chapter 15.

REFERENCES

1. Freud, S.: "Inhibition, Symptoms and Anxiety" (1926), in *Standard Edition*, 1959, vol. XX, p. 75.
2. A general discussion of neurotic reactions from the psychoanalytic point of view appears in:
   Fenichel, O.: *The Psychoanalytic Theory of Neurosis*, New York, W. W. Norton & Company, Inc., 1945.
3. Kolb, L. C.: "Anxiety and the Anxiety States," *J. Chronic Dis.*, 9:199, 1959.

4. Cannon, W. B.: *The Wisdom of the Body,* New York, W. W. Norton & Company, Inc., 1932.
5. Weiss, E., and O. S. English: *Psychosomatic Medicine,* 3d ed., Philadelphia, W. B. Saunders Company, 1957.
6. Dunbar, H. F.: *Psychosomatic Diagnosis,* New York, Paul B. Hoeber, Inc., 1943.
7. Alexander, Franz: *Psychosomatic Medicine,* New York, W. W. Norton & Company, Inc., 1950.
   ———— and T. M. French (eds.): *Studies in Psychosomatic Medicine,* New York, The Ronald Press Company, 1948.
   ———— and T. S. Szasz: "The Psychosomatic Approach in Medicine," in F. Alexander, and H. Ross (eds.), *Dynamic Psychiatry,* Chicago, The University of Chicago Press, 1952.
8. Grinker, R. R.: *Psychosomatic Research,* New York, W. W. Norton & Company, Inc., 1953.
   Kubie, L. S.: "The Problem of Specificity in the Psychosomatic Process," in E. D. Wittkower and R. A. Cleghorn, *Recent Developments in Psychosomatic Medicine,* Philadelphia, J. B. Lippincott Company, 1957.
9. Janet, P. M.: *The Major Symptoms of Hysterias,* 2d ed., New York, The Macmillan Company, 1929.
10. Breuer, J., and S. Freud: "Studies in Hysteria" (1895), in *Standard Edition,* 1955, vol. II, p. 1.
11. Marmor, J.: "Orality in the Hysterical Personality," *J. Amer. Psychoanal. Ass.,* 1:656, 1954.
    Chodoff, P. A., and H. Lyons: "Hysteria, the Hysterical Personality, and 'Hysterical' Conversion," *Amer. J. Psychiat.,* 114:734, 1958.
12. Chodoff, P. A.: "Reexamination of Some Aspects of Conversion Hysteria," *Psychiatry,* 17:75, 1954.
    Ziegler, F., J. Imboden, and E. Meyer: "Contemporary Conversion Symptomatology," *Amer. J. Psychiat.,* 116:901, 1960.
13. Prince, M.: *The Dissociation of a Personality,* New York, Longmans, Green & Co., Inc., 1905.
    Thigpen, H., and H. M. Cleckley: *The Three Faces of Eve,* New York, McGraw-Hill Book Company, 1957.
14. Freud, S.: "Analysis of a Phobia in a Five Year Old Boy" (1909), in *Standard Edition,* 1955, vol. X, p. 3.
    ————: "Obsessions and Phobias: Their Psychical Mechanisms and Their Aetiology" (1895), in *Standard Edition,* 1962, vol. III, p. 69.
15. Leonard, W. E.: *The Locomotive God,* New York, Century Company, 1927.
16. Eysenck, H. J. (ed.): *Behaviour Therapy and the Neuroses,* New York, Pergamon Press, 1960.
17. Stoeckle, J. D., and G. E. Davidson: "Bodily Complaints and Other Symptoms of Depressive Reaction," *J.A.M.A.,* 180:134, 1962.
18. Freud, Sigmund: "Mourning and Melancholia" (1917), in *Standard Edition,* 1957, vol. XIV, p. 237.
19. Daniels, R. S.: "Psychotherapy of Depression," *Postgrad. Med.,* 32:436, 1962.

Chapter 11

PSYCHOTIC REACTIONS

When psychiatric diagnosis was based on a relatively superficial description of manifest symptoms, the distinction between psychosis and neurosis was not hard to make. The conditions which required mental-hospital care were psychotic; the conditions which were consistent with adaptation outside of a hospital were *ipso facto* neurotic. With modern refinements of diagnosis, however, the line between the two groups has become blurred, as it has been discovered that from the viewpoint of personality structure, some ambulatory patients have much more in common with most hospitalized patients than they have with most ambulatory patients, and vice versa [1].

It is still easy to distinguish between relatively severe psychotic reactions, such as hebephrenic schizophrenia, and relatively benign neurotic reactions. It is harder, however, to find a formula that will consistently differentiate between severe neurotic reactions and mild psychotic reactions—between severe neurotic depressions and mild psychotic depressions, for example.

To complicate the problem, there is some evidence that a neurosis can become a psychosis, although some psychiatrists believe that an apparent transition simply means that the psychosis was present but latent all along. The argument is more vigorously pursued in the case of patients who at one time are considered neurotic but who later show signs of schizophrenia than in the parallel case of the compulsive neurotic who develops an involutional depression, where the depression is considered a new and separate entity superimposed on the neurosis.

It may no longer be possible to find consistent, mutually exclusive definitions of neurosis and psychosis. Since these terms are honored by tradition and fixed in the literature, however, they at least deserve working definitions. In typical neurotic reactions, as discussed in the last chapter, the patient meets his problem by a partial regression to a point of fixation while retaining his capacity to meet many if not most problems on an adult level. Although preoccupied with his symptoms, he continues to be concerned with his relationships to other people. Generally speaking, the neurotic retreats on one front but maintains his positions elsewhere, whereas in the typical psychotic reaction, the retreat has become a rout and the regression is total or close to it. Consequently, the psychotic is preoccupied with himself virtually to the exclusion of other relationships and may lose contact with his environment completely, although in less severe regressions he retains a tenuous semblance of relationship to the world about him. As a result of his failure to make a realistic adaptation, he often behaves in such a peculiar or dangerous manner that hospital care is necessary.

The collapse of the patient's integration in the reactions commonly classified as psychotic may be due primarily to organic causes—either systemic disease or disease of the central nervous system. This group of psychotic reactions is described in the next chapter. The causes of the reactions described in this chapter may also have an organic component, although the exact nature of any organic component is as yet undetermined, but the contribution of psychologic and social factors is more clearly delineated. The end results of the two types of psychotic reaction may be difficult to distinguish, and both the general physician and the psychiatrist should be alert to the possibilities of coexisting organic disease in any psychotic reaction, no matter how obvious the psychologic basis appears.

Four major groups of psychotic reactions have causes which appear to be chiefly psychologic. These are *schizophrenic, paranoid, manic-depressive,* and *involutional reactions.* They are closely related to one another, and in many psychotic patients, characteristics of two or more groups may be discerned.

SCHIZOPHRENIC REACTIONS

Of the four major groups of psychotic reactions, schizophrenic reaction is the most common. It often occurs in adolescence, and even when the overt symptoms develop many years later, the personality characteristics on which they are superimposed usually become apparent in adolescence.

Patients with the diagnosis of schizophrenia occupy approximately one-half of all mental hospital beds—or one-fourth of all hospital beds in the United States. More patients are hospitalized with schizophrenia than with any other disease. These observations alone make it clear that schizophrenia presents economic and health problems of major proportions. Since it often appears in adolescence or shortly after, since it does not shorten life, and since the response to treatment in many patients is relatively poor, the average hospital stay for schizophrenia is longer than for most other forms of illness. The turnover in hospitalized cases is therefore low, and the incidence in the general population is not so high as the hospital census might at first suggest. On the other hand, many schizophrenics do not require hospital care and are not recorded in these statistics.

The Swiss psychiatrist Bleuler coined the term "schizophrenia" (split personality) as a more accurate descriptive term than its predecessor, "dementia praecox" [2]. Bleuler believed that the implications of Kraepelin's term, "dementia praecox"—that the illness consistently began in early life and that it produced intellectual deterioration—were both inaccurate and unduly limiting. He was the first to observe that the most dramatic symptoms of the illness—delusions and hallucinations—were not the schizophrenic's primary problem but were secondary, or restitutive, symptoms, evidence of the patient's effort to restore his relationship to reality. Bleuler's list of basic, or primary, symptoms is often referred to as the "four A's." They include: (1) Affective disturbances—emotional flatness or inappropriateness; (2) Association looseness—the disturbance in thinking that results in transitions that presumably have their own logic which is not evident to nonschizophrenics [3]; (3) Autism—the almost exclusive use of the self as the point of reference in the schizophrenic's thinking; and (4) Ambivalence, which although evident to a degree in most relationships, dominates the relationships of the schizophrenic.

Early Schizophrenia

The psychiatrist usually sees referred schizophrenics when their symptoms are pronounced and well established; other physicians, as well as clergymen and caseworkers in social agencies, are more likely to see early cases, when the symptoms are not clear-cut and the diagnosis is more difficult. Early diagnostic indications are therefore much more important to the reader who is not planning to become a psychiatrist than are the various types and subtypes of the full-blown symptom picture.

The most frequent presenting complaints of the early schizophrenic are hypochondriacal. A youth, usually in late adolescence or the early twenties, may request a physical examination to determine the cause of a pain or a peculiar sensation. The first indication of schizophrenia may be the somewhat bizarre or unusual terms in which the symptom is described or the disproportionate emphasis given to relatively minor complaints. The following case shows how a patient may express in a peculiar way symptoms which would appear to have serious significance, yet worry more about a minute cosmetic defect.

> A young man complained of headaches and chest pain. When asked for a more explicit description of his symptoms, he said that the pain in his chest made it feel like jelly and that his head felt "like a big mass of fluid in the brain." He also was concerned, without objective evidence, that his right eye was becoming smaller and that his hands were becoming atrophied. He worried most, however, about a slight loss of hair in the area surrounding a mole above his left ear.

The initial diagnostic impression of early schizophrenia was later confirmed. There were no physical findings to account for any but the last complaint and no evidence of organic disease of the central nervous system, which, particularly in early stages, may resemble schizophrenia.

In many cases, the bizarre nature of the patient's complaints is not as obvious as in the case quoted above, and the physician must rely for diagnostic evidence on rather indefinable, subjective nuances of manner or attitude. The physician's first hint may be a somewhat frustrating inability to establish communication or rapport with the patient, as if a barrier existed between them. Sometimes the patient seems to lack appropriate emotional responses; he may smile without apparent reason or fail to show feeling when there appears to be good cause. He may relate colorful details of his personal and sex life with disconcerting abruptness and without the expected reserve or embarrassment. His manner of speech may be somewhat stilted, and his posture and body movements may seem a little awkward and uncomfortable. A physician who has known him over several years may recognize a personality change in the direction of shyness and withdrawal. The early schizophrenic finds it hard to concentrate on problems outside himself and is so preoccupied with his own thoughts or daydreams that his schoolwork or job efficiency suffers. He becomes to some degree forgetful and may in addition be secretive, suspicious, irritable, depressed, or sleepless. He not only appears to be detached but may complain that things no longer seem real to him or that he feels as if he were standing to one side and observing himself in action (the symptom of *depersonalization*).

Often his parents bring him for examination because of one or more of these symptoms. They may report that he insists on performing some incomprehensible routine, such as reversing the mattress before going to bed, or that he has unaccountably taken a perfectly good radio apart or that he has accused them of putting saltpeter in his food. Some patients, however, maintain a reasonably adequate façade, so that the personality in general remains apparently intact save for occasional pathologic out-croppings. This course may go on indefinitely, or else one of the incidents may develop into a major episode.

Usually the onset is insidious, occurring in adolescence or somewhat later, although it may begin in childhood (page 300) or as late as middle age. Often, once it becomes evident that the patient is ill, relatives can recall incidents of peculiar thinking or behavior which happened many years before but which they then rationalized as quirks or habits of no particular consequence.

Occasionally the onset is acute. The patient, who may or may not have shown earlier signs of withdrawal, rapidly stops communicating with his environment or suddenly lashes out in a random and desperate fashion without apparent concern for or awareness of his own safety. An episode of this type (often called *catatonic excitement*) is a medical emergency, since the patient may injure himself or others or drive himself to exhaus-tion. While arrangements are made for psychiatric care, the patient should be hospitalized and treated with sedatives.

Even when a patient stops communicating with his surroundings, he is aware of their existence, since he can relate his observations of them when the episode is over. It is therefore a mistake to conclude that he has lost all contact with his environment, even though he may appear to be completely withdrawn.

The Causes of Schizophrenia: Theoretic Considerations

The schizophrenic behaves as if he had abandoned all attempts to adapt to his environment and as if he had become so frightened of the world around him that regression seemed his only recourse. In extreme cases, the schizophrenic is reduced to a state even more helpless than that of the infant, a state in which he cannot, or at least does not, let others know when he is uncomfortable. A severely regressed patient often re-fuses to eat, apparently afraid that those about him will hurt him even when they want to give him food. These observations suggest that he has become conditioned to regard all other people as dangerous and threaten-ing, presumably because of deprivation and frustration in his earliest ex-periences with other people. Exploration of the personality development of schizophrenics supports this hypothesis and usually shows that throughout his later developmental steps, he held this concept of people, so that when a threatening situation causes him to begin to regress, he has no safe foothold as he slips down the developmental ladder. Sexuality, aggression, and dependency are all too dangerous, and his adaptation as a schizophrenic can be described as almost predependent.

The hypothesis that early deprivation and frustration are important factors in causing schizophrenia is strengthened by evidence from studies of the parents of schizophrenics. Bateson, Jackson, and their associates [4] observed the interaction between schizophrenic patients and their families and concluded that schizophrenia represents the child's solution to the "double bind" in which his parents place him by simultaneous communications requiring opposite responses. The parent's verbal communication means to the child, "Treat me as a loving mother who wants you to come to her," but at the same time she freezes when he does come, so that the nonverbal communication, evident to the child but not to the parent, means, "Stay away from me, I can't stand you." Unable to avoid the parent's displeasure either by coming or by staying away, the child solves the problem by regression to a point where he is no longer concerned about relationships with others and so can be indifferent to parental displeasure.

A somewhat similar theory has been proposed by Johnson and her associates [5]. In a high proportion of schizophrenics, they found historical evidence of parental assault, often sexual assault, in childhood or adolescence. Afterwards the parent denied the assault, insisting to the child that it did not happen. The child, in order to maintain even a distorted relationship with his parent, had to reject the evidence of his own senses, and thus the foundations of the schizophrenic departure from reality were laid.

Other investigators, noting that the mothers of schizophrenics frequently combine a basic lack of maternal warmth with an anxious conscientious determination to do everything the right way for their infants (see page 93), conclude that this type of mother is pathogenic for schizophrenia [6]. Lidz and his group, who have studied the family as a whole, have observed a lack of constructive integration within the families of schizophrenics, particularly female schizophrenics, often producing a "marital schism," with an atmosphere of rivalry and anxiety, in which each parent demands the child's allegiance against the other [7]. In families of male schizophrenics, they more often observe a "marital skew," by which they mean that one parent, more realistic in his thinking but more passive than his spouse, gives in to the other's aggressiveness and accepts the other's distorted, often psychotic, thinking as more realistic than his own.

As in the case of psychosomatic illnesses, there is probably no single developmental pattern that is sufficient to account for the psychologic determinants of schizophrenia. Instead, there is probably a field of interacting determinants, with varying valences in different cases [8]. With a high titer of "double bind," there may be less evidence of "marital skew," and vice versa. Cultural factors play a part; schizophrenia occurs more frequently at the lower end of society's socioeconomic distribution curve [9]. Furthermore, the fact that similar family patterns and experiences of deprivation and frustration may be found in the histories of many persons who do not become schizophrenic suggests that factors other than psychologic and social also contribute to the cause of schizophrenia. The extreme sensitivity and vulnerability of the schizophrenic and his apparent inability to obtain satisfaction from experiences usually considered pleasurable intimate that he is in some way basically predisposed to respond to one or a combination of interpersonal stresses by developing the psychosis. The components of the predisposition are not at all clearly understood; there is probably an hereditary element [10], and there may be biochemical or endocrine abnormalities of one kind or another [11]. The evidence for any of these presumably responsible factors is not as yet clear enough to justify saying that the cause of schizophrenia is known.

Secondary Symptoms: Delusions and Hallucinations

Just as in rheumatic fever, however, understanding of the causes of the illness does not need to be complete in order to evaluate the patient's reaction to it or even to formulate the mechanics of the pathologic process. In schizophrenia and in organic illnesses which simulate schizophrenia, the personality often appears to be trying to avoid total disintegration by distorting its perception of reality. The function of proper reality testing, or evaluation of the environment, is sacrificed so that some semblance of internal integration can be maintained. As his fear of people causes him to lose contact with the environment as it is, the schizophrenic struggles to provide a new environment to which he can adjust. The major symptoms of his unrealistic evaluation are delusions, or false beliefs, and hallucinations, or false perceptions. (For diagram, see Appendix B, Figure 19.)

Delusions are classified in the following four categories:

Delusions of Reference. The patient with delusions of reference believes that casual or unrelated actions by others have reference to him. Thus, when he sees two acquaintances chatting across the room, he may develop the idea, fixed and unassailable by logical explanation, that their conversation refers to him. He appears to be trying to counteract his own feeling that he is losing touch with his environment by developing the belief that those around him are much more concerned with him than they really are. He may carry this to the point of believing that random comments made on the radio or in the newspapers concern him.

Delusions of Grandeur. A patient's belief that he is extremely wealthy, exalted in rank, or unusually powerful may follow sequentially from his delusions of reference: If everyone is talking about him, he must be very important. It is more likely, however, that delusions of grandeur result from the patient's attempt to distort the world so that he is assured a place of significance.

Some investigators believe that delusions of grandeur and certain other schizophrenic phenomena reflect a regression to an infantile concept of the world. According to this concept, the infant, primarily concerned with himself and with only a vague perception of anything outside of himself, interprets the response of others to his needs as evidence of his control over his environment. Until he can extend his concept of the world beyond himself, it is impossible for him to interpret mother's provision of food in response to his hunger as her voluntary, independent decision, and so he assumes that his wish somehow controls her response. He is thus *omnipotent,* at least as far as his tiny world is concerned; as he grows up, his world expands, but if later he undergoes the deep regression of the severe schizophrenic, he reapplies the notion of his own omnipotence to the world as he perceives it.

Delusions of Persecution. Most of us occasionally try to shift the blame for our own troubles onto others. When this tendency to *project* responsibility is applied to unconscious, unacceptable drives and when it becomes fixed past the point of being modifiable by logic, it forms the basis of the delusion of persecution, in which the patient believes that others are plotting against him or injuring him in some way. By projecting the source of the unacceptable drive from himself to the environment, he changes "I am angry at him" to "He is angry at me" or "I am sexually interested in him" to "He is sexually interested in me." (For diagram, see Appendix B, Figure 20.)

Somatic Delusions. The patient with somatic delusions is convinced that he is suffering from a specific physical illness or deformity. He may believe, for example, that his stomach has turned to stone or that he has syphilis. Since these delusions indicate the patient's belief in his own partial destruction, they are often found in guilt-ridden depressions and are more commonly observed in involutional psychotic reactions than in schizophrenia. The somatic delusion differs from hypochondriacal or phobic displacements, in which the patient fears that something may be wrong with his stomach or that he may have syphilis but does not "know" that a specific change has taken place. Sometimes it is difficult to distinguish the two; a phobia of cancer may imperceptibly change into a delusion that the cancer exists.

By mechanisms not altogether clear, the schizophrenic usually seems to mobilize evidence to back up delusional defenses by false perceptions, or hallucinations [12]. These are most frequently auditory but may be visual, olfactory, or gustatory or may even involve skin sensation. Thus the patient who suffers from delusions of reference and persecution may not only *believe* that his associates are talking about him and plotting against him but may also *hear* their voices, *see* them at the window, *smell* gas in the room, or *taste* poison in his food.

Hallucinations occur not only in schizophrenics but in patients with organic disease of the brain and can be produced artificially by stimulation of parts of the brain and by administration of small doses of certain "psychotomimetic" drugs, such as mescaline and lysergic acid diethylamide (LSD) [13]. The similarity of schizophrenic and organic hallucinations has encouraged many investigators to believe that there is a predominantly biochemical cause of schizophrenia. There are differences between the two types of hallucinatory experiences, however, that cast doubt on the validity of the analogy; for example, schizophrenics have a preponderance of auditory hallucinations, while hallucinations of drug origin are more likely to be visual.

Although it is possible to explain delusions in strictly psychologic terms, hallucinations are more likely to be products of psychologic stimuli on an organically predisposed substrate. Their *content* may be described in symbolic terms, but their *existence* requires an additional explanation.

PARANOID REACTIONS

Illnesses in which delusions of persecution and corresponding hallucinations dominate the symptomatology are called *paranoid: paranoid schizophrenic reactions* when other schizophrenic manifestations are present; *paranoid states* when the personality is otherwise relatively intact. Freud's classic study of the Schreber case [14] convinced him that the nature of the projected conflict in all paranoid disturbances is closely related to homosexuality. Later investigators who have studied paranoid disturbances with similar thoroughness have demonstrated a high incidence of homosexual conflicts, or at least of the type of conflict which in some circumstances leads to homosexuality. In all probability, however, other conflicts related to hostile feelings can also be projected to form symptoms of paranoid illness [15].

The concept that delusions and hallucinations protect the patient against more serious personality collapse helps explain his resistance to any attempts to demonstrate their unrealistic nature. Occasionally, he may take action which seems to him appropriate in response to his delusions. He may complain to the authorities, start lawsuits, or even physically attack his presumed persecutors, usually in the early phases of his illness. Presidents have been assassinated and physicians killed by paranoid individuals, but for the most part, their actions are confined to threats and complaints, particularly if in the past they have shown no unusual tendencies to act on impulse.

The diagnosis of paranoid disturbances is often difficult, especially in early cases. When there is a precedent or a possibility that a patient's accusations may be true, as in the following case, the diagnosis presents a formidable problem.

A thirty-year-old mother of four children asked her family doctor for medication to help her sleep. She attributed her sleeplessness to her worry over her husband's infidelity. For the last two years, she said, he had been making certain prolonged stops on his laundry route, and she had good reason—lipstick on his handkerchiefs, for example—to believe that he was being intimate with another woman. He had in fact acknowledged that he had been unfaithful two years ago after she found letters from a girl friend in his bureau drawer. Since then he had consistently denied any extra marital relationships, in spite of the evidence she produced.

The physician knew that her husband was a somewhat irresponsible man who was frequently in debt and occasionally drank to excess. He had even heard rumors which tended to confirm his patient's story. (He later discovered that the rumors originated with her complaints to her neighbors about her husband.)

The doctor pointed out that a prescription for sleeping pills was not the way to solve the problem and, with the permission and encouragement of the patient, made an appointment to see her husband. The husband was a somewhat inarticulate individual, who sheepishly acknowledged his earlier affair but repeated his denial that it had continued. He maintained that his schedule did not permit time for dalliance en route and said that he could not argue with his wife about the lipstick marks, because he was color-blind. The physician doubted his story but could not decide how to proceed. He temporized by prescribing a week's supply of sleeping medication for the patient and considered referring them to a marriage counseling agency.

At the time of the next appointment, however, the wife seemed more tense and upset than before and insisted on going over the details of her grievances. The doctor wondered how she could check up so assiduously on her husband's laundry route when she had a household and four children to care for. When he discovered that she assigned her oldest boy to follow her husband on a bicycle in order to time the stops, he began to question her judgment. He asked a few more questions and found that she could still smell suspicious perfume on her husband's clothes after they had been to the cleaners and in storage all summer. He also discovered that in the last two years she had become so preoccupied with her suspicions that she had neglected her housework and her children. When discussing other subjects, such as her children's health, she showed an inappropriate lack of concern, or "flatness" of affect. The changes had come on so gradually that they had not been evident to her relatives, although they had been noted by casual acquaintances.

The doctor referred her to a psychiatrist, who confirmed the doctor's supposition that she was suffering from paranoid delusions and visual and olfactory hallucinations and corroborated his diagnosis of paranoid schizophrenia.

SUBTYPES AND COURSE OF SCHIZOPHRENIA

The German psychiatrist Kraepelin developed the first workable classification of schizophrenia, then called dementia praecox [16]. He divided the illness into four major subtypes: paranoid, catatonic, hebephrenic, and simple. The paranoid type remains a reasonably well-defined and frequently encountered entity, but the incidence of clean-cut examples of the other three types has diminished considerably. Although in all probability this is partly attributable to refinements of diagnosis and to earlier and more effective treatment measures, the major determinant of the apparent change in symptom spectrum is more likely cultural and parallels a similar change in neurotic symptoms (see page 233).

The hebephrenic is seldom seen outside of a mental hospital, and the symptoms of the catatonic are so dramatic that the necessity for immediate psychiatric referral is usually obvious. The student should be able to recognize them, however, and to differentiate them from other conditions with similar symptoms.

Hebephrenic Schizophrenia

Some patients show signs of the *hebephrenic* symptom picture from the time of onset; others develop it as the illness progresses. Hebephrenics become more and more detached and withdrawn, and their private worlds become increasingly remote from our understanding. They lose interest in their appearance and clothing; they may gorge themselves or may refuse or forget to eat; they ignore their excretory functions; their speech usually becomes impossible to understand and is filled with stereotyped repetitions (verbigerations) and word inventions (neologisms) of their own. They giggle in a silly but humorless manner, apparently in response to auditory hallucinations, and often repeat peculiar gestures or posturings. They have regressed and distorted reality to a point where they appear to be reasonably well satisfied, and most of them lack the incentive for the long uphill fight. Although generally the prognosis is poor, an occasional hebephrenic patient responds spontaneously or with treatment, even when the illness has persisted for years, and the physician should encourage families of hospitalized patients to do what they can to strengthen any threads of contact with reality that the patient retains.

Catatonic Schizophrenia

Withdrawal in the *catatonic* type of schizophrenia is usually characterized by relative or complete immobility, muteness, negativism, and an apparent oblivion to physical needs or to the surroundings. In severe cases of catatonic stupor, the patient's limbs can be molded into awkward or uncomfortable positions; since the patients seem to lack the capacity for voluntary movement or for discomfort, they retain these positions for long periods of time. The catatonic *stupor* may be punctuated by sudden outbursts of wild, destructive, apparently purposeless activity, or catatonic *excitement,* in which the patient appears to be oblivious to pain or to his safety. The catatonic patient's symptoms suggest that his only alternative to the uncontrolled expression of his impulses is complete inhibition of all behavior. However, in spite of the severity of symptoms, the relatively early onset, and the dramatic extent of regression, the catatonic has the best prognosis for recovery from the episode of the various forms of schizophrenic reaction.

Simple Schizophrenia

A patient with *simple schizophrenia* appears to give up trying to adapt himself to his environment more gradually and with much less fear than other schizophrenics. He makes few attempts to restore his relationships and consequently seldom has delusions or hallucinations, although his thinking is usually bizarre. He slowly loses interest in his friends, family, work, and activities and becomes detached and preoccupied. If someone takes responsibility for him, he will accept passively whatever he is given; if he is on his own, he may become a vagrant or hobo. He often gets into minor trouble with the law because he cannot work out realistic solutions even for his relatively simple needs. He is usually harmless, seldom disturbs others enough to require hospital care, and is not uncomfortable enough to seek treatment on his own.

It is difficult to differentiate mild simple schizophrenics from *schizoid personalities* and mild paranoid states from *paranoid personalities*. In their use of distortion or projection, schizoid and paranoid personalities appear to reach a state of equilibrium in which they retain just enough contact with reality to make a marginal adjustment but in which they reduce their contacts with people to a minimum, either by withdrawal into private worlds of fantasy or by retreat into an armed fortress of suspicion. These conditions differ from schizophrenic or paranoid reactions only in the degree of personality involvement, and the patients are subject to acute psychotic episodes when under increased environmental pressure.

Mixed, Schizoaffective, and "Pseudoneurotic" Forms of Schizophrenia

As the incidence of clearly defined examples of hebephrenic, catatonic, and simple schizophrenia has diminished, other, less well-defined types have emerged. Many, if not most, schizophrenic patients show evidences in varying proportions of the symptoms of the different subgroups and are called, for the lack of a more specific term, *mixed*, or *undifferentiated*, types. Others combine schizophrenic thinking with the emotional characteristics of affective disorders and are called *schizoaffective* types.

A third type, called by Hoch and Polatin [17] *pseudoneurotic schizophrenia*, bears such a close relationship to neurosis that it has been called a "borderline state," and many psychiatrists, particularly in Europe, do not include it among the schizophrenic reactions. Regardless of its classification, however, it is important for the student to recognize a condition that appears to be neurotic but that, under unusual pressure, either from the environment or from treatment, shows evidence of schizophrenic responses.

Under ordinary circumstances, a pseudoneurotic patient uses neurotic mechanisms. If he can use repression reasonably well, he may even appear outwardly well adjusted, at least in superficial relationships, though repressed tension may be expressed in psychophysiologic reactions. If his previous conditioning leads to the use of isolation and reaction formation, he appears to be an obsessive-compulsive, while if displacement is the mechanism of choice, his symptoms are hypochondriacal or phobic. Generally, however, his anxiety is so great that no one mechanism suffices, and he uses a variety of mechanisms simultaneously.

As long as nothing interferes with the ability of these patients to handle their conflicts and relationships by neurotic mechanisms, they maintain a tenuous contact with reality; but when external or internal pressures are increased past their capacity to handle them in a neurotic manner, they fall back to the use of reality-distorting mechanisms. The following case illustrates the manner in which some of these patients oscillate between psychosis and the appearance of neurosis.

A thirty-five-year-old woman had visited a psychiatric clinic intermittently for fifteen years. She would appear after an interval of absence from the clinic, complaining of fatigue, weakness, and vague hypochondriacal aches and pains. Although she continued to work and to maintain casual social contacts, she usually complained of depression, loneliness, and boredom.

As long as her physician kept the focus of the interviews on her symptoms and her day-to-day adjustment, she continued to present the same complaints; but when he attempted to probe deeper into her personality and talk about her earlier relationships, she began to complain that things seemed unreal to her and that others were talking about her and working against her. Her hypochondriacal complaints became less intense but more peculiar; for example, instead of worrying over the possibility that she had gallbladder trouble, she began to speculate in a rather detached fashion that someone might have put poison in her food to cause her pains.

At this point, she would voluntarily interrupt treatment, almost as if she realized that further discussion of her deeper feelings might lead to a complete break with reality. She would fail to appear for her next appointment but would return a few months later with her original complaints restored.

Not all patients with this type of schizophrenia can as readily resume the neurotic mask once it has been removed. Therefore, a therapist should attempt to expose neurotic mechanisms by treatment directed toward insight development only when he is reasonably sure that these mechanisms are not protecting his patient against a latent psychotic reaction. Psychoses can be treated psychotherapeutically, but their treatment presents a formidable challenge. Under ordinary circumstances, if there is serious danger of allowing a latent psychotic reaction to be set in motion, the physician should devote his efforts to strengthening the neurotic shell even if he must occasionally cater to relatively incapacitating compulsive or hypochondriacal symptoms. For most of these patients, a neurotic adjustment is the best that can be expected, and the physician should assiduously support it.

The Course and Prognosis in Schizophrenia

The course of schizophrenia varies. At one time, schizophrenia was thought to progress inevitably to a deterioration resembling in some ways that of senility; hence the earlier term "dementia praecox," or dementia of youth. Some schizophrenics apparently deteriorate, although there is no evidence that the deterioration is the result of organic processes or that it is not potentially reversible. However, with modern methods of treatment and, perhaps, partly as a result of changes in the character of schizophrenia over the last half century, many patients are now able to make a "social recovery," so that although still handicapped they can make a marginal adjustment to society's demands. Still others, particularly those in whom the onset has been acute, approximate a full recovery, although a thorough evaluation usually discloses residual evidence of schizophrenic thought processes or disturbances in affect. The prognosis of schizophrenia, therefore, is no longer so gloomy as it once was.

Specific treatment measures in schizophrenic and paranoid reactions will be discussed later in this chapter.

AFFECTIVE REACTIONS

Schizophrenic reactions and affective (manic-depressive or psychotic-depressive) reactions have long been considered separate disease entities. Schizophrenia was defined as a progressive disorder of thinking occurring in introverts of slender physique, and manic-depressive reactions were defined as periodic disorders of mood occurring in extroverts of stocky physique. Unfortunately for the cause of neat and unequivocal classifications of disease, there are many exceptions to these stereotypes. Furthermore, the substantial group of schizoaffective disorders combine characteristics of both, and some patients progress in their symptoms from an early manic-depressive to a late schizophrenic picture. Many authorities believe that the thinking disorder of schizophrenia is secondary to a basic disorder of affect, and some contend that schizophrenic and manic-depressive reactions are variations of the same disease. However, if the dichotomy between the two is recognized as more arbitrary than absolute, the classifications can be useful, particularly in estimating prognosis and in planning treatments.

Psychotic Depressions

The most common manifestations of affective reactions are recurrent depressions. These depressions often follow the loss of somebody or something of significance to the patient, and the dynamics [18] resemble the dynamics of neurotic depression (see page 242). In both types of depression, patients usually demonstrate an habitual pattern of repression of hostility, derived from an early atmosphere which threatened the loss of love if they expressed hostility.

The degree and extent of manic-depressive or psychotic depressions, however, are out of proportion to the precipitating factors, and in some instances, the precipitating factor is either nonexistent or apparently so insignificant that it is entirely overlooked, so that the depression seems to originate spontaneously, or *endogenously*.

Moreover, hereditary factors seem to contribute to the predisposition to manic-depressive reactions. Also suggesting a constitutional component is the fact that the reaction usually occurs in so-called *cyclothymic personalities*, patients whose personalities are characterized by apparently spontaneous mood swings. A constitutional, or endogenous, factor is probably essential to the development of a manic-depressive reaction; both psychologic and constitutional factors probably contribute to its severity [19].

Another peculiarity of manic-depressive reactions is the occurrence in many cases of episodes of excitement or elation during which the patient seems to be trying his best to throw off depression. These episodes are called *mania*. Many manic-depressive patients do not have manic attacks; some who have manic attacks do not have depressions; and in those who have both types, the sequence varies. The onset is usually somewhat later than the onset of schizophrenia, although it can occur for the first time at any time in adult life. The episode of depression is customarily self-limited, although there is a tendency for succeeding attacks to occur at progressively shorter intervals and to last progressively longer.

The psychotic depression resulting from a manic-depressive reaction is hard to differentiate from a severe neurotic depression unless the patient has a history of manic attacks. In both conditions, the patients are sad and tearful and are so preoccupied with their depression that they lose their initiative and interest in their surroundings. Both types may be retarded, in the sense of a slowing down of speech, movement, and physiologic functions, although in a variant of psychotic depression, the *agitated depression*, the patient demonstrates almost the opposite behavior—pacing the floor, wringing his hands, and talking incessantly about his sins or his somatic delusions [20]. The psychotic depressive is more likely to focus on his unworthiness per se, while the neurotic depressive sees his unworthiness more in relation to his loss. Both suffer from insomnia, although the typical patterns of insomnia differ—the patient with a neurotic depression usually finds it hard to get to sleep, while the patient with a psychotic depression customarily awakens early in the morning and cannot get back to sleep.

The physician, social worker, or clergyman usually first encounters depression in its early and less severe stages when the patient is still able to conceal his feelings. Evidence of concealed depression should be looked for in patients whose complaints are hypochondriacal or psychosomatic or in patients who drink or eat to excess.

Suicide

The risk of suicide is greatest in the early stages of depression and again toward the end of treatment, when the patient apparently is close to recovery. In the depths of his depression, he is usually too retarded to make the effort, but since his ability to act usually returns while he still retains severe feelings of guilt, he is most dangerous to himself as he begins to improve.

Suicide ranks at least ninth as a cause of death in the United States; since many suicides are not reported, the actual rank may be higher than ninth [21]. Although depressed patients usually plan their attempts far in advance, they may act on impulse. No clear-cut criteria for diagnosing possible suicide exist; it can occur in all forms of depression as well as in schizophrenic, paranoid, and neurotic reactions. Even a gesture toward suicide by a dependent or hysterical personality who wants only to gain attention may backfire and result in death.

The danger signals, therefore, are numerous. In spite of a persistent popular belief to the contrary, a patient is dangerous to himself if he talks openly of suicide. He also is dangerous if he implies suicidal intentions by reiterating his belief that he is hurting his family through living or by insisting that he is too much of a burden for them to carry. Overwhelming guilt or hopelessness and excessive fear of punishment, of mental or physical illness, or of insomnia should cause the physician concern. Loss of appetite, when accompanied by weight loss, represents a warning. Partial recovery, particularly when it is unaccountably rapid or when it is associated with an insistence on greater privacy and solitude, is a dangerous phase. The doctor should carefully evaluate the suicidal risk in a patient with a history of previous attempts or with a history of suicide in a relative or friend with whom he may identify. Thoughts of suicide are almost universal in depression, and the patient who maintains that for religious or other reasons he has never considered it may be attempting to forestall interference with his plans.

Physicians and other therapists often hesitate to ask a patient directly about suicide lest they "put ideas in his head"; however, if tact is used, this question not only is less dangerous than it appears but may be lifesaving. The problem can be approached indirectly, for example, by asking him what thoughts or plans he has for the future. If he replies that he has no future or that his case is hopeless or that his family would be happier without him, he is obviously dangerous to himself. On the other hand, a reply indicating his expectations of returning home or to work should be explored further to make sure it is not a cover for a suicide plan. Whenever there is a question of possible suicide, psychiatric consultation should be obtained.

Although the risk of suicide must always be kept in mind in the treatment of depression, it is impossible altogether to avoid taking risks. No hospital is suicideproof, and preliminary measures to bring about hospitalization may increase the risk by reducing the patient's self-esteem. The prospect of hospital care is often interpreted by the depressed patient as confirmatory evidence that he is unloved and unworthy and that everyone would be better off if he were dead. In this situation, clinical judgment is of the greatest importance, as the physician balances one risk against another. To make the situation even more complicated, the pessimistic doctor's expectation of suicide, subtly or unsubtly conveyed to the patient, may contribute to its expression, in much the same way as a parent's expectation of his child's antisocial behavior contributes to its expression (see Chapter 14).

The Manic Phase

The characteristic symptom of the manic phase is restless, purposeless activity. The patient talks, thinks, and moves at a stepped-up pace, but he never concentrates on one thought or one activity for very long. Although his behavior is usually described as elation, he characteristically displays a great deal of resentment and hostility, particularly toward his family. He strikes out at them abruptly, usually in a vicious but short-lived verbal attack, then goes on to something else. While in depression, his feelings of guilt and his need of punishment for his anger appear to dominate his personality; in mania, his hostility breaks loose and he acts as if he were in full flight from his pursuing superego, never permitting himself to stand still lest his guilt catch up with him. Although running full tilt, he is not aware of his flight; he is superficially self-confident and grandiose, displaying the opposite of (and perhaps compensating for) the feelings of worthlessness which characterize depression.

> A thirty-five-year-old housewife was hospitalized with manic symptoms. In the two months before coming to the hospital, she had become increasingly restless and sleepless. She energetically started numerous projects, which she quickly abandoned after making innumerable phone calls to influential members of the community. She boasted of her accomplishments, meddled in other people's business, and discussed her private affairs and

family quarrels with anyone who would listen. She finally became too busy to eat, talked incessantly in a rambling, disconnected manner, and was admitted to the hospital.

During the history taking, she described her condition as follows: "My mother threw me out of the house. . . . I'm suing my parents for one million bucks. . . . Money is their language. . . . I've had nothing but grief for thirty-five years. . . . The hospital is the worst place in the world for me. . . . I should be out. . . . I should get an annulment. . . . My husband wants to perjure himself to get a divorce . . . the accusations against my morals. . . . I'm well, but they're not. . . . I've been under the roughest restrictions. . . . That's the life I can't stand. . . . My children need help—you can't take a mother like me away without trouble. . . . They need a psychiatrist. . . . I know Dr. B.—he and I are the smartest people in town. . . . I get anything the doctors can't handle. . . . I should stand up for myself—I was never permitted to stand up for myself. . . . My son was slow in talking. The doctor said: 'How do you expect him to talk—you talk all the time.' . . . I've spent most of my life studying—I always made A's—my mother wanted me to. . . . My mother needed someone to care for her. . . . She should go to a psychiatrist—I'll be damned if I will go on giving her free psychiatric care for nothing. . . . My doctor's humoring rather than hurting my mother. . . . I know how to get out of here . . . but it's better than being at home. . . . What's the difference what psychiatric patients I take care of—I study the cases and I do the psychoanalysis. . . . Nobody around here is smarter than I am. Maybe Albert Einstein was—though I wouldn't really know."

In the early stages of mania, the patient may jeopardize his financial position and his good name in the community both by taking abortive action on his unrealistic, grandiose schemes and by his uninhibited though short-lived hostile attacks on anyone who crosses him. The patient's family at first finds it hard to recognize the nature of his illness and the consequences of not protecting him from his own impulsive actions. Often the family physician, as a trusted friend of long standing, can help them to understand the need for hospitalization.

The prognosis is good for attacks of manic or depressive reactions, although recurrence is common and is difficult to prevent. The attacks, untreated, last from a few weeks to several years. Some individuals, however, seem to have incorporated mildly manic, or *hypomanic,* characteristics into their personality structures and to operate constantly at a stepped-up pace. Other personalities appear always to carry a mild load of depression and pessimism. These individuals, particularly those who demonstrate chronic depression, usually have been seriously deprived of affection during their most dependent period.

Involutional psychotic reactions symptomatically resemble manic-depressive depressions and were once considered part of the same group of emotional illnesses. They differ, however, in cause and in dynamics, and since they are so closely associated with menopause and retirement, they are considered in the section in which these events are discussed.

TREATMENT OF PSYCHOTIC REACTIONS

Most people look to their family physician or their clergyman for advice when concerned about a mentally ill relative [22]. Therefore, both physician and clergyman need information about appropriate emergency referral procedures and about community resources for psychiatric care. Even after a patient is under care, the family physician and the clergyman, as well as the hospital social worker, can maintain important links between a patient in a mental hospital and his relatives. The relatives are often frightened by the changes in the patient and discouraged about the future. Even though the mental-hospital staff recognizes and understands their feelings, the relatives are reassured if the physician they know best continues to take an interest in the patient, keeps in touch with the psychiatrist, and seems to know what is going on. The clergyman has a parallel role, although his continuing contact with the hospital staff is usually with the hospital chaplain.

There are three major types of treatment for psychotic reactions, corresponding to the three major groups of contributing causes. These are (1) social, or milieu, (2) individual psychologic, and (3) "biologic." One, two, or all three types of treatment may be used concurrently [23].

Social or Milieu Treatment

The social vector of treatment seeks to reestablish the psychotic patient's contact with reality by encouraging his participation in group activities, the most traditional of which are occupational and recreational therapy. Occupational therapy has advanced tremendously in recent years; instead of supervising a daily hour or so of basket weaving for everyone, the trained occupational therapist, guided by the psychiatrist, works out a carefully graded program for each patient, with concern for his individual interests, his capacities, his illness, and his particular type of conflict. The patient is kept busy during most of the day; and when he is not working, recreational therapists take over to help him reestablish social and recreational contact. All this is done in a prescribed milieu in which nurses and aides respond to each individual patient with appropriate therapeutic attitudes. A manic patient, for instance, may not be permitted visitors or access to group activities which are liable to over-stimulate him, while an attitude of kind firmness is usually prescribed for a depressed patient and a schizophrenic is gently encouraged toward social participation. The patient is helped to make successful adaptations to an artificially maneuvered but gradually more complex environment until he gains confidence in himself and again can face the outside world. Hospitals vary, of course, in their facilities for milieu therapy; in the long run, however, a comprehensive, not necessarily elaborate milieu program reduces the period of hospitalization for a great many patients and probably more than pays for itself [24].

In an effort to counteract the relatively complete isolation from responsibility characteristic of patients in most hospitals, many centers have experimented with techniques for letting patients make or assist in making decisions about ward management and, with certain restrictions, about their treatment. Maxwell Jones's concept of a hospital as a "therapeutic community" [25] makes doctors, nursing staff, maintenance staff, and patients coparticipants in a therapeutic endeavor. The delegation of traditional medical decisions to patient-staff committees requires a willingness on the part of the psychiatrist really to surrender some of his authority and does not come easily to everyone. There seem to be distinct advantages, however, in maintaining patients' responsibility for decisions about themselves. The active role that patients accept in their treatment helps to restore or to maintain their self-esteem and eases the transition from the hospital to the more independent existence outside.

Group therapy, or the psychotherapeutic treatment of patients in groups, combines the social and the individual psychologic vectors in that it uses the presence and support of a group of fellow sufferers to help both in desensitizing the individual members to their conflicts and in improving their capacity for reality testing.

Individual Psychologic Treatment

Individual psychotherapy aimed at modifying the basic personality structure of patients with psychotic reactions requires a great deal of time, expense, and skill [26]. More modest efforts, however, aimed at the restoration of previous, less incapacitating defenses, are an important part of treatment in any case and often should be continued for a long period. Social workers and psychologists carry out this phase of treatment under psychiatric guidance in many aftercare clinics. In areas where facilities for psychiatric care are limited, the family physician may be the most appropriate and available source of follow-up psychotherapy.

"Biologic" Treatment

The "biologic" approaches to treatment include the use of drugs, electrically induced convulsions, and surgery. Sequential insulin comas, formerly a popular method of treating schizophrenia, have not been shown to be effective enough to justify the danger involved in their use. Prefrontal lobotomy and other forms of surgical treatment for schizophrenia, for persistent depressions, and particularly for severe obsessive-compulsive reactions are still advocated by a few investigators. The side effects and social consequences of these operations, however, are often of such gravity that a thorough evaluation of all facets of the problem should precede their use.

Electric Convulsive Treatment (ECT). Electrically induced convulsive seizures have been most effective in psychotic depressions, although they are useful in controlling manic attacks and, to a lesser degree, in some cases of schizophrenia. The frequency and total number of convulsions in a course of treatment vary; a typical course may consist of eight to twelve or sometimes up to twenty treatments, usually administered on alternate days. The danger to life is slight, and although an occasional fracture has resulted from the convulsions, the drugs that are now used to reduce their violence minimize the risk. If this type of treatment is going to be effective, the patient usually begins to respond after three or four treatments, although some cases respond somewhat later. A few cases resist treatment and become chronically ill. None of the many theories which have been proposed to account for the success of electric convulsive treatments has been substantiated, and the reasons for their success remain obscure. In recent years, hospitals that have been able to develop intensive programs in the social and psychologic vectors of treatment, assisted by mood-elevating drugs, have greatly reduced their use of electric convulsive treatments. In many settings, however, and for certain patients in any setting, this type of treatment remains valuable [27].

Drug Treatment. For many years, sedative drugs have been used as adjuncts in the symptomatic treatment of psychotic reactions. Bromides, barbiturates, chloral hydrate, and paraldehyde were usually prescribed, but all had disadvantages, primarily unpleasant or dangerous side effects. The psychiatrist prescribed them mainly in emergencies and sought to discontinue their use as soon as possible.

The discovery of chlorpromazine and the use of rauwolfia compounds in mental illness, shortly after World War II, has changed the picture. These drugs, happily named "tranquilizers" instead of "sedatives," at first appeared to have a specific action against the symptoms of schizophrenia. Later, the specificity of their action was questioned, although their site of action (on the brain stem primarily, instead of on the brain stem and cortex alike) appears to give chlorpromazine in particular definite superiority over conventional sedatives in the management of patients with delusions, hallucinations, and the associated emotional distress. Chlorpromazine and similar drugs have made it possible to control symptoms to the point where many schizophrenics can adjust at home instead of requiring continued hospital care. The policy of discontinuing medication as soon as possible, therefore, has been replaced by the indefinite use of medication as a sustaining agent. Often the patient's physician will be asked to continue and oversee its prescription after the patient is discharged.

Chlorpromazine is not free from side effects, however, and is not consistently effective in controlling psychotic symptoms. A great number of other phenothiazines, variations on the chlorpromazine theme, and many new departures in the field of tranquilizers have therefore appeared and doubtless will continue to appear (see Table II, page 345) [28]. These new drugs are produced with such frequency that any assessment of their relative merits soon becomes obsolete; in any case, the physician's follow-up treatment of discharged psychotic patients should be carried on in close collaboration with the hospital from which he has been discharged.

The follow-up care of patients on tranquilizing medication cannot be considered easy. Some patients refuse or forget to take medication, others relapse in spite of medication, and a substantial number create social problems of such severity that the advantages to them of remaining outside the hospital may be counteracted by the disadvanatages to their families and to others.

A schizophrenic patient discharged on a substantial maintenance dose of chlorpromazine continued to hallucinate, although he was able to resume work of a highly intellectual character. He complained that on the recommended dose, the hallucinated voices interfered with his concentration, but that if he increased the dose to the point where the voices were sufficiently subdued so that he could ignore them, he was too groggy to work. Neither juggling the dosage nor the substitution of alternative drugs solved his problem to his satisfaction, but he was able to remain outside the hospital.

His inability to concentrate made him irritable, and he demanded complete silence in his home, harshly punishing his children if they failed to conform to his restrictive regime. His residual paranoid symptoms led to the loss of his job, and he was unable to obtain another. He refused to help around the house, as he considered such activity to be beneath his dignity, but freely criticized his wife for the inadequacy of her housekeeping, which she tried her best to complete after a full day's work in a store. His oldest son left home after a particularly bitter argument following an attempt to protect his mother from critical abuse. The patient refused voluntary hospital admission, and his wife, although recognizing that his behavior was destroying the family, could not bring herself to take legal steps to return him. She also realized that since, in medication, he was sufficiently in contact to be able to malinger health when he so desired, he could easily have convinced the doctors at the overcrowded hospital that he was well enough to leave, and so there was not much point in forcing his return.

At this writing, it is difficult to predict or to determine when, if ever, a patient who has been discharged on drugs can discontinue their use without risk of relapse. Any reduction of dosage or discontinuance contemplated by the general physician caring for a discharged mental patient should be undertaken in consultation with the psychiatrist who originally prescribed the medication.

Psychomotor stimulants, particularly drugs in the amphetamine group, have been used for some time in the treatment of psychotic depressions but have rather serious side effects. Lately, new groups of antidepressant drugs have been found useful; at current writing, the iminodibenzil derivatives seem to be the most effective and least dangerous (see Table III, page 345) [29]. Since depressions tend to be self-limited, these drugs are customarily prescribed over a relatively brief period of time. All these drugs are potentially dangerous, and the physician using them must be thoroughly familiar with their indications, contraindications, and side effects. They may produce a rebound phenomenon in the form of intensified depression after the initial reaction wears off, and they may serve to conceal an increasing severity of the depression with its concomitant danger of suicide.

In spite of their limitations, these medications can be used effectively by the physician in the outpatient treatment of mild endogenous depressions. In all cases, however, the use of the drug should be combined with regular psychologic support and surveillance, particularly with respect to the suicide risk.

For depressed patients, a physician should prescribe only a small supply of any potentially dangerous drug. Although a patient who is determined to commit suicide will ordinarily find one way or another to carry it out, there is no need to put a gun in his hand. Even when supplies are limited, some people will hoard medications over a long period of time for suicide attempts; on the other hand, to withhold relief from insomnia on the suspicion of suicide plans may hasten the execution of such plans. When there is much doubt, it is safest to obtain psychiatric consultation or to hospitalize the patient.

Aftercare

A particularly crucial period in the course of all psychotic reactions is the patient's return from the hospital. He has behind him a history of failure to adapt his drives and conflicts to the demands of his environment. If he has been schizophrenic, he has regressed to a childlike phase of development and has met his problems by grossly distorting reality. In the hospital, he has been nursed back into contact with an artifically structured, protected environment. He has been encouraged to participate in relatively simple activities in company with others who also have been unable to cope with the world's demands. Particularly if he has been at an undermanned state hospital, he probably has seen his hospital physician rather infrequently, and their conversations have been unavoidably limited to discussing his symptoms, his adjustment to the hospital, and his future plans.

He has improved to the point where further hospital treatment is no longer necessary. He must return to the environment to which he could not adjust before, complicated now by the regrettable but currently almost unavoidable social stigma of mental illness. Even though his family may have learned to understand him, they will still find it difficult to be natural with him. Understandably, they fear that he will relapse or behave peculiarly in the presence of outsiders, and they find it hard, particularly at first, to have much confidence in him.

Many hospitals attempt to ease the transition by intermediate treatment facilities such as night hospitals, which permit the patient to resume his work before cutting his hospital contacts completely, and day hospitals, in which treatment can continue while the patient readjusts to his home at night and on weekends. Unfortunately, too many American mental hospitals are so remote from patients' homes and jobs that day- and night-hospital programs are not feasible and the discharged patient abruptly loses the protection of the hospital and of those on whom he has relied for support while struggling to regain his emotional balance at home. At this point, help from someone who is more objective than his family and who understands his problems of adjustment may be the crucial ingredient in his rehabilitation. The family physician is often in the best position to give him the protection he needs, particularly during this transitional period. Along with the drugs he prescribes, he can protect the patient through the medium of psychologic support (see Chapter 15); he can give the patient opportunities to discuss the problems he finds in adjusting, and he can encourage his realistic efforts to adapt himself. When the patient reveals the presence of residual psychotic symptoms, the physician's calm and objective attitude reassures him. He should not argue or even attempt to unravel the unconscious meaning of symptoms, but as soon as he can determine that they are residual and not evidence of relapse, he should switch the focus of the interview to the patient's constructive achievements and plans. He should be careful not to measure his patient's adjustment by his own standards; a convalescent schizophrenic should not always be urged to socialize and to force himself to participate in group social activity. To do so may frighten him into a relapse, whereas if he is helped to live a relatively secluded life and is permitted to limit his social contacts, he has a better chance to remain outside the hospital and to live a useful, although perhaps unconventional, life. If he continues to gain confidence in himself, he may on his own initiative gradually extend his social frontiers. Recovery in the sense of attaining a conventional adjustment, however, is rather infrequent except in acute cases.

The same techniques apply to the treatment of milder schizophrenia which has not required hospitalization. The physician, by being available at times of increased stress, can help the patient over the difficult period and may protect him from the necessity of hospital treatment. As in the case cited on page 211, however, remaining outside of the hospital may not be an unmixed blessing, and the impact of a patient on his children and on other members of his family should be assessed and considered in deciding on the most appropriate locus of treatment.

SUMMARY

In this chapter, the major groups of psychotic reactions—schizophrenic, paranoid, and affective—were discussed, with emphasis on their early manifestations and care rather than on the aspects more typical of hospitalized patients. The physician, clergyman, and social worker all may contribute substantially to the psychiatric care of psychotic patients in three areas: early recognition, assistance to families during the patient's hospitalization, and aftercare.

REFERENCES

1. Beck, A. T., et al.: "Reliability of Psychiatric Diagnosis," *Amer. J. Psychiat.*, 119:351, 1962.

Bowman, K. M., and M. Rose: "Criticism of Terms 'Psychosis,' 'Psychoneurosis' and 'Neurosis,' "*Amer. J. Psychiat.*, 108:161, 1951.

2. Bleuler, Eugen: *Dementia Praecox, or the Group of Schizophrenias,* New York, International Universities Press, Inc., 1952.

3. Kasanin, J. S. (ed.): *Language and Thought in Schizophrenia,* Berkeley, Calif., University of California Press, 1944.

4. Bateson, G., D. D. Jackson, J. Haley, and J. Weakland: "Toward a Theory of Schizophrenia," *Behav. Sci.,* 1:251, 1956.
Haley, J.: "An Interactional Description of Schizophrenia," *Psychiatry,* 22:321, 1959.

5. Johnson, A. M., et al.: "Studies in Schizophrenia at the Mayo Clinic," *Psychiatry,* 19:137, 1956.

6. Reichard, S., and C. Tillman: "Patterns of Parent-Child Relationship in Schizophrenia," *Psychiatry,* 13:247, 1950.
See also: Sullivan, H. S.: *Schizophrenia as a Human Process,* New York, W. W. Norton & Company, Inc., 1962.

7. Fleck, S., T. Lidz, and A. R. Cornelison: "Comparison of Parent-Child Relationships of Male and Female Schizophrenic Patients," *Arch. Gen. Psychiat. (Chicago),* 8:1, 1963.
Lidz, T., A. R. Cornelison, S. Fleck, and D. Terry: "The Intrafamilial Environment of Schizophrenic Patients II. Marital Schism and Marital Skew," *Amer. J. Psychiat.,* 114:241, 1957.

8. Arieti, S.: *The Interpretation of Schizophrenia,* New York, Robert Brunner, Publisher, 1955.
Fessel, W. J.: "Interaction of Multiple Determinants of Schizophrenia," *Arch. Gen. Psychiat. (Chicago),* 11:1, 1964.

9. Hollingshead, A., and F. Redlich: *Social Class and Mental Illness: A Community Study,* New York, John Wiley & Sons, Inc., 1958.
Meyers, J. K., and B. H. Roberts: *Family and Class Dynamics in Mental Illness,* New York, John Wiley & Sons, Inc., 1959.

10. See reference 1, Chapter 4.

11. Benjamin, J. D.: "Some Considerations in Biological Research in Schizophrenia," *Psychosom. Med.,* 30:427, 1958.
Hoskins, R. G.: *The Biology of Schizophrenia,* New York, W. W. Norton & Company, Inc., 1946.

12. West, L. J. (ed.): *Hallucinations,* New York, Grune & Stratton, Inc., 1962.

13. Cholden, L. (ed.): *Lysergic Acid Diethylamide and Mescaline in Experimental Psychiatry,* New York, Grune & Stratton, Inc., 1956.
Unger, S. M.: "Mescaline, LSD, Psilocybin and Personality Change," *Psychiatry,* 26:111, 1963.

14. Freud, S.: "Psychoanalytical Notes upon an Autobiographical Account of a Case of Paranoia" (1911) in *Standard Edition,* 1958, vol. XII, p. 1.

15. Waelder, R.: "The Structure of Paranoid Ideas," *Int. J. Psychoanal.,* 32:167, 1951.

16. Braceland, F. J.: "Kraepelin: His System and His Influences," *Amer. J. Psychiat.,* 113:871, 1957.

Kraepelin, E.: *Dementia Praecox and Paraphrenia*, Edinburgh, Livingston, 1925.

17. Hoch, P. H., and P. Polatin: "Pseudoneurotic Forms of Schizophrenia," *Psychiat. Quart.*, 23:248, 1949.
———, et al.: "The Course and Outcome of Pseudoneurotic Schizophrenia," *Amer. J. Psychiat.*, 119:106, 1962.

18. Rado, Sandor: "Psychodynamics of Depression from the Etiologic Point of View," *Psychosom. Med.*, 13:51, 1951.

19. Bellak, L.: *Manic-Depressive Psychosis and Allied Conditions*, New York, Grune & Stratton, Inc., 1952.

20. Schwartz, D. A.: "The Agitated Depression," *Psychiat. Quart.*, 35:758, 1961.

21. Offenkrantz, W.: "Depression and Suicide in General Medical Practice," *Amer. Practitioner*, 13:427, 1962.
Stengel, E.: "Recent Research into Suicide and Attempted Suicide," *Amer. J. Psychiat.*, 118:725, 1962.

22. Gurrin, G., J. Veroff, and S. Field: *Americans View Their Mental Health*, New York, Basic Books, Inc., Publishers, 1960.
The impact of mental illness on the family is described in: Spiegel, J. P. and N. W. Bell: "The Family of the Psychiatric Patient," in Arieti, S. (ed.): *American Handbook of Psychiatry*, New York, Basic Books, Inc., Publishers, 1959, vol. I, p. 114.

23. Linn, L.: *A Handbook of Hospital Psychiatry*, New York, International Universities Press, Inc., 1955.

24. The use of social or milieu therapy is described in:
Artiss, Kenneth L.: *Milieu Therapy in Schizophrenia*, New York, Grune & Stratton, Inc., 1962.
Cumming, John, and Elaine Cumming: *Ego and Milieu; Theory and Practice of Environmental Therapy*, New York, Atherton Press, 1962.
Group for the Advancement of Psychiatry, Report No. 51. *Toward Therapeutic Care*, 1961.

25. Jones, Maxwell: *The Therapeutic Community*, New York, Basic Books, Inc., Publishers, 1953.
———: "Towards a Clarification of the Therapeutic Community Concept," *Brit. J. Med. Psychol.*, 32:200, 1959.

26. The use of psychotherapy in psychotic reactions is described in:
Arieti, S.: "Psychotherapy of Schizophrenia," *Arch. Gen. Psychiat. (Chicago)*, 6:112, 1962.
Federn, P.: *Ego Psychology and the Psychoses*, New York, Basic Books, Inc., Publishers, 1952.
Fromm-Reichmann, F.: *Principles of Intensive Psychotherapy*, Chicago, The University of Chicago Press, 1950.
Will, O. A.: "Human Relatedness and the Schizophrenic Reaction," *Psychiatry*, 22:205, 1959.

27. The use of shock treatment is described in:
Regan, Peter: "Effective Utilization of Electroconvulsive Treatment," *Amer. J. Psychiat.*, 114:351, 1957.

28. Welsh, A. L.: "The Newer Tranquilizing Drugs," *Med. Clin. N. Amer.,* 48:459, 1964.
29. Cole, J. O.: "Therapeutic Efficacy of Antidepressant Drugs," *J.A.M.A.,* 190: 448, 1964.
   Hordern, A.: "The Antidepressant Drugs," *New Eng. J. Med.,* 272:1159, 1965.
   Overall, J. E., et al.: "Imipramine and Thioridazine in Depressed and Schizophrenic Patients: Are There Specific Antidepressant Drugs?" *J.A.M.A.,* 189:605, 1964.
   Siegler, P. E.:"Current Status of Drug Treatment of the Depressive State," *Med. Clin. N. Amer.,* 48:483, 1964.

Chapter 12

ORGANIC CONDITIONS

The chronic organic brain syndrome is primarily distinguishable from psychiatric conditions of predominantly psychologic origin by the presence of *dementia,* or decreased intelligence, most dramatically signaled by memory disturbances. Later, disturbances in *sensorium, orientation,* and *judgment* make their appearance.

In the early stages or in mild cases, however, the chronic brain syndrome may be difficult to diagnose, and the first symptoms are often hard to distinguish from schizophrenia, depressions, paranoid states, or neurosis. The patient's adaptive capacity can be weakened by organic factors as well as by social or psychologic factors, and as a result the same kind of threatened breakthrough of impulse leads first to anxiety and then to the mobilization of defense mechanisms characteristic of the individual concerned. A patient's symptoms may not offer clues to the presence of organic illness, and it is essential for the physician to keep in mind the possibility of an organic component in emotional illness even if at first sight it appears typical of psychologically determined conditions. Careful attention to the mental-status examination, particularly to the section on sensorium and mental competence, helps bring to light latent evidence of organic impairment. The social worker, psychologist, and pastoral counselor, handicapped by the lack of a medical background, must make certain that their clients or parishioners are adequately protected against the failure to diagnose organic factors, both by careful initial medical evaluation and by continuing medical evaluation during the course of treatment.

My purpose in this chapter is to provide an overview of the organic disorders, primarily to help the student recognize them and take them into consideration in his diagnostic evaluations. I am not attempting to provide a comprehensive survey of all the organic psychoses; I am not including the pathologic and laboratory data, nor am I specifying the characteristic neurologic findings in these conditions. The material in the chapter should help the student in nonmedical disciplines become alert to signals that require special consultation beyond his customary consultations with his medical collaborators. The medical student, however, should amplify his knowledge of these conditions by further reading [1].

ACUTE BRAIN SYNDROME

The acute brain syndrome, or delirium, appears to be rapid in onset and usually dramatic in its manifestations, although premonitory signs of anxiety, restlessness, and suspiciousness are often present and almost as often overlooked [2]. Once in full swing, the evidence cannot be overlooked; the combination of restlessness and excitement on the one hand and confusion and disorientation on the other, together with hallucinations and delusions, makes the delirious patient a severe management problem. He needs constant nursing care to protect him from suicide or from injuring himself or others in his desperate attempts to avoid or combat his hallucinated tormenters and to help him restore his orientation to reality. To help overcome his confusion, he needs the reassurance, insofar as possible, of familiar sounds, sights, and voices, and he needs patient explanation of what is happening to him. He needs proper sedation to calm his restlessness and excitement. Barbiturates are contraindicated, as they often intensify excitement; chloral hydrate, paraldehyde or the phenothiazines are less risky. Mechanical restraints increase the patient's panic and should be avoided. Nutrition and fluid balance must be maintained, and the most important measure of all is finding and, if possible, counteracting the specific cause.

SENILE DEMENTIA AND CEREBRAL ARTERIOSCLEROSIS

Senile dementia is probably the most commonly encountered organic psychosis, and as medicine prolongs the average life-span, it is becoming increasingly prevalent. The most common symptom is the loss of memory for recent events. As the patient's adaptive capacity progressively deteriorates, it becomes more difficult for him to focus his attention on the current environment and to develop new methods of handling problems. The result is disorientation and confusion and a lack of flexibility and spontaneity.

Before memory defects become evident, the weakening of a patient's ability to inhibit may be reflected in emotional imbalance and in the emergence of specific psychiatric symptom pictures. These pictures usually represent exaggerations of previous personality characteristics; thus, suspicious people become paranoid, pessimistic people become depressed, and sensitive people become hypersensitive. The symptom pictures form the basis for a subclassification of senile dementia into the following five major groups:

1. The simple deteriorating type, without particular predilection for a characteristic psychotic picture
2. The delirious and confused type, in which loss of orientation apparently takes place more rapidly and in such a way that the patient becomes panicky rather than resigned
3. The depressed and agitated type, often confused with involutional or manic-depressive depressions
4. The paranoid type, which resembles the paranoid state
5. The presbyophrenic type, which resembles schizophrenia

Although the clinician should be alert to the possibility of an organic element in any elderly psychotic patient, he should never assume that a psychotic older person is necessarily senile. The same psychologic factors that operate in younger patients may precipitate depressions, paranoid states, and even schizophrenia in the older age groups [3].

The eventual prognosis of senile dementia is poor, but the course of deterioration is not fixed. As previously stated (page 209), the development of dementia in the senile patient is not strictly in proportion to the extent of brain damage [4]. If he has built up a substantial reserve capacity for adaptation through successful early life experiences, he will be able to adapt to the increased stress caused by his reduced organic capacity and so postpone for a while the development of the usual clinical manifestations. As time goes on, however, senile patients slowly regress to a stage of narcissistic dependency, so that eventually they are concerned only about their own needs and childishly demand their own way. As their deterioration progresses, they become disoriented, not knowing where they are or what day it is, and finally they lose contact completely with their environment.

By the time symptoms are manifest, it is difficult, if not impossible, to increase a patient's adaptive reserves. It may be possible, however, to help him reduce current stresses. Sometimes a patient's family may overprotect and infantilize a grandparent with beginning signs of enfeeblement. Clarification of the importance of maintaining as much activity as possible and perhaps some attention to factors in the family leading to their overprotection can be helpful in postponing the necessity for hospitalization.

The *disengagement,* or withdrawal from social contact, characteristic of many aged persons may be symptomatic of their increasing inability to adapt to the demands of others [5]. In older people, human relationships often appear to be replaced to a degree by attachments to places and to physical objects. Moving the elderly, therefore, should be avoided whenever possible, and when moving is necessary, the older person's attachment to objects should be respected [6]. Thus, when an elderly person becomes physically unable to maintain independent existence and must move to a nursing home, his wishes with regard to keeping his furniture and other personal belongings should be respected insofar as possible, even though the objects themselves may appear to be old-fashioned and unattractive. Peculiarities in life patterns should also be respected when they do not interfere with the patient's health.

> An elderly gentleman was hospitalized with senile dementia. For the first two or three weeks, he was irritable and depressed as well as mildly demented. When it was discovered that for years he had never gone to sleep until midnight and had preferred to sleep in a chair instead of a bed, these modifications in his hospital routine were introduced. His depression lifted, he became less irritable, and although his dementia remained, he was able to adapt himself to his new environment with greater ease [7].

Senile dementia and *cerebral arteriosclerosis* have many characteristics in common [8]. Cerebral arteriosclerosis is usually considered to be earlier in onset—often in the seventh decade rather than in the eighth or ninth—and to be associated more frequently with focal neurologic findings. The pathology of senile dementia is more diffuse and presumably is primarily due to intrinsic degeneration of the nerve cells. By contrast, the pathology in cerebral arteriosclerosis is secondary to vascular changes and, at least in early stages, is more likely to be focal than diffuse. Once the pathologic process has progressed to the point of requiring hospital care, however, the differences between senile dementia and cerebral arteriosclerosis tend to disappear, and the antemortem diagnosis of one or the other is often not confirmed by the postmortem findings.

Two relatively rare conditions occurring earlier in life symptomatically resemble senile dementia and the classic form of cerebral arteriosclerosis. These conditions are Alzheimer's disease, or presenile dementia, and Pick's disease.

TOXIC AND METABOLIC CONDITIONS

The toxin responsible for the majority of disturbances in this group is alcohol. Earlier (page 109), some of the elements in the psychopathology of alcoholism were discussed and also some of the basic principles in the management of delirium were mentioned (page 210).

The acute delirium associated with alcohol is called *delirium tremens*. Delirium tremens develops acutely during a period of heavy drinking or shortly after its termination. Beginning with irritability, tremor, and mounting apprehension, its main symptoms are visual hallucinations, which often terrify the patient to the point of panic. Although frequently the subject of humor and often considered with little sympathy as the just consequences of self-indulgence, delirium tremens should be taken seriously, as the suffering is intense and the mortality high [9].

Treatment is essentially the same as for other forms of delirium. Since vitamin deficiencies and interference with carbohydrate metabolism have been implicated along with alcohol in the cause of this condition, B-complex vitamins, glucose, and small doses of insulin are used in its treatment. Several other adjuncts to treatment, such as the administration of steroids, have their advocates, although at present writing their effectiveness has not been substantiated.

Another relatively acute sequel of alcoholism, *alcoholic hallucinosis,* differs from delirium tremens in that the hallucinations are predominantly auditory instead of visual, the physical signs are less marked, and the onset is more insidious. The full-blown picture resembles an acute paranoid schizophrenia, although the prognosis for the attack is considerably better.

The chronic psychotic conditions associated with alcohol customarily resemble organic psychoses due to other, generalized causes. Polyneuritis and other evidence of nutritional deficiencies, particularly vitamin deficiencies, often accompany the psychosis, and two special types of chronic, dementing psychosis are occasionally seen. The characteristic feature of *Korsakoff's psychosis* is *confabulation*. Confabulation is the production of fantasied, inaccurate accounts of a patient's activity, which he develops apparently in an effort to fill in recent memory gaps. In Korsakoff's psychosis, the gaps appear to be extensions of the "blackouts" characteristic of acute alcoholism. The distinguishing characteristic of *Wernicke's encephalopathy* is diplopia, due to damage to the cranial nerve nuclei. The damage may extend to cause a complete ophthalmoplegia.

Somewhat similar patterns of psychosis result from any agent that can cause acute or chronic damage to the brain. The agents listed below are the most common, but they by no means include every possibility.

1. Drugs, particularly bromides and amphetamines. Although sleeplessness is an early sign of psychosis, the physician should not overlook

the possibility that a psychosis may be related to medication taken by the patient for relief of insomnia due to other causes. Amphetamine psychoses, often simulating paranoid schizophrenia, may follow extensive use of the drug for mood elevation or for weight reduction.

2. Hormones, particularly steroids and occasionally thyroid hormones. Psychoses following steroid administration may be due, at least in part, to the distortion of body image brought about by these substances [10]. Any patient under intensive steroid treatment requires an adequate opportunity to talk with his doctor about his dismay and apprehension concerning the side effects. The acne, hirsutism, and change in facial contour have a particularly profound significance to adolescent and postadolescent girls.

3. Chemicals and gases such as carbon monoxide. Lead encephalopathy is fortunately less commonly encountered in children than it was before the paint industry took precautionary measures. It is still, however, a potential danger.

4. Vitamin and hormone deficiencies. The classic deficiency psychosis is pellagra, fortunately no longer frequent in the United States as a social phenomenon of poverty. A nutritional component similar to pellagra may contribute, however, to the psychotic conditions associated with aging. Elderly people, particularly if somewhat depressed, may restrict their diets either quantitatively or qualitatively, or both, and a condition that appears to be due to senile dementia or cerebral arteriosclerosis may respond, at least in part, to improved diet. Myxedema and Addison's disease also may be accompanied by psychotic manifestations.

5. Metabolic disturbances. Uremia is often associated with delirium. The baffling metabolic disturbances of porphyria may simulate conversion reactions and other diseases primarily of psychologic origin. Complicating the picture is evidence that attacks of porphyria in constitutionally predisposed individuals may be precipitated by emotional stress as well as by alcohol and barbiturates. Since barbiturates are commonly prescribed for the relief of symptoms of emotional disorder, the understanding of porphyria presents an interesting challenge in the coordination of constitutional, toxic, and emotional factors.

HEAD INJURIES

A history of head injury traditionally has provided a convenient rationalization for virtually any psychotic disturbance. It maintains the self-esteem of the parents of a mentally defective child [11], and it helps to protect the patient with a conversion reaction from the anxiety associated with the exploration of his conflicts and interpersonal relationships. However, recognition of the facility with which this explanation can be

used as rationalization should not deter the physician from careful evaluation of organic factors in patients with psychiatric symptoms following
head injury, since the consequences of brain injury may not only give
clear-cut organic pictures, as in the "punch-drunk" fighter, but may contribute more subtly to other symptom complexes. Brain injury is indeed
an important cause of mental retardation and has been implicated in the
development of behavior disorders and hyperactivity in children.

A difficult medical-legal problem is often presented by the *postconcussion syndrome* [12]. After a head injury, patients frequently complain of
headache, dizziness, fatigue, insomnia, and a decreased tolerance for stress
of any kind. The weakening of adaptive capacity removes barriers to the
emergence of impulses, leading to emotional instability and irritability,
and reduces the ability to compensate for the effects of toxins, particularly
alcohol, which further weaken the already weakened ego. Frequently patients will be so distressed by their inability to "hold their liquor" following head injuries that they will give up drinking altogether.

The possibility of financial compensation that so often follows head injury increases secondary gains and frequently prolongs the period of a patient's disability. The threat of the original injury, the vagueness of the
postconcussion syndrome, and the combination of fact and folklore concerning the sequelae of head injury all encourage the development of
quasi-neurologic symptoms typical of conversion reactions. However, the
prospect of compensation is not in itself evidence of a psychologic overlay
to an organic condition nor is its absence enough to rule out the possibility, since secondary gains can be found in areas other than financial
compensation.

A third consideration in the differential diagnosis of postconcussion
states is malingering, or conscious simulation of symptoms. The obvious
nature of the relationship between financial compensation and the continuation of symptoms without organic basis at first makes it easy to assume
that the symptoms are consciously simulated. Careful study, however,
demonstrates that this assumption holds true for only a small proportion
of these patients and shows that for the vast majority the symptoms are
unconsciously determined.

By far the best treatment of any condition associated with compensation is prevention. Extremely careful management is indicated, therefore,
early in the course of the treatment of head injury. The best prevention
includes the prescription of a gradual return to activity, encouraged by as
optimistic an expectation as the conditions warrant. The subjective nature
of many symptoms of injury, however, makes it difficult to know when
gentle but firm encouragement to increased activity past the patient's own

estimation of his tolerance is warranted. To reduce the chances of a compensation neurosis, the physician should be careful neither to suggest symptoms nor to predict a longer disability than is likely to be the case under optimal circumstances.

EPILEPSY

The relationship of psychiatric conditions to epilepsy is still not at all clear. How much of the psychologic symptomatology is due to the seizure per se, how much is due to the feeling of isolation and the constant fear of the attack that are virtually inevitable in an epileptic, and how much is related to medication is difficult to determine. Finally, emotional stress has been given some consideration in attempting to understand the periodicity of the attacks and their occurrence in only a limited number of individuals with typical electroencephalographic patterns.

The psychologic disturbances which are associated with epilepsy include the following:

1. Episodes resembling dissociative reactions or acute catatonic schizophrenic reactions. These epidodes occur apparently without precipitating cause and are usually self-limited.

2. Episodic outbursts of destructive behavior, especially in children.

3. Episodes of mental dullness and other psychiatric symptoms which may resemble schizophrenia and which are often accompanied by hallucinatory experiences. These attacks are self-limited, although they may last longer than the usual seizure. Patients with temporal lobe foci are prone to develop this type of attack [13].

4. Chronic personality disturbances. There are several types of personality disturbances associated with epilepsy. The so-called "epileptic personality," however, is neither so typical nor so prevalent as was once assumed. The personality disturbances may be due primarily to brain injuries, therapeutic drugs, or the psychologic effect of the disease and so may have only a secondary relationship to epilepsy.

Treatment of the psychiatric symptoms associated with epilepsy is not specific but depends on the elucidation of the cause in each indvidual case.

TUMORS, HEREDITY, AND INFECTIONS

Psychosis Due to Brain Tumor

Brain tumors may simulate senile dementia, schizophrenia, or virtually any emotionally caused illness [14].

A thirty-five-year-old man entered a hospital emergency room in a state of great agitation and vociferously asserted that his wife was trying to poison him. He maintained that she wished to get rid of him in order to marry a former boyfriend. He gave a rather inconsistent story of the behavior that had made him suspicious and said that his suspicions had recently become confirmed when he noted a peculiar taste and odor in his food.

He was admitted to the psychiatric service with a provisional diagnosis of paranoid schizophrenia. There, more careful investigation revealed that the "peculiar odor" occurred in spells not necessarily associated with eating, and a thorough neurologic work-up revealed the presence of an uncus tumor. The patient, a mildly paranoid personality, had rationalized his symptoms into a paranoid system.

Psychosis Due to Heredity

The most dramatic example of a *hereditary psychosis* is Huntington's chorea. This condition is a Mendelian dominant which usually develops in the fourth decade of life and is associated with degeneration in the caudate nucleus and putamen, as well as in the cortex. The patient develops progressive dementia associated with choreiform movements. Treatment, unfortunately, is only symptomatic.

Psychosis Due to Infectious Causes

The classic example of chronic psychosis due to infection is general paresis, caused by syphilitic infection of the central nervous system [15]. Since the introduction of penicillin as a treatment of early syphilis, this condition has become rare, although it has not completely disappeared. Initially, it may resemble virtually any psychiatric condition, although in common with other organic psychoses it is characterized by a progressive dementia with loss of judgment. Grandiose delusions are somewhat more common in this condition than in schizophrenia. A juvenile form of paresis was once frequently encountered among children with congenital syphilis but is now a rarity, at least in the United States.

Some forms of encephalitis are followed by organic psychosis, and in children this condition has been associated with the development of conduct disorders, probably a result of organic weakening of the inhibitory elements of the ego.

The most frequent psychiatric manifestation of infection is the acute brain syndrome, or delirium (see page 280). Almost any severe infection may cause delirium, particularly in children and the aged. Although usually transient, deliriums are potentially dangerous because of exhaustion secondary to the patient's panic.

SUMMARY

In this chapter, the major types of organic conditions producing psychiatric symptoms were briefly outlined. The effects of aging, toxins, metabolic disturbances, injuries, epilepsy, tumors, infections, and heredity in causing acute and chronic conditions were discussed. The importance of proper evaluation of the contributions made by organic factors was emphasized.

REFERENCES

1. Arieti, S. (ed.): *American Handbook of Psychiatry,* New York, Basic Books, Inc., Publishers, 1959, vol. II, part 8, p. 1003.
   Dewan, J. G., and W. B. Spaulding: *The Organic Psychosis, a Guide to Diagnosis,* Toronto, Canada, University of Toronto Press, 1958.
2. Engel, G. L., and J. Romano: "Delirium: A Syndrome of Cerebral Insufficiency," *J. Chronic Dis.,* 9:260, 1959.
3. Kay, D. W. K., and M. Roth: "Environmental and Hereditary Factors in the Schizophrenias of Old Age," *J. Ment. Sci.,* 107:649, 1961.
4. Rothschild, D.: "Pathological Changes in Senile Psychoses and Their Psychobiologic Significance," *Amer. J. Psychiat.,* 93:757, 1937.
   See, however:
   Corsellis, J. A. N.: *Mental Illness and the Aging Brain,* Fairlawn, N.J., Oxford University Press, 1962.
5. Cumming, E., and W. E. Henry: *Growing Old: The Process of Disengagement,* New York, Basic Books, Inc., Publishers, 1961.
6. Aldrich, C. K.: "Relocation of the Aged and Disabled: A Mortality Study," *J. Amer. Geriat. Soc.,* 11:185, 1963.
7. Davidson, R.: Personal Communication.
8. Kaplan, O. J. (ed.): *Mental Disorders in Later Life,* 2d ed., Stanford, Calif., Stanford University Press, 1956.
   Allison, R. S.: *The Senile Brain: A Clinical Study,* Baltimore, The Williams & Wilkins Company, 1962.
9. Tavel, M. E.: "A New Outlook at an Old Syndrome: Delirium Tremens," *AMA Arch. Intern. Med.,* 109:129, 1962.
10. Rome, H. P., and F. J. Braceland: "Psychological Response to Corticotropin, Cortisone and Related Steroid Substances," *J.A.M.A.,* 148:27, 1952.
11. Eisenberg, L.: "Psychiatric Implications of Brain Damage in Children," *Psychiat. Quart.,* 31:72, 1957.
12. Ross, W. D.: *Practical Psychiatry for Industrial Physicians,* Springfield, Ill., Charles C Thomas, Publisher, 1956, pp. 158 and 255.
13. Glaser, G. H.: "The Problem of Psychosis in Psychomotor Temporal Lobe Epileptics," *Epilepsia,* 5:271, 1964.
    Mulder, D. W., and D. Daly: "Psychiatric Symptoms Associated with Lesions of the Temporal Lobe," *J.A.M.A.,* 150:173, 1952.
14. Strauss, H.: "Intracranial Neoplasms Masked as Depressions and Diagnosed

with the Aid of Electroencephalography," *J. Nerv. Ment. Dis.*, 12:185, 1955.

Waggoner, R. W., and B. K. Bagchi: "Initial Masking of Organic Brain Changes by Psychic Symptoms," *Amer. J. Psychiat.*, 110:904, 1954.

15. Wagner-Jauregg, J., and W. L. Bruetsch: "The History of the Malaria Treatment of General Paresis," *Amer. J. Psychiat.*, 102:577, 1946.

Chapter 13

MENTAL RETARDATION
AND LEARNING BLOCKS

CAUSES AND DIAGNOSIS OF MENTAL RETARDATION

As stated earlier (page 84), hereditary factors apparently set limits to an individual's potential for intellectual achievement, and if cultural, educational, and emotional factors are optimal and if there is no damage to the brain, differences in intellectual capacity can be attributed to hereditary causes. The distribution of intellectual potential among the general population presumably follows a normal (Gaussian) curve (Figure 4), with a bulge at the lower end. Low intelligence is a handicap in adaptation; when intelligence is low enough significantly to handicap adaptation, the individual is considered mentally retarded. The point on the curve below which mental retardation is diagnosed is somewhat arbitrary; in actual experience, it varies considerable according to the complexity of the social environment. For example, a man who could function adequately as a sheepherder in an isolated rural area might be considered mentally retarded in an urban society.

Hereditary, cultural, and educational causes theoretically account for virtually all the distribution of intelligence along the normal, symmetrical curve. The bulge at the lower end (shaded in Figure 4) represents mental retardation due to a group of specific metabolic errors, injuries, and severe emotional illnesses. This group of causes, therefore, accounts for a disproportionate number of the most severely retarded.

In some types of intellectual retardation, when the evidence is obvious, the physician can make the diagnosis as early as the first day of a child's life. The more common, milder degrees of retardation, however, do not become evident until later, when parents, teachers, physicians, or other observers notice that the child's maturation is slow. Parents understandably tend to avoid facing the unpleasant fact that they have a handicapped child and often either deny the evidence of intellectual defect or rationalize it as the effect of physical illness or diet or anything else which offers

them a possible way of avoiding the unavoidable. Although more objective observers may have realized for years that something was wrong, the
parents may not seek help for a retarded child until confronted with in-
controvertible evidence of school failure. Even then, they generally find
their misfortune difficult to face and anxiously try to pin the blame on the
schools. Occasionally the teacher, but more often the school psychologist,

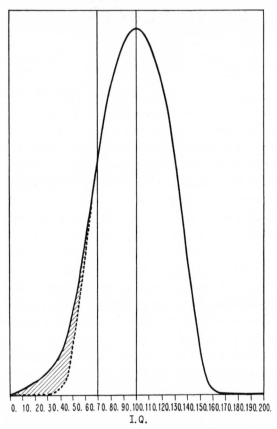

0. 10. 20. 30. 40. 50. 60. 70. 80. 90.100.110.120.130.140.150.160.170.180.190.200.
                                    I.Q.

FIGURE 4. Theoretical distribution of intelligence test scores in the total population.

nurse, or social worker is the first professionally trained person to discuss
the problem with the parents.

When the parents can no longer avoid facing the problem, they may
reveal that the child's defect has a meaning to them deeper than the blow
to their pride. Some of them believe the defect in their child is a punishment for previous sins. The mother, in particular, may tie it up with an
earlier sexual indiscretion and may believe that bearing a defective child
is appropriate retribution for her sexual offense. In the eyes of the guilt-

ridden parent, the punishment should fit the crime, and he (or she) will interpret a defective child as a cross to be borne indefinitely, even if other children in the family must be neglected or suffer embarrassment.

The presence of the defective child is in itself a potential source of guilt as well as of shame for the parents. They are ashamed of having a defective child, and they may be ashamed of being ashamed. Furthermore, the child's defect encourages the parents' ambivalence and the wish, either conscious or repressed, that the child had not been born alive or that an illness or accident had proven fatal or that in some other way the burden of the defective child had been removed. Whether the parents recognize their guilt for their destructive wish or whether they repress it and overcompensate by overprotection, their guilt interferes with their objectivity in planning for the child. Parents may interpret other congenital defects in the same way, and the physician who recognizes and understands the basis for this attitude can help the parents express and resolve enough of their guilt feelings so that they can view more objectively the needs of the defective child in the perspective of the needs of the whole family. He can also understand the part guilt may be playing in the genesis of the exaggerated grief some parents display at the death of a severely handicapped child.

Since parents who seek help for a retarded child from a pediatrician or general practitioner often screen their anxiety by presenting an apparently unrelated complaint, it may take some time in the course of the history taking for their real purpose to become evident. A doctor who knows the family usually is prepared for the eventual disclosure, but in any case, the parents should be permitted to present the problem in their own way. Eventually, after they have discussed the details of pregnancy and birth and the child's developmental and health history, it becomes obvious both to parents and to physician that the child is not performing at the level expected for his age.

When the nature of the problem has been established, the parents usually need to ventilate their feelings before the extent of the problem can be explored. Although guilt is probably the most difficult feeling for the parents to express, they may also need help in expressing other feelings about their child: grief at the child's helplessness and inability to appreciate the world they know, anger at the fate that has saddled them with a child in whom they cannot have the usual kind of pride, fear and despair about the future. The ventilation of feeling may require several sessions, but it is necessary before the parents can begin to plan or even to see the extent and implications of the problem.

The next step is to encourage the parents to review the specific differences they have noticed between the child and his contemporaries. With this approach, parents usually can arrive at a fairly accurate estimate of their child's developmental age, helping to prepare themselves for eventual acceptance of the extent of the defect and for later planning.

When they are encouraged to discuss their theories about the cause of the retardation, parents may attach the blame to a minor head injury, overlooking earlier evidence of retardation, or they may convince themselves, without objective evidence, that the damage was caused by injury or asphyxia at birth. Even if the physician recognizes that this explanation is a rationalization to avoid facing a possible hereditary cause, there is often no advantage in confronting the parents with the facts. It is important, however, carefully to evaluate the child for signs of possible brain damage during the complete physical, neurologic, psychologic, and laboratory examinations which every suspected mentally retarded patient requires.

Young children with brain damage from birth injury or other causes occasionally demonstrate hyperactive, distractible, and impulsive behavior that makes them difficult to manage. Although they may have average general intelligence, they often have specific defects in integration and conceptualization that lead to reading problems and difficulties in abstract thinking and that may give the impression of generalized mental retardation. Since there are seldom any gross neurologic findings, it may be difficult to differentiate this type of brain damage from similar symptoms due to emotional causes. The electroencephalogram is sometimes helpful in making the diagnosis.

Besides brain damage, mongolism should be considered, as well as the inborn errors of metabolism such as phenylketonuria and galactosemia. It is extremely important to diagnose the kinds of metabolic error for which treatment is available early enough in a child's life so that permanent damage can be forestalled. Tests for phenylketones, for example, should be run routinely on the urine of infants.

Measurement and Classification

The degree of mental retardation can best be determined by psychologic testing. Simple screening tests can be used to determine rough approximations of intelligence, but they are not accurate enough for establishing a diagnosis of mental deficiency. When mental deficiency is suspected, the psychiatrist, pediatrician, or other physician without specific training in this field should rely on a psychologist for choosing, administering, and interpreting tests. A report from a competent psychologist gives much more than a single numerical score; it indicates variations in the child's capacities, it reports observations of his performance and attitudes, and it usually provides some clue to the probable causes of the retardation.

Parents often rely on the physician for an explanation of the psychologic report, and he should be familiar with the terminology most commonly used. The numerical result is usually given in terms of *intelligence quotient* or of *mental age*. The mental age of the average child is the same as his chronologic age; in superior children, the mental age is higher, and in retarded children, lower. Thus, an eight-year-old child who manipulates, calculates, reads, thinks, and learns as fast as an average child of six, taking into consideration individual variations in specific abilities, has a mental age of six.

The intelligence quotient, or IQ, is the result of dividing the mental age by the chronologic age and multiplying by 100. The IQ of the average child, therefore, is 100. The IQ of the eight-year-old who has a mental age of six is determined as follows:

$$\frac{(MA)\ 6}{(CA)\ 8} \times 100 = 75$$

The IQ as a yardstick has the advantage of remaining approximately constant under ordinary circumstances throughout childhood, while the mental age continues to increase in the same ratio. Thus, by the time he is twelve, the child mentioned above should have a mental age of nine, but his IQ should remain the same:

$$\frac{(MA)\ 9}{(CA)\ 12} \times 100 = 75$$

Intelligence, at least as measured by the standard tests, levels off at about sixteen, which is therefore taken as the adult base line. The mental age of the child in the example will stabilize at about twelve, and in adult life his IQ will continue to be:

$$\frac{(MA)\ 12}{(CA)\ 16} \times 100 = 75$$

Mental retardation is classified into four general categories according to the degree of defect, as measured by the IQ. These categories—severe, moderate, mild, and borderline—are shown in Figure 5. In adult life, severe cases remain helpless and require constant care; moderate cases can care for themselves to some degree within the protection of an institution or home; mild cases can manage outside of institutions when the environmental demands are minimal, but they lack the judgment to deal with new or stress situations; borderline cases often make a satisfactory adjustment, although they tend to be easily influenced or exploited.

The IQ, however, may vary. It does not necessarily reveal the patient's potential abilities; it may only reveal the level at which he is operating at the time of testing. A great many factors can cause him to perform at a level below his true ability. Physical illness, particularly when it affects his eyes, ears, or coordination, makes it hard for a child to do his best on tests; a limited cultural or educational background seriously handicaps him; and emotional disturbances can interfere with his performance. The

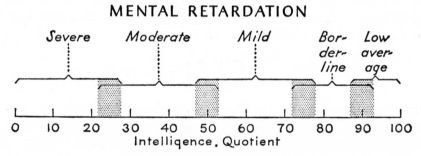

FIGURE 5. Classification of Mental Retardation.

trained psychologist often can detect underachievement on tests and thus can contribute more to the diagnosis than simply the degree of retardation.

A substantial number of the mentally retarded are handicapped primarily as a result of cultural deprivation. Without the opportunity in their homes to develop a readiness to learn, culturally deprived children cannot take advantage of their education, and the gap between their abilities and the abilities of the normal child progressively increases. Prevention of culturally determined mental retardation is far easier than treatment; reports from special nursery schools which prepare these children for schooling have been encouraging.

References to more complete surveys of the causes of mental deficiency and the diagnostic methods for their determination will be found at the end of this chapter [1].

TREATMENT OF MENTAL RETARDATION

Proper management of the child whose intelligence is limited by heredity or organic disease may improve his ability to make the best of his resources, but as far as we know, such children will always be limited. It is difficult for parents to accept this prognosis, but if they are convinced of the thoroughness of the examination and if they have confidence in the physician, they can be helped to make realistic plans for the future.

The parents have both the right and the responsibility to make their own choice among the available alternatives and should not be hurried or overridden. The doctor can best help the parents find their own answers by making the alternatives clear.

Possible plans include home care, boarding-home placement, a private school, and a state institution. In recent years, day-care centers for retarded children have been developed which, in many cases, provide an acceptable compromise between home and institutional care.

The doctor can help the parents express their fear, on the one hand, that as the child grows older his defect will become more obvious and playmates may treat him cruelly and their concern, on the other hand, that the child would be treated impersonally in an institution. He can help them weigh objectively the importance of the intensive personal care which can be given to a defective child at home against the importance of the relatively normal home environment that they can provide for themselves and especially for their normal children if they arrange for outside care of the defective child. If they decide on care away from home, the doctor can help them in overcoming the guilt which often follows the parents' relief once the child has gone.

Occasionally, as in the following example, he may be asked to support a plan which he knows is unrealistic. If he firmly holds to realistic planning, however, he will be more helpful in the long run to the child, to the parents, and to himself.

A pediatrician, responding to tremendous pressure from a mother, recommended to the school authorities that her moderately retarded child be permitted to attend first grade "so as to gain the benefits of social contacts with other children of her age." The teacher made heroic attempts to protect the girl from ridicule and to help the others to understand her. The child, however, constantly disrupted the schoolroom, to the detriment of the teaching program, and had to be transferred to a special school. Although the pediatrician had made the recommendation reluctantly, he became the scapegoat for the failure of the plan.

The question of school promotion is often raised with respect to the borderline mental defective. If he is retained in the same grade year after year, he becomes conspicuous, feels inadequate, and as a result may develop behavior problems. On the other hand, "social" or routine promotions without achievement carry the weaker student intellectually farther and farther away from his level of performance. The best solution yet discovered appears to be the special class, if it can be established without unduly stigmatizing its pupils. In many communities, however, special classes are not available. The physician, because of his profession, has an unusual opportunity to exert influence toward the institution of special classes in public schools as well as toward other improved facilities for handicapped children.

EMOTIONAL BLOCKS TO LEARNING

Although organic limitations cause most intellectual retardation, emotional blocks to learning can simulate mental deficiency. Sometimes parents make such unreasonable intellectual demands on a child that he seems to feel that it is hopeless to satisfy them and abandons the effort. Other children find that refusal to learn is their only means of self-assertion. Still other children may be so dependent and insecure that they are afraid to learn and thereby jeopardize the protection that comes with helplessness.

A child may fail to learn because he has been severely punished at an early age for sexual curiosity. If the incident occurs when he is too young to distinguish sexual curiosity from other forms of curiosity, he may interpret his punishment as the result of the curiosity per se rather than of its sexual implications; and if the punishment or threat was severe enough, he may attempt to protect himself by inhibiting all curiosity and therefore all learning. In the same way, if learning acquires a forbidden, aggressive connotation, the child may inhibit all learning as he attempts to keep all signs of aggression out of sight. Observing the relationship between child and parents often gives a clue to the nature of the problem, as in the following case.

> A five-year-old child was referred to a clinic in a nearby city because of slowness of learning. He was hospitalized for examination, and although the initial testing revealed an IQ of 69, the nurses noted that as he became accustomed to the warm and friendly attitude on the ward, he appeared to brighten up. They also noted that at visiting hours the parents, middle-aged people with high intellectual standards, greeted him with derogatory remarks and irritated criticism. During visiting hours, the child lapsed back into slow, colorless, retarded behavior.

Further study confirmed the suspicion that the parents expected too much of the child, and thorough psychologic evaluation showed that his abilities were greater than his performance. A social worker began a series of interviews with the parents. Tactfully and with patience, she helped them understand and resolve some of their ambivalent feelings about their child. The social worker supported them in their conscientious efforts to be good parents and helped them to accept more comfortably the fact that their child had no more than average intelligence. After three months in the accepting and uncritical atmosphere of the hospital, the child's intelligence test showed an IQ of 95. Although the child's return from the hospital was somewhat difficult for all concerned, he maintained his improvement, and the parents were able to temper their criticisms to a more realistic level.

A program of this type has crucial importance in the prevention of severe social and emotional incapacity. Although the physician cannot be expected to carry out all the details of the program, he may be the key to its success through his early use of diagnostic skills, his knowledge of appropriate community resources, and his psychologic support of the family struggling through the problems of treatment.

Some children have trouble in reading, although in other intellectual functions they are not handicapped. Many reading problems result from confusion of the sequence of letters; thus, "salt" is read "slat" or even "last." Some children persist in a tendency to confuse letters which are mirror images: *b* and *d*, *p* and *q*. The exact cause of such reading problems is not clear. Many investigators believe that altered cerebral dominance is responsible, although others are not convinced. The physician should refer patients with reading problems for psychologic testing, just as he refers patients with low intelligence. In cases of reading disability, he should also be alert for signs of emotional stress and should not assume an organic brain defect in every case.

An eight-and-a-half-year-old boy was referred for neurologic examination because he could not read. He was good in arithmetic and apparently of superior intelligence (a later IQ was 124). Although no mention of other problems had been made in the referral, the parents, when interviewed separately, revealed that their son was enuretic, had frequent temper tantrums and nightmares, and made a poor social adjustment with other children. The boy was the battleground for bickering between the parents and was constantly threatened, both directly and indirectly, by the imminent breakup of the family home.

The physician's neurologic examination found nothing abnormal, and psychologic tests showed no signs of specific, organic language disabilities. Meanwhile, he discussed with the parents the effect of the emotional climate at home on the child's troubles. They agreed to seek professional help for their marital problems and arranged to have their son helped by a tutor trained in remedial reading.

In this case, the emotional problem appeared to be primary and the reading difficulty secondary. Almost any reading problem or other educational deficiency, however, may precipitate emotional upsets in the family, and it is often difficult to dissect out the primary factor. The existence of emotional turmoil in such a family by no means implicates emotions as the primary cause of the disability [2].

CHILDHOOD SCHIZOPHRENIA AND AUTISM

The extreme withdrawal and preoccupation with internal psychologic stimuli characteristic of children who suffer from severe childhood schizophrenia or autism seriously interfere with learning and often cause these children to be considered mentally retarded. In the following case, many years passed before the correct diagnosis was made.

> The customarily docile, mute, and vacant existence of a forty-eight-year-old female patient in an institution for the mentally retarded was interrupted by her transfer to a new institution. Apparently disturbed by her new surroundings, she became mildly agitated, pacing the floor and talking to herself in a low voice. Occasionally, she would interrupt her stereotyped behavior pattern with a lucid and intelligent observation; thus, when an attendant was struggling to put shoes on some severely retarded women, the patient stopped pacing to ask, appropriately, "Why don't you use a shoehorn?"
>
> The history revealed that the patient had been a withdrawn, preoccupied, irritable child, who constantly played with her fingers and face. Her family considered her stupid, and after a brief and completely unsuccessful trial at school at the age of seven, followed by an intelligence test with a reported IQ of 40, she was adjudged mentally retarded and placed in an institution. For forty-one years, she had vegetated in the institution; the record showed only that she had received competent medical care for physical illnesses and that two subsequent tests had indicated IQ's of 7 and 23. The fortuitous combination of a transfer and an unusually alert attendant finally led to a psychiatric evaluation and to a revision of the diagnosis to schizophrenia.

The childhood diagnosis of this patient was either childhood schizophrenia or infantile autism. Infantile autism is a condition in some ways similar to childhood schizophrenia that develops in the first year of life and is often mistaken for mental retardation. The child either does not "learn" to talk or uses speech inappropriately; he is not able to evaluate the environment correctly; he resists change, often with outbursts of temper or anxiety; and he seems preoccupied with stereotyped actions and inanimate objects. In contrast to most mentally retarded children, however, he avoids rather than seeks out human contacts and relationships.

Both autism and childhood schizophrenia are difficult to treat, and the odds are that this patient's course would not have been dramatically different if she had been properly diagnosed in the first place. As more knowledge and facilities for the treatment of autistic and schizophrenic children become available, however, the importance of making correct diagnoses increases [3].

Before closing this chapter on intellectual deficits, mention should be made of the child of superior intelligence who adjusts poorly to school simply because he is bored. Promoting him may solve his intellectual problems, but only at the expense of producing social problems, since he is then placed with pupils of greater social maturity. Just as for the borderline defective, special classes are indicated, or opportunities for extra work with greater intellectual challenge should be provided.

SUMMARY

In this chapter, the causes, classification, and management of intellectual deficits, both general and specific, were briefly outlined. The primary focus was on the approach and the point of view of the physician and on the areas in which he can best cooperate with the specialist. The importance of considering emotional blocks to learning, childhood schizophrenia, and infantile autism in the differential diagnosis of mental retardation was emphasized.

REFERENCES

1. Two general references on mental retardation are:
   "Mental Retardation: A handbook for the Physician," *J.A.M.A.*, 191:183, 1965.
   Piaget, J.: *The Origins of Intelligence in Children* (1936), New York, International Universities Press, Inc., 1952.
   Two useful reports on the subject are:
   Group for the Advancement of Psychiatry: Report No. 43, *Basic Considerations in Mental Retardation*, 1959.
   Group for the Advancement of Psychiatry: Report No. 56, *Mental Retardation: A Family Crisis—the Therapeutic Role of the Physician*, 1963.
   For a more extensive discussion, see:
   Masland, L., S. B. Sarason, and T. Gladwin: *Mental Subnormality: Biological, Psychological, and Cultural Factors*, New York, Basic Books, Inc., Publishers, 1958.
   See also:

The President's Panel on Mental Retardation: *Proposed Program for National Action to Combat Mental Retardation,* report to the President, Washington, U.S. Government Printing Office, 1962.

For parents:

French, E., and J. C. Scott: *Child in the Shadows: A Manual for Parents of Retarded Children,* Philadelphia, J. B. Lippincott Company, 1960.

2. See reference 15, Chapter 5.

3. For further study of autism and childhood schizophrenia, see:

Bettelheim, Bruno: *Truants from Life: The Rehabilitation of Emotionally Disturbed Children,* New York, The Free Press of Glencoe, 1955.

Despert, J. L.: "Some Considerations Relating to the Genesis of Autistic Behavior in Children," *Amer. J. Orthopsychiat.,* 21:335, 1951.

Goldfarb, W.: "An Investigation of Childhood Schizophrenia," *Arch. Gen. Psychiat. (Chicago),* 11:620, 1964.

Kanner, L.: "Autistic Disturbances of Affective Contact," *The Nervous Child,* 2:217, 1943.

Chapter 14

SOCIOPATHIC PERSONALITY DISTURBANCES

Recently, psychiatry has become more actively concerned than ever before with the attempt to understand the causes of disorders of conduct or behavior. For many years, with a few distinguished exceptions, psychiatrists generally seemed content to categorize most offenders against society's laws and customs either as normal individuals who had deliberately chosen to misbehave and hence should be held responsible or as "psychopathic personalities" with an inborn incapacity to behave in accordance with society's demands or to learn by experience. According to this concept, the church and the law should discipline the first group and society should be protected from the second; in either case, psychiatrists had little to offer.

The fatalistic concept of the psychopathic personality as an inherited abnormality was fostered by the writings of Lombroso [1], who considered that the criminal type represented a biologic return to savagery. Although the anthropologic assumptions on which the Lombroso hypothesis was based have long been proven incorrect, the concept continues to survive. Reports of families in which the incidence of criminal behavior was high—the well-known Jukes and Kallikaks, for example—were interpreted to mean that tendencies toward crime were inherited [2]. Later, more scientific approaches through studies of twins [3], of body build [4], and of electroencephalographic abnormalities [5] all seemed to confirm the heredity hypothesis, although exceptions were numerous, and the effects of early environment were often uncritically assumed to be evidences of hereditary taint. Some child psychiatrists, impressed with the frequency of behavior problems among children who have suffered from encephalitis and with the high incidence of electroencephalographic abnormality among all delinquents, are still convinced that the cause of delinquency is primarily organic.

Meanwhile, the psychiatrist's major concern with crime was in the area of overlap between the law and mental illness [6]. If *A* attacked *B* in response to a delusion that *B* was persecuting *A*, should *A* be held as responsible as a person without delusions, or should his act be considered a symptom and *A* be given psychiatric treatment? Although at first glance the answer seems obvious enough, society was concerned that if the paranoid patient was relieved of responsibility, the door would be opened for any criminal who could find a symptom—alcoholism, depression, phobias, even the psychopathic personality—to get off scot-free. If emotional health is defined as satisfactory adaptation, then any crime could be considered a symptom of a temporary or permanent failure of adaptation.

The psychiatrist's goal in studying criminal responsibility was not to relieve the criminal of responsibility, although in isolated instances it often appeared that way, but to learn more about human behavior, and as in nuclear physics or any other science, his research could not very well be curtailed because its consequences might be troublesome to society. Actually, the discovery of causes of criminal behavior outside of the individual's control does not require society to license such behavior; the history of the legal commitment of the mentally ill is evidence that society can limit the freedom of anyone who gives it offense, regardless of the causes.

CAUSES OF BEHAVIOR DISORDERS

The forensic psychiatrist's concern with problems of criminal responsibility, together with the child psychiatrist's concern with behavior problems, has led in recent years to a more careful scrutiny of the causes of criminal behavior. This scrutiny, in turn, has led to increasing skepticism about the central role of hereditary factors. As the difficulty of differentiating between the effects of heredity and the effects of early environment has become more apparent, the significance of twin and genetic studies has become less clear. Follow-up studies have cast some doubt on the assumption that the so-called psychopathic personality never changes his behavior patterns [7], and evidence from electroencephalographic studies has been more equivocal than at first seemed likely.

Meanwhile, the effects of social and psychologic factors have been more thoroughly investigated [8]. Alexander showed that a group of "neurotic" delinquents "acted out" unacceptable drives by indirect, modified expression through antisocial behavior [9]. The process of modification of a drive so as to conceal its true nature has been discussed with reference to the excessive hunger of the obese. In much the same way, part of the need to receive affection can be modified to a drive to accumulate possessions or, more specifically, to take possessions from the desired source of affection or his symbolic representative. Thus, a child who has all the possessions he needs but not enough affection may steal from his mother's pocketbook and eventually from the pocketbook of someone else who represents his mother. Many, perhaps the majority, of child psychiatrists now emphasize the role of early maternal deprivation, with the implication that the child seeks through delinquent behavior to extract from society a material substitute for his mother's love or to get indirect revenge for his deprivation [10].

Among other social factors, poverty, poor housing, the anonymity of urban life, and family disorganization have all been shown to be spawning grounds for delinquency. One sociologic theory postulates that the underprivileged youth becomes delinquent because of his lack of a place in society and because of the unbridgable gap between the middle-class goals which society encourages him to aspire to and his opportunity to attain them. Another theory postulates a "delinquency subculture" among underprivileged adolescents, with standards and goals virtually opposite to the standards and goals of the culture as a whole [11].

A challenging approach to the behavior problems of children was provided by Johnson and Szurek [12]. Their studies stemmed from an interview one of them had with a boy and his father. The boy had been referred to the child-guidance clinic for investigation of frequent running away from home. As he told his story, the doctors noticed that the father kept prompting him, supplying additional details, and evincing a great deal of interest in each step of each episode, while the son played up to his father's interest with appropriate embellishments of his story. Although the father's attitude changed at the end of the story and he expressed conventional criticism of the boy's behavior, the doctors were struck by the father's evident vicarious participation in his son's wanderings. On investigation, they found that, although the father had reluctantly given up his occupation of long-distance truck driving to settle down in family life, he had not abandoned his fascination with travel. It became quite clear that, after each episode, he had enjoyed hearing about each step of his son's wanderings and that the son was well aware of the pleasure his miniature travels afforded his father. He also was aware of the lack of conviction with which the paternal prohibitions against this kind of behavior were stated, and he responded to the father's subtle, unconscious encouragement to continue his behavior.

From this beginning, Johnson and Szurek extended their exploration of childhood and adolescent behavior problems and concluded that among their patients parental expectation, unconscious sanction, and vicarious gratification were significant determinants of the specific antisocial mode of drive expression. They considered that parental expectation or sanction produced a specific defect in the child's conscience or superego which rendered the child unable to restrain a particular type of behavior, and they labeled the defect in inhibition the "superego lacuna." They found that the particular type of behavior which the parent suspects in the child was specifically related to the parent's own unconscious conflicts. Usually the parent, without realizing it, not only sanctions but encourages such behavior and derives vicarious, although unconscious, satisfaction from it, meanwhile consciously condemning it and self-righteously punishing the child for it. The parent usually selects—again unconsciously—one of his children for the scapegoat role, and this child goes on to express to some degree the promiscuous, perverse, violent, or other concealed antisocial drives of the parent. This sequence of events has been implicated in the causes of theft, fire setting, sexual deviations, murder, and many other forms of antisocial behavior [13].

Johnson and Szurek thus postulated two interacting sets of dynamic factors: one determining the neurotic conflict and the other determining the choice of symptom. They restricted this concept to "neurotic delinquency," consisting of the "acting out" of conflict-conditioned impulses by children of otherwise conventional or conforming families; they did not consider that it was applicable to delinquency occuring in socially deprived settings or to delinquency following organic brain damage.

I doubt, however, whether there is such a clear-cut difference between parental and societal expectations as they imply; instead, I suspect that parental, peer-group or gang, and community expectations of delinquent behavior all can contribute in much the same way and to varying degrees in varying situations. For example, essentially the same kind of dynamics seems to operate to sanction antisocial behavior in the following two cases.

> 1. The fifteen-year-old son of a civic leader burglarized a home. The boy's mother said that she had anticipated this kind of incident ever since at the age of nine he had stolen a pack of cigarettes. At the time, instead of making it clear to the child that such actions were unacceptable, administering appropriate discipline, and then assuming that the child would learn from the experience not to steal, the mother categorized the child as a potential thief. With this expectation in mind (as a result of internal conflicts of her own), she routinely watched and checked up on him, and he became aware that she expected him to steal. Without his mother's confidence that he could restrain his impulses, he could hardly be expected to develop confidence in himself, and so her expectations were rewarded.

2. Another fifteen-year-old boy burglarized a home. He was the illegitimate son of a promiscuous, impoverished woman who lived in a high-delinquency area. The mother, police, schoolteacher, and neighborhood worker all agreed that with his background this boy was destined to get into trouble, and as soon as trouble occurred, they immediately thought of him. Thus, his total environment expected him to steal; without anyone's confidence in his ability to restrain his impulses, he had no support for developing confidence in himself, and society's expectations were rewarded.

DIAGNOSIS OF BEHAVIOR DISORDERS

The more general applicability of expectation as a determinant sanctioning antisocial behavior suggests that not only neurotic delinquency but any delinquent behavior should be scrutinized from two viewpoints: first, the nature of the *drive* that is expressed in the behavior, and second, the nature of the *sanctions* that permit its expression.

In most cases, not one but several interacting determinants—biologic, psychologic, and social—contribute to the drive and to the sanctions. Anyone who attempts to understand why a crime is committed, therefore, needs answers to the following questions:

1. With respect to the drive expressed through the antisocial behavior:
   a. To what extent is its choice and strength affected by hereditary factors? Freedman has shown that offenders are not indiscriminately criminal but tend to repeat offenses reflecting one of three basic groups of drives, which he calls aggressive, sexual, and acquisitive [14]. To the extent that inherited factors contribute to temperament, they presumably affect the relative strength of the three groups of drives. The temperamentally aggressive child, however, can be expected both to develop more neurotic conflict about aggression and to mobilize more expectations of aggressive behavior in his environment than the temperamentally more passive child. The influence of temperament, therefore, must be considered in relationship to other factors. In somewhat the same fashion, the individual with a mesomorphic constitution has the physical equipment to be more active and aggressive and so may develop stronger aggressive drives and, secondarily, more external problems around aggression [4].
   b. To what extent is the strength of the drive affected by organic factors? Although organic brain damage is more likely to diminish the strength of controls of behavior than to increase directly the strength of drives, the stimulating effects of increased irritability of lower centers in some types of brain damage and the secondary effects of endocrine dis-

turbances should be given consideration. Both drives and sanctions are affected in the *epileptic equivalent,* a type of seizure state in which the patient carries out sudden, apparently unmotivated aggressive action which may well be antisocial in character. An increase in drive stemming indirectly from organic factors is seen in the familiar compensatory response to such organic handicaps as small stature or disfigurement.

c. To what extent is the choice and strength of the drive affected by psychologic factors? Early emotional deprivation may be important in building up a backlog of rage against the depriving parent which can be displaced or transferred to symbolic substitutes in antisocial activity. Later sources of neurotic conflict may also have contributed to the intensity of the drive that finds its outlet in antisocial action. Psychotic mechanisms may also intensify drives, although the psychosis usually primarily affects restraints.

d. To what extent is the choice and strength of drive affected by social factors? For example, a high level of aggression may result in part from frustration secondary to the inability of an underprivileged youth to see the possibility of attaining standard middle-class goals.

The fact that these questions should be asked does not mean that all or any of them must be answered in the affirmative. The strength and quality of a delinquent patient's drives may be within normal limits by genetic, organic, psychologic, and social standards. Man does not come into the world civilized, and it would be a mistake to assume that the drives expressed in antisocial behavior are *ipso facto* abnormal.

> For example, the adolescent son of a respectable citizen stole an automobile in such a way that he was readily apprehended. Study of the family revealed a long-standing impasse between mother and son over the son's habit of eating between meals. The conflict had become intensified as his adolescent appetite led to recurrent raids on the refrigerator and the cookie jar. Instead of working out the problem with him in a reasonable manner, however, the mother undertook various defensive stratagems and maneuvers, including padlocking the cupboards and refrigerator, and the son responded in turn by picking the locks. She interpreted this behavior as evidence that he was an innate thief instead of seeing it in the more conventional context of adolescent challenge and a game that had gone a bit too far. The boy, unable to extricate himself from the situation and now frightened at the implication of the mother's subtly conveyed expectations, had no confidence in his ability to resist the temptation to steal a car when an opportunity presented. He succeeded, however, in completely botching the job, suggesting that he was trying to signal his need for help.
>
> The mother was helped, through brief treatment, to understand the

nature and effect of her expectations, and the boy was helped to revise his self-concept so that he no longer considered himself defenseless against his acquisitive impulses. At the termination of treatment, some residual problems of relationship between mother and son persisted, but they seemed to be within normal limits and the boy seemed capable of managing his part in them. No identifiable signs of neurosis appeared, and ten years later, he was socially conforming and generally successful.

2. *With respect to the sanctions for antisocial behavior:*

Although there is not always evidence of pathologic distortion of the antisocial impulse, there is almost always evidence of pathologic sanction of antisocial behavior. In investigating this aspect, trouble may be found in one or more of the same four areas that were searched in exploring the nature of the antisocial drive.

a. How significant are hereditary sanctions? The possibility of mental retardation must be considered in this context, since the capacity to set limits to drive expression is reduced by low intelligence. Even this factor cannot be considered in isolation but must be seen in relation to psychologic and social factors, since the family and society frequently expect the mentally handicapped to have reduced impulse control, and their expectations influence his behavior. There is no reliable evidence whatsoever that inherited factors in themselves determine theft, arson, murder, or any other specific type of antisocial behavior. If society expects the son of a thief to be a thief, the expectation rather than the genes may determine the behavior.

b. How significant are organic sanctions? The solubility of the superego in alcohol is a familiar phenomenon and demonstrates that toxic factors permit the release of otherwise inhibited behavior. Any temporary or permanent damage to the brain, whether of encephalitic or other origin and with or without electroencephalographic evidence, reduces the ego's general capacity to inhibit, although the specific type of behavior thus released is usually primarily determined by other factors.

A more indirectly organic sanction might be called anthropologic. If an individual *looks* like a criminal, the people in his environment may expect him to *behave* like a criminal, and in this indirect manner the Lombroso hypothesis may appear to have some validity. The same rationale may apply to the grand mal epileptic; the violence of the seizure encourages the observer to anticipate (and so, in some cases, indirectly to sanction) violence in other areas.

c. How significant are psychologic factors? For example, early deprivation affects not only the drives but also the sanctions in relation to antisocial behavior, in that lack of early security makes identification with parents or other models difficult and so interferes with the normal process of internalization of restraints and with the development of the superego or conscience. The antisocial behavior of a psychotic patient is often in response to the psychologic sanctions stemming from delusions or hallucinations.

d. How significant are social sanctions? Expectations of conforming and nonconforming behavior by parents, groups, communities, and the culture as a whole may to some extent balance each other out. Firm and unequivocal parental expectation of conforming behavior may be sufficient to counterbalance the group's expectation of delinquent behavior in a delinquent subculture, just as parental expectation of delinquent behavior may counteract the cultural restraints in a more conventional milieu. There are innumerable influences beyond the family and peer group that provide a shifting spectrum of expectation of social and antisocial behavior: church, school, neighborhood club, police, newspapers, and so on. A family or a group rendered unusually apprehensive by a particularly outrageous crime may temporarily increase its expectation of similar behavior on the part of its children or members and so may inadvertently contribute to the apparent contagiousness of criminal behavior. Finally, whenever, as now, cultural patterns are changing in the direction of greater freedom for youth, a rise in delinquency rates may be due in part to increased expectations of delinquency, since many parents equate freedom with sanction for antisocial behavior.

Cultural Considerations

The definition of delinquent or antisocial behavior varies from culture to culture and from time to time within a culture. Premarital sexual relations, for example, were until recently considered a priori evidence of delinquency in Western culture; cultural attitudes are now much more tolerant, although legal and, for the most part, religious prohibitions remain. Since no convincing case for mental health can be made either way, the physician, psychiatrist, or other professional is no more than a neutral observer of this development, although as a citizen he is entitled to an opinion in the same way as the next man. As an observer, however, he must take cognizance of the tensions between generations that result from this cultural change, tensions that in many ways parallel those between the immigrant parent, holding to Old World values, and his second-generation child, struggling to identify with the patterns of the New World. In any event, the cultural change, coupled with their observations of adolescent rebellion, make the parents fear and expect the worst; and in the same manner as in clearly antisocial behavior, the parents' expectation contributes to the attainment of the result they anticipate. The following excerpt from a recorded interview with a girl who had become pregnant outside of marriage illustrates the dynamics of this self-fulfilling prophecy. She is speaking of her mother:

Patient: I would probably have been much stronger willed if I hadn't had her nagging at me all the time, saying I was doing things which I wasn't doing.

Doctor: Yes.

Patient: When you are accused of doing things you haven't done, you might as well go out and do the sort of thing. Then you can be accused of something. I mean, I do, deep down—well, I don't suppose one can blame somebody else for one's own actions, but . . . I mean she used to lock me out at night if I wasn't in by a certain time, and I was left standing on the doorstep many a night, and that's without doing anything. So that maybe, had she been less suspicious of what I was up to, it might never have happened.

The problem of the unmarried mother may be more complicated, as in the following example.

When an unmarried girl of good family became pregnant for the third time, the family physician sought psychiatric consultation. In the course of his diagnostic evaluation, the psychiatrist recognized her partial fixation at the dependency level and saw that to her an illegitimate baby meant someone all her own whom she could protect and control and on whose affection, therefore, she felt she could depend.

Understanding the nature of the drive, however, did not help him understand why she expressed it so directly and in such a socially unacceptable way. While investigating her background, he learned that all through her adolescence her mother had been afraid that she would become involved in sexual misbehavior. She warned her before every date and cross-examined her afterwards; she checked on her evening visits to girl friends to make sure there were no unauthorized boys present; and she forbade baby-sitting, fearing the opportunity for clandestine meetings with boys.

Since her mother did not suspect her of shoplifting (she did not inspect her handbag every time she returned from a department store), the daughter never thought of stealing anything, but since it was clear that her mother expected her to misbehave sexually, she had developed no inner controls to prevent it.

TYPES OF BEHAVIOR DISORDERS

The *symptoms* of behavior disorders are, by definition, acts which are not condoned by the society in which the patient lives. The degree or amount of such behavior necessary before an individual is categorized as suffering from a behavior disorder depends to a great extent on the type of behavior; one murder usually makes a murderer, but driving a car faster than the law allows usually must become habitual before the fast driver acquires a clinical label.

Antisocial Reaction

In the most extreme form, the antisocial individual expresses his demands and his aggression without inhibition or consideration of his environment. This type of person was once said to have constitutional psychopathic inferiority, later he was said to have a psychopathic personality, and now, in the standard nomenclature of psychiatric illnesses, he is classified as manifesting an *antisocial reaction.* In much the same fashion as the infant, he wants what he wants when he wants it, can tolerate no delay, and cannot seem to learn by experience. Since he either has not received affection or has not been able to assimilate affection, he has not learned to give affection. He is entirely self-centered, using relationships with others only to exploit them. Life to him is a struggle for survival, with no holds barred, in an unfriendly world. Since he has no altruistic motives, he cannot understand altruism in others, and he will not hestitate to rob the man who befriends him. Since he has no sense of guilt or responsibility, he can lie convincingly. If he sees any advantage to himself, he may attempt to dupe the physician by malingering, or consciously simulating illness. He will feign penitence and an interest in rehabilitation if he thinks it will get him out of trouble, but he lacks the capacity for significant relations with others which is the prerequisite of successful psychotherapy.

> A prison chaplain was so impressed by the stated good intentions of a young prisoner convicted for auto theft that he helped him secure a parole and find a job, offering him board and room until he received his first paycheck. Two nights later, the former prisoner stole everything of value he could find in the house, damaged the furnishings looking for more, and disappeared in his benefactor's car.

Patients of this type are lonely and pitiful figures, but since they cannot as yet be successfully treated, they must be restrained from damaging their environments. They usually spend much of their lives in prison, and until we learn to reverse the clock and undo the destruction to personality or to brain which has occurred in early childhood, they are likely to continue to require custodial care. This extreme form of antisocial reaction is fortunately not too common, but less extreme forms are found all along the continuum from the hypothetic patient with no controls to the patient with adequate controls.

Generalized sanction for antisocial behavior may result when parents fail to set any limits to the behavior of their children. These children do not suffer from a basic deprivation of affection, and they can identify with their parents enough to develop consciences, but they have not had a chance to establish their own controls under parental protection. As a result, they find it difficult to avoid the direct expression of drives that they realize are antisocial and afterwards feel guilty about. To protect themselves from guilt, they often develop their own rather peculiar and constrictive limits, as in the following example.

> A young man serving his second reformatory term for impulsive acts of car theft stated that he and his sister always had been permitted to do exactly as they wished. Apparently, neither parent ever indicated the advisability of limiting any activity. He never planned his escapades; in fact, he went out of his way to avoid contacts that might lead to trouble, and he felt conscience-stricken after each episode. At the scene of his last theft, he had "accidentally" left his wristwatch engraved with his name. Although he would not acknowledge it, he seemed to be seeking imprisonment in order to protect himself from the expression of drives he could not control. Under the rigid restrictions of incarceration, he was much less tense and anxious than when he was at home.
>
> His sister led a friendless, completely routinized life between home and work. It developed, however, that it was not dislike of friends or distaste for other activities that kept her life so constricted but fear of her inability to control her impulses once they became stimulated. If she went to the movies, she let herself be picked up; if she dated, she had intercourse; if she went through the stores, she shoplifted. This behavior made her feel extremely guilty, and realizing that she had weak controls, she thought it safest to keep away from temptation.

Thus, in a family where no limits were set by the parents, the children had no guidance in setting up their own patterns of control. As a result, one child expressed his impulses in antisocial behavior, while the other set up extreme and artificial limits for her own protection. Incarceration actually may relieve anxiety in patients who are realistic enough or who have enough conscience to feel horrified at their own behavior but who lack the capacity to inhibit it. An example is a youth who is reported to have written on the wall after one of his series of murders: "Catch me before I kill again; I cannot help myself." [15]

Dyssocial Reaction

What is delinquent behavior in one culture may be conventional behavior in another. Thus, the son of a hill-country moonshiner may be secure and law-abiding except for the illegal manufacture of liquor, or a second-generation Oriental may smoke opium but otherwise conform to our society's expectations. A person in this behavior category, classified as a *dyssocial reaction,* may have had plenty of security and affection so that his ego is strong. His superego, too, may be strong insofar as it reflects family mores, so that his only delinquent behavior is that which the family condones. He can postpone gratification of his drives, he can learn from experience, he can give affection, and he can be generous and unselfish. These qualities make him susceptible to change, particularly at adolescence when, in seeking emancipation from family control, he may set up as an ideal a parent substitute outside the family group. (See diagram, Appendix B, figure 21.)

For example, the adolescent son of immigrant parents often adopts as an ideal someone who is the epitome of the native American. He may then express his rebellion against his parents by completely rejecting their cultural pattern and taking on the cultural pattern of the ideal. He may choose a teacher, a clergyman, the family doctor, or almost any adult as his ideal; in any case, an adult who understands his problems but respects his cultural heritage can help him eventually compromise, so that he modifies rather than rejects his heritage.

When delinquent behavior is part of the family pattern, the tendency to search for a new ideal may give the adolescent an opportunity to strengthen his superego. In this situation, the teacher, minister, or doctor can help him modify his character structure to prevent delinquency. Similar opportunities may be found by scoutmasters, social workers, policemen, probation officers, citizen volunteers such as Big Brothers and Big Sisters, and many others in contact with young people. To do so, the adult must not be too aggressive in setting up a working relationship. The most effective relationships usually develop as by-products of contacts initiated for another reason.

> During the course of a prolonged illness, an eighteen-year-old youth began to show a great deal of interest in medicine and particularly in his doctor. The doctor recognized that he had become an ideal to his patient and spent extra time talking with him. Eventually the boy revealed that he had begun to participate, although with mixed feelings, in the extralegal gambling business which his father concealed behind his apparently

respectable café. Although the boy appeared to have genuine affection for his father, he did not entirely accept his father's way of life.

Revelations of this type often tempt the doctor, and particularly the minister, to preach little sermons on the advantages of respectability. If he can restrain himself long enough to evaluate the situation, however, he usually finds evidence which suggests another tack. In this case, the doctor discovered that the boy was already concerned about the problem, although sensitive to intimations of disloyalty to his father. The doctor realized that his patient might interpret unprovoked criticism of his father's morality as a personal attack on his father and might then feel obliged to defend not only his father but everything his father did.

Anyone who wants to provide an adolescent with a supplementary pattern for identification and help him plug the leak in his conscience accomplishes more by example than by precept. He must therefore be personally incorruptible, although not self-righteous. In this case, the doctor accepted the boy as a friend and tried to understand him—without, however, condoning his or his father's antisocial behavior. Furthermore, and most important, he had confidence in the boy's capacity to adopt new standards. Any child, adolescent, or adult who has the capacity for significant relationships and who is striving to emulate the qualities of people he selects as ideals needs their confidence in his eventual ability to do so. If the possibility of being duped by an adolescent is a major threat to the physician or clergyman, he will find it difficult if not impossible to have enough trust to strengthen the adolescent's own controls. For the same reason, a probation officer or anyone else in authority finds it difficult to treat and at the same time to check up on a delinquent.

TREATMENT OF THE NEUROTIC DELINQUENT

Treatment of the patient with a neurotic type of delinquency requires the same degree of incorruptibility. The goal of treatment is to strengthen the patient's controls through identification with a substitute parent who neither expects nor condones his antisocial behavior. Until he has a chance to discover more constructive outlets for the drives he has been expressing through antisocial behavior, however, he must resort to inhibition, in which he usually has little confidence. The consequent threatened breakthrough is a source of anxiety to him, which he attempts to alleviate by seeking permission, as it were, from his new object of identification for a return to the old antisocial outlets. Subtly, therefore, he tests out the strength of the therapist's controls by attempting to involve him in minor conspiracies or to get him to condone minor peccadilloes.

Johnson and Szurek have strongly emphasized the danger of stirring up the latent drives by exploring their origins before the control system has been buttressed [12]. For example, if, as usually occurs, the first step in the treatment of an adolescent peeping tom consists of an exploration of the basic reasons for the abnormally strong voyeuristic drive, the drive, stirred up by the exploration, might well find expression in more voyeuristic behavior before the conflict can be resolved. In order to avoid the dangerous consequences of even a temporary increase in antisocial behavior, its expression should be blocked by repairing, as it were, the specific superego weakness which sanctions the behavior before focusing on its basic causes. This procedure requires either removal of the child from the home or, preferably, the collaborative treatment of the parent, so that he can be helped not to continue, unconsciously yet effectively, to encourage his child's voyeurism. Only when the adolescent's superego has been shored up, so to speak, through a combination of an understanding of the cause of the defect, an incorporation of the therapist's more realistic standards, a revised self-concept, in which peeping behavior is not condoned, and a reduction in parental pressure for vicarious gratification of the parent's repressed voyeurism, should the therapist turn his attention to the resolution of the neurotic intensification of the voyeuristic impulse. Meanwhile, the patient, no longer permitting himself to discharge his tensions by action, may find the customary defenses of repression strained and may fall back on a neurotic solution. In this case, he might conceivably develop an hysterical blindness to protect himself from voyeuristic temptation. Such evidence of neurotic conflict would be anticipated, however, as a sign of progress in the course of the eventual resolution of the whole problem and would be treated in the conventional psychotherapeutic manner.

As indicated in this example, the prognosis of treatment of children or adolescents is poor unless, while it is carried out, the parent who is unconsciously encouraging the behavior either is being treated concurrently or is not in close contact with the child. If the responsible parent remains untreated and in contact with the child, he will, in spite of his good intentions, unconsciously sabotage the child's treatment. Although the actual treatment is usually carried out by psychiatrists in collaboration with psychiatric social workers, the physician or clergyman often can encourage the parents to participate by interpreting their cooperation as a valuable contribution to the treatment plan. On the other hand, attempts to force cooperation by accusations or blame usually fail. Since the parents are more horrified than anyone else by the child's behavior and are completely unaware of their part in it, they will resist any initial implication that they are responsible.

Once an individual has been identified as a criminal, society's expectations and consequent sanctions for repeated behavior of a similar kind mount rapidly, recidivism is the rule, and rehabilitation becomes more difficult. It is therefore particularly important to strengthen preventive forces in all areas that contribute to delinquency. In any community, social services to combat early deprivation are essential, as are whatever forces that can be brought to bear to strengthen individual personality development and to discourage the development of neurotic conflict. Efforts to prevent brain damage and efforts to curb the excessive use of drugs and alcohol are also important, as are measures to improve the lot of the underprivileged. Perhaps the major challenge, however, is in the field of community expectations. To begin to meet this challenge requires, I suspect, more intensive studies of community morale than have so far been carried out, studies which take advantage of such social experiments as slum clearance and the development of new housing areas. Furthermore, society must soon start to develop ways of doing something about the new double standard of morality whereby it is legitimate to cheat an institution but not to cheat an individual. The fine line of demarcation a father draws between maintaining integrity in a poker game with his friends and cheating on his income tax may not be so clear to his child, who may find in his father's behavior sanction for the direct antisocial expression of his acquisitive impulses.

SUMMARY

Three general categories of delinquency were described: the antisocial reaction, the dyssocial reaction, and the neurotic form of delinquency. In assessing the causes of any of these types of delinquent or antisocial behavior, two sets of causes must be explored: (1) the biologic, psychologic, and social factors contributing to the choice and strength of the drive that finds its expression in the specific type of behavior; and (2) the biologic, psychologic, and social factors contributing to the internal sanctions that permit its expression.

REFERENCES

1. Lombroso, C.: *L'uomo delinquente* (Delinquent Man), Milan, Italy, U. Hoepli, 1876.
2. Dugdale, R. L.: *The Jukes: A Study in Crime, Pauperism, Disease and Heredity*, New York, G. P. Putnam's Sons, 1910.
3. Lange, J.: *Crime and Destiny*, New York, C. Boni, 1930.

4. Glueck, S., and E. Glueck: *Physique and Delinquency*, New York, Harper & Row, Publishers, Inc., 1956.
5. Gottschalk, L. A.: "Psychologic Conflict and Electroencephalographic Patterns," *Arch. Neurol. Psychiat.*, 73:656, 1955.
   Kurland, H. D., C. T. Yeager, and R. S. Arthur: "Psychophysiologic Aspects of Severe Behavior Disorders," *Arch. Gen. Psychiat. (Chicago)*, 8:599, 1963.
   Simon, B., J. L. O'Leary, and J. J. Ryan: "Cerebral Dysrhythmias and Psychopathic Personalities," *Arch. Neurol. Psychiat.*, 56:677, 1946.
   Walter, W.: *The Living Brain*, New York, W. W. Norton & Company, Inc., 1953.
6. Diamond, B. L.: "Isaac Ray and the Trial of Daniel McNaughton," *Amer. J. Psychiat.*, 112:651, 1956.
   Group for the Advancement of Psychiatry: Report No. 26, *Criminal Responsibility and Psychiatric Expert Testimony*, 1954.
7. Gibbens, T. C. N., D. A. Pond, and D. Stafford-Clark: "A Follow-up Study of Criminal Psychopaths," *J. Ment. Sci.*, 105:118, 1959.
8. Aichhorn, A.: *Wayward Youth*, New York, The Viking Press, Inc., 1935.
   Glueck, S., and E. T. Glueck: *Family Environment and Delinquency*, Boston, Houghton Mifflin Company, 1962.
   Healy, W., and A. Bronner: *New Light on Delinquency and Its Treatment*, New Haven, Conn., Yale University Institute of Human Relations Publications, 1936.
9. Alexander, F.: "The Neurotic Character," *Int. J. Psychoanal.*, 11:292, 1930.
   Kobrin, S.: "The Chicago Area Project—a 25 Year Assessment," *Ann. Amer. Acad. Polit. Sci.*, 322:19, 1959.
10. Bowlby, J.: *Maternal Care and Maternal Health*, Geneva, World Health Organization, 1952.
11. Cohen, A. K.: *Delinquent Boys: The Culture of the Gang*, New York, The Free Press of Glencoe, 1955.
    Stein, H. D., and R. A. Cloward (eds.): *Social Perspectives on Behavior*, New York, The Free Press of Glencoe, 1958.
12. Johnson, A. M., and S. A. Szurek: "Etiology of Antisocial Behavior in Delinquents and Psychopaths," *J.A.M.A.*, 154:814, 1954.
    ——— and ———: "The Genesis of Antisocial Acting-out in Children and Adults," *Psychoanal. Quart.*, 21:323, 1952.
13. Giffin, M. E., A. M. Johnson, and E. M. Litin: "Specific Factors Determining Anti-social Acting Out," *Amer. J. Orthopsychiat.*, 24:668, 1954.
14. Freedman, L. Z.: "Sexual, Aggressive and Acquisitive Deviates: A Preliminary Note," *J. Nerv. Ment. Dis.*, 132:44, 1961.
15. Kennedy, F., H. R. Hoffmann, and W. H. Haines: "A Study of William Heirens," *Amer. J. Psychiat.*, 104:113, 1947.

Part Four

MANAGEMENT OF
EMOTIONAL DISORDERS

Chapter 15

OFFICE TREATMENT

In the chapter on diagnosis (Chapter 3), the importance of constant and careful concern for the possibility of an organic component in virtually any emotional disturbance was stressed. For the fullest protection of the patient, anyone undertaking the treatment of emotional disturbances should have medical training. There are, however, many more people with emotional distress who seek or need psychologic help or for whom society considers psychologic help appropriate than there are physicians with enough interest or time or specific training to help them. Furthermore, there is by no means a clear line of demarcation between emotional illness and many of the family, social, spiritual, or educational problems that are traditionally the concern of the social worker, probation officer, clergyman, teacher, or psychologist. As the gap between the community's demand for treatment and the medically trained supply of therapists has steadily widened, it has become clear that the medical profession cannot claim a monopoly of the provision of psychologic help. The burden must be shared, and traditional jurisdictional disputes—between, for example, psychologist and psychiatrist—must be resolved in the interest of providing the kind and amount of help, complete with adequate safeguards, that the community deserves and is being educated to expect. Psychiatrists can contribute to the extension of safe treatment resources by developing their consultation and teaching skills and by devoting a substantial portion of their time to working as consultants to general practitioners and to nonmedical agencies. Physicians can contribute by improving and utilizing their diagnostic and treatment skills in this area and by working out plans for collaboration with nonmedical therapists for the medical protection of the latters' clients. Nonmedical therapists, particularly those who do not work in medical settings, can contribute by taking the initiative to ensure that their clients are medically as adequately protected as possible.

In the remainder of this chapter, the concepts and techniques of treatment are discussed primarily with the physician in mind as therapist, and so the settings for the illustrative examples are medical. With the exception of medication, however, most of the concepts and techniques discussed can be used by the social worker, clinical psychologist, pastoral counselor, or other professionally trained therapist.

THE EVALUATION OF PSYCHOTHERAPY

Granting that the patient or client deserves adequate medical protection, what assurance does he have that the treatment he so anxiously seeks will do him any good? Considering the public demand for and confidence in psychotherapy, social casework, and counseling, and considering the substantial number of professional personnel trained to carry out these procedures, it is surprising and even at first sight alarming to find so few scientifically controlled studies testing their efficacy. Numerous explanations have been advanced to account for the paucity of such studies; perhaps the two most valid explanations concern the absence of satisfactory criteria of improvement and the difficulty encountered in finding satisfactory control subjects [1].

Efforts to establish satisfactory criteria of improvement run into two kinds of trouble: First, since virtually everyone has symptoms or traits which can be considered neurotic, there is no clear-cut point, short of an unrealistic and probably unattainable perfection, at which treatment can be considered complete; and second, the process of self-scrutiny associated with psychotherapy often mobilizes the patient's wish to resolve previously unrecognized conflicts or his wish to relieve symptoms which previously had not been identified as symptoms.

> A young woman's only conscious reason for seeking help was persistent lying, which she did not believe she was able to control. In the course of the ensuing psychotherapy, which was primarily directed toward developing her confidence in her ability to control her lying, she realized that one of the motives for her lying was to buttress her low self-esteem. She thus identified low self-esteem as a "new" problem and began to explore its origins. She discovered that it was related to her mother's depreciation of her, and she realized that her lack of confidence in herself bound her to her parents in an angry but dependent way. She thus identified a third problem, the hostile-dependent tie to her parents. She then proceeded to use therapy effectively to help emancipate herself. Rejoicing in her newfound independence, she took a position in another city.
>
> Sometime later, she requested treatment again, this time complaining of anxiety and depression precipitated by her engagement to an eligible young man.

How can the first treatment experience be evaluated? From the point of view of relief of the presenting symptom, it was an unqualified success—there was no evidence of continued lying after the first few sessions. From the point of view of the development of maturity, it was a qualified success—she became more independent and her self-esteem was raised, but she did not progress to the point where she could view the imminence of marriage with reasonable equanimity. From the point of view of prevention of further trouble, her psychotherapy must be considered unsuccessful, since the later anxiety and depression were more disabling to her than the original lying. Depending on the criterion, therefore, it can be evaluated as successful, partially successful, or unsuccessful.

Was the first phase of treatment prematurely terminated? Should she have been influenced to continue it to the point of resolution of her conflicts about marriage? In retrospect, assuming the continued success of treatment, continuation would have prevented the development of the later and more disabling symptoms. To influence her to continue, however, would have required the first psychiatrist to emphasize her residual weaknesses rather than her newfound strength; in so doing, he might have lowered the self-esteem that had been so carefully built up. More important, it would have prolonged her dependent relationship to her therapist at a time when she was enthusiastic about trying out her new independence. He believed that she needed to use this opportunity, just as an adolescent needs successful independent accomplishment to strengthen his independent self-concept.

It might have been justifiable to interfere with the patient's move toward independence if the therapist could have predicted the sequel. However, many, if not most, people who have broken hostile-dependent ties to parents work out satisfactory interdependent relationships in marriage without psychotherapeutic help, and it is hard to predict which ones can do it on their own and which ones will need help. It is also possible that this patient eventually would have resolved her problem by herself if further help had not been available, since spontaneous improvement seems to be reasonably common in people with emotional distress. Furthermore, potentially therapeutic and contratherapeutic influences abound in the daily life of patients, so that it is extremely difficult to determine with any degree of precision how much of a patient's improvement or failure to improve can be attributed to psychotherapy.

This discussion is not meant to suggest that research in psychotherapy is useless but is meant to point out that it is more complicated and difficult than it might appear at first glance. Although several fruitful investigations have been made in this field [2], more research is badly needed and should be enthusiastically supported by psychotherapists of every theoretic persuasion.

A Subjective Appraisal

The research in psychotherapy that is currently available often seems contradictory, and its appraisal inevitably has a considerable subjective bias. Granting this bias, my own appraisal of the evidence that is available leads me to believe that for most psychiatric patients who do not require hospital care, psychotherapeutic treatment based on an understanding of psychodynamics and balanced by due consideration for social and biologic factors is potentially the most efficient and effective approach now available. I further believe that the experience, professional discipline, and theoretic background of the therapist are less significant in the determination of outcome than is usually assumed, that the importance of the first few contacts is greater than is usually assumed, and that the average therapist's major handicap is not knowing when to quit. The great initial advantage of the psychodynamically trained therapist in understanding his patient's psychology can be lost if his depreciation of short-term treatment, aimed at symptom relief rather than at personality change, leads him to carry the patient past "... the point where his natural growth ... can be resumed." As Alexander goes on to say, "... treating beyond this point—or 'infantilization'—interferes with the natural growth potential and tempts the patient's ego to take the easy path of continuing dependency." [3] If the therapist scales his therapeutic ambitions to the patient's motivation and is ready to terminate when the patient gives the signals, his successes may be more modest but they will be more frequent.

Most of the remainder of this chapter is devoted to a description of the kind of psychodynamically oriented, limited-goal, short-term psychotherapy that I believe can be carried out successfully not only by psychiatrists, but by physicians who are not psychiatrists and by many other professionally trained counselors.

Treatment Goals

Generally speaking, the goals of treatment of emotional distress are two: (1) the relief of symptoms, and the maintenance of that relief, and (2) the development of increased capacity for mature adaptation, particularly in social, sexual, and vocational areas. With an appropriately motivated patient, the therapist can sometimes achieve both goals simultaneously, although he may find that if he relieves symptoms successfully, the patient will lose interest in working toward increased maturity, or that, in the patient's progress toward maturity, he will face new and anxiety-producing challenges which in turn will provoke new symptoms. Keeping both goals in view, the therapist should decide which goal has priority on the basis of his diagnosis, of his estimate of the patient's motivation and the amount of anxiety he can tolerate, and of the available facilities for treatment.

The details of the treatment plan depend primarily on the diagnosis, which consists of a careful assessment of organic, social, developmental, and psychodynamic factors and their interrelationships (see Chapter 3). Since the fine points of diagnosis are subject to modification and refinement as treatment or the passage of time add new considerations, the details of any plan should be subject to change. When the treatment plan is flexible, the therapist is prepared to switch to more conservative, symptomatic relief if emotional danger signs develop or to an exploration of more ambitious psychotherapeutic possibilities if he discovers unexpected strengths in the patient's personality. He should be prepared to terminate treatment ahead of schedule if its goal has been accomplished, avoiding the excessive dependency which develops when treatment efforts are unnecessarily prolonged at the initiative of the therapist.

THE THERAPIST'S PERSONAL QUALIFICATIONS

Flexibility, therefore, is a desirable personal qualification for the therapist. Perhaps more important is a capacity for *empathy*, the "objective and insightful awareness of the feelings, emotions and behavior of another person, their meaning and significance." [4] A strong interest in helping people is another qualification which is relatively easy to meet, however, since it usually is a major determinant in choosing medicine or any of the other helping professions. The therapist's interest, empathy, and wish to help, conveyed not so much verbally as in the subtleties of his attitude, make it possible for his patient to trust him in the same way that a child trusts his parent when he senses his love and interest.

No matter how much he loves his child, however, the wise parent sets constructive limits to his child's behavior; in the same way, the therapist's wish to help his patient, client, or parishioner should not keep him from setting constructive limits to the amount and kind of help he gives. In medical practice, whenever it is in his patient's best interests, the physician should kindly but firmly apportion the time he spends with his patient just as he limits the number of sleeping capsules he prescribes, even if the patient pleads for more. If a doctor cannot set limits, some patients, with or without conscious intent, exploit his interest, take up more and more of his time, and look for more and more regressive dependency satisfactions

from treatment. Such a patient eventually loses sight of his original problem, while the doctor gradually becomes disgusted with the increasing,
unproductive drain on his own emotional resources, and the relationship
may end amid mutual frustration and anger. In the case of Mrs. Brown,
the patient with the multiple complaints discussed in Chapter 1 and sub-
sequently, Dr. Wilson had not limited the amount of time and attention
he gave her, and she was increasingly turning to him for dependency
satisfactions. Earnestly wishing to help her, Dr. Wilson indirectly and
inadvertently encouraged her unconscious expectations that he would
take complete responsibility for her; but as she expected and demanded
more and more of his time, he began to find caring for her burdensome
and irritating. Eventually he would be forced to call a halt to her demands, but by that time she would have become so dependent on him
that any limits he set would be interpreted as rejection rather than as the
requirements of reality. If, however, he had set realistic limits from the
outset, he could have helped her without stirring up her unrealistic expectations.

The patient's best interests do not always require the physician to set
limits to his help. Particularly in acute episodes of pain, grief, or panic,
the patient may need more than anything else the freely given time of his
doctor. Unless the condition is acute, however, the doctor must be able to
ration his time objectively, in the interests of both his patient and himself.

Transference

In helping people with emotional problems, a therapist needs to recognize and tolerate both his own and his patient's feelings. As the earlier
part of this book has indicated, a significant part, if not the most important part, of emotional disturbance is rooted in residual angry, affectionate, or anxious feelings which usually originated with the child's relationship to his parents. When a doctor treats a patient, he acts in a quasi-
parental role and, as such, receives the same kind of feelings by *transfer*
that were directed toward the parents. The patient may or may not be
aware of the inner nature of these transferred emotions, and the doctor's
own personality may make it difficult for him to see the problem objectively. For example, the doctor may perceive that some of his patient's
feelings are hostile; unless he also recognizes the occasions when they represent earlier associations to someone in authority or when they are
transferred from someone else to him as a substitute target, he will feel that
his efforts are unappreciated and will resent the patient's attitude or
actions. Even if the patient does not show overt anger, he may act without

conscious intent in a way that makes the doctor feel defeated, frustrated, and anxious, and the doctor may cover up his anxiety by blaming the patient [5].

Mrs. Brown did not consciously intend to irritate Dr. Wilson, but since her anxiety and her pains occurred in the middle of the night and since Dr. Wilson rewarded her symptoms by giving her attention, care, and the opportunity for a confidential talk, her unconscious dependency needs caused her to exploit the situation. Dr. Wilson's consequent irritation was understandable; he felt that his early-morning pilgrimages were unnecessary, he sensed that he was being exploited, and he had the frustrating feeling that he was not doing his job correctly and did not know why. But the irritation was also preventable. He could have prevented it by understanding his patient better and so reducing his own anxiety and by kindly and firmly setting limits *before* he became irritated. After he had become irritated, it was doubly difficult for him to be objective. Dr. Wilson, however, was objective enough in retrospect to observe that when he scolded Mrs. Brown, she became worse instead of better. He also saw that his treatment plan was not accomplishing its purpose and needed reevaluation.

A doctor's angry feelings are not always preventable or unjustified. When he feels that his toes are being stepped on, deliberately and unreasonably, he helps the patient most if he shows his irritation in such a way that the patient understands that the doctor is not rejecting *him* in the sense of withdrawing his interest and concern but that he is angry at his *behavior*. On the other hand, the doctor cannot assume complacently that any irritation a patient shows is transferred from his unloving parent. For example, some patients are annoyed when a physician makes no attempt to schedule appointments but consistently asks them to come at 10 and sees them at 11:30. The housewife and mechanic and lawyer who are losing valuable working time during the wait become angry, not at their fathers but at the doctor, although if they are afraid that showing anger will jeopardize their relationships of dependency on him, they may conceal it from him.

Use of Authority

Another possible basis for the doctor's anger is the patient's failure to follow his suggestions. A doctor is accustomed to prescribing in a rather arbitrary fashion, and his patient is seldom in a position to question a prescription of codeine or penicillin or a recommendation to go to the hospital. When the patient fails to carry out the doctor's orders, however, the physician should be more concerned about the reason for the failure than the implied challenge to his authority. When the prescription is for a change in habit patterns or way of life, particularly when it is a habit such as smoking which the patient may have trouble controlling, the physician should be particularly careful not to take personal umbrage at failure, or his attempt to help the patient become more mature will be over-shadowed by his attempt to enforce compliance with his orders. He must enforce some of his recommendations, of course, or abandon the attempt to treat the patient, but the essential orders are usually few in number.

A doctor's attempt to control in an authoritarian manner usually results from his own anxiety. He has decided on a course and has given directions which he assumes will be followed; when his directions are not followed and he does not know what to do next, he tries to counteract his rising anxiety by berating the patient and trying to force him to conform. He thus compounds the problem and re-creates the hostility-dependency dilemma of the training period—the patient again must abandon either his self-assertion or his dependency relationship. Capitulation may satisfy the doctor, but it represents the patient's partial regression to an earlier level and his temporary abandonment of the strivings for independence on which his steps toward maturity are based. Usually, the course of treatment can be discussed and explained to the patient in such a way that he becomes a participant in its planning and can follow it without seeming to abandon his independence. Although the physician's and the clergyman's basic training predisposes them to greater reliance on authority than is the case with social workers or psychologists, the temptation to fall back on authoritarian techniques under stress is common to therapists of any professional background.

If he is not careful, the therapist's interest in his patient may cause him to overidentify and to see problems from the patient's own subjective point of view rather than from that of a more objective observer. This attitude jeopardizes his effectiveness, particularly when he overidentifies with one party to a marital or parent-child problem. Ideally, his interest should be warm as well as objective, and his desire to help should be coupled with the knowledge and the ability to set the conditions for the help he wishes to give.

Response to Shame

A doctor who is interested in people can learn to be sensitive to his patients' individual motives, values, and attitudes, as well as to their reactions to him and to others. He does not try to fit patients into his own preconceived patterns, and he respects their right to have viewpoints different from his own. He neither condemns nor moralizes, although he should not condone antisocial behavior. When a patient tells a doctor something he is ashamed of, he is not asking the doctor to tell him he should be ashamed—he already knows it, or he would not be discussing the problem in the doctor's office. He is looking for help in living with or understanding his shame or in preventing a repetition of whatever caused his shame. If the nature of the problem makes the doctor feel uncomfortable, particularly if he does not feel capable of handling the situation, he may be tempted to cover up his own anxiety by moralistic condemnation. Moralizing or condemning, however, merely convinces the patient that his needs are not understood and makes him feel more alone with his problems.

The doctor's or clergyman's temptation to moralize is often particularly strong when a mother discusses her child's problem with him. It may be obvious to him that she is to blame for the child's problem, but accusation or reproof will only cause her to retreat; he will help the child most in the long run by responding primarily to the mother's wish to help her child. The patient or the mother who says, in effect, "I am ashamed of what I have done," is seldom helped by a response which communicates, "You are a bad person and you certainly should be ashamed." He is almost sure to be helped by a response that communicates, "I can (or I will try to) understand how ashamed you feel, and I am interested in helping you understand it better, make amends if necessary, and avoid similar troubles in the future."

The physician needs patience to tolerate the failure of a patient to be as mature as the doctor thinks he should be. He can also use a sense of humor, combined with the knowledge of when not to be facetious, an ability to take the patient's problems seriously even if they appear to be inconsequential, a capacity correctly to assess and appropriately to manage erotically tinged transferred feelings in either the patient or himself, and above all, a willingness to submit his own feelings and reactions to continual and intensive self-scrutiny.

Training

Although success in psychotherapy depends to a major degree on the personal characteristics of the therapist, it is also influenced by training. Lectures and readings can provide an introduction and a theoretic outline for the prospective psychotherapist, but individual differences among trainees in communication style and in blind spots are so great that individualization of teaching is generally considered essential. In virtually all training programs, therefore, careful attention to the interaction between patient and trainee is given by experienced therapists in regular supervisory sessions. The purpose is not only to help the trainee avoid mistakes but also to help him understand himself and his own responses to the patient. In the course of learning about his responses to patients, a trainee may find some areas in which his objectivity is blocked by mild neurotic problems that are not otherwise sufficiently handicapping to require treatment. Consequently, he may decide to seek psychotherapy for himself, and so a substantial proportion of psychotherapists have themselves experienced psychotherapy.

LEVELS OF TREATMENT

Emotional disturbances occur when a person cannot satisfactorily integrate the external stresses of his environment and the internal pressures of his unconscious drives and conflicts. Treatment, therefore, is directed toward one or more of these general goals:

1. Strengthening the adaptive functions of the personality (by *psychologic support*)
2. Reducing environmental stresses (by *environmental modification*)
3. Reducing internal pressures (by *intensive psychotherapy*)

These three general goals roughly correspond to the goals of treatment in heart disease. The physician tries to strengthen the cardiac patient's ability to adapt to his illness by prescribing rest, medication, or diet; he may attempt to reduce the amount of stress on the heart by prescribing a more sedentary occupation or a first-floor apartment; in some cases, he may believe that the best treatment requires modifying the internal structure of the heart by surgery. The family doctor, sometimes after consultation with a cardiologist, may carry out the first two treatment procedures; cardiac surgery, however, requires the services of a specialist. In a similar way, the family doctor, sometimes after consultation with a psychiatrist, may give psychologic support and arrange for environmental modification in emotional illness, whereas intensive psychotherapy requires a specialist's care. (For diagram, see Appendix B, Figure 22.)

Outside of the field of medicine, the techniques of environmental modification and psychologic support are regularly used by social workers, pastoral and school counselors, psychologists, and other professionally qualified nonmedical therapists. Most nonmedical therapists do not undertake intensive psychotherapy, although some psychologists and social workers have had advanced training in this technique beyond their basic professional training. The ethical nonmedical therapist who carries out intensive psychotherapy makes sure that adequate medical safeguards are provided for his client throughout the course of the treatment.

PSYCHOLOGIC SUPPORT

When a physician gives a patient psychologic support, he is helping him use his own adaptive functions to solve his emotional problems [6]. Since the techniques of psychologic support are directed toward the goal of self-help, the physician should be careful not to assume responsibility for a patient's problems except as part of a long-term plan with relative self-sufficiency as its goal. Otherwise, by taking the patient's problems on himself, the doctor supports the patient's dependency instead of building up his strength.

Psychologic support is most effective when a patient has temporarily regressed because of a difficult situation. As discussed in Chapter 1, acute physical illness may produce this type of stress, and in such situations the physician should combine psychologic support with specific medical treatment. Psychologic support may also help a patient cope with chronic illness or other stress, and it can help a patient who is close to psychosis preserve enough integration to prevent the psychosis from developing.

The function of psychologic support is to strengthen the ego and its protective mechanisms. It does not attempt to uncover unconscious material; on the contrary, it helps the patient do a better job of repression. It encourages sublimation and may support such mechanisms as reaction formation where necessary to prevent personality disintegration. It does not modify fixations or long-standing regression, although it is an essential adjunct to intensive psychotherapy.

The four primary techniques of psychologic support are empathic listening, justified reassurance, cautious clarification, and the restrained use of medication.

Empathic Listening

The basic technique of psychologic support is so unspectacular that most students underestimate its effectiveness. It is simply the process of empathic listening to the patient's expression of his thoughts and feelings. By the end of the preliminary history taking, some patients already sense the value of talking to an understanding individual whom they consider capable of helping them, although others still need encouragement and most patients should be told that the doctor expects them to benefit by their self-revelation.

During the interviews, the doctor encourages the patient to talk about his current situation, his problems, and his reactions, especially as they apply to his illness. As the patient continues the discussion he initiated during the diagnostic process, he amplifies and revises the material, often repeating the same things. Repetition of material about interpersonal relationships in an understanding atmosphere often brings him closer to the release of associated feelings; repeated description of symptoms, however, should be gently discouraged because it deflects the focus of the interview away from material of primary significance.

In most cases, the patient has never revealed his feelings to anyone who is not intimately involved in the situations which produced them. He may find it hard to express himself, and because the expression of feelings at first makes him uncomfortable, he may appeal to the doctor for interpretation, advice, a lecture, a prescription—anything to protect him from the painful process of self-revelation. If the doctor believes that the feelings are too much for the patient to tolerate at the moment, he may come to the rescue and change the subject temporarily. In most cases, however, he should encourage the patient to continue by telling him gently that it is perhaps premature to expect to find solutions at this point and by showing his interest and attention to the patient's problem with remarks such as, "I'd like to know a few more details about . . ." or "I'm interested in hearing more about your feelings at that time." He should avoid fixing the patient with a critical stare or suggesting in any way that the patient is on trial. The doctor's attitude—uncritical, patient, accepting, and interested—reassures the patient. His feelings appear less dangerous than he had thought; encouraged, he permits himself gradually to reveal more of them. Meanwhile, the physician does not minimize the patient's fears, nor does he press him to disclose more than he wants to; instead, in his manner and in the show of continued interest, he conveys to the patient the belief—when justified—that together they can eventually work out better solutions to his problems and that the patient will be able to carry them out.

Reassurance

The second technique of psychologic support is reassurance. The best reassurance is the least formalized: the doctor's attitude of interest, understanding, and hope. Verbal reassurance should be given only when justified and when based on facts (see discussion of the possible exception to this rule, page 16). When reassurance proves false, the patient loses confidence in anything the doctor says.

Information about the nature of an illness or about the prescribed treatment comes under the head of reassurance when it relieves a patient's apprehension. To relieve apprehension, the information must be relevant to the specific misconception which contributes to the fear. The source of confusion may not spontaneously occur to the physician, who often tends to assume too much medical sophistication on the patient's part.

The physician should therefore find out why the patient is troubled before attempting to counteract the apprehension by giving information. If a patient anticipating prostatectomy, for example, fears castration more than death, a physician who limits his reassurance to the chances of survival misses the point. In any case, information or instruction should be given in lay terms, but not condescendingly.

Too much information may make a patient more apprehensive rather than less, especially when it includes serious possibilities and more particularly when no steps are planned at the time to do something about the disturbing possibilities.

> A young woman who complained of headaches had X-rays taken. The doctor reassured her that there was no physical cause for her symptoms and attempted to reinforce his reassurance by showing her the films. While looking at them together, he noted an area of increased density and said, "There's a remote possibility that this might be the beginning of a brain tumor; I really don't think you have one, and I wouldn't advise doing anything about it now, but I'd like to check up on it again in a couple of months."
>
> The patient became very agitated, left her job, and returned to her home in another city, convinced that she was going to die. There, a complete examination showed no signs of a brain tumor.

Fortunately, this patient did not have such a strong tendency to hypochondriacal displacement that her apprehension could not be relieved by the repeated examination and subsequent discussion. In susceptible people, however, information given in this fashion precipitates serious and often incapacitating hypochondriacal preoccupations (see Chapter 10). The physician needs the courage of his convictions about the present illness; like anybody else, the neurotic patient can develop an organic condition, but the patient is not helped to overcome his present condition by stated or implied warnings about what the future may bring. A positive diagnosis is the best protection for both patient and physician—a diagnosis that convinces him that the symptoms under consideration today are due to emotional causes.

Articles and books about emotional illness either treat the subject so sketchily that the patient learns little of value or are so comprehensive that he is likely to read into his own case dynamics and diagnoses which do not apply to him. When the doctor believes that reading can be prescribed safely, the patient should be given ample opportunity to discuss and relieve any extraneous worries it stirs up. Many patients with emotional illness are omnivorous readers in psychiatric and pseudopsychiatric literature, but it often seems to disturb them more when they do it on prescription than when they read on their own initiative.

The type of information and instruction a doctor gives should depend to some extent on the patient's personality structure. Overdependent patients generally respond best to clear-cut and definite directions and prefer to leave the rationale for the directions up to the physician. Patients who do not tolerate dependency well, however, respond better if they are given some information about their illnesses so that they can understand the reasons for the prescribed course of treatment. A technique which is appropriate for one patient may not be appropriate for another.

> Two women were discussing their medical problems. One, an insecure individual who attempted to counteract her insecurity by maintaining control over other people, said, "Dr. A. was so arbitrary I couldn't stand him. He would just order me to do this and that and never tell me why. Now I go to Dr. B., who always takes time to explain the reasons for everything he asks me to do."
>
> The other, a rather overtly dependent person, replied, "I couldn't stand Dr. B.'s insistence on telling me all about everything that's wrong with me. I finally gave up and went to Dr. A. He makes me feel so safe; I can leave everything up to him and just follow his instructions, and I know things will turn out all right."

Dr. B.'s approach was suited to the first patient, and Dr. A.'s to the second. It should be possible, however, for a physician to individualize his approach, at least to some extent, according to the patient's particular emotional needs.

Reassuring a patient that he has no organic illness will help him only if it does not minimize his condition or imply that it is under voluntary control. Statements like, "It's just your imagination" or "Don't worry; there's nothing really wrong with you," usually mean to the patient that the doctor is belittling his symptoms. He is not reassured but merely convinced that the doctor does not understand them. Instead, it is usually more helpful to say: "I can understand how symptoms as severe as yours would make you suspect that there must be something wrong organically. However, although the symptoms certainly are severe, they are clearly due to the tension we have been talking about and not to any organic condition." (See page 74.) Sometimes the physician can reassure a patient by explaining symptoms of anxiety in terms of autonomic nervous-system function. Such explanations show the patient the relevance of exploring his emotions and reassure him that the physician does not consider his symptoms imaginary.

Advice

As the patient expresses his feelings, the doctor's understanding and his hopeful attitude are often enough to give the patient confidence in his ability to find his own answers to his problems. Other patients, however, expect the doctor to tell them how to solve their difficulties. Habit, pressure from the patient, and limitations of time all conspire in encouraging the doctor to give his patient ready-made answers. But unless his diagnosis has given him good reason to adopt an authoritative approach, he should resist this temptation and should instead let his patient know why he will accomplish more by finding his own solutions.

The doctor should give advice on medical problems, of course, but he should be extremely conservative in advising the patient on personal relationships or on the conduct of his social and economic life. By encouraging any constructive steps or plans the patient has undertaken, the doctor shows confidence in the patient's ability to take care of future as well as current crises. On the other hand, whenever he supplies the patient with definite answers to a personal problem, he suggests indirectly that he thinks him incapable of working out a satisfactory solution on his own, and the patient will have less confidence in his ability to master the next problem. The physician should provide answers, therefore, only in situations where long-term advantages must be sacrificed for immediate solutions which the patient cannot provide for himself. Thus, the husband of a harmlessly psychotic woman can be helped by psychologic support to clear up the ambivalent feelings which prevent him from deciding whether to hospitalize her or to keep her at home, but if the wife is dangerously psychotic, he must be advised firmly to hospitalize her at once, and help with his ambivalence must wait until later.

The physician should never advise marriage, divorce, or having children, and should be very cautious about advising a patient to leave home, even when, as in the following case, the advice seems logical.

A twenty-six-year-old woman complained bitterly of her unhappiness at home. She resented her mother's exploitation, her father's criticism, and her brother's preferred position. Since she earned a comfortable salary and could afford to live elsewhere, her doctor advised her to move. With some trepidation, she followed his advice, but soon she grew anxious, worried about her parents' quarrels, inefficient in her work, and finally too upset to take care of herself.

She moved back home, and although conditions there remained the same, her unsuccessful attempt to escape had so drained her confidence that she rejected the doctor's efforts to help her understand and resolve the hostile-dependent tie which bound her to her parents' home.

The doctor had advised an obviously appropriate course of action, but in precisely this situation—when a person of adequate intelligence does not do the obvious—he should hesitate to advise. The course was clear to him and should have been clear to her, but her feelings were blocking her vision. Instead of advising her to break through the block, he should have helped her discover why it was there.

A doctor's advice to pursue a course which has already been tried and found impossible frustrates a patient. He is likely to conclude that his doctor does not understand him if he is told to relax when he has tried to relax and cannot or if he is advised to forget his worries when his reason for seeing the doctor is his inability to forget them. Before giving advice in personal or family problems, therefore, a doctor should ask himself:

Is the solution obvious to the patient as well as to the doctor? If it is, do
    not advise.
Can the patient follow the advice? If he cannot, do not advise.
Can he work out his own answers, with the doctor's help? If he can and
    if it is possible to wait until he does, do not advise.

Clarification

The patient deserves an explanation, however, of the kind of help he can expect from the doctor, even though it is not the type of help he hoped for. If, when he asks advice, he is told: "This is your problem; you have to work it out," he is entitled to wonder what advantage there is in seeing the doctor. On the other hand, if he is told: "I suspect that this is a question only you can decide, but since you are having trouble making a decision, we might sit down and talk it over. Perhaps together we can find out what is causing the trouble and help you to come to a decision," the patient will grasp the idea that the doctor is interested and will help him, even if he will not decide the course of action for him.

With a statement of this type, the doctor introduces an important technique of psychologic support: clarification. By making observations, rewording concepts, pointing out similarities and differences, and interpreting attitudes and activities of the patient and of those about him, the doctor attempts to help the patient cope with his problems more realistically.

Clarification helps the patient to stay on the track, as it were—to avoid the tendency to wander on to peripheral or secondary subjects and to persevere in the direction of a particular, specific goal of treatment. Short-term, limited-goal psychotherapy requires a good deal more activity on the therapist's part than is appropriate in more ambitious and slower-moving types of treatment; through clarification, the therapist helps the patient to outline his specific treatment goals and to focus on one more or less circumscribed problem at a time.

Clarification is also used to give information and instruction, to help the patient define the relative merits of alternative courses, and to help him understand his own emotions and attitudes and the emotions and attitudes of those about him. It may be used to encourage a patient to face new problems or new facets of his old problems. Although exposing new conflicts may be helpful to the patient, it also may carry both patient and doctor on to the consideration of more problems than the patient needs to overcome or wants to tackle and into areas of psychopathology that the doctor is not prepared to treat. Use of this technique therefore requires caution, and it should be employed only to clarify material already on or close to the patient's conscious level; it should not be used to attempt to bring deep, unconscious material to the surface or it may lead to more anxiety than supportive treatment can handle.

When, in helping a patient make a decision, a doctor tries to clarify the alternatives, he may find it difficult to refrain from exerting pressure on behalf of the course he favors. For example, the doctor who tries to clarify with a patient the pros and cons of putting an elderly and infirm relative in a home for the aged may inadvertently overemphasize the advantages of the home and the disadvantages of the *status quo*. In so doing, he is giving advice and taking some of the responsibility for the decision instead of clarifying the alternatives and helping the patient make his own decision. The difference is small but important, for advice fosters dependency and clarification encourages responsibility. Appropriate clarification in this case usually follows a discussion of the patient's feelings about the move and is in terms such as these: "I suspect that what this all amounts to is that the longer he stays with you, the more bored he gets and the more you resent his complaints and criticism. You don't like to feel resentful, but you also know that he would resent moving, and you'd feel bad about that, too. It's going to be tough for both of you, either way." The goal of this bit of clarification is to help the patient drop the fruitless search for a painless way out and turn his attention to the more profitable exploration of which course will most benefit all concerned. However, if the doctor says, "The longer he stays with you, the more you resent his complaints and criticism, and this will get worse and worse, while the initial resentment he might feel about moving will soon wear off," he is giving advice and directly influencing the decision. (If the particular situation is so urgent that he believes he must exert his influence toward one or another alternative, he should recognize that he is giving advice and not using clarification.) If the patient is led by his dependency on the doctor to send his parent to the home, he may feel very guilty about it afterwards, when the doctor is no longer there to take the responsibility. If he decides instead that he can tolerate his own resentment more easily than his parent's and keeps him at home, he will add to his anxiety by going against the doctor's advice.

Clarification of attitudes may be overdone. The obstetrician who tells his patient that she vomits because she really does not want to have a baby is carrying clarification too far. In this case, the doctor can make more appropriate use of this technique if he first helps the patient express at length her anxieties about her capacity to be an adequate mother and then says, "It seems to me that although you are looking forward to the baby, you are also so apprehensive about its implications and your ability to make a successful adjustment to all the changes it will make in your life that at times it must hardly seem worth it." Clarification of this type does not represent accusation. It implies understanding on the doctor's part and focuses the interview on the patient's fears. Her fears may well have caused her to wish heartily that she were not pregnant, but this wish is so repugnant to her that she has repressed it. No advantage is gained by confronting her with her unconscious rejection of the child, particularly if it can be eradicated by counteracting the fears that caused it.

Premature confrontation may precipitate a serious breakdown of a patient's defenses against anxiety. For example, our old friend Dr. Wilson believed that Mrs. Brown had protected herself from anxiety by repressing her anger at her mother for exploiting her and preferring her sister. If he had said, "It looks to me as if you really hated your mother," it could have jarred her hostility into awareness too abruptly and frightened her unduly, or else she might have rejected the interpretation in order to protect her defenses. In either case, no benefit would have come from it.

A therapist should respect a patient's neurotic defenses, therefore, until he can see definite advantages from breaking them down.

If Dr. Wilson felt that it would be helpful to explore this area of feeling, he might test Mrs. Brown's awareness of it by a comment such as: "In some ways, you are still playing the Cinderella role you played as a child. I wonder if the reasons that led you to accept the role at that time are still as compelling."

She might in response reveal a greater acceptance of her resentment than Dr. Wilson anticipated, in which case he could be less hesitant about pursuing the subject further. On the other hand, she might reiterate a feeling that she was simply inferior to her sister, to which Dr. Wilson might respond with a raised eyebrow or other indication that he was not so sure that was the whole story. This subtle indication of his appraisal of her might well be more supportive than a reassuring statement, which she might easily reject as insincere or based on inadequate knowledge.

The patient who represses hostile feelings does so because he is afraid of them, and so his fear of hostility must be counteracted before he can recognize the existence of hostility. Clarification of specific hostilities that a patient may harbor should be delayed, therefore, until he has been helped to become less frightened of hostile feelings in general.

Clarifying the attitudes of other people in the patient's environment also must be done with care. The danger here is that the patient will exploit the opportunity to justify his current disability. For example, if a patient is told, "Naturally you don't want to be a mother, because your own mother wanted you to be a boy," she may conclude that since her present attitude is due entirely to her mother's attitude, there is nothing she can do about it. In order for clarification to be a prelude to a constructive change rather than a justification for the unproductive *status quo*, the doctor should emphasize the difference rather than the similarity between the two situations, as: "You've told me before that you think you first got the feeling of inferiority and resentment of woman's role from your mother's attitude toward girls, and you seem to have assumed that she was right in her generalization. Today, though, you've been telling me that your mother's preference for boys was a result of specific troubles in her own background. Perhaps the basis for your generalization needs looking into."

An overenthusiastic clarification of the attitudes or characteristics of others may give the patient a weapon to use against someone else. A doctor, trying to encourage a domineering wife to give her husband a break, said, "Your husband's behavior sounds more immature than deliberately unhelpful; perhaps if he had a chance to make more decisions and take more responsibility, he could become more mature," only to find that she then belabored her husband with the epithet "immature" every time he did something she disliked. A more supportive and probably equally accurate clarification might be: "As you've described this problem about responsibility, I've wondered a little whether you think your husband seldom takes a stand because he can't or because he has decided it's worth giving in to keep the peace." Even if the patient is convinced of one alternative, presenting the other as a possibility may lead to its exploration.

As many of the foregoing examples suggest, clarification requires on the part of the doctor a greater awareness of the personality dynamics of the individual patient than at first seems necessary. However, clarification used appropriately is worth the effort, because it expedites the progress of treatment toward a goal and counteracts the tendency of treatment to deteriorate into a prolonged recital of symptoms, complaints, and past misfortunes.

Time Problems

The *modus operandi* contributes significantly to the success of psychologic support. Privacy and the feeling that the doctor is giving his undivided attention are necessary. A patient should know how long an interview will last, so that he can pace himself and can touch on a disturbing subject at the end of an interview without feeling that he must discuss it in detail in the same session. Patients often need a chance to go home and digest the therapist's immediate reaction to the disturbing subject before feeling comfortable enough to pursue it further.

Some physicians complain that a psychotherapeutic approach takes too much time. It is estimated, however, that including the time he spends telephoning the pharmacist, talking with the nurse or technician, and completing his records, the family physician devotes at least fifteen or twenty minutes of his time to the average patient contact. Psychologic support of a chronically hypochondriacal patient, for example, should not require much more than twenty minutes at each visit, and some general physicians report that regularly spaced ten-minute interviews seem satisfactory. Twenty minutes, or even ten minutes, of psychologic support, however, may seem much longer to the physician than the same period of time spent in his customary routine. He spends most of his office hours in active pursuit of well-defined goals, driven by the pressure of waiting patients and unfinished paper work, and he may find it hard to reverse his usual procedure and listen patiently and somewhat passively to what may at the moment appear rambling or even irrelevant and inconsequential talk. This is perhaps the major obstacle to the doctor's use of psychologic support—the fact that he must adjust to a technique which is in so many ways the antithesis of everything else he does. To use it effectively, he must have faith in its validity and confidence in his ability to use it constructively; otherwise he may be tempted to substitute simpler and faster but antiquated and less effective alternatives, such as baseless reassurance, superfluous vitamins, or indiscriminate use of sedatives.

In cases of relatively recent regression, longer sessions are usually more effective in helping the patient progress to a more mature level of adjustment. Longer sessions cause a considerable drain on a physician's time, however, especially if they continue for an extended period, and he is probably wise to prevent too much of a strain on his own good intentions by adjusting his fees in proportion to the time he plans to spend. The patient should be informed, in advance, of the cost of treatment; when he understands that all the talk has a purpose, he is usually glad to pay his way.

Some physicians object to increasing their fees for longer sessions, maintaining that since they do not punch time clocks on anyone else, there is no reason why they should on patients with emotional illness. If they do not set proportionate fees, however, they tend to cut their sessions short on busy days, which means most days, or to postpone these sessions to the end of their office hours, when they are tired and their patients know it. Eventually they cannot help resenting the extra time involved and will begin to find reasons for using shortcuts or to drop the patients from treatment prematurely. Even when the doctor gets so much extra satisfaction from this type of work that he does not mind the time it takes, undercharging can be detrimental to the patient. Some patients feel uncomfortable in taking more than their share, and if they feel that they are not paying their way, they may be so preoccupied by their concern about the doctor's time that they either do not give their full attention to the subject at hand or else hesitate to express themselves fully and freely. For the more overtly dependent patient, to be a "special case" encourages his fantasy that he has at last become someone's favorite child, with the associated expectation that the "parent" will take care of all his needs. In the interests of strengthening the patient's autonomous efforts to help himself, therefore, it is wise to set realistic fees and so discourage this type of regression.

Social workers, psychologists, and psychiatrists, accustomed to long interviews in their training, often have time problems which are the opposite of the physician's. The convenient and traditional hour—whether a full hour or the psychoanalyst's fifty-minute hour—easily becomes the prototype for all interviews, and patients and clients who might benefit more from briefer periods to help protect them from too intensive an involvement in treatment may nevertheless be assigned longer sessions almost through force of habit.

Another time problem concerns the duration of treatment. Although many of the benefits of treatment can be lost by premature termination or by undue prolongation, choosing the right time to stop is not easy. Some patients need treatment within limits for almost indefinite periods, if the goal is to keep a psychotic or infantile personality propped up; other patients, reasonably healthy personalities with circumscribed problems, may need no more than two or three (or even one) interviews. As stated earlier, a therapist with overambitious goals may expect a patient to seek more personality change than he is prepared to undertake; once a patient senses this expectation, he tends to slip into a more dependent role, as if to say: "This is your idea, Doctor, so you go right ahead and take care of me," and so treatment bogs down. Treatment also may be unduly prolonged if the doctor is too hesitant to risk antagonizing the patient by suggesting termination at an appropriate time, just as it may be foreshortened if the doctor is too impatient or angry.

The following factors are significant in determining appropriate duration and termination of treatment:

1. *Diagnosis and planning of treatment,* including a priority list of problem areas, described not so much in terms of symptoms ("depression") as in terms of dynamics ("fear of hostile feelings").

2. *Focus* on one problem area at a time, with a recapitulation as each goal is reached. The recapitulation should provide the background for one of the following: change of focus to the next problem area, revision of the plan in the light of new developments, or termination. Termination is indicated if the patient is content with his progress and the doctor does not anticipate regression before the patient has had the opportunity to consolidate his gains or if further progress cannot be expected.

3. *Self-awareness,* on the doctor's part, of such feelings as affection for or dependency on the patient, guilt about his affectionate feelings or about his failure to be more helpful, anger at the patient or fear of the patient's anger, and inability to admit defeat.

Medication

Medications such as sedatives, tranquilizers, or antidepressant drugs can be valuable temporary adjuncts to supportive treatment, particularly when the patient's level of anxiety is too high for him to use support effectively [7]. They are most useful in acute conditions with a substantial situational factor. In chronic conditions, the danger of addiction or habituation should be kept in mind, particularly with patients who have strong dependency fixations. Although the degree of physical dependence varies among different drugs, psychologic dependence can develop on any drug.

The widespread use of sedatives, tranquilizers, and "energizers" makes it necessary for the physician to be constantly alert to the possibility of toxic delirium in patients with illnesses apparently of emotional origin. Often the symptoms are not dramatic; the toxic effects of the drug may merely accentuate the symptoms for which the patient originally took it.

Prescribing medications without making efforts to discover and remove the cause of the symptom is usually unsatisfactory. The following comments by Barhash [8] refer specifically to the use of barbiturates in chronic insomnia but apply as well to any drug used for the treatment of chronic states of tension.

> The course is so regular that it can generally be charted in advance. The patient takes the prescribed dose and gets relief. Several weeks later the effectiveness of the original dose has worn off, and he is getting no more sleep with it than he was getting before starting medication. Either on the suggestion of the physician or without asking for such advice, he keeps increasing the dose, always with the result that the increased dose at first brings relief, only to have it wear off in a shorter or longer period of time. At last he ends up taking as much of the drug as he dares or as much as his physician will allow him or as much as he can take without feeling drowsy all the next day. What has happened to his sleep in the meantime? He still sleeps just about as little as he slept before he started taking barbiturates. Then he decides to go to another physician and ... begins a new course with a different sedative. But he's only on a merry-go-round—always on the way back to where he started from and getting very dizzy in the process.

Many patients with insomnia fear sleep more than they fear staying awake. Sleep reduces the effectiveness of any defenses against anxiety, and since the defenses of most patients with chronic insomnia are not functioning well even when they are awake, they grimly hold on to consciousness. Such a patient will say, "I'm just about to doze off when I awaken with a start—then I'm wide awake and can't go to sleep for hours," or "If I do go to sleep, I have terrible nightmares; I wake up in the middle of them, and I'm so scared I can't go back to sleep." Although the causes are usually different, the mechanisms have much in common with the sleep problems of the one-year-old child or the delirious patient.

Daytime medication to counteract anxiety or depression should follow the same general rule: Use only as an adjunct to supportive treatment during limited periods of unusual stress. When a condition has been thoroughly evaluated and the doctor is convinced that maintenance treatment is the only possible means of help, medication can be used over longer periods of time. Schizophrenic patients usually fall into this group; in the masked or pseudoneurotic form of schizophrenia maintenance medication is often helpful in maintaining the patient's current "neurotic" adjustment and preventing psychotic decompensation. Patients with depressions due to manic-depressive or involutional disorders may require maintenance treatment with anti-depressant drugs for the duration of the episode.

The accompanying tables briefly survey the indications, contraindications and side-effects of tranquilizers, sedatives and hypnotics, and anti-depressant drugs, and a representative list of each. The spectrum of useful drugs in psychiatry changes so rapidly, however, that any list compiled for a textbook is likely to be out of date by the time the book is published. The information included in the tables should be modified regularly, therefore, as more information becomes available.

Table I. SEDATIVES AND HYPNOTICS

Mode of action: central-nervous-system depressants.
Effective in control of anxiety and insomnia.
Dosage varies, although tolerance may develop.
Chemically, most sedatives are barbiturates, although a number of other types of drug have sedative effect.
Paradoxical effects (excitement) and *sensitivity* are common with barbiturates. Drowsiness and confusion are common *side effects.* Hangover and depression are frequent *aftereffects,* often leading to habituation and occasionally leading to suicide attempts. Convulsions may occur on withdrawal.
Selected sedatives, for daytime sedative control of anxiety and tension:
   Phenobarbital, daily dosage 60 to 120 mg is most frequently prescribed. A newer drug, less predictable but reported to be particularly useful in alcoholic withdrawal, is:
   Chlordiazepoxide (Librium), daily dosage 20 to 40 mg.
Similar in composition is:
   Diazepam (Valium), daily dosage 20 to 40 mg.
In some patients,
   Meprobamate (Miltown, Equanil), daily dosage 1.5 to 3 Gm
seems to produce sedation with fewer side effects, and the margin of safety is considered greater.
Another nonbarbiturate in common use is:
   Hydroxyzine (Vistaryl, Atarax), daily dosage 75 to 400 mg.
   Selected hypnotics, for insomnia:
   Secobarbital (Seconal), average dose 100 mg
is considered the shortest-acting.
   Pentobarbital (Nembutal), average dose 100 mg
is the standard hypnotic.
   Amobarbital (Amytal), average dose 100 mg
is a little longer-acting.

Nonbarbiturate hypnotics, recommended for alcoholics and patients with organic brain disease, include:

Chloral hydrate, average dose 0.5 Gm.

Paraldehyde, average dose 15 ml.

Table II. TRANQUILIZERS

Mode of action appears to be depression of subcortical area of brain.

Effectiveness greatest in agitation and psychomotor hyperactivity in schizophrenic, paranoid, and manic states. Often used as maintenance medication in chronic schizophrenia.

Dosage often initially high but usually can be reduced as time goes on to find the lowest effective dose. Excessive dosage may lead to depression.

Chemically, the major tranquilizers are, for the most part, phenothiazines.

Paradoxical effects; sensitivity leading to agranulocytosis, skin reactions, etc.; and *side effects* (drowsiness, postural hypotension, jaundice, extrapyramidal symptoms, atropinelike effects) are common. The physician prescribing any tranquilizer should be familiar with and on the alert for the characteristic side effects and sensitivities associated with the particular drug he chooses.

Selected tranquilizers: There are many varieties of phenothiazine, with more emerging every month; sometimes after experience with them, investigators find side effects and contraindications that are not evident at first. Apparently there are idiosyncratic responses to tranquilizers, and some patients respond better to one of the less frequently used drugs than they do to the commoner drugs.

As of 1965, the most generally useful for the agitated psychotic patient seems to be:

Chlorpromazine (Thorazine), daily dosage 75 to 2,000 mg.

For retarded or catatonic schizophrenic patients, a more useful alternative seems to be:

Trifluoperazine (Stellazine), daily dosage 4 to 40 mg.

A phenothiazine useful in conjunction with antidepressants in the treatment of agitated depression is:

Thioridazine (Mellaril), daily dosage 40 to 1,000 mg.

Other phenothiazines currently used extensively include:

Perphenazine (Trilafon), daily dosage 6 to 64 mg.

Prochlorperazine (Compazine), daily dosage 15 to 150 mg

as well as promazine (Sparine) and triflupromazine (Vesprin), and fluphenazine (Permitil or Prolixin). The rauwolfia alkaloids, included among the major tranquilizers although not phenothiazine derivatives, are now relatively less frequently used.

Chlorpromazine and sodium amytal, as well as other tranquilizers, can be used parenterally in emergencies.

Table III. "ANTIDEPRESSANTS"

Mode of action not clearly determined and may not be as specific as originally appeared.

Effectiveness probably greatest in depressions with a high "endogenous" component, although specific advantages and indications are in question.

Dosage required for effective treatment is usually above the minimum recommended and is difficult to determine because the effects often do not become apparent for as long as ten days to three weeks.

Chemically, there are two major groups of antidepressants: monoamine oxidase inhibitors and iminodibenzil derivatives.

Sensitivity can occur, and *side effects,* usually of atropinelike quality, may occur, including hypotension and urinary retention. Monoamine oxidase inhibitors have more serious side effects, including hypertensive crises when administered with amphetamines, iminodibenzil derivatives, certain cheeses and other substances containing tyramine.

Selected antidepressants: At present the iminodibenzils are rapidly replacing the more dangerous monoamine oxidase inhibitors as the drugs of choice. The two most commonly employed are:

   Imprimamine (Tofranil), daily dosage 100 to 300 mg.
   Amitriptyline (Elavil), daily dosage 100 to 300 mg.

The monoamine oxidase inhibitors, sometimes used with great care if the iminodibenzils are ineffective, include:

   Tranylcypromine (Parnate), daily dosage 10 to 30 mg

for more retarded depressions, and

   Phenelzine (Nardil), daily dosage 15 to 45 mg.

Another group of drugs extensively used at one time for depression is the amphetamines. The risk of addiction, potentiated by the brief effect with rebound depression, and the occurrence of paranoid-type psychoses have brought these drugs into disfavor.

The cultural pattern in some communities leads patients to believe that they are not getting their money's worth unless they leave the doctor's office with a prescription or even a bottle of medicine. The physician who tries to avoid fulfilling this expectation may find it more trouble than it is worth, but in the long run he will probably have better results if he does not overemphasize medication. When the doctor assures the patient that the medication will cure him, he is using direct suggestion. Although the effects of suggestion, whether in the form of medicine, electrical gadgets, or words, are often dramatic, they are usually short-lived. When the effects of one magical elixir wear off, the patient comes back for another formula, and the doctor eventually is hard-pressed for new ideas. Meanwhile, the patient has become more dependent on the doctor, but nothing has been done to strengthen his adaptive functions, reduce his environmental stress, or relieve his inner burden of conflict.

For these reasons, placebos, inert substances represented as potent drugs, are of limited use in treatment (see page 76). When a patient discovers the true nature of the placebo, as he almost always does, he feels duped and usually more anxious and distrustful of people than ever. Medication may be prescribed in homeopathic doses, particularly when the physician is worried about the possibility of addiction, but it should contain active ingredients and the patient should be informed that it is simply for symptomatic relief.

Physical and occupational therapy may also be used as adjuncts to psychologic support. Their arrangement requires more initial effort on the doctor's part, but once he becomes accustomed to using them, he may find them more helpful in many instances than medication.

Case Example

Listening with understanding, warranted reassurance, cautious clarification, and the judicious use of medication are, then, the four primary techniques of psychological support. The following case illustrates a physician's use of psychologic support in a relatively well-circumscribed emotional problem.

A physician diagnosed an anxiety reaction in a middle-aged spinster who complained of perodic episodes of tension, depression, headache, and palpitation. Since her episodes consistently occurred in the middle of her menstrual cycle and since she studiously avoided any mention of sex in her history, the physician suspected a sexual component in the background of her anxiety. He did not press her for details in this area, however, but suggested a series of weekly half-hour interviews, to which she somewhat skeptically agreed. Meanwhile, he prescribed a mild sedative, to be used only during the episodes of anxiety.

During the first few exploratory interviews, the patient discussed her symptoms, her job, her family, and her friends. The physician encouraged her to take the initiative in selecting topics for discussion and showed her that he was interested in the facets of her current adjustment which she believed were significant. Although she brought out a few problems, he noted that she talked about them in a rather matter-of-fact and unemotional manner. When she asked him if they were accomplishing anything, he assured her that it might take some time for any results to be evident and that as she became accustomed to talking with him, it would be easier for her to express her feelings as well as her thoughts.

After this indirect encouragement and a long preamble in which she emphasized the effort it required to reveal her feelings to anyone, she confided in the fifth interview that she was deeply troubled by a strong sexual urge for two or three days each month. She dreaded these days, felt extremely guilty about her feelings, and had tried to eliminate them without success by cold baths, exercise, and whiskey. As she discussed them, her usual imperturbability was replaced by tears and agitation, and she interspersed her account with apologies for her show of emotion.

The physician did not interrupt her account but indicated by his attitude that he was interested, sympathetic, and uncritical. At the conclusion, he showed his understanding of her immediate discomfort by saying, "Telling me this has really been awfully hard for you, hasn't it?"

This statement produced more tears, followed by a repetition of her comment that revealing her emotions was indeed extremely hard for her. The physician then said, "From what you have said, it sounds as if you felt that having sexual feelings is somehow not normal." (At this point, he was primarily interested in discovering the basis for her guilt. He wanted to leave the impression that he did not consider her feelings abnormal, and yet he did not want to bluntly confront her with her naïveté and risk appearing to ridicule her.) She replied that she had always assumed that it was abnormal for a woman to have sexual feelings but that she had never discussed the subject with anyone and that the books she had read only seemed to confuse her. The doctor reassured her by saying that he knew it was a difficult subject to discuss, although he avoided such comments as, "You're no different from any other woman," in order not to discourage her from continuing the discussion later on. By this time, she had composed herself, and since the interview time had run out, she left, with the comment that she had realized all along that she should talk about this subject but that it had taken some time to overcome her embarrassment. She felt relieved now that she had broken the ice.

At the beginning of the next interview, she again apologized for her emotional outburst. The physician said, "I know it was hard for you, but perhaps we will find it was worth it." (Note that he did not lecture her on the value of expressing emotion or the importance of revealing everything to her doctor. He was not trying to remodel her personality but simply to help her over a specific psychologic hurdle.)

He then asked her to tell him of the development of her attitudes about sex. (Since she had introduced the subject, he now felt free to explore it further.) She described the care with which all references to anything sexual were censored in her home, the anxiety she experienced when she began to menstruate, and the fear with which she had approached dates or any contact with boys. As she again discussed her current problem, this time with more composure, she said, "Last time, I got the impression from you that my feelings were not so unusual." The physician then clarified the problem in terms which were not critical of the patient: "No, they are not unusual; actually, they are probably more often present than absent, although since people don't ordinarily talk about the subject very freely, it's easy to get the idea that you're alone in having them."

The patient then asked, "What will I do about them?" (Here the physician was careful not to appear to recommend acting out the feelings by intercourse, masturbation, etc.) The reply was, "That is a difficult problem, I'm sure, and there aren't any easy answers. However, when you understand a feeling and can discuss it with someone, it may prove easier to tolerate." He also prescribed a mild sedative for the two or three days each month that she was most troubled.

The patient returned for three more visits. She found that discussing the problem was progressively less disturbing to her and observed that her preoccupation was considerably reduced and her symptoms relieved. Stating that she now believed she could manage the situation, she terminated treatment. Her physician assured her of his continued interest in her and indicated his readiness to resume their discussions in the future if she should encounter other problems for which discussion might be helpful.

She had not indicated dissatisfaction with her unmarried state, and he did not take the initiative in exploring this or other possible sources of conflict to which she had apparently made a satisfactory adjustment. To have done so would have risked precipitating unnecessary anxiety and depression, without any assurance that she would benefit.

The physician anticipated that this patient was likely to choose him as the object of the sexual feelings she was for the first time accepting as a legitimate part of her being. He therefore was particularly careful not to encourage her by word or gesture to imagine that he might respond in kind.

Extra time in the office, social contacts outside the office, phyical contact (whether through physical examination or through friendly pats on the back), increased familiarity (as by changing to the use of her first name), all might have been unconsciously interpreted as seductive by this patient. It is much easier for the psychiatrist than for other physicians to set up his pattern of practice so to avoid these symbols of encouragement and still convey his empathy and understanding. To the extent possible, however, the physician who is not a psychiatrist should take similar precautions in his psychotherapy. The physician's anticipation of the possibility of his patient's sexual attraction to him not only alerts him to take measures to avoid its unnecessary encouragement but also prepares him to respond constructively and without embarrassment to its revelation. Most patients are ashamed of any sexual attraction that may develop to their therapists and can use help in feeling less ashamed, in accepting the frustration inevitable under the circumstances, and in understanding the origins of the attraction.

ENVIRONMENTAL MODIFICATION

As used here, the term "environmental modification" refers to steps taken by or at the suggestion of the therapist to change the patient's physical or social surroundings in order to reduce the external pressures on him. Primarily, these steps are taken when the environmental pressures are intrinsically overwhelming (as when a soldier with combat exhaustion is temporarily removed from combat for treatment) or when the personality is too weak to respond to support (as when patients with schizophrenic or severe depressive reactions require hospitalization). As a secondary or supplementary measure, environmental modification is used as follows:

1. When pressure from the environment is unnecessary and modifiable. For example, unnecessary restrictions on parental visiting may be removed to aid in treating the anxiety of a hospitalized child.

2. As an adjunct to supportive measures. The returned state-hospital patient may need help in locating a job; the lonely elderly patient or overburdened housewife often can make use of the doctor's suggestions in

finding recreational facilities; temporary assistance in child care may help a mother respond to supportive measures.

3. When psychologic support is not enough and intensive psychotherapy is not practicable. Some women who deeply resent the feminine role but who are not in a position to undertake the kind of intensive treatment that might modify their resentment can be better mothers if they get outside jobs for a while and hire housekeepers to care for their children and to do their housework. Particularly in cases like the last one, the environment cannot be modified arbitrarily or without the patient's concurrence. If, as happens more often than not, the woman who is resentful of the feminine role feels guilty about her resentment and defends herself against her guilt by overprotecting her children and overdoing her housework, she will object to any suggestion that would relieve her of these duties. If her objections are summarily overridden, she will consciously or unconsciously find ways to sabotage the plan. Often, however, focusing the discussion in an uncritical manner on the ostensible basis for objections to proposed environmental modification can help the patient to arrive at an acceptable compromise or even to risk facing the underlying conflict.

In any of these situations, environmental modification should not be used alone, particularly when the change is temporary and the patient must eventually return to the same set of environmental pressures. Patients under emotional tensions, for example, frequently feel fatigued and believe that all they need is a respite from their daily routine. Simply to prescribe rest, however, is seldom helpful. In the first place, the patient often takes the recommendation to mean that his doctor does not believe him able to cope with his day-to-day problems; consequently, at the end of the prescribed rest he will have less confidence in his own ability than before, and his tensions will increase. Rest encourages him to be dependent, and the attention he gets becomes a secondary gain which encourages the regressive rather than the progressive elements in his personality. A prescription of rest may also suggest to the patient that the doctor really thinks he has organic illness and so may strengthen his hypochondriacal displacements. Furthermore, rest may withdraw sublimative outlets for a patient's tension and so increase his problem. For example, a man who uses bowling or wood chopping as an indirect expression of hostile feelings will lose this sublimative outlet if he is ordered to avoid all physical activity. Finally, if rest is prescribed in the form of a vacation or change of scenery, it may deprive a patient of sustaining personal relationships in his own environment and add feelings of isolation and depression, which in some cases may even increase the risk of suicide. Rest has a place in psychiatric therapy, but most cases benefit far more from the suggestion to carry on in spite of symptoms.

When a therapist does suggest an environmental change, he should be sure it can be reversed. If he saddles himself with the responsibility for a relatively irreversible step, such as a change in occupation, he encourages the patient to blame him for whatever goes wrong in the new situation and to depend on him for direction in other major steps. At the same time he compounds the patient's original problem with the pressure of new adaptations. Major irreversible changes in a patient's life are best reserved until he has regained the capacity to make his own decisions.

Community Resources

Before recommending environmental changes, the therapist should know whether they are possible and, if possible, something about the resources for carrying them out. Otherwise, he may recommend an impossible course, stirring up needless conflicts. Community agencies have their own rules and policies, and the therapist should suggest that a patient talk with the agency representatives about the possibility of a course of action rather than promise a service which he does not control.

No therapist, whatever his professional identification, can be expected to know in detail all the functions, rules, and personnel of all the agencies for helping people in his community. His work can often be simplified, however, and his time saved if he knows something about the following:

Medical and psychiatric clinics and hospitals, nursing homes, and rehabilitation centers.

Public-assistance programs and the administration of relief, old-age
assistance, and aid for dependent children.

Facilities for children, including child-placement and adoption agencies, school social workers and counselors, child-guidance clinics,
special schools, and residential treatment centers.

Facilities for the aged and handicapped, including homes, day-care
centers, and public housing, as well as counseling, guidance, and
recreational services.

Family agencies providing casework services for marital counseling and
similar problems. Homemaker services in some cities help maintain
family solidarity by providing families with experienced housekeepers
skilled in handling children during short-term crises, such as a
mother's illness.

Law enforcement and probation offices.

Special groups, such as Alcoholics Anonymous.

Services offered by visiting nurses, the Red Cross, and organizations
   directed to specific health problems, such as tuberculosis, cancer, or
   mental deficiency.

The churches. Clergymen and psychiatrists have made great progress in recent years in learning to work together to help people with
   emotional disturbances. Although their methods and specific areas
   of operation differ, their efforts supplement each other and are
   by no means mutually exclusive. The discovery that this cooperation is possible often surprises a patient, but he is reassured to
   find that his faith and his ego can be simultaneously strengthened.

When specific community facilities are inadequate or lacking, the
therapist may decide to take over as best he can. This is usually more
difficult than it appears. For example, a physician who is impatient with
the red tape of conventional adoption practice may be tempted to take
matters into his own hands and arrange an adoption. At first glance, it
seems perfectly safe.

> An unmarried college girl confided to her physician that she was preg-
> nant by a classmate. She definitely did not want to marry the boy; she
> wanted to avoid publicity but lacked funds to spend the last months of
> pregnancy in seclusion. Her doctor knew a wealthy couple who had asked
> him to be on the lookout for a suitable child they could adopt. They had
> applied to an adoption agency but were dissatisfied with the delay in proc-
> essing and the lack of assurance that the agency would eventually find a
> child for them. The childless couple, the pregnant girl, and the boy were of
> approximately the same intellectual, cultural, and religious backgrounds,
> and the couple would be delighted to pay the girl's expenses at a retreat
> for unmarried mothers.

Although tempted to make everyone happy by arranging an adoption
in this situation, the physician hesitated. He was aware of the following
possible misadventures that might befall such an apparently mutually satisfactory arrangement:

1. The girl might later admit that she was unsure who the child's father
was or that he was really someone who would not meet the qualification
set down by the adoptive parents. (Adoption agencies have the time and
resources to make the painstaking investigations often necessary to establish paternity.)

2. After the baby was born, the girl might change her mind about giving him up or might decide to marry the father and keep the baby.

3. The identity of one or the other of the parties might be accidentally

revealed. Such secrets are easier to keep within a community agency than among the patients of one physician. When such information leaks out, problems are likely to arise, particularly if the mother, feeling guilty at having given up her child, seeks to check up on his care. Even if the secret is kept, the mother may greatly inconvenience the doctor by the pressure she exerts on him to reveal her child's whereabouts.

4. If the child should be born with a congenital defect, the adopting parents might decide not to accept him.

5. Any of several possible complex legal problems could develop, with the doctor involved in a bitter and time-consuming battle.

6. If the couple had marital differences, their real reason for wanting to adopt a child might be their hope that the baby would somehow resolve them. Instead, the adoption might bring the conflict out into the open, and the child's economic security would then be counterbalanced by emotional insecurity.

Present-day adoption agencies are designed to forestall these problems as much as possible. Physicians can best expedite satisfactory adoptions by supporting the agencies of their communities in instituting and carrying out modern adoption practices which provide for a minimum of delay between application and determination of eligibility. In similar fashion, they can use their influence in the community to inaugurate or strengthen other types of social and welfare agencies.

PSYCHIATRIC CONSULTATION AND REFERRAL

Several considerations determine the use of psychiatric consultation and referral. The physician or the nonmedical therapist, in collaboration with his medical colleague, will routinely refer patients who are suicidal or homicidal or who cannot be cared for outside a psychiatric hospital. He usually refers patients when he is in doubt about diagnosis or treatment plan or when he feels unwilling or unable to carry out appropriate treatment. He may also make a referral if the situation requires treatment of children [9], group therapy [10], or specialized techniques such as hypnosis [11] and he lacks the relevant experience.

The availability and expense of psychiatric treatment are important considerations. There are not enough psychiatrists to meet the demand in most communities, and many of them prefer to work with specific types of patients. Some are chiefly interested in hospitalized patients, while others restrict their practices to outpatient psychotherapy. Psychoanalysts —psychiatrists who have completed additional psychoanalytic training —do an extremely intensive investigation of the patient's unconscious drives and mechanisms in an effort to modify the basic personality structure. Though at first glance this would seem to be the ideal approach to any problem, only a small proportion of psychiatric patients are suitable for psychoanalysis. The patient must be intelligent and well motivated and must have enough ego strength to be able to cope with the anxiety released by the penetration of his defenses. Since each psychoanalysis requires an enormous amount of time, the patient must be able to afford it. Even if all these conditions are favorable, however, there is seldom an advantage in carrying out a radical program of treatment if conservative measures will suffice. Psychoanalysis is an ordeal not only for the patient but for his family, who must make new adaptations to any changes that take place in his personality.

Most outpatient psychiatric treatment or psychotherapy is somewhat more searching than the relatively simple supportive measures described earlier in this chapter, but it does not penetrate as deeply into the unconscious as psychoanalysis. Although special training is needed for carrying out intensive treatment, it may be helpful to the physician, clergyman, social worker, or other professional person who refers patients for this kind of care to know something of its goals and methods. The bibliography at the end of this chapter contains several references describing intensive psychotherapy in some detail [12].

Psychotherapy of this type usually takes a long time, and the psychiatrist is limited, although to a lesser degree than the psychoanalyst, in the number of patients he can accept. When he sees a patient in consultation, he may decide not to accept him for psychotherapy, either because he has concluded that the case is not suitable or because he does not have room in his schedule for more treatment cases. Most psychiatrists have found that if it is to be effective, psychotherapy cannot be fitted in haphazardly at odd hours; it requires regularly scheduled appointments of consistent length. They must either re-refer patients for whom they have no room or put them on a waiting list.

Accordingly, the referring physician or other professional person should not promise his patient in advance that the psychiatrist will treat him nor, under any circumstances, that he will cure him. Occasionally, a doctor uses the promise of a cure to overcome a patient's resistance to referral. It is a good idea to indicate confidence in the consultant, but if this is carried too far, the patient begins to expect dramatic results. He then becomes discouraged if the consultant cannot treat him or sends him back to his physician for psychologic support. Even if he does start treatment, he may be discouraged when he discovers how long, tedious, and unspectacular the process is. Psychotherapy, as well as psychoanalysis, is too often oversold or undersold; it is neither magic nor futile but a technique which, when applied skillfully to appropriate patients under reasonably favorable circumstances, has a good chance of bringing about relative improvement.

The physician, therefore, should refer his patient for consultation, not for treatment. Besides avoiding unrealistic expectations, the physician in so doing shows that he is still interested in the patient. Patients referred to psychiatrists often feel that their doctors are contemptuous of them and are trying to get rid of them. A referral for consultation, however, implies that the shift is a temporary one and that the referring physician is seeking help in deciding what he should do next. This approach reassures the patient, if he senses that the doctor is sincere, and it helps him overcome some of his hesitancy in participating in the consultation.

Although the patient usually assumes that the psychiatrist's conclusions will be communicated to his doctor, it is neither necessary nor advisable for the patient to know everything the psychiatrist says about him. Reading the psychiatrist's report to the patient or permitting the patient to read it comes under the heading of overenthusiastic clarification and almost always arouses more anxieties than it relieves. The patient should know the nature of the treatment plan but generally should be spared diagnostic terms and dynamic formulations.

Since the patient has chosen the referring physician for his doctor, he presumably has primary confidence in him. The physician therefore should discuss frankly the reasons for the consultation and the identity of the consultant. When this information is withheld or disguised, the patient feels duped and angry upon discovering that he is seeing a psychiatrist. Diagnosis then becomes more difficult, treatment becomes almost impossible, and the patient feels he can no longer trust the referring physician.

Many patients object at first to seeing a psychiatrist. Some feel that psychiatrists treat only the insane; others are fearful of being turned over by a physician they trust to one they do not know and whose interest and trustworthiness they have had no chance to assess. Still other patients resist referral even when they understand the function of psychiatry in their cases and when they are assured of the continuing respect and interest of their doctors. They are often patients who find it hard to accept dependency without the rationalization which organic disease provides. They are convinced that they ought to be able to take care of their own problems, and the recognition that they cannot is a blow to their self-esteem. In such cases, the physician can usually delay referral until he has, by supportive measures, helped them to accept it. The progress toward acceptance is hastened if the physician stands firmly but patiently on his diagnosis and his recommendation for eventual consultation, even though the patient may try to cajole him to temporize by treating borderline organic possibilities. If the physician capitulates and tells the patient he will "try vitamins for a while on the chance that it might be a vitamin deficiency," he strengthens the patient's conviction of an organic cause for his illness and makes eventual referral more difficult.

Sometimes the patient is much more receptive to the referral than the doctor believes.

> A patient entering a psychiatrist's office for a consultation looked around and remarked, "You're a psychiatrist, aren't you?" When he asked if this surprised her, she said, "No, I thought that's what Dr. X meant, but he kept putting me off and told me he just wanted a colleague to see me. I've thought I needed a psychiatrist all along."

In emergencies, the patient can have no choice in referral. The doctor often must talk with the family and help them to see the importance of taking appropriate steps to hospitalize and protect the patient. The relatives may need a good deal of support and explanation to overcome uncertainty, particularly if they fear that the patient will later resent their interference.

When such considerations as distance or availability make outpatient psychiatric treatment impractical, the psychiatrist may suggest that the physician continue to give psychologic support. Ideally, this suggestion goes farther than a simple recommendation; the psychiatrist should indicate his evaluation of areas to be supported, problems to be avoided, and so on, while the physician checks back occasionally to make progress reports and discuss new developments. When consultation is followed up in this way, the physician gains the continued support of the psychiatrist, and the psychiatrist gains the opportunity to break through the isolation which unfortunately has all too often surrounded his medical specialty.

SUMMARY

The plan of treatment of each individual emotional disturbance should evolve from the diagnosis and should integrate goals of symptomatic relief and greater maturity. Among the characteristics that the therapist should possess, besides a basic interest in helping people, are sensitivity, flexibility, objectivity in the face of dependency and hostility, and the capacity to set limits.

The basic treatment technique is psychologic support through which the therapist tries to strengthen the patient's weakened integrating forces and which indirectly encourages him to work out his own solutions to his emotional problems. He listens to the patient's expression of feelings and gives attention, understanding, appropriate reassurance, advice only when definitely indicated, and cautious clarification of goals, alternatives, attitudes, and areas of confusion.

He may supplement psychologic support by conservative suggestions for environmental modification and by a careful use of adjunct medication. He uses psychologic support to help the patient make the best use of psychiatric consultation or referral when indicated.

REFERENCES

1. Group for the Advancement of Psychiatry: Report No. 42, *Some Observations on Controls in Psychiatric Research*, 1959.
2. Knight, R. P.: "An Evaluation of Psychotherapeutic Techniques," *Bull. Menninger Clin.*, 16:112, 1952.
   Malan, D. H.: *A Study of Brief Psychotherapy*, Springfield, Ill., Charles C Thomas, Publisher, 1963.
   Wallerstein, R. S. (ed.): "The Psychotherapy Research Project of the Menninger Foundation," *Bull. Menninger Clin.*, 20:221, 1956.
   Ward, C. H.: "Psychotherapy Research: Dilemmas and Directions," *Arch. Gen. Psychiat. (Chicago)*, 10:596, 1964.
   Breger, L. and J. L. McGaugh: "A Critique and Reformulation of Learning Theory Approaches to Psychotherapy and Neurosis," *Psychol. Bull.*, 63:338, 1965.
   Goldstein, A. P.: *Therapist-Patient Expectations in Psychotherapy*, New York, The Macmillan Company, 1962.
3. Alexander, F.: "Psychoanalysis and the Human Condition," in J. Marmorston and E. Stainbrook (eds.), *Psychoanalysis and the Human Situation*, New York, Vantage Press, 1964.
4. *Psychiatric Glossary*, 2nd ed., Washington, D.C., American Psychiatric Association, 1964.
5. Freud, S.: "The Dynamics of Transference" (1912), in *Standard Edition*, 1958, vol. XII, p. 97.
6. Goldman, George S.: "Reparative Psychotherapy," in Rado, Sandor, and George E. Daniels (eds.), *Changing Concepts from Psychoanalytic Medicine*, New York, Grune and Stratton, Inc., p. 101, 1956.
   Bellak, L., and L. Small: *Emergency Psychotherapy and Brief Psychotherapy*, New York, Grune & Stratton, 1965.
   Castelnuovo-Tedesco, P.: *The Twenty-Minute Hour: A Guide to Brief Psychotherapy for the Physician*, Little, Brown and Company, Boston, 1965.
7. Uhr, L., and J. B. Miller (eds.): *Drugs and Behavior*, New York, John Wiley & Sons, Inc., 1960.

Wikler, A.: *The Relation of Psychiatry to Pharmacology,* Baltimore, The Williams and Wilkins Company, 1957.

See also, references 28 and 29, Chapter 11.

8. Barhash, A. Z.: "Psychiatric Techniques in General Practice," *J.A.M.A.,* 146:1585, 1951.

9. Lippman, H. S.: *Treatment of the Child in Emotional Conflict,* 2d ed., New York, McGraw-Hill Book Company, 1962.

10. Powdermaker, F., and J. D. Frank: *Group Psychotherapy,* Cambridge, Mass., Harvard University Press, 1953.

    Mullan, H., and M. Rosenbaum: *Group Psychotherapy: Theory and Practice,* New York, The Free Press of Glencoe, 1962.

11. Group for the Advancement of Psychiatry: Symposium No. 8, *Medical Uses of Hypnosis,* 1962.

    Kaufman, M. R.: "Hypnosis in Psychotherapy Today," *Arch. Gen. Psychiat. (Chicago),* 4:30, 1961.

12. Colby, K. M.: *A Primer for Psychotherapists,* New York, The Ronald Press Company, 1951.

    Levine, M.: "Principles of Psychiatric Treatment," in F. Alexander and H. Ross (eds.), *Dynamic Psychiatry,* Chicago, The University of Chicago Press, 1952, chap. XI.

    Tarachow, J.: *An Introduction to Psychotherapy,* New York, International Universities Press, Inc., 1963.

Appendix A

CLINICAL DIAGNOSIS AND CLASSIFICATION

Clinical diagnosis and classification in psychiatry are complicated by the fact that patients with emotional illness seldom fall into specific diagnostic categories. They usually demonstrate overlapping patterns, often with a changing emphasis from time to time. For understanding and treating patients, genetic and dynamic considerations are generally more helpful than clinical labels.

Clinical diagnosis is important, however, particularly as an aid to teaching and research. The following list is taken, with code numbers, from part of the section on Diseases of the Psychobiological Unit (pp. 89 ff.) in the fourth edition (1952) of the *Standard Nomenclature of Diseases and Operations.** This section is divided into three major groups. A representative sample of the first group, Disorders Caused by or Associated with Impairment of Brain Tissue Function, is included in the scope of this book (See Chapter 12), and the second group, Mental Deficiency, is discussed in Chapter 13. The third group listed below consists of Disorders of Psychogenic Origin or Without Clearly Defined Physical Cause or Structural Change in the Brain, many of which are mentioned in the text. For most effective use the reader should consider the diagnostic categories to be guideposts on the diagnostic continuum rather than discrete entities.

In the following list the number in the left-hand margin is the code number from the *Standard Nomenclature;* the number in the right-hand column is the page or pages in this book where the disorder is described.

ACUTE BRAIN DISORDERS

009–100	Acute brain syndrome associated with intracranial infection	287
000–100	Acute brain syndrome associated with systemic infection	287

* New York, The Blakiston Division, McGraw-Hill Book Company, Inc.

000–3..	Acute brain syndrome, drug or poison intoxication	
000–3312	Acute brain syndrome, alcohol intoxication	283
000–33122	Acute hallucinosis	283
000–33123	Delirium tremens	283
000–4..	Acute brain syndrome associated with trauma	284
000–5..	Acute brain syndrome associated with circulatory disturbance	282
000–550	Acute brain syndrome associated with convulsive disorder	286
000–7..	Acute brain syndrome with metabolic disturbance	284
000–8..	Acute brain syndrome associated with intracranial neoplasm	286
000–900	Acute brain syndrome with disease of unknown or uncertain cause	
000–xx0	Acute brain syndrome of unknown cause	

CHRONIC BRAIN DISORDERS

009–0..	Chronic brain syndrome associated with congenital cranial anomaly, congenital spastic paraplegia or Mongolism, or due to prenatal maternal infectious disease	291
0..–147.0	Chronic brain syndrome associated with central nervous system syphilis	287
009–1...0	Chronic brain syndrome associated with cranial infection other than syphilis	287
009–300	Chronic brain syndrome associated with intoxication.	283
009–3312	Chronic brain syndrome, alcohol intoxication	283
009–050	Chronic brain syndrome associated with birth trauma	291
009–400	Chronic brain syndrome associated with brain trauma	285
009–516	Chronic brain syndrome associated with cerebral arteriosclerosis	282
009–5..	Chronic brain syndrome associated with circulatory disturbance other than cerebral arteriosclerosis.	282
009–550	Chronic brain syndrome associated with convulsive disorder	286
009–79x	Chronic brain syndrome associated with senile brain disease	279
009–700	Chronic brain syndrome associated with other disturbance of metabolism, growth or nutrition (includes presenile, glandular, pellagra, familial amaurosis)	284
009–8..	Chronic brain syndrome associated with intracranial neoplasm.	286
009–900	Chronic brain syndrome associated with diseases of unknown or uncertain cause (includes multiple sclerosis, Huntington's chorea, Pick's disease and other diseases of familial or hereditary nature)	287

Appendix B

A SCHEMATIC REPRESENTATION OF PERSONALITY AND SOME OF ITS FUNCTIONS AND DISORDERS

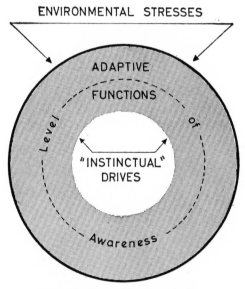

Figure 6. Personality Organization.

This basic diagram illustrates in a rough way the buffering position of the adaptive functions in their relationships to environmental stress and to the impact of drives. The diagram is not meant to correlate with anatomical structure, but simply to indicate the background for a conception of the equilibrium of forces within the personality and between the personality and its environment. The center of the diagram represents the origin of the drives; the outer part represents the environment to which the individual must adjust. The middle, shaded part represents the "ego," within which lies the psychological adaptive functions which expedite the individual's adjustment. In the diagram this zone is divided by a broken line which represents the level of awareness. The individual is aware of or can focus his attention at will on the functions of the part of his personality outside the dotted line; he is not aware (he is unconscious) of activity occurring in the inner part. The level of awareness is shown as a broken line to indicate that it is not a sharp demarcation, and that there is a twilight zone of thoughts and feelings which at times appear in awareness and at other times remain unconscious. (See discussion on pp. 41–42.)

Each of the subsequent figures represents a section of Figure 6.

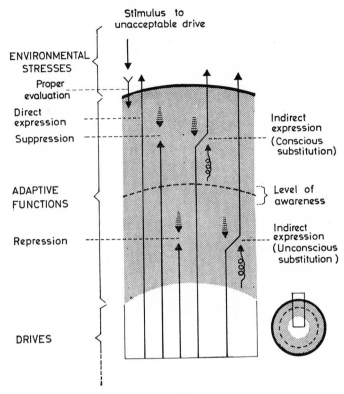

Figure 7. Adaptive Function.

This diagram illustrates various psychologic adaptive functions in their relationship to environmental stress and to the impact of drives. The arrows on the far left illustrate the adaptive function of evaluation, in this case, evaluation of the significance of an external stressful stimulus that stirs up an unacceptable drive. The other arrows indicate alternative responses: direct expression of the drive in spite of its unacceptability; conscious inhibition, or suppression, and its unconscious counterpart, repression; and finally substitute or indirect expression, either consciously or unconsciously carried out. (See discussion on pp. 42–43.)

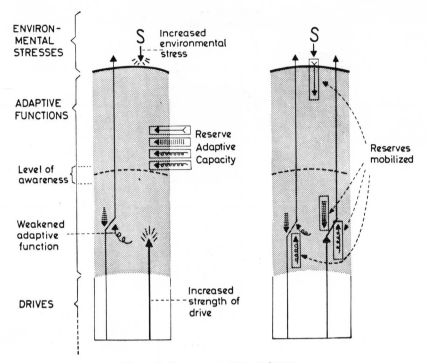

ENVIRON-
MENTAL
STRESSES

ADAPTIVE
FUNCTIONS

Level of
awareness

Weakened
adaptive
function

DRIVES

S Increased
environmental
stress

Reserve
Adaptive
Capacity

Increased
strength of
drive

S

Reserves
mobilized

Figure 8. Response to Potential Crisis.

This double diagram illustrates the ego's mobilization of reserve adaptive capacity to cope with a potential crisis, or breakdown in emotional homeostasis. In the hypothetical situation pictured on the left, breakdown is imminent as a result of three factors: increased environmental stress, increased strength of the unacceptable drive, and weakened adaptive functions. Reserve strength is available, however, and, as shown on the right, can be mobilized in the emergency to strengthen inhibition and to find new substitute outlets. At the same time there is enough left over to evaluate the new environmental stresses. The diagram is somewhat oversimplified; the time factor, for example, is difficult to illustrate. If the threat persists, the reserve strengths may begin to wear thin and homeostasis again may be endangered. (See discussion on p. 44.)

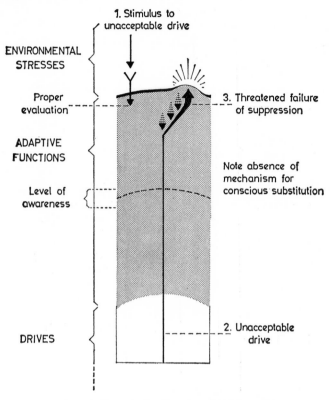

Figure 9. Threatened Failure of Suppression.

The ability to consciously inhibit (suppress) is giving way under the pressure of a strong unacceptable drive that has been stimulated by an environmental stress. The stress has been evaluated properly but no appropriate substitute outlet for the drive has been found, and so it threatens to erupt in direct expression. (See discussion, p. 45.)

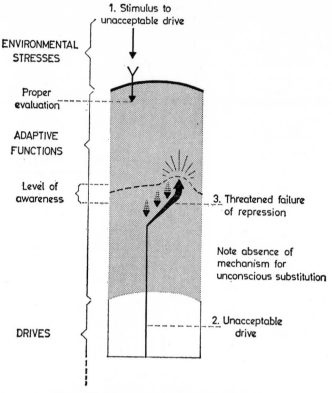

Figure 10. Threatened Failure of Repression.

The same type of situation as shown in Figure 9 is presented, with one important difference. The stressful stimulus and the proper evaluation are the same, but the attempt at inhibition and the unsuccessful attempt to find an appropriate substitute outlet take place below instead of above the level of awareness—they are unconscious instead of conscious processes. Instead of threatening to erupt in the form of direct expression, therefore, the drive threatens to erupt into consciousness, after which it may or may not be directly expressed. Since he does not know what he is repressing, the subject of this diagram has no way of knowing how he would cope with it; he apparently is so afraid that he cannot cope with it that at all costs he must keep it out of consciousness. (See discussion on p. 45.)

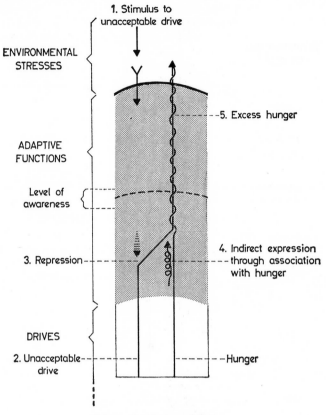

Figure 11. Fusion of Drives.

This shows the resolution, by association or fusion of the unacceptable drive with an acceptable drive, of the kind of threatening situation illustrated in Figure 10. Since the fusion takes place below the level of awareness, the individual is not aware that his unacceptable drive exists; instead, he recognizes that the intensity of his acceptable drive is increased substantially. Thus, in the case described on page 104, a man's hunger, normally no more than enough to support his metabolic processes, is amplified by fusion so that his appetite is increased. In his case, his attempts at suppression of his hunger are not effective, and the result is obesity. (See discussion on pp. 47–48.)

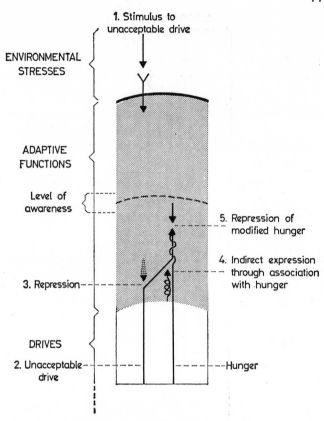

Figure 12. Repression of Fused Drives.

This is a variation of the dynamic situation illustrated in Figure 11. In this case, although fusion of an unacceptable drive with an acceptable drive (hunger) occurs, the fusion does not make it possible for the unacceptable drive to be expressed indirectly. Instead, the disguise fails, the acceptable drive becomes unacceptable, the reinforced hunger drive is repressed, and severe appetite loss (anorexia nervosa) results. (See discussion on p. 48.)

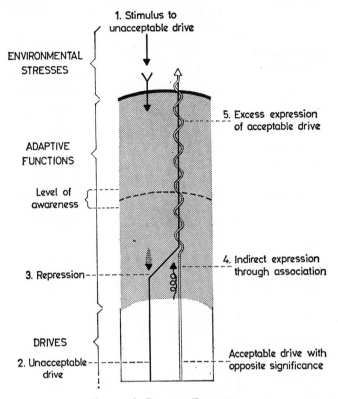

Figure 13. Reaction Formation.

A special case of the association or fusion of drives shown in Figure 11 is represented here. The unacceptable (black) drive is fused with its opposite (white) drive, so that the amplified acceptable drive performs, in effect, a double function: it not only conceals its unacceptable component but also, at the same time, by an excess of the acceptable component, seems to advertise its freedom from any taint of unacceptability. "How could anyone think I have any black (or anger or sex)" it seems to be saying, "when I am so very, very white (or loving, or pure)?" (See discussion on p. 139.)

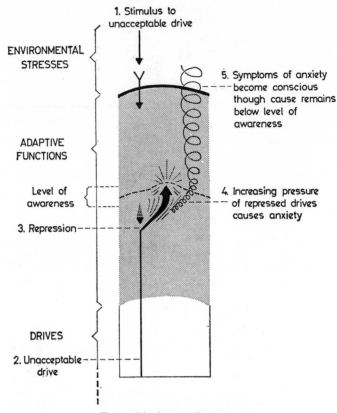

Figure 14. Anxiety Reaction.

This diagram, illustrating the anxiety reaction or its special case, the psycho-physiological reaction, is an extension of Figure 10, which represented the threatened failure of repression. The threat is frightening, but since it is all below the level of awareness, the individual is not conscious of the cause of his anxiety. He is conscious, however, of the physiological signs of his anxiety, represented in the diagram by the spiral line. (See discussion on p. 221.)

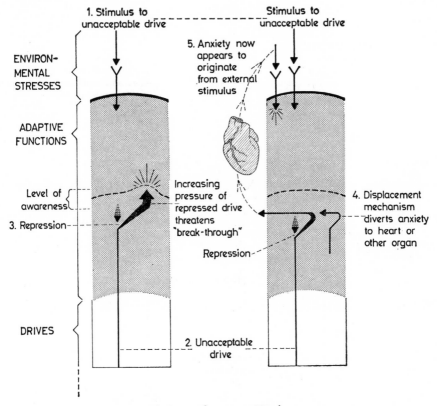

1. Stimulus to unacceptable drive   Stimulus to unacceptable drive

5. Anxiety now appears to originate from external stimulus

ENVIRON-
MENTAL
STRESSES

ADAPTIVE
FUNCTIONS

Level of awareness

3. Repression

Increasing pressure of repressed drive threatens "break-through"

Repression

4. Displacement mechanism diverts anxiety to heart or other organ

DRIVES

2. Unacceptable drive

Figure 15. Rationalization or Displacement.

This double diagram shows the effect of rationalization or displacement in diverting the apparent source of anxiety from within the personality to a part of the body perceived by the patient as being outside of the personality. In the left-hand diagram the familiar threatened failure of repression is depicted; the patient knows or is about to know that he is anxious but does not know why. In the right-hand diagram an unconscious mechanism has displaced the apparent source of the anxiety to the heart, or has rationalized its manifestations as having come from the heart. The former, apparently causeless, anxiety can now masquerade as fear of heart disease, or its manifestations can be rationalized as caused by heart disease. Since the difference between displacement and rationalization is largely a matter of time—one acts as if to forestall anxiety, the other as if to explain anxiety—the same diagram must suffice for both. (See discussion on pp. 224–227.)

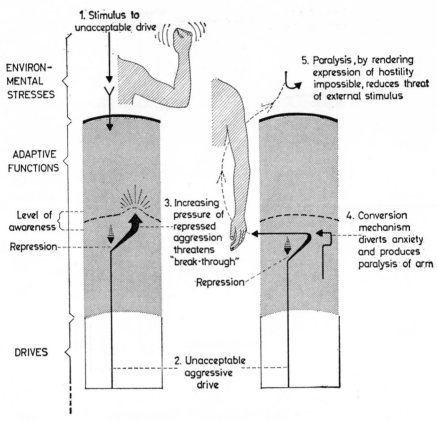

Figure 16. Conversion Reaction.

The double diagram shows the effect of the conversion mechanism. In this case, an external stimulus has stirred up the aggressive drive in a patient whose past experience has made unacceptable the direct or indirect expression, or even the recognition, of aggression. He acts as if he were afraid that if he knew how angry he was, he would kill someone. The conversion mechanism brings about a paralysis of the arm—the weapon, as it were, with which he could kill. Without a weapon, he need not fear the consequences of his anger; freed of that part of his anxiety, he can redeploy his defenses to conceal the existence of his anger more effectively through repression. (See discussion on pp. 230–231.)

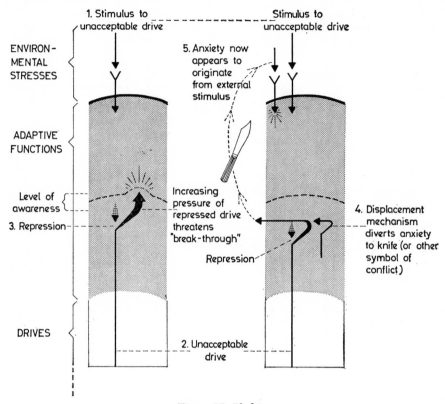

Figure 17. Phobia.

Displacement of the patient's apparent source of anxiety from an inner, unknown source to an outer, recognized source is depicted. The mechanism is the same as the hypochondriacal displacement illustrated in Figure 15, but the apparent source is different. In the phobia, the outer, recognized source is symbolically linked with the conflict, and is not part of the patient's body. (See discussion on p. 239.)

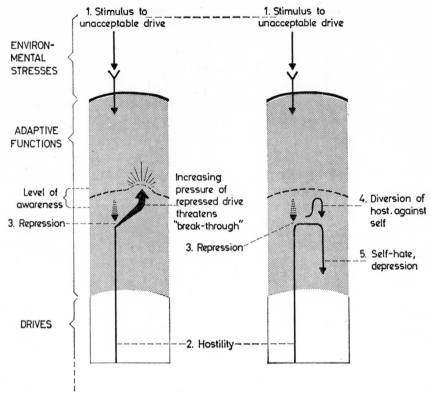

Figure 18. Depression.

This diagram illustrates the type of depression resulting from hostility turned against the self. It is a bit difficult to diagram accurately because, although the mechanism and the hostile drive both remain unconscious, the patient is aware of the feelings of worthlessness and depression that result. (See discussion on p. 243.)

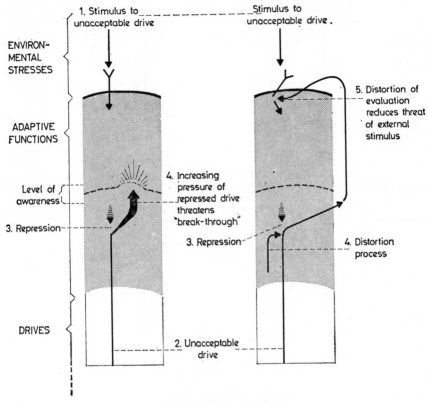

Figure 19. Psychosis.

Collapse of the adaptive function of evaluation in some types of psychoses is represented in this diagram. Without correct evaluation, the stimulus to the unacceptable drive is no longer perceived as it really is. (See discussion on p. 255.)

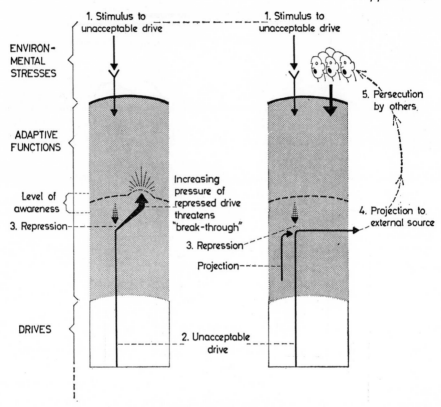

Figure 20. Projection.

This diagram illustrates the mechanism of projection as seen in paranoid disorders. In one way it resembles displacement (Figure 17), in that an external threat is substituted for an internal threat. In another way, however, it differs in that the source of the *drive* rather than simply the source of the *fear* appears to be outside of the self. (See discussion on p. 256.)

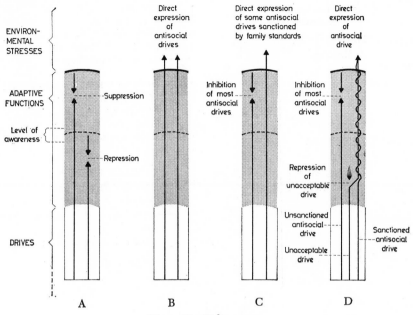

Figure 21. Delinquency.

This four-part diagram illustrates the major types of delinquency. Segment *A* represents the person with a healthy conscience who, by suppression or repression, inhibits any antisocial drives that might be stirred up. Segment *B* shows the direct, uninhibited expression of antisocial drives in the essentially conscienceless *antisocial reaction. C* shows the selective inhibition of some antisocial drives and the sanctioned expression of others in the *dyssocial reaction. D* represents the *neurotic delinquent,* in which some repressed drives—unacceptable, although not necessarily antisocial—are fused with and expressed through a particular antisocial activity sanctioned by parental expectations. (See discussion on pp. 312, 314, and 306.)   i

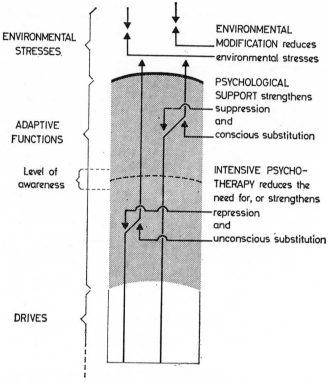

Figure 22. Levels of Treatment.

Illustrated here are the major targets of intervention in milder psychiatric illness. Medication (not illustrated) usually is effective by reducing the strength of drives although at the same time, it may complicate the therapeutic task by reducing the effectiveness of repression and suppression. (See discussion on p. 330.)

INDEX